MASTERS OF
CHINESE POLITICAL THOUGHT

Masters of Chinese Political Thought

From the Beginnings to the Han Dynasty

EDITED BY SEBASTIAN DE GRAZIA

Preface by Frederick W. Mote

The Viking Press | New York

To Renzo Sereno

It is because I have
not been given a
chance that I have
become so handy.

    —*Analects,* 9:6

PREFACE

by Frederick W. Mote

Chinese political thought has guided the political and social life of mankind's largest and longest-enduring state. Just as general statements about political science are deficient when formulated without reference to Chinese man's accumulated political experience, so the general questions that occur to political philosophers, and to historians of political thought, acquire an added measure of breadth and interest when they incorporate awareness of the ideas which the Chinese tradition has generated. But even if that were not so, there still would be for many persons an intrinsic interest in the political and social and ethical points of view which the great East Asian civilization, at one time or another in its vast and rich history, has found to be worthy of thoughtful man's consideration.

Sebastian de Grazia has brought to his study of Chinese political philosophy the thoughtful mind of a man deeply cultivated in the West's intellectual traditions. He has selected a large number of passages, of chapters, of sections from the canonical works, of discourses from the theoreticians—selections which have seemed to him most useful for conveying the fullness of Chinese political thought in its Golden Age. As he has noted in his Foreword, all Chinese thought thereafter, in some sense, is footnotes to these great monuments, even when those footnotes have assumed great bulk and range; and that they did, for the continuous tradition of Chinese political thought has remained vigorous and central to Chinese life through two intervening millennia. Yet it is to the classical period that we must constantly turn, and to which this book brings us.

The selections are not in all cases those which a sinologist might make, and therein lies much of their interest, for the sinologist as for the political philosopher. Another kind of eye has searched the Chinese past, and a mind attuned somewhat differently from that of the usual student of China has dictated the emphases evident here. This collection, drawn from the founding masters of the Chinese political tradition themselves, brings us rich fare.

Princeton University, October 1972

FOREWORD

The period covered in this volume goes from the very beginnings of Chinese political thought, sometime prior to 1000 B.C., to the appearance of the Han Dynasty, 221 B.C. The era is roughly comparable to the Homeric and classical Greek, not alone in chronology but in beauty of language, fertility of imagination, and influence on all succeeding centuries.

Alfred North Whitehead, in a well-appreciated remark, said that the history of Western philosophy is but a series of footnotes to Plato. In the same sense and to an even greater degree, Chinese philosophy is a series of footnotes to the few masters of this volume. Some of the earliest are anonymous, but of the ten who can be identified by name, nine by the Chinese themselves have been traditionally called "tzŭ" (as in Hsün Tzŭ) meaning *Master*. Their fascinating writings make up the documents that Chinese philosophers have drawn on for three thousand years. The Confucian, the mandarin, the famous scholar-official of the Chinese empire, based his education and his study for official examinations on the *Four Books* and the *Six Classics*, all of which are well represented here. (See Table 3.)

This volume also contains writings from the great masterpieces of Taoism, one of the world's most important philosophies, one with important ramifications today. Taoism was not canonical reading for the mandarins; yet it drew almost all men of learning irresistibly. The Confucian ruling class was attracted also to another school, but less forcefully and for different reasons. This was the so-called Legalist school of statecraft, represented here by its two greatest works, the *Book of Lord Shang* and the *Han Fei Tzŭ*. They formulated the tough, calculated approach to politics that officials almost everywhere, it seems, often find necessary to adopt but rarely wish to profess.

The Confucian's profession of faith was humanistic. He was, therefore, opposed to war in principle. But principle in politics, in China, too, is often accommodated to something else. War was all too frequently there to contend with. Military writers had their place. Of them none was so intriguing as the remarkable Sun Tzŭ, a military man, presumably a general, of the fourth century B.C. whose brilliance and style have propelled him into the twentieth century. Mao Tsê-tung's military doctrines draw upon his.

Probably the one master whom Confucians most generally disliked was a man whose opposition to war they shared—Mo Tzŭ. What they could not abide was his attack on the family. Nonetheless, for sheer boldness and diversity, Mo Tzŭ ranks as one of the most original and interesting thinkers in the history of political philosophy.

The influence of these early great writings can be clearly seen in all subsequent political philosophers from the Han Dynasty to the People's Republic. Most observers view China's present political doctrine as a new departure, stepping off from Marx and Lenin and other communist writers. But to break a tradition as long and strong as that of the masters, one must fight hard, and acknowledge that the struggle is against formidable foes. Mao Tsê-tung's poem "Snow" indicates where one break must be made—with the model kings of antiquity.

> Now they are all past and gone.
> To find men truly great and noble
> We must look here in the present.

There are further breaks to make—to jump from a cosmos of harmony to one of struggle and from a world of resilient, complementary change to one of harsh, dialectical contradiction. These are just two examples; there are other beliefs the new rulers of China hold to, or fight against, that come also from the archaic and classical ages, from the very masters of political thought of this volume. Their greatness and inspiration invented China, created the culture through which one could hope to transform the world within and beyond the Great Wall into something better.

On this greatness and inspiration no rulers of China, if Chinese, can ever resolutely turn their backs.

ACKNOWLEDGMENTS

My fullest thanks go to Professors Frederick W. Mote and Angus C. Graham for their careful, critical reading of the manuscript, and for their encouragement too, without which this long effort would have sputtered out. My thanks also to Professor Jessie G. Lutz for her expert reading, to Mrs. James Y. Lee for help with individual passages of translation, to Anne M. Birrell for thoughtful suggestions and research assistance in the early stages of the work, to Sally Runyon, Wendy Ashmore, and Gail Hunton for research help throughout. The Chinese calligraphy that graces the jacket of the book and each selection heading I owe to Mrs. Chien-chin Wang. My debt is also great to the learned and accomplished translators on whose works I have so largely banked.

CONTENTS

TABLES

MASTERS OF
CHINESE POLITICAL THOUGHT

1

Literature of Kings: The *Six Classics*

Why do you not obey the King
and make the Mandate of Heaven resplendent?
—*Book of Documents,* To Fang

Contrary to what is generally believed, historically, China is not very old. (See Table I.) The Great City Shang flourished about 1450 B.C. Much earlier than this historians have not been able to go. The other river-valley civilizations of the world—Egypt, the Fertile Crescent, and the Indus—are much more ancient. But there are stories reported in Chou and Han literature that give China a long legendary if not historical past.

China's legendary past, some hold, begins with P'an Ku,* creator of heaven and earth. P'an Ku, though, appears in China, it now seems, no earlier than the third century A.D., an émigré possibly from India. More purely Chinese and more ancient in origin are the twelve Emperors of Heaven, eleven of Earth, and nine of Mankind who follow one another in fraternal succession. Then, after sixteen kings about whom nothing except their names is mentioned, appear Three Sovereigns: Fu Hsi, inventor of writing, hunting, fishing, and animal husbandry; Shên Nung, "the Divine Cultivator," patron of agriculture, trade, and medicine; and in the twenty-seventh century B.C., Huang-ti or the Yellow Emperor. His wife wove the first cloth, began the culture of silk, built the first house, brewed the first herbal remedy, worked out the first calendar, and lit the first fire.

* In the romanization of proper nouns the Wade-Giles standard will be followed.

TABLE I. Political and Military Events
in China and the Rest of the World *

China	B.C.	Rest of World
	3000	Archaic period: Egypt, 3000–2780 Old Kingdom: Egypt, 2780–2260 BRONZE AGE: Mesopotamia, Egypt, Iran, Indus cities, 3000–2000
		Akkadian Empire: Mesopotamia, 2750 Ur Dynasty, c. 2500 Sargon of Akkad, 2264
		Minoan Empire: Crete, 2200–1500
EMERGENCE FROM STONE AGE	2000	Hammurabi of Babylon, 2067–2025 Middle Kingdom: Egypt, 2000 Ur Dynasty III, 2000 Aryans: India, 2000–1200 Hebraic Heroes: Abraham, Jacob, Joseph, 2000–1225
		BRONZE AGE: Europe
Shang Dynasty, 1766–1122 Emperor T'ang, 1751–1738		Assyrians: West Asia, c. 1850 Hittites: Asia Minor, 1800 Aegeans: Greece, 1800
	1750	
		Stonehenge: England
		Late Minoan Empire, fl. 1600 Late Egyptian Empire, 1580–1090
BRONZE AGE	1500	
		Hittite Empire: Asia Minor, 1400– 1200
	1250	
King Wên of Chou, 1231–1135		Phoenician city states, 1200–774
Emperor Chou, ruled 1154–1122 Chou Dynasty 1111–256 King Wu, ruled 1111–1104		Sack of Troy, 1184

* This table follows conventional chronology. A discussion of the methods, sources, and problems of such dating can be found in William L. Langer, ed., *An Encyclopedia of World History*, 4th ed., rev. (Boston: Houghton Mifflin Co., 1968).

TABLE I. (*Continued*)

China	B.C.	Rest of World
Duke of Chou, ruled c. 1104–1067		IRON AGE: 1100
		Kingdoms of Saul, David, Solomon:
		Israel, 1028–933
Western Chou · 1121–771	1000	
		Great Assyrian Empire, 933–624
		Greek Aristocracies, 900–600
		Founding of Carthage, 814
Multi-State System	750	Roman monarchy: Rome, c. 753
		Age of Tyrants: Greece, 600–500
722–256		Cyrus the Great: Persia, 550–529
"Spring and Autumn		Persian Empire, 550–336
Era," 722–481		Multi-State System: India, 550–321
		Darius, c. 558–486
		Roman Republic, 509
IRON AGE	500	Buddhism: India, c. 500
		Graeco-Persian Wars, 490–479
		Periclean Age in Athens, 495–429
"Warring States		Peloponnesian Wars, 431–404
Era," 403–221		Isocrates, 436–338
		Alexander the Great, ruled 336–323
Eastern Chou		Maurya Dynasty: India, 321–184
		Punic Wars, 264–146
	250	Parthian Empire, fl. c. 250
Ch'in Dynasty: The First Empire, 221–207		
Unification of multi-states into empire		Macedonian Wars, 215–146
Han Dynasty, 206 B.C.–220 A.D.		
State Monopolies	150	
Military Campaigns west and east under Han Emperor Wu, 140–87		
Confucianism, a state cult, 136		
	100	Hinduism: India, c. 100
		Julius Caesar, ruled 49–44
		Western Roman Empire, 31 B.C.–476 A.D.

At this point in the chronology, Ssŭ-ma Ch'ien (c. 145–c. 90 B.C.), compiler of the great first general history of China, settles on the Yellow Emperor as the first human ruler, the founder-hero from whom all subsequent sovereigns of China must claim descent. All those previous to him are divinities. Under the Yellow Emperor and his four successors—Chuan Hsü, K'u, Yao, and Shun—the world enjoyed a golden age of perfect government.

None of these men built a dynasty. Judging their sons unworthy of them, they transmitted the throne to others. Of the three great and virtuous kings of the twenty-fourth to twenty-second centuries B.C., namely, Yao, Shun, and Yü, Yao abdicated and gave the throne to a good and capable commoner, Shun, who afterward himself abdicated in favor of Yü, the great hydraulic engineer. Yü mastered the floods and tamed the rivers for irrigation. He also founded the one and only dynasty that preceded the Shang—the Hsia.

There is a legend of the fall of man connected with the Hsia's introduction of dynastic succession. Until their rule, perfect government, a monocracy or nonhereditary monarchy, had brought Heaven and Earth into the harmony of a Golden Age. But then—how it happened is unclear—men, true civilized men—that is, the Chinese—learned to do evil from barbarians beyond the pale. Punishment had to be instituted and, since rulers could not be counted on to be good enough to abdicate, the expedient of dynastic succession was adopted. Heredity instead of merit became the basis of rulership; bad kings inevitably cropped up.

To return to the line of venerable kings: if we now add the founder of the Shang Dynasty, T'ang, to the cofounders of the Chou—Kings Wên and Wu, plus the Duke of Chou (regent for the boy king)—the list is about complete. Table 2 gives their names in approximate chronological order. There are various and overlapping pieces of this mythology whose names, dates, and places do not always match.

The Chou inserted themselves into the genealogy of the Shang as gracefully as they could. Some ancient genealogist linked them to Hou Chi, "he who rules the millet," sometimes called the Millet Prince or God of Millet, the grain god, a male personified as Ch'i, son of K'u, an early successor of the Yellow Emperor. Thus, the royal house of Chou belonged to the first families, having descended from the most respectable ancestry, even though down an obscure line.

TABLE 2. Legendary Heroes and Model Kings*

THE THREE SOVEREIGNS (Ruled 2674–2574 B.C.)	Fu Hsi, Inventor of writing, hunting, fishing, and animal husbandry Shên Nung, Divine Cultivator, patron of agriculture, trade, and medicine Huang-ti, Yellow Emperor	THE FIVE EMPERORS

Shao-Hao (ruled 2574–2490 B.C.)
Chuan Hsü (ruled 2490–2413 B.C.)
K'u (ruled 2412–2342 B.C.)
Hou Chi,
   God of Millet
   or Millet Prince,
   called Ch'i, son of K'u (ruled 2342–2334 B.C.)
Yao (ruled 2333–2233 B.C.)
Shun (ruled 2233–2183 B.C.)

THE THREE DYNASTIES OF ANTIQUITY

Dynasty	Ruler	
Hsia (2183–1751 B.C.)	Yü	Founder of Hsia Dynasty (ruled 2183–2177 B.C.)
Shang (or Yin) (1751–1111 B.C.)	T'ang	Founder of Shang Dynasty (ruled 1751–1738 B.C.)
Chou (1111–256 B.C.)	Ch'ang, Wên Wang	the Accomplished King, Founder of Chou Dynasty
	Fa, Wu Wang	the Martial King, Cofounder of Chou Dynasty (ruled 1111–1104 B.C.)
	Tan, Chou Kung	Duke of Chou, Regent to heir apparent Ch'êng (ruled 1104–1067 B.C.)

* The dates in this table are taken from Tung Tso-pin, *Chronological Tables of Chinese History:* 2 vols. (Hong Kong: Hong Kong University Press, 1960). They are all legendary except for those of the Shang and Chou Dynasties. The persons named as the Three Sovereigns and the Five Emperors often vary in different Chinese works. Thus in Ssŭ-ma Chien's *Historical Records* the Five Emperors are listed as Huang-ti, Chuan Hsü, Ti K'u, Yao, and Shun; the Three Kings as Yü, T'ang, and the two kings Wên and Wu taken as one.

The list above can be given much more detail, of course. The Chinese have usually attributed invention of great ideas or things (for instance, well-digging) to legendary persons, most of them ministers of the Yellow Emperor (for example, Hou Chi). Variations in dating can be supplied, too, such as the legendary versus the literary dates of the Yellow Emperor. From one or another version of this list, Chinese philosophers chose their heroes. Usually they began from the point where rulers were no longer gods but mortals—that is, from the period of the entirely legendary Yellow Emperor downward (and that is the span of most interest to us).

The Taoists selected, perhaps even invented, the Yellow Emperor because of his ability to govern perfectly without effort. Confucius exalted Yao, Shun, and the Duke of Chou in particular, as virtuous rulers. Mo Tzŭ went back beyond the Chou to include the kings of the Shang and Hsia, thus making all the Three Dynasties of Antiquity his reservoir of model kings. He chose as exemplars Yao, Shun, Yü, T'ang, Wên, and Wu. Mencius, with his interest in commoners, added Yü to Confucius's Yao and Shun. He also admired T'ang of Shang, Wên and Wu, and the Duke of Chou.

The materials most philosophers drew upon come from one main source—the great literature of the Chou. Principally this was what came to be called the *Six Classics*. (See Table 3.) Much of what these works tell is colored by their intent to persuade readers of the virtue and greatness of the Chou, and some of them may have been mellowed by Confucian editing. The student of politics, however, is accustomed to the suave sound of rhetoric and insistent beat of propaganda. All he need know is that these works, the classical literature of ancient China, consist of writings produced by the Chou ruling class. He will then look on them less as historical than as political documents, important for the theory of rulership.

Yet once the *Book of Documents* is read, Confucianism no longer seems so startlingly new, nor does any other Chinese political philosophy until the ideological invasions first of Buddhism, and in modern times, of democracy and communism. Two millennia of Chinese statesmen, historians, thinkers, and men of letters have put their faith in the words of the model kings as recorded in the ancient documents. The Chou texts embodied in the *Six Classics* educated the scholar, the official, the gentleman, the poet; they formed his character, informed his mind. Even mod-

TABLE 3. The *Six Classics* and the *Four Books*

The *Six Classics**	The *Four Books*‡
1. *Book of Changes (I Ching)* (sometimes called *Book of Divination* or *Classic of Changes*)	1. *Great Learning (Ta Hsüeh)*
2. *Book of Documents (Shu Ching)* (sometimes called *Book of History* or *Classic of Documents*)	2. *Doctrine of the Mean (Chung Yung) (Mean-in-Action)*
3. *Book of Songs (Shih Ching)* (*Book of Odes, Book of Poetry*, or *Classic of Songs*)	3. *Analects (Lun Yü)* (*The Analects of Confucius*)
4. *Book of Rites (I Li)* (*Record of Rituals* or *Ceremonial Records*)	4. *Mencius (Mêng Tzŭ)*
5. *Book of Music (Yüeh Ching)* (Classic of Music)†	
6. *Spring and Autumn Annals (Ch'un Ch'iu)*	

* The listing is given in customary Confucian order. The selections from the *Six Classics* given in succeeding chapters, however, follow an order adapted to the political and historical text of the book.

† Lost in the late centuries B.C. For this reason the *Six Classics* are often called the *Five Classics*. These works all seemed to have appeared between the eleventh and third centuries B.C. and to have been compiled between the eighth and second centuries B.C. The word *ching* appearing in most of them means a scripture or sacred book.

‡ Put together as the *Four Books* by the philosopher Chu Hsi in the twelfth century B.C.

ernist reformers of the nineteenth and twentieth centuries are rooted in the words and ideas of the Chou.

We begin now with the earliest of the masterpieces, the *Book of Documents*, the likely creation of the Duke of Chou, Confucius's idol.

2

Book of Documents

The king said, Oh Fêng, be careful. . . . Grandly take as
pattern the active virtue of the ancients.
                                    —*Book of Documents*, K'ang Kao

On the surface the *Book of Documents* is a group of important speeches,
letters, and prayers collected originally, perhaps, for the state archives.
Some go back prior to 1000 B.C., to just after the Chou conquest of the
Shang. The style is appropriately archaic.

The political theory of the Chou was a universal kingship deriving its
just powers from the universal T'ien (Heaven).* When political thought
first appears in China, a king of the imperial house would invest his
dukes with a mandate to rule. The king himself could rule only because
he too had received a mandate, the Mandate of T'ien. T'ien granted the
Mandate only to one king on earth, who then became known as the Son
of T'ien, a title equivalent to Emperor. As the *Book of Documents* puts it,
"The Son of T'ien is father and mother of the people and thereby king
over the whole world." The title carries no connotation of divine heredity. Rather it describes how the Emperor should act: to maintain the
peace and harmony of T'ien's design as an obedient, true son would do.
And it prescribes one-man rule. The charge to rule is conditional.
Should the emperor be wicked, T'ien will withdraw the Mandate and
wreak ruin and destruction on his head. The Chinese did not relinquish
this theory of kingship until the twentieth century.

---

* Henceforth throughout the book, including the translations, we shall retain the
Chinese "T'ien" and not use the common translation "Heaven." Any name—
Heaven, God, Nature, Sky-deity, Providence—given in translation to the object of
greatest reverence in another culture bears inappropriate connotations. See note 16, p.
393 below.

The famous historian, Ssŭ-ma Ch'ien, remarked that Confucius, finding that the *Book of Documents* had become defective, arranged the events and speeches in proper order.

The following pronouncements, counsels, and philosophical principles comprise some of the most fundamental political documents of China.

BOOK OF DOCUMENTS

(Shu Ching)

Selections

Declaration of Emperor Yao (Yao tien)

Examining into antiquity we find that the emperor Yao was called
Fang-Hsün. He was reverent, enlightened, accomplished, sincere, and
mild. He was truly respectful and could be modest. He extensively covered the four extreme points of the world. He reached to Heaven above
and Earth below. He was able to make bright his lofty virtue, and so he
made affectionate the nine branches of the family. When the nine
branches of the family had become harmonious, he distinguished and
honoured the hundred clans. When the hundred clans had become illus-

From Bernhard Karlgren, tr., *Book of Documents* (reprinted from the *Museum of Far
Eastern Antiquities, Bulletin* 22; Stockholm: Museum of Far Eastern Antiquities, 1950),
translation slightly modified. Reprinted with the kind permission of the translator.

trious, he harmonized the myriad states. The numerous people were amply nourished and prosperous and then became concordant. And then he charged Hsi and Ho[1] reverently to follow the august T'ien and calculate and delineate the sun, the moon, and the other heavenly bodies and respectfully give the people the seasons.

o o o o

The emperor said: Oh, you Hsi and Ho, the year has three hundred sixty-six days, by means of an intercalary month you should fix the four seasons and complete the year. If you earnestly control all the functionaries, the achievements will all be resplendent. The emperor said: Who will carefully attend to this? I will raise and use him. Fang Ch'i[2] said: Your heir-son Chu is enlightened. The emperor said: Alas, he is deceitful and quarrelsome, will he do? The emperor said: Who will carefully attend to my affairs? Huan Tou said: Oh, Kung Kung everywhere has accumulated and exhibited his merits. The emperor said: Alas, he smoothly speaks but his actions are perverse. He is in appearance respectful, but he swells up to the sky. The emperor said: Oh, you Ssŭ Yüeh, voluminously the great waters everywhere are injurious, extensively they embrace the mountains and rise above the hills, vastly they swell up to the sky. The lower people groan. Is there anybody whom I could let regulate it? All said: Oh, Kun, indeed! The emperor said: Oh, he is offensive. He neglects my orders, he ruins his kin. Ssŭ Yüeh said: He is remarkable. Try him, and if he will do, then employ him. The emperor said: Go, and be reverent. After nine years the work was not achieved. The emperor said: Oh, you Ssŭ Yüeh, I have been in the high position on the throne seventy years. If you can execute T'ien's mandate, I shall yield my high position. Ssŭ Yüeh said: I have not the virtue, I should disgrace the emperor's high position. The emperor said: Promote one already illustrious, or raise one humble and mean. All to the emperor said: There is an unmarried man in a low position, called Shun of Yü. The emperor said: Yes, I have heard of him; what is he like? Ssŭ Yüeh said: He is the son of a blind man; his father was stupid, his mother was deceitful, his brother, Hsiang, was arrogant; he has been able to be concordant and to be grandly filial; he has controlled himself and has not come to wickedness. The emperor said: I will try him; I will wive him, and observe his behaviour towards my two daughters. He directed and sent down his two daughters to the nook of the Kuei river, to be wives in the Yü house. The emperor said: Be reverent! Shun carefully displayed the five rules;[3] the five rules then could be followed. He was appointed to the general management, the general management was orderly. He received the guests at the four gates, the four gates were stately. He was sent into the great hill-foot forest; violent wind, thunder, and rain did not lead him astray. The emperor said: Come, you Shun, in the affairs on which you have been consulted, I have examined your words; your words have been accomplished and been capable of yielding fine results during three years; do you ascend to the emperor's throne. Shun considered himself inferior in virtue and was not pleased with the proposal. But in the first month, the first day he accepted the abdication of Yao in the temple of the Accomplished Ancestors.

o   o   o   o

In five years he went once round to the fiefs, and four times all the princes came to court. They extensively made reports by their words; they were clearly tested by their achievements; they were endowed with chariots and garments according to their works. He delimited the twelve provinces, and raised altars on twelve mountains, and he deepened the rivers. He made a full description of the legal punishments. Banishment is the mitigation of the five principal punishments,[4] the whip is the punishment of the magistrate's courts, the rod is the punishment of the schools, fines are the punishment for redeemable crimes. Offences by mishap are pardoned, but those who are self-reliant and persist are punished as miscreants. Be reverent, be reverent! The punishments, to them you should carefully attend! He banished Kung Kung to Yu-chou, he banished Huan Tou to Ch'ung-shan; he made the San Miao skulk in San-wei, he killed Kun on Yü-shan.[5] After these four condemnations, all in the world submitted.

Declaration of Emperor Shun (Shun tien)

In the twenty-eighth year, Fang-hsün died, the people were as if mourning for a dead father or mother, for three years[6] within the four seas[7] they stopped and quieted the eight kinds of music. In the first month, on the first day Shun went to the temple of the Accomplished Ancestors. He consulted with Ssŭ Yüeh to open up the four gates[8] so as to make clear the four views and to observe everything in the realm. He said: Oh, you twelve Pastors,[9] be reverent! Now be gentle with the distant ones and kind to the near ones, treat generously the virtuous men and trust the great men, and balk the insinuating ones; then the Man and I barbarians will follow and submit. Shun said: Oh, you Ssŭ Yüeh, is there anybody who can start achievements and make resplendent the emperor's undertakings? I shall make him occupy the general management, to assist in the affairs helping them out with their tasks. All said: Po Yü, master of the official works. The emperor said: Yes. Oh, you Yü, you shall regulate water and land, in this be energetic! Yü saluted and bowed down the head and ceded to Chi, Hsieh and Kao Yao.[10] The emperor said: Oh yes, you shall go! The emperor said: Ch'i, the multitudinous people will presently starve, you shall be Ruler of the Millet, sow those hundred cereals. The emperor said: The hundred families[11] are not affectionate, the five classes are not compliant, you shall be Master of the Multitude, and respectfully propagate the five instructions; they depend upon large-mindedness. The emperor said: Kao Yao, the Man and I barbarians disturb the Hsia; they are robbers and bandits and villains and traitors. You shall be judge. The five punishments have their applications; in the five applications there are three accommodations. The five banishments have their placings; in the five placings there are three dwellings. If you are discerning, you can be trusted. The emperor said: Who will carefully attend to my works? All said: Ch'ui! The emperor said: Yes. Oh, you Ch'ui, you shall be Master of Works. Ch'ui saluted and bowed down the head and ceded to Shu, Ch'iang, and Po Yü. The emperor said: Yes, go, you shall cooperate with them! The emperor said: Who will carefully attend to my herbs and trees, birds and beasts in the highlands and the lowlands? All said: I! The emperor said: Yes. Oh, you I, you shall be my Forester. I saluted and bowed down the head and ceded to Chu, Hu, Hsiung, and P'i. The emperor said: Yes, go, you shall act in harmony with them. The emperor said: Oh, Ssŭ Yüeh, is there anybody who can direct my three categories of rites? All said: Po I. The emperor said: Yes. Oh, you Po, you shall be Master of Rites. Morning and night, be respectful; in your straightness, be pure. Po saluted and bowed down the head and ceded to K'uei and Lung. The emperor said: Yes, go and be respectful! The emperor said: K'uei, I charge you to be Director of Music, to teach the descendant sons, to be straight and yet mild, large-minded and yet careful, firm and yet not tyrannical, great and yet not arrogant. Poetry expresses the mind, the song is a chanting of its words, the notes depend upon the mode of the chanting, the pitch-pipes harmonize the notes. When the eight sounds can be harmonized and not encroach upon each other, Spirits and men will be brought into harmony.[12] K'uei said: Oh, when I strike the stone, when I knock on the stone, all the animals follow it and dance. The emperor said: Lung, I hate those who speak slanderously and act destructively and who agitate and alarm my multitude. I charge you to be conveyer of words, morning and night to give out and bring in reports of my decrees; be truthful. The emperor said: Oh, you twenty-two men, be respectful, now you shall assist me in the works assigned by T'icn. Every three years he examined the achievements of his subordinates. After three examinations he degraded or promoted the unenlightened and the enlightened. The achievements were all resplendent. He detached and sent to the north the San Miao.

When Shun was thirty years of age, he was called and employed for thirty years; he was on the throne for fifty years and then ascending to his place in Heaven he died.

Counsels of Minister Kao Yao (Kao Yao mo)

Examining into antiquity we find that Kao Yao said: If the ruler sincerely pursues the course of his virtue, the counsels will be enlightened and the aid will be harmonious. Yü said: Yes, but how? Kao Yao said: Oh, he should be careful about his person, the cultivation of it should be perpetual. If he amply regulates his nine family branches, all the enlightened ones will energetically be wings to him; the fact that his influence on his nearest kin can reach to more distant people lies in this. Yü did reverence to the splendid words and said: Yes. Kao Yao said: Oh, it lies in knowing men, it lies in giving peace to the people. Yü said: Alas, that both these things are as they should be, even the Emperor finds it difficult to bring about. If the ruler knows men, he is wise, and he can nominate proper men for office; if he gives peace to the people, he is kind; the numerous people cherish him in their hearts. If he can be wise and kind, what anxiety need there be in regard to Huan Tou, what displacement need there be in regard to the lord of Miao, what fear need there be in regard to smart talk, a fine appearance, and great artfulness? Kao Yao said: Oh, in the actions there are nine virtues; when we say that this man has virtue, we mean that he initiates the various works. Yü said: Which are the virtues? Kao Yao said: He is large-minded and yet apprehensive, he is soft and yet steadfast, he is sincere and yet respectful, he is regulating and yet cautious, he is docile and yet bold, he is straight and yet mild, he is great and yet punctilious, he is hard and yet just, he is strong and yet righteous. Displaying his constant norms hc is auspicious indeed!

o   o   o   o

T'ien gives charges to those who have virtue, there are five degrees of garments and their five classes of emblems. T'ien punishes those who have guilt, there are five punishments and their five applications. In the affairs of government let us be energetic, let us be energetic! T'ien's hearing and seeing work through our people's hearing and seeing, T'ien's discernment and severity work through our people's discernment and severity against bad rulers. There is correspondence between the upper and the lower world. Be careful, you possessors of the soil.

o   o   o   o

The emperor said: Come, Yü, you also have splendid words. Yü did obeisance and said: Oh, emperor, what can I say? I think of daily being diligent. Kao Yao said: Ah, but how? Yü said: The great waters swelled up to the sky, vastly they embraced the mountains and rose above the hills, the lower people were killed and submerged. I mounted my four conveyances, and all along the mountains I cut down the trees. Together with I, I gave to the multitudes the game of the mountains. I cut passages for the nine rivers and brought them to the seas; I deepened the channels and canals and brought them to the rivers. Together with Chi, I sowed and gave to the multitudes the hard-gotten grain and the game. I exchanged and transferred those who had and those who had not any hoards of stores. The multitudinous people then had grain-food. The myriad states have become well-ordered. Kao Yao said: Yes, we shall take as norm your splendid words. Yü said: Oh, emperor, be careful about your being in the high position. The emperor said: Yes. Yü said:

Be quiet in the position which you occupy, if you attend to the smallest beginnings, you will have peace. Your assistants should be virtuous, if you act through them, there will be a grand response from the people. They will wait for your will, and so it will be manifest that you have received your mandate from Shang Ti, T'ien will renew its mandate and apply blessings. The emperor said: Oh, ministers, associates! Associates, ministers! Yü said: Yes. The emperor said: My ministers are my legs and arms, ears and eyes. I desire to succour my people, do you assist me! I desire to spread my powers through the four quarters, do you act for me! I desire to see the symbols of the ancient men.

o   o   o   o

K'uei said: The sounding-boxes, the singing *ch'iu* stone, the small leathern drum, the guitar, and the lute, when with them one sings, the Spirits of the ancestors come, Shun's guests[13] are in their high positions at the sacrifice. All the princes are virtuously modest. Below, there are the flutes, the hand-drums, and the drums, with them there are the hammer and the *chu* and *yü* sounding-boxes; the reed organs and the bells are in between. Birds and beasts dance. When the *shao*-music of the Pan-flutes is achieved in nine parts, the male and female phoenixes come and put in an appearance. K'uei said: Oh, when I strike the stone, when I knock on the stone, all the animals follow it and dance, all the governors become truly harmonious.

o   o   o   o

The Battle of Kan (Kan shih)

There was a great battle in Kan. One convoked the six minister-generals. The king said: Oh, you six ministers, I solemnly declare and tell you. The lord of Hu violates and despises the five elements,[14] he neglects and discards the three governing forces.[15] T'ien therefore cuts off his appointment. He further said: During the day, now with the lord of Hu I shall fight about the fate to be decided in one day; and you, ministers, dignitaries, and commoners, I do not covet your fields or your guarded lands. Now I execute T'ien's punishment. If those on the left do not do their duty on the left, you do not execute my orders. If those on the right do not do their duty on the right, you do not execute my orders. If the charioteers do not correctly manage their horses, you do not execute my orders. If you obey my orders, you will be rewarded in the temple of my ancestors; if you do not obey my orders, you will be killed at the altar of the Soil; then I will kill you with your wives and children.

Decree of Emperor T'ang (T'ang shih)

The king said: Come, you multitudes, all listen to my words. It is not that I, the small child, dare act so as to start rebellion. The lord of Hsia has much guilt, T'ien has charged me to kill him. Now, you multitude there, you say: Our ruler, king Chieh, has no compassionate care for our multitude, he sets aside our husbandry works and has an injurious government. I have heard the words of you all; the lord of Hsia has guilt, I fear Shang Ti,[16] I dare not but punish him. Now you will surely say that Hsia's guilt is such as I say. The Hsia king in all ways obstructs the efforts of the multitude, in all ways he injures the city of Hsia, the multitude are all slack and disaffected. They say: That one, Chieh, daily injures and destroys, I and you shall all together perish. Such is the conduct of the king of Hsia. Now I will necessarily march. May you support me, the One Man, the sovereign, to apply T'ien's punishment. I will then greatly reward you. May there be none of you who do not believe me. I do not eat my words. If you do not obey the words of this proclamation, I will kill you with your wives and children; there will be nobody who will be pardoned.

Great Plan (Hung fan)

In the thirteenth year, the king consulted the prince of Chi. The king spoke and said: Oh, prince of Chi, T'ien shelters and raises the people here below, it aids and harmonizes its living conditions; I do not know whereby its constant norms get their proper order. The prince of Chi spoke and said: I have heard that in ancient times Kun obstructed the inundating waters, and brought disorder into the arrangement of the five elements. The Sovereign [Ti] then was roused and angry, and did not give him the Great Plan in nine sections, whereby the constant norms were destroyed. As to Kun, he was killed and died, and Yü then succeeded him and rose. T'ien then gave Yü the Great Plan in nine sections, whereby the constant norms get their proper order.

o   o   o   o

First, the five elements: the first is called water, the second fire, the third wood, the fourth metal, the fifth earth. Water is said to soak and descend; fire is said to blaze and ascend; wood is said to curve or be straight; metal is said to obey and change; earth is said to take seeds and give crops. That which soaks and descends produces saltness; that which blazes and ascends produces bitterness; that which curves or is straight produces sourness; that which obeys and changes produces acridity; that which takes seeds and gives crops produces sweetness.

Second: the five conducts. The first is called the appearance; the second speech; the third seeing; the fourth hearing; the fifth thinking. The appearance is said to be respectful, the speech reasonable, the seeing clear, the hearing perceptive, the thinking liberal. Being respectful produces gravity; being reasonable produces orderliness; being clear-sighted produces wisdom; being perceptive in hearing produces deliberation; being liberal-minded produces sagacity.

Third: the eight rules of government. The first is called the rule pertaining to food; the second, merchandise; the third, sacrifices; the fourth, the director of works; the fifth, the director of the multitude; the sixth, the director of crimes; the seventh, official guests; the eighth, the army.

Fourth: the five regulators. The first is called the year, the second the month, the third the day, the fourth the stars and constellations, the fifth the calendaric calculations.

Fifth: the august correctness. When the august one firmly establishes the correctness he possesses, he thereby brings together those five felicities and largely bestows them upon his people; then the people become endowed with your correctness, and you can preserve the correctness. Among all the people, the fact that there will be no licentious factions, and nobody will take conspiratory action, is because the august one creates correctness. Among all the people, when some have plans, have activity, have self-control, you should bear them in mind; those who do not conform to the correctness, but do not fall into evil, the august one should receive them. You should make serene your mien and say: What I love is virtue, and then you should give them emoluments. Those men thus will think of the august one's correctness. Do not oppress those who are helpless and alone, while fearing those who are high and illustrious. When there are men who have ability and activity, cause them to bring forth their achievements, and the state will be prosperous. All the principal men, when they have been remunerated, then they will be good. If you cannot cause them to have friendliness towards your house, those men then will commit offences. As to those who are not good, even though you give them emoluments, in acting for you they will use wickedness. Have nothing onesided, nothing oblique, and follow the king's righteousness; have no predilections and follow the king's way; have no aversions and follow the king's road; have nothing onesided, nothing partial, the king's way is smooth and easy; have nothing partial, nothing onesided, the king's way is well-arranged; have nothing deflected, nothing perverse, the king's way is straight. If you bring together those who have correctness, then they will turn to the one who has correctness, yourself. Thus: As to the king, the propagation and teaching of correctness, this he makes his norm, this he complies with, and with the Sovereign [deity] he will then comply. As to all the people, the propagation and teaching of correctness, this they comply with, this they carry into practice, and thereby they will come near to the glory of the Son of T'ien. Thus: the Son of T'ien is father and mother of the people and thereby king over the whole world.

Sixth: the three virtues. The first is called straightness; the second is called hardness predominating; the third is called softness predominating. For treating the peaceful ones, there is the straightness; for the violent and offensive ones, there is the hardness predominating; for the concordant and friendly ones there is the softness predominating. For those who are plunged and soaked in wine and pleasures there is the hardness predominating, for those who are high-standing and enlightened there is the softness predominating. It is the ruler who dispenses favours, it is the ruler who dispenses punishments, it is the ruler who eats the precious food. As to the subjects, it should never occur that they dispense favours, dispense punishments, and eat the precious food. If it occurs that subjects dispense favours, dispense punishments, and eat the precious food, it is injurious to your house and baleful to your state. The men in office thereby become partial and perverse, the people become offensive and wicked.

Seventh: the elucidators of doubt. One selects and establishes diviners by tortoise and diviners by milfoil. And then one makes denominations for the tortoise and milfoil oracles. They are called oracles about rain, clearing up, fog, calamity, and victory; and they are called the lower trigram and the upper trigram. In all there are seven. The tortoise oracles are five, the applications of the milfoil oracles are two, with extensive combinations of them. One appoints those men to perform the tortoise oracles and the milfoil oracles. When three men prognosticate, one follows the pronouncements of two men.

Now you have a great doubt; then consult with your heart, consult with the dignitaries and noblemen, consult with the common people, consult with the tortoise and milfoil oracles. Now you consent to a certain action, the tortoise consents, the milfoil consents, the dignitaries and noblemen consent, the common people consent; that is called the great concord; your person will be prosperous and strong, your sons and grandsons will be great; it is auspicious. Now you consent, the tortoise consents, the milfoil consents, but the dignitaries and noblemen oppose, the common people oppose; it is still auspicious. The dignitaries and noblemen consent, the tortoise consents, the milfoil consents, but you oppose and the common people oppose; it is still auspicious. The common people consent, the tortoise consents, the milfoil consents, but you oppose and the dignitaries and noblemen oppose; it is still auspicious. Now you consent, the tortoise consents, but the milfoil opposes, the dignitaries and noblemen oppose, the common people oppose: in internal affairs it is auspicious, in external affairs outside the state it is baleful. When tortoise and milfoil both go counter to men, to remain still is auspicious, to act is baleful.

Eighth: the various verifications. They are called rain, sunshine, heat, cold, wind, and their seasonableness; when the five come in a complete way, and each in its order, all the plants are rich and luxuriant. If one of them is complete to the extreme, it is baleful; if one is lacking to the extreme, it is baleful. Some are called the lucky verifications. Gravity— seasonable rain responds to it; orderliness—seasonable sunshine responds to it; wisdom—seasonable heat responds to it; deliberation—seasonable cold responds to it; sageness—seasonable wind responds to it. Some are called unlucky verifications. Wildness—constant rain responds to it; incorrectness—constant sunshine responds to it; indolence—constant heat responds to it; rashness—constant cold responds to it; stupidity—constant wind responds to it. He said: What the king scrutinizes is the year for its natural phenomena, the dignitaries and noblemen the months, the many lower officials the days for verifications of their government. When in years, months, and days the seasonableness has no changes, the many cereals ripen, the administration is enlightened, talented men of the people are distinguished, the house is peaceful and at ease. When in days, months, and years the seasonableness has changes the many cereals do not ripen, the administration is stupid and unenlightened, talented men of the people are in petty positions, the house is not at peace. What the common people scrutinize is the stars. There are stars which favour wind, there are stars which favour rain. Owing to the course of sun and moon there is winter and summer. According as the moons follow the stars, there is wind and rain.

Ninth: the five felicities. The first is called long life, the second riches, the third ease and tranquillity, the fourth the cultivation of a fine virtue, the fifth the achievement of a naturally ended life.

The six calamities: the first is called premature death, the second sickness, the third sorrow, the fourth poverty, the fifth ugliness, the sixth weakness.

The Metal Coffer (Chin t'êng)

After the victory over the Shang, in the second year, the king fell ill and was not happy. The two princes Shao Kung and T'ai Kung said: We shall for the king solemnly take tortoise oracle.

Chou Kung[17] said: One cannot distress our former kings. The prince then proffered himself. He made three altars on the same arena. He made an altar on the southern side, facing north. Chou Kung took his place there. He held upright, a *pi* jade disc and he grasped a *kuei* tessera. And so he addressed T'ai Wang, Wang Chi, and Wên Wang.[18]

The scribe then put on tablets the prayer, saying: Your chief descendant So-and-so has met with an epidemic sickness and is violently ill. If you three kings really owe a great son to T'ien,[19] then substitute me, Tan, for So-and-so's person. I am good and compliant, clever and capable, I have much talent and much skill, I can serve the Spirits. Your principal descendant does not, like me, Tan, have much talent and much skill, he cannot serve the Spirits. But he has been appointed in the Sovereign's hall, extensively to possess the regions of the four quarters and thereby be able firmly to establish your descendants on the earth here below. Of the people of the four quarters, there are none who do not revere and fear him. Oh, do not let fall the precious mandate sent down by T'ien, then our former kings will also forever have a reliance and resort.[20] Now I will announce the inquiry to the great tortoise. If you grant me my wish I will with the *pi* jade disc and the *kuei* tessera return and wait for your order. If you do not grant me my wish, I will shut up the jade disc and the tessera.[21]

Then he divined with the three tortoises, all in the same way were auspicious. He opened the bamboo tubes and looked at the documents. They likewise indicated that this was auspicious. The prince said: According to the content of the oracles, the king will suffer no harm.

The king said: I, the little child, anew have obtained an appointment from the three kings; for a distant end I shall plan; what I now expect is that they will care about me, the One Man.

When the prince had returned, he placed the tablets in the metal-bound coffer. The next day the king got better.

When Wu Wang had died, Kuan Shu and all his younger brothers spread talk in the state, saying: The prince will do no good to the infant.[22]

Chou Kung then said to the two princes: If I do not correct them, I shall have nothing to answer our former kings. Chou Kung dwelt in the East for two years, and then the criminal men were apprehended. Afterwards, the prince made an ode and presented it to the king, it was called *Ch'i-yao.* The king still did not dare to blame the prince.

In the autumn, when there was great ripeness, when they had not yet reaped, T'ien made great thunder and rain with wind, all the grain laid itself down, great trees then were uprooted. The people of the land greatly feared. The king and dignitaries all capped themselves in order to open the books of the metal-bound coffer. And then they got hold of the words by which Chou Kung proffered himself to take the place of Wu Wang. The two princes and the king then asked about it with the scribe and all the functionaries. They answered and said: It is true, alas! But the prince ordered that we should not dare to speak about it.

The king held the document and wept, and said: Let us not solemnly take tortoise oracle. Formerly the prince toiled for the royal house, but I, young man, have not had the means of knowing it. Now T'ien has set in motion its terror in order to signalize Chou Kung's virtue. I, the little child, will in person go and meet him, the rites of our royal house also justify this.

When the king came out to the suburbs on his way to meet Chou Kung, T'ien made rain and turned the wind and the grain all rose up. The two princes ordered the people of the state, in regard to all great trees which had been overthrown, to raise them all and earth them up. The year then was greatly fruitful.

Counsels to Prince Fêng of K'ang (K'ang kao)

In the third month, on the second day, Chou Kung first laid the foundations and made a new big city, at Lo in the eastern state. The people from the four quarters greatly concurred and convened. From the *hou*, *tien*, and *nan* states, and from the *ts'ai* and *wei* zones, the various officers and the scattered people willingly appeared for service in Chou. Chou Kung encouraged them all. And then he grandly announced the work to be done. The king spoke thus: Oh you leading prince, my younger brother, youngster Fêng! Your greatly illustrious father Wên Wang was able to make bright the virtue and to be careful about the punishments. He dared not maltreat the widowers and widows. Very meritorious, very respectful, very majestic, he was illustrious among the people. And so he created our section of the Hsia countries. In our one or two states there was thereby created order, and our western territories relied on him; it was seen and heard by Shang Ti and Ti favoured him. T'ien then grandly ordered Wên Wang to kill the great Yin[23] and grandly receive its mandate; its states and people became orderly. Your sovereign elder brother has exerted himself, and thus you, youngster Fêng, are here in the eastern territory.

The king said: Oh, Fêng, consider! Now the people will be disposed respectfully to follow your father Wên, to continue what they have heard and to follow the virtuous words. Go and widely seek from the Yin's former wise kings, thereby protecting and governing the people. You should grandly and far think of Shang's old and accomplished men, comprehend their minds, and understand their instructions. You should, besides that, seek information from the ancient former wise kings and so tranquillize and protect the people. You will be grandly protected by T'ien, a compliant virtue will be abundant in your person, you will not neglect to be intent on the king's orders. The king said: Oh, youngster Fêng, exert yourself intensely and be careful. T'ien's majesty is not to be relied on. The people's feelings are greatly visible, the small people are difficult to keep in order. Go and do your very best. Do not repose and love idleness, and you will well govern the people. I have heard the saying: dissatisfaction does not depend on whether the matter is great or whether it is small. Make compliant those who are not compliant, make energetic those who are not energetic. Yes, you are a youngster, but you shall manage great things; when your king has received and taken in his care the Yin people, you shall help the king to consolidate T'ien's mandate, and make of them a new people. The king said: Oh, Fêng, be careful and enlightened in regard to your punishments. If somebody has made a small offence, if it is not an offence by mishap but a persistence and he himself has committed what is unlawful according to his set purpose, even if his offence is small, then you cannot but kill him. If he has a great offence, if it is not a persistence but an offence by mishap, done by chance, when you have justly probed to the end his guilt, then you cannot kill him. The king said: Oh, Fêng, if you have order in that, you will make greatly illustrious your management. The people will with force strive to be concordant. As if there were a sickness to be got rid of, so the people will entirely throw away its faults; as if one protected an infant, so the people will become peaceful and well-governed. Is it not you, Fêng, who punish people and kill people?—do not erroneously punish or kill people. And again, is it not you, Fêng, who cut the nose or the legs off people?—do not erroneously cut the nose or legs off people. The king said: In judicial affairs you should set forth those items of the law, and follow those laws of the Yin that have good principles. And again he said: Having tried a case of arrest, reflect upon it five or six days, nay even to a decade or a season, and then grandly decide the tried case of arrest. The king said: You should set forth those items of the law and take for punishments and verdicts the norms of the Yin. Use their just punishments and just killings. Do not use them so as to agree with you, Fêng. Then you will be entirely compliant, saying: It is in order; yet saying modestly: There has not yet been a sufficient compliance. Yes, you are a youngster, but there is nobody who has a heart like you, Fêng; and my heart and my virtue you know. All people who draw guilt upon themselves, being robbers and thieves and villains and traitors, who kill and destroy and go for spoil, and are forceful and do not fear death, there are none who do not detest them. The king said: Fêng, when the primary evil-doers are greatly detested, how much the more then the unfilial and the unbrotherly? When a son does not respectfully manage his service to his father, he greatly hurts his father's heart. The one in a position of father cannot cherish his son but hates his son, the one in a position of younger brother does not think of T'ien's clear laws and so he cannot respect his elder brother. The elder brother likewise does not think of his tender younger brother's pitiableness and is greatly unfriendly towards his younger brother. If we are pitying to these, and they are not considered as offenders by us, the rulers, the norms given by T'ien to our people will be greatly brought into disorder. I say, may you speedily follow Wên Wang's rules of punishments, and punish these without pardon. Those who are not compliant should be greatly subjected to rules. How much the more then the provincial tutors of the noble youths, the administrators and the petty officers of various ranks? When they on their own account promulgate penal innovations, and do not think of or employ the greatly renowned ones among the people and distress their ruler, then they lead on to wickedness, and I detest them. Indeed, you should speedily, according to these norms of right, kill them all. And further, being ruler and president, if you do not treat your house-people well, and your petty officers and your provincial administrators, but are terrorizing and tyrannical and greatly set aside the royal orders, then with immorality you govern. You should in everything respect the rules, and, following them, make the people opulent; thinking of Wên Wang's care and caution, you should make the people opulent, saying: May I only attain to him! Then I, the One Man, will be pleased. The king said: Fêng, when it is at fault, the people should be guided to happiness and peace. I always think of the virtue of Yin's former wise kings, in order to tranquillize and govern the people, and I actively seek it. All the more since at present the people go wherever they are guided; if one does not guide them, there will be no government in their state. The king said: Fêng, I cannot but scrutinize. I will tell you the principles of virtue in the application of the punishments. Now the people are not quiet, they have not yet settled their minds. I have guided them, but repeatedly they have not concurred with my directions. If there is any fault, T'ien will punish and kill me, and I shall not resent it. As to their crimes my responsibility does not depend on whether they are great, it does not depend on whether they are many—how much the more, then, when they upwards are manifest to and heard by T'ien! The king said: Oh, Fêng, be careful. Do not create animosity, do not use bad counsels and bad norms. May your decisions be correct and reliable. Grandly take as pattern the active virtue of the ancients. Thereby make steady your heart, take care of your virtue, make far-reaching your plans and intentions, then you will make the people tranquil, and I will not remove you or cut you off. The king said: Oh, now, you youngster Fêng! The mandate is not irremovable. You should think of it. May it not happen that I cut off your enjoyment of the fief. Make illustrious the mandate you manage. Think highly of what you have now heard, and so tranquillize and govern the people. The king spoke thus: Go, you Fêng, do not set aside your respectful care; constantly listen to my admonishments; then you will, with the people of Yin as your subjects, from generation to generation enjoy your fief.

Duke of Chou's Address to Restless Shang Nobles (To fang)

In the fifth month, on the day *ting-hai*, the king came from Yen and arrived in Tsung Chou. Chou Kung said: The king has spoken thus: I will discourse and tell you four states and numerous other regions, you officials and common people of the prince of Yin. I grandly give you my commands. May none of you fail to take cognizance. You greatly despise T'ien's command, and do not perpetually and reverently think of the sacrifices. God descended and ascended with Chieh, the Hsia king, but the lord of Hsia increased his pleasurable ease, and he was not willing solicitously to speak to the people. He was greatly licentious and darkened, and could not for a whole day be stimulated by Ti's guidance. This is what you have heard. Despising Ti's command, he could not set free those of the people who had been assigned for punishment, and so he greatly sent down punishments, and he heavily disordered the realm. And then he was familiar with the disorderly ones in the interior.[24]

He could not excellently take care of the multitude. He did not grandly bring them forward to reverence. He was greatly lazy towards the people. Also the people of the lord of Hsia, their grief and annoyance became daily more intense. He destroyed and injured the city of Hsia. T'ien then sought a new lord for the people, and grandly it sent down its illustrious and felicitous mandate to Ch'êng T'ang of Shang, and it punished and destroyed the lord of Hsia. T'ien's not giving favour to Hsia was definite; having the righteous people of your numerous regions he still could not continue long in the ample enjoyment of the mandate. Hsia's trusted officers were greatly unable brightly to protect and to give bounties to the people. And so, together with them he oppressed the people, so that in the numerous actions he was greatly unable to condone the accused. Then Ch'êng T'ang, having your numerous regions, could supersede Hsia and become the lord of the people. He was careful about those who were assigned for punishments and so he stimulated the people. The people imitated him and were stimulated. Right up to Ti I there were none who did not make bright their virtue and be careful about the punishments, and thus they also could stimulate the people. Trying the cases of arrest, they destroyed and put to death those who had many crimes, and thus stimulated the people; they set free the innocent, and thus could also stimulate the people. But now, when it came to your sovereign, the last Yin king, he could not, having your numerous regions, enjoy T'ien's mandate.

Oh! The king has spoken thus: I inform and tell you in your numerous regions, it was not that T'ien thus did away with the lords of Hsia, it was not that T'ien thus did away with the lords of Yin. But it was that your sovereign, having your numerous regions, despised T'ien's command; he was greatly licentious and dissolute and had ill fame. It was that the lord of Hsia despised his government work, and he did not achieve the enjoyment of the mandate. T'ien sent down that ruin, and a feudal prince superseded him. It was that your last king of Shang enjoyed his pleasurable ease, despised his government work, and did not bring pure sacrifices. T'ien then sent down that ruin. The wise, if he does not think, will become foolish, the foolish, if he can think, will become wise. T'ien for five years waited and gave respite to him, so that his sons and grandsons would grandly be the lords of the people, but he could not think or be wise. T'ien then searched in your numerous regions and greatly shook you by its severity; it would condone those who had regard for T'ien, but in your numerous regions there were none who were able to have regard for it.

But our king of Chou excellently took care of the people, he was able to use the virtue, and preside over the sacrifices to the Spirits and to T'ien. T'ien then instructed us to avail ourselves of its grace, it selected us and gave us Yin's mandate, to rule over your numerous regions. Now, how dare I make these many declarations? I grandly send down orders to the men of your four states. Why do you not make them truly opulent in your numerous regions? Why do you not support and assist and guide our king of Chou, to enjoy T'ien's mandate? Now, may you still dwell in your dwellings and cultivate your fields. Why do you not obey the king and make T'ien's mandate resplendent? You have been guided, but repeatedly you have been unruly. Your hearts are not yet affectionate.

You do not greatly consolidate T'ien's mandate. You recklessly reject the command of T'ien. You yourselves do unlawful things and despise being faithful to your superiors. I will therefore instruct and tell you. I will therefore put fear into you and arrest you for trial, even twice, even thrice. If there are those who do not obey the orders which I have sent down to you, I will greatly punish and kill them. It is not that the character which we Chou have is unruly, it is that you yourselves draw upon yourselves guilt.

o   o   o   o

May you, from this city Lo, forever forcefully cultivate your fields. T'ien will endow you and pity you. We, lords of Chou, will greatly help and reward you. We will promote and select you to be in the king's court. We will give you high offices, to have work among the great dignitaries.

o   o   o   o

Establishing Government (Li chêng)

o   o   o   o

From of old, the Shang men and our Wên Wang of Chou, when they established a government, when they nominated a manager, a pastor, and a man of law, they could put them in the high positions, and they could let them continue. Thus they caused them to govern. As to the empire, it has never occurred that in establishing a government one has employed insincere men. Those who were not docile in their virtue, those were not illustrious in their generation. From this time forth, in establishing the government may you not use insincere men. May there be good men; use them and stimulate them to assist in the government of our state. Now, accomplished son of Wu, accomplished grandson of Wên, young son and king, may you not err in regard to the many legal prosecutions, for those there is the pastor in office. May you be able to examine your weapons, and thus step up in the footsteps of Yü, and everywhere travel in the world, as far as to the extreme points of the seas, there being no place that does not submit as a dependency, so that you display Wên Wang's bright virtue and extol Wu Wang's brilliant deeds.

Oh, from this time forth, when the posterior kings establish their government, may they be able to use permanent men in office.

o   o   o   o

Deathbed Commands (Ku ming)

In the fourth month, on the second day, the king was ill. On the day *chia-tzŭ*, the king poured water over his face, the assistants put on him the cap and the robe, and he leaned on a jade stool. He called together the grand guardian Shih, the prince of Jui, the prince of T'ung, the prince of Pi, the prince of Wei, the prince of Mao, the instructor, the chief of the tiger braves, the various governors and managers of affairs.

The king said: Oh, the sickness greatly advances, there is imminent risk. An extreme illness is daily approaching; it has tarried long. I fear that I shall not be able to make a solemn declaration about the subsequent matters. Now I minutely instruct and order you. The former rulers Wên Wang and Wu Wang displayed their brightness one after the other and set forth their refinement. In spreading their instructions they toiled, but in toiling they did not go too far. Thus they could reach to Yin and achieve the great mandate. I, the succeeding stupid one, have respectfully applied T'ien's majesty, and continued to keep to Wên's and Wu's great instructions, and not dared foolishly to transgress them.

Now T'ien has sent down a sickness that is fatal, I cannot rise, I cannot get my mind clear. May you clearly understand these words of mine, and thus carefully guard my eldest son, Chao, and grandly help him over in the difficulties. Be gentle with the distant ones, be kind to the near ones. Tranquillize and stimulate all the small and great states. You should think of how a man governs himself in dignity. You should not, because Chao is covetous, make him presents in improper quantities.

Now, when they had received the king's order, they returned. One brought the stitched garments into the courtyard. The next day, an *I-ch'ou* day, the king died. The grand guardian gave order to Chung Huan and Nan-kung Mao and made them assist him. The prince of Ch'i, Lü Chi, with two men with shield and dagger-axes and tiger braves, one hundred men, went to meet the son Chao outside the south gate, and invited him to enter the Bright Room and carefully attend to those who sojourn in the clan temple.[25]

On the day *ting-mao* order was given to make a document about the measures prescribed by the dead king. On the seventh day, a *kuei-yu* day, the leader-premier ordered the officers to exact the materials for the burial. Servants displayed the screen ornamented with axes and the stitched garments of the king. Between the windows, facing the south, they spread out double bamboo-strip mats with black-and-white-silk borders, and the traditional stool with varicoloured jades. In the space along the western wall, facing the east, they spread out double smooth rush mats with stitched borders, and a traditional stool with striped cowries. In the space along the eastern wall, facing west, they spread out double sumptuous mats with painted borders, and a traditional stool with carved jades. In the western side-room, facing the south, they spread out double young-bamboo mats with dark, ample borders and a traditional stool with lacquer. There were quintuple jades and old treasures. The red sacrificial jade knife, the large grand *kuei* tessera, the great jade *pi* disk, the rounded-top *kuei* tessera, and the pointed-top *kuei* tessera were in the space along the western wall, the great jade, the jade of the I tribes, the great *ch'iu* jade and the drawing-tablet of the River were in the space along the east wall, the dancing garments of Yin, the great shell and the big drum were in the western room, the dagger-axe of Tui, the Bow of Ho, the bamboo arrows of Ch'ui were in the eastern room. The grand chariot was in front of the guests' staircase, the adjunct chariot was in front of the eastern staircase, the foremost chariot was before the left gate-room, the next-following chariot was before the right gate-room.

Two men with sparrow-caps holding *hui* lances stood inside the Last gate [farthest from the south]. Four men with black-mottled caps, holding dagger-axes with the edge upwards, stood on both sides of the staircases and the corners of the raised hall-platform. One man, with state cap, holding a *liu* axe, stood in the eastern part of the open hall, one man, with state cap, holding a *yüeh* axe, stood in the western part of the hall, one man, with state cap, holding a *k'uei* lance, stood at the eastern extreme end of the hall, one man with state cap, holding a *ch'ü* lance, stood at the western extreme end of the hall, one man, with state cap, holding a *tui* lance, stood at the side staircase north from the hall.

The king had hempen state cap and skirt with black-and-white axe-shaped ornaments and ascended by the guests' staircase, the ministers and feudatory rulers had hempen state caps and ant-coloured skirts, they entered and went to their positions. The grand guardian, the grand scribe, and the grand master of rites all had hempen state caps and red skirts. The grand guardian held the grand *kuei* tessera, the high master of rites held a *chia* vessel and libation ladle; they ascended by the eastern staircase.

The grand scribe held the document and ascended by the guests' staircase. He presented to the king the written-down order of the dead king. He said: The august sovereign, leaning on the jade stool, brought forward and manifested his last will. He ordered you to follow up the instructions, to look down upon and govern the state of Chou, to follow the great laws, to make the whole world harmonious and concordant. . . .

The Prince of Lü's Code of Punishment (Lü hsing)

○   ○   ○   ○

The king said: Oh, come, possessors of states and possessors of lands. I will tell you about litigations and punishments. Now, when you tranquillize the people, what should you select, if not the proper men, what should you carefully attend to, if not the punishments, what should you plan for, if not the attainment of the highest standards? When both parties have appeared fully prepared with testimonies, the court assessors deal with the five kinds of pleading. When by the five kinds of pleading one has ascertained and verified the guilt, one attributes the case to one of the five punishments; if the five punishments are not found adequate, one attributes it to one of the five redemption-fines; if the five redemption-fines are not applicable, one attributes it to the five cases of errors. The shortcomings called the five cases of error are officialism, insubordination, bribery, hoarding, and office-seeking. These offences are on a par. May you investigate it. In doubtful cases of the five punishments there is condoning; in doubtful cases of the five redemption-fines there is condoning. May you investigate it. You should ascertain and verify and act in concert with public opinion; you should minutely make investigation. If the guilt is not ascertained, you should not deal with the case. You should all stand in awe of T'ien's majesty.

○   ○   ○   ○

The kinds of crimes falling under the five punishments are three thousand. In graver and lighter cases, you should with precedents compare the offences. Do not admit false and disorderly pleadings. Do not use what is obsolete. What you should study is the law. May you investigate it.

In regard to a higher punishment, when the crime tends towards the lighter side, it should be downwards applied; in regard to a lower punishment, when the crime tends towards the heavier side, it should be upwards applied. For the lighter or heavier redemption-fines there is the balance of circumstances. The punishments and fines are in certain ages light, in certain ages heavy. For adjusting what is not just there are reasons and leading principles.

Through the correcting by fines, there is no death, but people come to the extreme in suffering. It is not the specious who should decide criminal cases, it is the good who should decide them. Everything depends on justness. Examine the pleadings with regard to the divergences, to find which not to follow and which to follow. Compassionately and carefully you should decide the criminal cases. Publicly open the law codex and together look for the answer; all will then, it is to be hoped, be just and correct. In punishing and in fining, may you examine it. When in a criminal case you have achieved your sure result, then commit to writing your sure result; the punishments should be recorded and completely indicated.

o   o   o   o

Now, when T'ien would aid the people, it has created a counterpart for itself here below. You should bring clarity into the pleadings from one of the parties only. In governing the people you should have nothing that is not just, and listen to both pleadings in the criminal cases. Do not perchance privately profit from the two pleading parties in criminal cases. Hoardings from criminal cases are no treasures. You only store up culpable deeds, and you will be requited by much guilt and punishment. What should be perpetually feared is the punishment of T'ien. It is not that T'ien is not just; it is man who should fully understand its decrees. If T'ien's punishments were not perfect, the common people would not have a good government under T'ien. The king said: Oh, you inheriting descendants! Henceforth, whom should you scrutinize? Is it not the virtuous ones in the midst of the people? May you enlightenedly listen to it.

For restraining the people there are the penal laws. The innumerable legal cases should be applied to the five proper norms, and when all is just there will be happiness. You who receive the king's fine multitude should scrutinize these rules of litigation and punishments.

3

Book of Songs

The King's business never ends.
My heart is sick and sad.
—*Book of Songs*, 145

The *Book of Songs* (tenth–sixth centuries B.C.) contains ballads (*fēng*, poetically the best of the lot), ceremonial songs (*yǎ*), and sacrificial odes (*sùng*). The songs and odes were part of court rites. Music set the rhythm and mood for performance of the ceremony. Officials wore pieces of jade, suspended from their clothing, that kept time with the bells. The songs and odes were gathered from the various regions of the Chou Dynasty in its early stage. Some of the ballads or folk songs seem to be from an even earlier time, from that of the Shang, predecessors of the Chou.

This collection of beautiful poetry, ranging from solemn dynastic hymns to delicate airs and lyrics of love, has been widely quoted by almost all philosophers and men of letters.

Sometimes the meaning of the verses is clear, sometimes it seems to be clear and is not. The custom of giving interpretations to the songs at variance with a literal reading, say, to words about a courtship, grew up early in ancient China. Often the underlying sense is supposed to be philosophic; more often it is supposed to be political. Frequently the political sense jabbed at the government and, therefore, with good reason, lay underground. A political light clearly bathes the lines "Chou is an old people but its mandate is new," but only interpretation and reinterpretation can reveal that "Cold is the north wind" should be read: Cruel and corrupt is this government. Also difficult to see is that the beautiful air:

If along the highroad
I caught hold of your sleeve,

> Do not hate me;
> Old ways take time to overcome.
>   —*Book of Songs*, 56

may be the lament of a courtier cast off by his duke. Whether taken in one sense or another or both, these songs are distillations of the flower of poetry.

BOOK OF SONGS

(Shih Ching)

Selections

Ballads

119

His furs of lamb's wool so glossy!
Truly he is steadfast and tough.
That great gentleman
Would give his life rather than fail his lord.

His furs of lamb's wool, facings of leopard's fur!
He is very martial and strong.

From Arthur Waley, tr., *Book of Songs* (Boston: Houghton Mifflin, 1937), translation
slightly modified.

That great gentleman
Is the upholder of right in this land.

His furs of lamb's wool so splendid,
His three festoons so gay!
That great gentleman
Is the first in all our land.

122

How few of us are left, how few!
Why do we not go back?
Were it not for our prince and his concerns,
What should we be doing here in the dew?

How few of us are left, how few!
Why do we not go back?
Were it not for our prince's own concerns,
What should we be doing here in the mud?

124

I climb that wooded hill
And look towards where my father is.
My father is saying, "Alas, my son is on service;
Day and night he knows no rest.
Grant that he is being careful of himself,
So that he may come back and not be left behind!"

I climb that bare hill
And look towards where my mother is.
My mother is saying, "Alas, my young one is on service;
Day and night he gets no sleep.
Grant that he is being careful of himself,
So that he may come back, and not be cast away."

I climb that ridge
And look towards where my elder brother is.
My brother is saying, "Alas, my young brother is on service;
Day and night he toils.

Grant that he is being careful of himself,
So that he may come back and not die."

232

Broken were our axes
And chipped our hatchets.
But since the Duke of Chou came to the East[1]
Throughout the kingdoms all is well.
He has shown compassion to us people,
He has greatly helped us.

Broken were our axes
And chipped our hoes.
But since the Duke of Chou came to the East
The whole land has been changed.
He has shown compassion to us people,
He has greatly blessed us.

Broken were our axes
And chipped our chisels.
But since the Duke of Chou came to the East
All the kingdoms are knit together.
He has shown compassion to us people,
He has been a great boon to us.

276

Big rat, big rat,
Do not gobble our millet!
Three years we have slaved for you,
Yet you take no notice of us.
At last we are going to leave you
And go to that happy land;
Happy land, happy land,
Where we shall have our place.

Big rat, big rat,
Do not gobble our corn!
Three years we have slaved for you,
Yet you give us no credit.

At last we are going to leave you
And go to that happy kingdom;
Happy kingdom, happy kingdom,
Where we shall get our due.

Big rat, big rat,
Do not eat our rice-shoots!
Three years we have slaved for you,
Yet you did nothing to reward us.
At last we are going to leave you
And go to those happy borders;
Happy borders, happy borders
Where no sad songs are sung.

Ceremonial Songs

127

Minister of War,
We are the king's claws and fangs.
Why should you roll us on from misery to misery,
Giving us no place to stop in or take rest?

Minister of War,
We are the king's claws and teeth.
Why should you roll us from misery to misery,
Giving us no place to come to and stay?

Minister of War,
Truly you are not wise.
Why should you roll us from misery to misery?
We have mothers who lack food.

130

What plant is not faded?
What day do we not march?
What man is not taken
To defend the four bounds?

What plant is not wilting?
What man is not taken from his wife?
Alas for us soldiers,
Treated as though we were not fellow-men!

Are we buffaloes, are we tigers
That our home should be these desolate wilds?
Alas for us soldiers,
Neither by day nor night can we rest!

The fox bumps and drags
Through the tall, thick grass.
Inch by inch move our barrows
As we push them along the track.

132

We bring out our carts
On to those pasture-grounds.
From where the Son of T'ien[2] is
Orders have come that we are to be here.
The grooms are told
To get the carts loaded up.
The king's service brings many hardships;
It makes swift calls upon us.

We bring out our carts
On to those outskirts.
Here we set up the standards,
There we raise the ox-tail banners,
The falcon-banner and the standards
That flutter, flutter.
Our sad hearts are very anxious;
The grooms are worn out.

The king has ordered Nan-chung[3]
To go and build a fort on the frontier.
To bring out the great concourse of chariots,
With dragon banners and standards so bright.
The Son of T'ien has ordered us

To build a fort on that frontier.
Terrible is Nan-chung;
The Hsien-yün[4] are undone.

Long ago, when we started,
The wine-millet and cooking-millet were in flower.
Now that we are on the march again
Snow falls upon the mire.
The king's service brings many hardships.
We have no time to rest or bide.
We do indeed long to return;
But we fear the writing on the tablets.[5]

"Dolefully cry the cicadas,
Hop and skip go the grasshoppers.
Before I saw my lord
My heart was full of grief.
But now that I have seen my lord
My heart is still." [6]
Terrible is Nan-chung;
Lo, he has stricken the warriors of the West!

The spring days are drawn out;
All plants and trees are in leaf.
Tuneful is the oriole's song.
The women gather aster in crowds.
We have bound the culprits; we have captured the chieftains,
And here we are home again!
Terrible is Nan-chung;
The Hsien-yün are levelled low.

145

WIFE: Tall grows that pear-tree,
Its fruit so fair to see.
The king's business never ends;
Day in, day out it claims us.

CHORUS: In spring-time, on a day so sunny—
Yet your heart full of grief?

The soldiers have leave!

WIFE: Tall grows that pear-tree,
Its leaves so thick.
The king's business never ends;
My heart is sick and sad.

CHORUS: Every plant and tree so leafy,
Yet your heart sad?
The soldiers are coming home!

SOLDIER: I climb that northern hill
To pluck the boxthorn.
The king's business never ends;
What will become of my father, of my mother?

CHORUS: Their wickered chariots drag painfully along,
Their horses are tired out.
But the soldiers have not far to go.

WIFE: If he were not expected and did not come
My heart would still be sad.
But he named a day, and that day is passed,
So that my torment is great indeed.

CHORUS: The tortoise and the yarrow-stalks agree;
Both tell glad news.
Your soldier is close at hand.

193

The fish are at home, at home among their water-plants,
Beautifully streaked are their heads.
The king is at home, at home in Hao,[7]
Content and happy he drinks his wine.

The fish are at home, at home among their water-plants,
Very pliant are their tails.
The king is at home, at home in Hao,
Drinking his wine, happy and content.

The fish are at home, at home among their water-plants,

Snuggling close to their reeds.
The king is at home, at home in Hao,
Very soft he lies.

202

We are drunk with wine,
We are sated with power.
Here's long life to you, our lord;
May blessings be vouchsafed to you forever.

We are drunk with wine,
All the dishes have gone the round.
Here's long life to you, our lord;
May their Shining Light[8] be vouchsafed to you.

May their Shining Light beam mildly upon you;
High fame and good end to all you do.
That good end is well assured;
The impersonator of the Ancient[9] tells a lucky story.

And what is his story?
"Your bowls and dishes are clean and good;
The friends that helped you
Helped with perfect manners.

Their manners were irreproachable;
My lord will have pious sons,
Pious sons in good store.
A good thing is given you forever."

And what is this good thing?
"Your house shall be raised,
My lord shall have long life,
Blessed shall be his inheritance for ever."

And what is this inheritance?
"T'ien will cover you with rewards.
My lord shall live long,

Have long life, and a gift as well."

And what is this gift?
"He gives to you a girl.
He gives to you a girl,
That you may in due time have grandsons and sons."

241

King Wên[10] is on high;
Oh, he shines in Heaven!
Chou is an old people
But its mandate is new.
The land of Chou became illustrious,
Blessed by God's charge.[11]
King Wên ascends and descends
On God's left hand, on His right.

Very diligent was King Wên,
His high fame does not cease;
He spread his bounties in Chou,
And now in his grandsons and sons,
In his grandsons and sons
The stem has branched
Into manifold generations,
And all the knights of Chou
Are glorious in their generation.

Glorious in their generation,
And their counsels well pondered.
Mighty were the many knights
That brought this kingdom to its birth.
This kingdom well they bore;
They were the prop of Chou.
Splendid were those many knights
Who gave comfort to Wên the king.

August is Wên the king;
Oh, to be reverenced in his glittering light!

Mighty the charge that T'ien gave him.
The grandsons and sons of the Shang,
Shang's grandsons and sons,
Their hosts were innumerable.
But God on high gave His command,
And by Chou they were subdued.

By Chou they were subdued;
T'ien's charge is not forever.
The knights of Yin,[12] big and little,
Made libations and offerings at the capital;
What they did was to make libations
Dressed in skirted robe and close cap.
O chosen servants of the king,
May you never thus shame your ancestors!

May you never shame your ancestors,
But rather tend their inward power,
That forever you may be linked to T'ien's charge
And bring to yourselves many blessings.
Before Yin lost its army
It was well linked to God above.
In Yin you should see as in a mirror
That T'ien's high charge is hard to keep.

The charge is not easy to keep.
Do not bring ruin on yourselves.
Send forth everywhere the light of your good fame;
Consider what T'ien did to the Yin.
High T'ien does its business
Without sound, without smell.
Make King Wên your example,
In whom all the peoples put their trust.

242

Mighty is God on high,
Ruler of His people below;
Swift and terrible is God on high,

His charge has many statutes.
T'ien gives birth to the multitudes of the people,
But its charge cannot be counted upon.
To begin well is common;
To end well is rare indeed.

King Wên said, "Come!
Come, you Yin and Shang!
Why these violent men,
Why these slaughterers—
Why are they in office, why are they in power?
T'ien has sent down to you an arrogant spirit;
What you exalt is violence."

King Wên said, "Come!
Come, you Yin and Shang,
And hold fast to what is seemly and fitting;
Your violence leads to much resentment.
Slanders you support and further,
To brigands and thieves you give entry,
Who curse, who use evil imprecations,
Without limit or end."

King Wên said, "Come!
Come, you Yin and Shang!
You rage and seethe in the Middle Kingdom,[13]
You count the heaping up of resentment as inward power;
You do not make bright your power,
So that none backs you, none is at your side.
No, your merit does not shine bright,
So that none cleaves to you nor comes to you."

King Wên said, "Come!
Come, you Yin and Shang!
T'ien did not flush you with wine.
Not good are the ways you follow;
Most disorderly are your manners.
Not heeding whether it is dawn or dusk

You shout and scream,
Turning day into night."

King Wên said, "Come!
Come, you Yin and Shang!
You are like grasshoppers, like cicadas,
Like frizzling water, like boiling soup;
Little and great you draw near to ruin.
Men long to walk in right ways,
But you rage in the Middle Kingdom,
And as far as the land of Kuei." [14]

King Wên said, "Come!
Come, you Yin and Shang!
It is not that God on high did not bless you;
It is that Yin does not follow the old ways.
Even if you have no old men ripe in judgment,
At least you have your statutes and laws.
Why is it that you do not listen,
But upset T'ien's great charge?"

King Wên said, "Come!
Come, you Yin and Shang!
There is a saying among men:
'When a towering tree crashes,
The branches and leaves are still unharmed;
It is the trunk that first decays.'
A mirror for Yin is not far off;
It is the times of the Lord of Hsia." [15]

243

God on high in sovereign might
Looked down majestically,
Gazed down upon the four quarters,
Examining the ills of the people.
Already in two kingdoms[16]
The governance had been all awry;
Then every land

He tested and surveyed.
God on high examined them
And hated the laxity of their rule.
So he turned his gaze to the west[17]
And here made his dwelling-place.

Cleared them, moved them,
The dead trees, the fallen trunks;
Trimmed them, levelled them,
The clumps and stumps;
Opened them, cleft them,
The tamarisk woods, the stave-tree woods;
Pulled them up, cut them back,
The wild mulberries, the cudranias.
God shifted his bright Power;
To fixed customs and rules he gave a path.
T'ien set up for itself a counterpart on earth;
Its charge was firmly awarded.

God examined his hills.
The oak-trees were uprooted,
The pines and cypresses were cleared.
God made a land, made a counterpart,
Beginning with T'ai-po and Wang Chi.[18]
Now this Wang Chi
Was of heart accommodating and friendly,
Friendly to his elder brother,
So that his luck was strong.
Great were the gifts that were bestowed upon him,
Blessings he received and no disasters,
Utterly he swayed the whole land.

Then came King Wên;
God set right measure to his thoughts,
Spread abroad his fair fame;
His power was very bright,
Very bright and very good.
Well he led, well lorded,

Was king over this great land.
Well he followed, well obeyed,
Obeyed—did King Wên.
His power was without flaw.
Having received God's blessing
He handed it down to grandsons and sons.

God said to King Wên:
"This is no time to be idle,
No time to indulge in your desires.
You must be first to seize the high places.
The people of Mi are in revolt.
They have dared to oppose the great kingdom.
They have invaded Yüan and Kung." [19]
The king blazed forth his anger;
He marshalled his armies,
To check the foe he attacked the armies,
He secured the safety of Chou,
He united all under Heaven.

They drew near to the capital,
Attacking from the borders of Yüan.
They began to climb our high ridges;
But never did they marshal their forces on our hills,
Our hills or slopes,
Never did they drink out of our wells,
Our wells, our pools.
The king made his dwelling in the foothills and plains,
Dwelt in the southern slopes of Mount Ch'i,
On the shores of the River Wei,
Pattern to all the myriad lands,
King of his subject peoples.

God said to King Wên,
"I am moved by your bright power.
Your high renown has not made you put on proud airs,
Your greatness has not made you change former ways,
You do not try to be clever or knowing,

But follow God's precepts."
God said to King Wên,
"Take counsel with your partner states,
Unite with your brothers young and old,
And with your scaling ladders and siege-platforms
Attack the castles of Ch'ung."

The siege-platforms trembled,
The walls of Ch'ung towered high.
The culprits were bound quietly,
Ears were cut off peacefully.
He made the sacrifice to T'ien and the sacrifice of propitiation.
He annexed the spirits of the land, he secured continuance of the an-
    cestral sacrifices,
And none anywhere dared affront him.
The siege-platforms shook,
So high were the walls of Ch'ung.
He attacked, he harried,
He cut off, he destroyed.
None anywhere dared oppose him.

267

    The guests are taking their seats;
    To left, to right they range themselves.
    The food-baskets and dishes are in their rows,
    With dainties and kernels displayed.
    The wine is soft and good,
    It is drunk very peaceably.
    The bells and drums are set,
    The brimming pledge-cup is raised.
    The great target is put up,
    The bows and arrows are tested,
    The bowmen are matched.
    "Present your deeds of archery,
    Shoot at that mark
    That you may be rewarded with the cup."

    Fluting they dance to reed-pipe and drum,

All the instruments perform in concert
As an offering to please the glorious ancestors,
That the rites may be complete.
For when all the rites are perfect,
Grandly, royally done,
The ancestors bestow great blessings;
Sons and grandsons may rejoice,
May rejoice and make music:
"Let each of you display his art."
The guests then receive the pledge-cup,
The house-men enter anew
And fill that empty cup,
That you may perform your songs.

When the guests first take their seats,
How decorous they are, how reverent!
While they are still sober
Their manner is dignified and correct;
But when they are drunk
Their manner is utterly changed.
They leave their seats and roam,
Cut capers, throw themselves about.
While they are still sober
Their manner is dignified and grave;
But when they are drunk
It becomes unseemly and rude;
For when people are drunk
They do not know what misdemeanours they commit.

When guests are drunk
They howl and bawl,
Upset my baskets and dishes,
Cut capers, lilt and lurch.
For when people are drunk
They do not know what blunders they commit.
Cap on one side, very insecure,
They cut capers lascivious.
If when they got drunk they went out,

They would receive their blessing like the rest.
But if they get drunk and stay,
The power of the feast is spoilt.
Drinking wine is very lucky,
Provided it is done with decency.

It is always the same when wine is drunk;
Some are tipsy, some are not.
So we appoint a master of ceremonies,
Or choose someone as recorder.
"That drunk man is not behaving nicely;
He is making the sober feel uncomfortable.
Pray do not mention at random
Things that do not belong together, that are quite silly.
What are not real words, do not say;
What leads nowhere, do not speak of,
Led on by drunkenness in your talk,
Bringing out 'rams' and 'hornless' side by side.
After the three cups you don't know what you are saying;
What will become of you if you insist on taking more?"

271

Grave and dignified manners
Are the helpmates of power.
Men indeed have a saying,
"There is none so wise but has his follies."
But ordinary people's follies
Are but sicknesses of their own.
It is the wise man's follies
That are a rampant pest.

Nothing is so strong as goodness;
On all sides men will take their lesson from it.
Valid are the works of inward power;
In all lands men will conform to them.
He who takes counsel widely, is final in his commands,
Far-seeing in his plans, timely in the announcing of them,
Scrupulously attentive to decorum,

Will become a pattern to his people.

But those that rule today
Have brought confusion and disorder into the government;
Have upset their power
By wild orgies of drinking.
So engrossed are you in your dissipations
That you do not think of your heritage,
Do not faithfully imitate the former kings,
Or strive to carry out their holy ordinances.

Therefore mighty T'ien is displeased;
Beware lest headlong as spring waters
You should be swept to ruin.
Rise early, go to bed at night;
Sprinkle and sweep your courtyard
So that it may be a pattern to the people.
Put in good order your chariots and horses,
Bows, arrows, and weapons of offence,
That you may be ready, should war arise,
To keep at due distance barbaric tribes.

Ascertain the views of gentlemen and commoners,
Give due warning of your princely measures,
Take precautions against the unforeseen,
Be cautious in your utterances.
Scrupulously observe all rules of decorum,
Be always mild and good-tempered.
A scratch on a sceptre of white jade
Can be polished away;
A slip of the tongue
Cannot ever be repaired.

Do not be rash in your words,
Do not say: "Let it pass.
Don't catch hold of my tongue!
What I am saying will go no further."
There can be nothing said that has not its answer,

No deed of Power that has not its reward.
Be gracious to friends and companions
And to the common people, my child.
So shall your sons and grandsons continue forever,
By the myriad peoples each accepted.

When receiving gentlemen of your acquaintance
Let your countenance be peaceable and mild;
Never for an instant be dissolute.
You are seen in your house;
You do not escape even in the curtained alcove.
Do not say: "Of the glorious ones
None is looking at me."
A visit from the Spirits
Can never be foreseen;
The better reason for not disgusting them.

Prince, let the exercise of your inner power
Be good and blessed.
Be very careful in your conduct,
Be correct in your manners,
Never usurp or go beyond your rights,
And few will not take you as their model:
"She threw me a peach
And I requited it with a plumb."
That kid with horns
Was truly a portent of disorder, my son!

Wood that is soft and pliant
We fit with strings.[20]
Reverence and goodness so mild
Are the foundations of inner power.
Mark how the wise man,
When I tell him of ancient sayings,
Follows the way of inner power.
Mark how the fool,
On the contrary, says that I am wrong,
And that everyone has a right to his ideas.

Alas, my son,
That you should still confuse right and wrong!
When I have not led you by the hand
I have pointed at the thing.
What I have not face to face declared to you
I have hoarsely whispered in your ear.
You may say to me, "You don't know";
But I am already a grandfather.
The people are short of supplies;
Who knew it early but deals with it late?

Oh, high T'ien so bright,
My life is most unhappy!
Seeing you so heedless
My heart is sorely grieved.
I instruct you in utmost detail;
But you listen to me very casually.
You do not treat my talks as lessons,
But on the contrary regard them as a joke.
You may say, "You don't know";
But I am in truth a very old man.

Alas, my son,
What I tell to you are the ways of the ancients.
If you take my advice
You will have small cause to repent.
T'ien is sending us calamities,
Is destroying the country.
You have not far to go for an example;
High T'ien does not chop and change.
By perverting your inner power,
You will reduce your people to great extremities.

280

    In flood those running waters
    Carry their tides to join the sea.
    Swift that flying kite
    Now flies, now lights.

Alas that of my brothers,
My countrymen and all my friends,
Though each has father, has mother,
None heeds the disorders of this land!

In flood those running waters
Spread out so wide, so wide.
Swift that flying kite;
Now flying, now soaring.
Thinking of those rebellious ones
I arise, I go.
The sorrows of my heart
I cannot banish or forget.

Swift that flying kite
Makes for that middle mound.
The false words of the people,
Why does no one stop them?
My friends, be on your guard;
Slanderous words are on the rise.

285

I climb those northern hills
And pluck the boxthorn.
Very strenuous are the knights,
Early and late upon their tasks;
The king's business never ends.
But for my father and mother I grieve.

"Everywhere under Heaven
Is no land that is not the king's.
To the borders of all those lands
None but is the king's slave."
But the ministers are not just;
Whatever is done, I bear the brunt alone.

[Like] a team of steeds so strong
The king's business bears down upon me.

Everyone congratulates me on my youthfulness,
Is surprised I am still so strong,
That with muscles still so tough
I build the frontiers on every hand.

Some people sit quietly at home;
Others wear themselves out in serving their country.
Some lie peacefully in bed;
Others are always on the move.

Some senselessly yell and bawl;
Others fret and toil.
Some loll about at their ease;
Others in the king's business are engrossed.

Some sunk in pleasure swill their wine;
Others are tortured by the fear of blame.
Some do nothing but scold or advise;
Others in every trouble must act.

288

Very leafy is that willow-tree,[21]
But I would not care to rest under it.
God on high is very bright;
Don't go too close to him!
Were I to reprove him,
Afterwards I should be slaughtered by him.

Very leafy is that willow-tree,
But I would not care to repose under it.
God on high is very bright;
Don't hurt yourself on him!
Were I to reprove him,
Afterwards I should be torn to pieces by him.

There is a bird, flies high,
Yes, soars to Heaven.
But that man's heart

Never could it reach.
Why should I rebuke him,
Only to be cruelly slain?

Sacrificial Odes

153

Mighty are you, Hou Chi,[22]
Full partner in T'ien's power.
That we, the thronging peoples, were raised up
Is all your doing.
You gave us wheat and barley
In obedience to God's command.
Not to this limit only or to that frontier,
But near, far, and forever throughout these lands of Hsia.[23]

156

Abundant is the year, with much millet, much rice;
But we have tall granaries,
To hold myriads, many myriads and millions of grain.
We make wine, make sweet liquor,
We offer it to ancestor, to ancestress,
We use it to fulfil all the rites,
To bring down blessings upon each and all.

205

Blind men, blind men[24]
In the courtyard of Chou.
We have set up the cross-board, the stand,
With the upright hooks, the standing plumes.
The little and big drums are hung for beating;
The tambourines and stone-chimes, the staff and clapper.
All is ready, and they play.
Pan-pipes and flute are ready and begin.
Sweetly blend the tones,
Solemn the melody of their bird-music.
The ancestors are listening;

As our guests[25] they have come,
To gaze long upon their victories.

221

He goes through his lands;
May high T'ien cherish him!
Truly the succession is with Chou.
See how they tremble before him!
Not one that fails to tremble and quake.
Submissive, yielding are all the Spirits,
Likewise the rivers and high hills.
Truly he alone is monarch.
Bright and glorious is Chou;
It has succeeded to the seat of power.
"Then put away your shields and axes,
Then case your arrows and bows;
I have store enough of good power
To spread over all the lands of Hsia."
And in truth, the king protected them.

254

Deep and wise was Shang,[26]
Always furthering its good omens.
The waters of the Flood spread wide.
Yü[27] ranged lands and realms on earth below;
Beyond, great kingdoms were his frontier,
And when this far-flung power had been made lasting
The clan of Sung was favoured;
God appointed its child to bear Shang.

The dark king[28] valiantly ruled;
The service of small states everywhere he received,
The service of great States everywhere he received.
He followed the precepts of ritual and did not overstep them;
He obeyed the showings of T'ien and carried them out.
Hsiang-t'u was very glorious;
Beyond the seas he ruled.

God's appointment did not fail;
In the time of T'ang[29] it was fulfilled.
T'ang came down in his due time,
Wise warnings daily multiplied,
Magnificent was the radiance that shone below.
God on high gazed down;
God appointed him to be a model to all the lands.
He received the big statutes, the little statutes,
He became a mark and signal to the lands below.

He bore the blessing of T'ien,
Neither violent nor slack,
Neither hard nor soft.
He spread his ordinances in gentle harmony,
A hundred blessings he gathered upon himself.
Great laws and little laws he received,
He became great protector of the lands below.
He bore the favour of T'ien.
Far and wide he showed his valour,
Was never shaken or moved,
Never feared nor trembled;
A hundred blessings he united in himself.

The warlike king gave the signal;
Firmly he grasped his battle-axe,
His wrath blazed like a fire.
None dare do us injury.
The stem had three sprouts;
None prospered nor grew.
All the regions were subdued;
Wei and Ku were smitten,
K'un-wu, and Chieh of Hsia.

Of old, in the middle time,
There were tremblings and dangers.
But truly T'ien cherished us;
It gave us a minister,
A true "holder of the balance,"
Who succoured the King of Shang.

4

Book of Changes

ENTHUSIASM. It is worthwhile to appoint aides
And to set armies marching.
—Book of Changes, 16

Ordinarily the interpretations that go with a divination method
would hold no more interest than the other astrological or numerologi-
cal, calendrical, and dream translations that were used by the Shang or
Chou and by other ancient empires of the world for political purposes.
The *Book of Changes*, however, with its ideas of heaven, earth, sun, moon,
wind, and thunder, has exerted a special influence on later cosmological
views, Han, Taoist, and Neo-Confucian, which were themselves often integrated with other theories, namely, the *yin* and *yang* and the five elements. (See Tables 4 and 5.) The resultant integrated systems required
for their handling a remarkable memory and logic. In fact, much of Chinese logical endeavor went into these intricate symbolic theories. Diviners and philosophers worked out many-columned tables and ingenious diagrams to ease their way in and out of complex tasks of
interpretation. Today the preliminary manipulations could easily be
handled by computers.

The *Book of Changes* also contains sophisticated political and philosophical discourse that has not only influenced philosophers in classical

TABLE 4. The Eight Trigrams Listed in Their Most Usual Order with Their Principal Attributes*

1. Ch'ien ☰	Heaven	Sky	Cold		Creative Active Strong Firm Light	Father
2. Tui ☱	Lake	Marsh	Rain	Autumn	Joyful Pleasurable	Youngest daughter
3. Li ☲	Fire	Lightning	Sun	Summer	Beautiful Depending Clinging	Middle daughter
4. Chên ☳	Thunder		Thunder	Spring	Active Moving Arousing	Eldest son
5. Sun ☴	Wind	Wood			Gentle Penetrating	Eldest daughter
6. K'an ☵	Water	Cloud A pit	Moon	Winter	Enveloping Dangerous	Middle son
7. Kên ☶	Mountain		Thunder		Stubborn Immovable Perverse	Youngest son
8. K'un ☷	Earth		Heat		Receptive Responsive Yielding Passive Weak Dark	Mother

* From John Blofeld, ed. and tr., *I Ching: The Book of Change.* Copyright © 1965 by George Allen & Unwin Ltd. Dutton Paperback edition. Reprinted by permission of E. P. Dutton & Co., Inc., and George Allen & Unwin Ltd.

times but also has been drawn on for maxims or gems of thought by Chinese statesmen ever since. This is apart from the *Book*'s use as an oracle.

In form the *Book of Changes* is a diviner's manual used to tell the future. The Shang used scapulomancy and tortoise-shell reading. The Chou used other materials too—milfoil and yarrow plants. The would-be diviner takes a number of yarrow stalks about a foot or two in length, divides them according to a set procedure, allowing the intervention of chance, and matches the result with a series of sixty-four hexagrams listed in the *Book*. (The method can be adapted, or, as purists would say, vulgarized, to the use of thin wooden rods and even to the tossing of coins.) When one throws the coins or counts through the stalks one assumes that the result means something more than mere chance. The configuration is simply, according to C. G. Jung, the distinguished psychoanalyst, "what it necessarily must be in a given 'situation,' inasmuch as anything happening in that moment belongs to it as an indispensable part of the picture."

The sixty-four hexagrams from which omens are drawn are built upon two trigrams of three horizontal lines each. A line may be either broken — — and therefore "yielding," or unbroken —— and therefore "firm." Broken lines are called *yin* lines; unbroken lines are *yang* lines. Under certain conditions there may be a "moving" *yin* line —x— , and a moving *yang* line —o—; these lines move in the direction of their opposites. This dynamic possibility allows for fuller integration of the *yin-yang* wherein all that is earthly, passive, negative, female, dark (*yin*) merges with the heavenly, active, positive, male, light (*yang*). The symbol of the *yin-yang* is beautifully designed to indicate this fluidity.

Symbol of the interaction of the Yin and the Yang.

There can be only eight trigrams; no more than this can be formed with the two kinds of lines, broken and unbroken.

Table 5. Mnemonic Uses of the Number Five in Ancient Chinese Discourse*

Five "Elements"	Wood	Fire	Earth	Metal	Water
Five Directions	East	South	Center	West	North
Five Colors	Green	Red	Yellow	White	Black
Four Seasons	Spring	Summer		Autumn	Winter
Five Flavors	Sour	Bitter	Sweet	Acrid	Salt
Five Odors	Goatish	Burning	Fragrant	Rank	Rotten
Five Grains	Wheat	Beans	Panicled Millet	Hemp	Millet
Five Sacrifices	Inner door	Hearth	Inner court (atrium)	Outer door	Well
Five Animals	Sheep	Fowl	Ox	Dog	Pig
Five Classes of Creatures	Scaly	Feathered	Naked	Hairy	Shell-covered
Five Organs	Spleen	Lungs	Heart	Liver	Kidneys
Five Numbers	8	7	5	9	6
Five Musical Notes	Chio	Chih	Kung	Shang	Yü

* This table based on the *Li Chi* is from H. G. Creel's *Sinism, A Study of the Evolution of the Chinese World-View* (Chicago: The Open Court Publishing Company, 1929), p. 34.

(1) (2) (3) (4)

(5) (6) (7) (8)

The Eight Trigrams, *Pa Kua.*

Each trigram has a meaning of its own that subsequent interpretations and commentaries have enriched. Table 4 lists their principal meanings.

In the *Book of Changes* the trigrams have all been combined by placing one above the other, giving the sum of sixty-four symbols. (Eight times eight trigrams equals sixty-four hexagrams.) There would be little in this manual did it contain the omens of the sixty-four hexagrams alone. Only the briefest oracle is given for any one hexagram taken as a whole. For example, for Hexagram 35,

Chin or Progress, the text reads: "Progress. The powerful is honored with large numbers of horses. He is granted audience three times in a single day." Then a brief oracle is given for each component line. For example, for the top line of the above hexagram the explanation reads: "Advancing [menacingly] with lowered horns is permissible only in order to punish one's own city. To be aware of danger brings good fortune. No blame. To persist brings humiliation." *

But the *Book of Changes* is really two books. The second book consists of appended commentaries called the *Ten Wings*. These attach many meanings in amplification or clarification of the original brief texts. Thus the commentary to the top line of Hexagram 35 adds a sober afterthought: " 'Only in order to punish one's own city.' The way is not yet clear." The appendices comment on the symbols of the hexagrams, on the sequence of the sixty-four of them, on the two trigrams that compose each, on the words of the text, and so on. The language is lapidary.

The word *ching* in the *Book of Changes'* title, *I Ching*, means a scripture or sacred book and was added by common usage a century or two after Confucius. The *I Ching* was the first of the Confucian classics to be so designated. According to Ssŭ-ma Ch'ien's history, Confucius was so delighted by the *I Ching* that he wore out the thong bindings of his copy three times. He also took upon himself the arranging of the *Ten Wings*. (Historians now generally assert that most of these appendices are additions made later, during either the First Empire or the Han Dynasty, that is, sometime between the third century B.C. and the third century A.D.) Ssŭ-ma Ch'ien said further that the inventor of the ingenious system was the model king, Wên of the ancient Chou.

If King Wên, the Duke of Chou, and Confucius did not compile, write, or edit the *Book of Changes*, some men of almost equally great gifts must have produced the work. Possibly none of the three greats mentioned were of a sufficiently mystical inclination. There are ancient lines in the *Book of Changes* that seem to have found their way to the exquisite mystical poem, the *Tao-tê-ching* (see Chapter 14), while others seem to have come from the *Tao-tê-ching* to elaborate the *Ten Wings*.

* From Richard Wilhelm, tr., *The I Ching or Book of Changes*, translated from the German by Cary F. Baynes, Bollingen Series XIX (Princeton: Princeton University Press, 1967); translation slightly modified.

BOOK OF CHANGES

(I Ching)

Selections

1. Ch'ien / The Creative[1]

above   Ch'ien   The Creative, Heaven

below   Ch'ien   The Creative, Heaven

The Judgment [2]
THE CREATIVE works sublime success,
Progressing through perseverance.

From Richard Wilhelm and Cary F. Baynes, trs., *The I Ching, or Book of Changes*, Bollingen Series XIX (Princeton: Princeton University Press, 3rd edn., 1967). Copyright © 1950, 1967 by the Bollingen Foundation, New York. Reprinted by permission of Princeton University Press and Routledge & Kegan Paul Ltd. Translation slightly modified.

COMMENTARY ON THE JUDGMENT

Great indeed is the sublimity of the Creative, to which all beings owe their beginning and which permeates all heaven.

The clouds pass and the rain does its work, and all individual beings flow into their forms.

Because the holy man is clear as to the end and the beginning, as to the way in which each of the six stages completes itself in its own time, he mounts on them toward heaven as though on six dragons.

The way of the Creative works through change and transformation, so that each thing receives its true nature and destiny and comes into permanent accord with the Great Harmony: this is what furthers and what perseveres.

He towers high above the multitude of beings, and all lands are united in peace.

The Image[3]
The movement of heaven is full of power.
Thus the superior man makes himself strong and untiring.

The Lines
Nine[4] at the beginning:
a) Hidden dragon.[5] Do not act.
b) "Hidden dragon. Do not act." For the light-giving force is still below.

Nine in the second place:
a) Dragon appearing in the field.
It furthers one to see the great man.
b) "Dragon appearing in the field." Already the influence of character reaches far.

Nine in the third place:
a) All day long the superior man is creatively active.
At nightfall his mind is still beset with cares.
Danger. No blame.
b) "All day long the superior man is creatively active." One goes to and fro on the right path.

Nine in the fourth place:

a) Waving flight over the depths.
No blame.

b) "Waving flight over the depths." Advance is not a mistake.

O Nine in the fifth place:

a) Flying dragon in the heavens.
It furthers one to see the great man.

b) "Flying dragon in the heavens." This shows the great man at work.

Nine at the top:

a) Arrogant dragon will have cause to repent.

b) "Arrogant dragon will have cause to repent." For what is at the full cannot last.

When all the lines are nines:

a) There appears a flight of dragons without heads.
Good fortune.

b) "All the lines are nines." It is the nature of T'ien not to appear as head.

2. *K'un / The Receptive*

above	K'un	The Receptive, Earth
below	K'un	The Receptive, Earth

The Judgment

THE RECEPTIVE brings about sublime success,
Gaining through the holding steady of a mare.
If the superior man undertakes something and tries to lead,
He goes astray;

But if he follows, he finds guidance.
It is worthwhile to find friends in the west and south,
To forgo friends in the east and north.
Quiet perseverance brings good fortune.

COMMENTARY ON THE JUDGMENT

Perfect indeed is the sublimity of the Receptive. All beings owe their birth to it, because it receives the heavenly with devotion.

The Receptive in its riches carries all things. Its nature is in harmony with the boundless. It embraces everything in its breadth and illumines everything in its greatness. Through it, all individual beings attain success.

A mare belongs to the creatures of the earth; she roams the earth without bound. Yielding, devoted, advancing through perseverance: thus the superior man has a direction for his way of life.

Taking the lead brings confusion because one loses his way. Following with devotion—thus does one attain his permanent place.

In the west and south one finds friends, so that he proceeds with people of his own kind. In the east and north one must do without friends, so that he finally attains good fortune.

The good fortune of rest and perseverance depends on our being in accord with the boundless nature of the earth.

The Image

The earth's condition is receptive devotion.
Thus the superior man who has breadth of character
Carries the outer world.

The Lines

Six at the beginning:
a) When there is hoarfrost underfoot,
Solid ice is not far off.
b) "When there is hoarfrost underfoot, solid ice is not far off."
When the dark power begins to grow rigid and continues in this way, things reach the point of solid ice.

O   Six in the second place:

a) Straight, square, great.
Without purpose.
Yet nothing remains unfurthered.

b) The movement of the six in the second place is straight and, because of this, square.[6]
"Without purpose, yet nothing remains unfurthered": for in the nature of the earth lies the light.

Six in the third place:

a) Hidden lines.
One is able to remain persevering.
If by chance you are in the service of a king,
Seek not works, but bring to completion.

b) "Hidden lines. One is able to remain persevering."
One must let them shine forth at the right time.
"If by chance you are in the service of a king. . . ."
This shows that the light of wisdom is great.

Six in the fourth place:

a) A tied-up sack. No blame, no praise.

b) "A tied-up sack. No blame." Through caution one remains free of harm.

Sixth in the fifth place:

a) A yellow lower garment brings supreme good fortune.

b) "A yellow lower garment brings supreme good fortune." Beauty is within.

Six at the top:

a) Dragons fight in the meadow.
Their blood is black and yellow.

b) "Dragons fight in the meadow." The way comes to an end.

When all the lines are sixes:

a) Lasting perseverance furthers.

b) "Lasting perseverance": it ends in great things.

4. Mêng / Youthful Folly

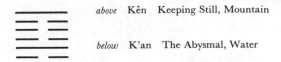

above Kên Keeping Still, Mountain

below K'an The Abysmal, Water

The Judgment

YOUTHFUL FOLLY has success.
It is not I who seek the young fool;
The young fool seeks me.
At the first oracle I inform him.
If he asks two or three times, it is importunity.
If he importunes, I give him no information.
Perseverance is worthwhile.

COMMENTARY ON THE JUDGMENT

YOUTHFUL FOLLY shows danger at the foot of a mountain. Danger and standstill: this is folly.

"Folly has success." One who succeeds hits upon the right time for his undertaking.

"It is not I who seek the young fool; the young fool seeks me." The two positions correspond.

"At the first oracle I answer," because the position is firm and central.

"If someone asks two or three times, it is importunity. If he importunes, I give no answer." To importune is folly.

To strengthen what is right in a fool is a holy task.

The Image

A spring wells up at the foot of the mountain:
The image of YOUTH.
Thus the superior man fosters his character
By thoroughness in all that he does.

The Lines

Six at the beginning:

a) To make a fool develop
It furthers one to apply discipline.
The fetters should be removed.
To go on in this way brings humiliation.

b) "It furthers one to apply discipline"—that is, in order to give emphasis to the law.

O Nine in the second place:

a) To bear with fools in kindliness brings good fortune.
To know how to take women
Brings good fortune.
The son is capable of taking charge of the household.

b) "The son is capable of taking charge of the household," for firm and yielding are in union.

Six in the third place:

a) Take not a maiden who, when she sees a man of bronze,
Loses possession of herself.
Nothing furthurs.

b) One should not take the maiden because her conduct is not in accord with order.

Six in the fourth place:

a) Entangled youthful folly brings humiliation.

b) The humiliation of entangled youthful folly comes from the fact that it of all things is furthest from what is real.

O Six in the fifth place:

a) Childlike folly brings good fortune.

b) The good fortune of the childlike fool comes from his being devoted and gentle.

Nine at the top:

a) In punishing folly
It does not further one
To commit transgressions.

The only thing that furthers
Is to prevent transgressions.

b) "It furthers to prevent transgressions," for then those above and those below conform to order.

7. *Shih / The Army*

above K'un The Receptive, Earth

below K'an The Abysmal, Water

The Judgment
THE ARMY. The army needs perseverance
And a strong man.
Good fortune without blame.

COMMENTARY ON THE JUDGMENT

THE ARMY means the masses. Perseverance means discipline.

The man who can effect discipline through the masses may attain mastery of the world.

The strong one is central and finds response.

One does a dangerous thing but finds devotion. The man who thus leads the world is followed by the people.

Good fortune. How could this be a mistake?

The Image
In the middle of the earth is water:
The image of THE ARMY.
Thus the superior man increases his masses
By sustaining the people.

The Lines
Six at the beginning:

a) An army must set forth in proper order.[7]

If the order is not good, misfortune threatens.

b) "An army must set forth in proper order." Losing order is unfortunate.

O Nine in the second place:

a) In the midst of the army.
Good fortune. No blame.
The king bestows a triple decoration.

b) "In the midst of the army. Good fortune." He receives grace from T'ien.
"The king bestows a triple decoration." He has the welfare of all countries at heart.

Six in the third place:

a) Perchance the army carries corpses in the wagon.
Misfortune.

b) "Perchance the army carries corpses in the wagon."
This is quite without merit.

Six in the fourth place:

a) The army retreats. No blame.

b) "The army retreats. No blame," for it does not deviate from the usual way.

O Six in the fifth place:

a) There is game in the field.
It is worth one's while to catch it.
Without blame.
Let the eldest lead the army.
The younger transports corpses;
Then persistence brings misfortune.

b) "Let the eldest lead the army," because he is central and correct.
"The younger transports corpses." Thus the right man is not put in charge.

Six at the top:

a) The great prince issues commands,
Founds states, vests families with fiefs.

Inferior people should not be employed.

b) "The great prince issues commands," in order to reward merit properly.

"Inferior people should not be employed," because they are certain to cause confusion in the country.

11. *T'ai / Peace*

above K'un The Receptive, Earth

below Ch'ien The Creative, Heaven

The Judgment

PEACE. The small departs,
The great approaches.
Good fortune. Success.

COMMENTARY ON THE JUDGMENT

PEACE. "The small departs, the great approaches.
Good fortune. Success."

In this way heaven and earth unite, and all beings come into the union.

Upper and lower unite, and they are of one will.

The light principle is within [Yang], the shadowy without [Yin]; strength is within and devotion without; the superior man is within, the inferior without.

The way of the superior man is waxing; the way of the inferior man is waning.

The Image

Heaven and earth unite: the image of PEACE.
Thus the ruler
Divides and completes the course of heaven and earth;
He furthers and regulates the gifts of heaven and earth,
And so aids the people.

12. P'i / Standstill [Stagnation]

above	Ch'ien The Creative, Heaven
below	K'un The Receptive, Earth

The Judgment

STANDSTILL. Evil people do not help
The perseverance of the superior man.
The great departs; the small approaches.

COMMENTARY ON THE JUDGMENT

"Evil people of the time of STANDSTILL do not help the perseverance
of the superior man. The great departs; the small approaches."

Thus heaven and earth do not unite, and all beings fail to achieve
union.

Upper and lower do not unite, and in the world, states go down
to ruin.

The shadowy is within, the light without; weakness is within
[Yin], firmness without [Yang]; the inferior is within, the superior
without. The way of the inferior is waxing, the way of the superior is
waning.

The Image

Heaven and earth do not unite:
The image of STANDSTILL.
Thus the superior man falls back upon his inner worth
In order to escape the difficulties.
He does not let himself to be honored with income and rank.

16. Yü / Enthusiasm

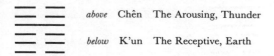

above Chên The Arousing, Thunder

below K'un The Receptive, Earth

The Judgment

ENTHUSIASM. It furthers one to install helpers
And to set armies marching.

COMMENTARY ON THE JUDGMENT

ENTHUSIASM. The firm finds correspondence, and its will is done.
Devotion to movement: this is ENTHUSIASM.

Because ENTHUSIASM shows devotion to movement, heaven and
earth are at its side. How much the more then is it possible to appoint helpers and set armies marching!

Heaven and earth move with devotion; therefore sun and moon
do not swerve from their courses, and the four seasons do not err.

The holy man moves with devotion; therefore fines and punishments become just, and the people obey. Great indeed is the meaning of the time of ENTHUSIASM.

The Image

Thunder comes resounding out of the earth:
The image of ENTHUSIASM.
Thus the ancient kings made music
In order to honor merit,
And offered it with splendor
To the Supreme Deity,
Inviting their ancestors to be present.

37. *Chia Jên / The Family [The Clan]*

═══ ═══ ══ ═ ══ ══ ═ ══ ═══════	*above* Sun The Gentle, Wind *below* Li The Clinging, Fire

The Judgment
THE FAMILY. The perseverance of the woman furthers.

COMMENTARY ON THE JUDGMENT

THE FAMILY. The correct place of the woman is within; the correct place of the man is without. That man and woman have their proper places is the greatest concept in nature.

Among the members of the family there are strict rulers; these are the parents. When the father is in truth a father and the son a son, when the elder brother is an elder brother and the younger brother a younger brother, the husband a husband and the wife a wife, then the house is on the right way.

When the family is set straight, the world is set in order.

The Image
Wind comes forth from fire:
The image of THE FAMILY.
Thus the superior man has substance in his words
And duration in his way of life.

43. *Kuai / Break-through (Resoluteness)*

═══ ═══ ═══════ ═══════ ═══════	*above* Tui The Joyous, Lake *below* Ch'ien The Creative, Heaven

The Judgment
BREAK-THROUGH. One must resolutely make the matter known
At the court of the king.
It must be announced truthfully. Danger.

It is necessary to notify one's own city.
It does not help just to resort to arms.
It helps one to undertake something.

COMMENTARY ON THE JUDGMENT

BREAK-THROUGH is the same as resoluteness. The firm resolutely dislodges the yielding. Strong and joyous—this means resolute and harmonious.

"One must make the matter known at the court of the king." The weak rests upon five hard lines.

Truthful announcement is fraught with danger. However, this danger leads to the light.

"It is necessary to notify one's own city. It does not help just to resort to arms." What that man holds high comes to nothing.

"It helps one to undertake something," because the firm grow and lead through to the end.

The Image
The lake has risen up to heaven:
The image of BREAK-THROUGH.
Thus the superior man
Distributes riches downward
And refrains from resting on his virtue.

44. Kou / Coming to Meet

above	Ch'ien	The Creative, Heaven
below	Sun	The Gentle, Wind

The Judgment
COMING TO MEET. The maiden is powerful.
One should not marry such a maiden.

COMMENTARY ON THE JUDGMENT

COMING TO MEET means encountering. The weak advances to meet the firm.

"One should not marry such a maiden." This means that one cannot live with her permanently.

When heaven and earth meet, all creatures settle into firm lines.

When the firm finds the middle and the right, everything under heaven prospers splendidly.

Great indeed is the meaning of the time of COMING TO MEET.

> *The Image*
> Under heaven, wind:
> The image of COMING TO MEET.
> Thus does the prince act when disseminating his commands
> And proclaiming them to the four quarters of heaven.

49. Ko / Revolution (Molting)

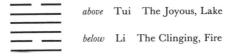

	above	Tui	The Joyous, Lake
	below	Li	The Clinging, Fire

> *The Judgment*
> REVOLUTION. On your own day
> You are believed.
> Supreme success,
> Furthering through perseverance.
> Remorse disappears.

COMMENTARY ON THE JUDGMENT

REVOLUTION. Water and fire subdue each other. Two daughters dwell together, but their views bar mutual understanding. This means revolution.

"On your own day you are believed": one brings about a revolution and in doing so is trusted.

Enlightenment, and thereby joyousness: you create great success through justice.

If in a revolution one hits upon the right thing, "remorse disappears."

Heaven and earth bring about revolution, and the four seasons complete themselves thereby.

T'ang and Wu brought about political revolutions because they were submissive toward heaven and in accord with men.

The time of REVOLUTION is truly great.

The Image
Fire in the lake: the image of REVOLUTION.
Thus the superior man
Sets the calendar in order
And makes the seasons clear.

5

The *Spring and Autumn Annals* with the *Commentary of Tso*

The grand historiographer wrote in his tablets—"Ts'ui Chu murdered his ruler."
—*Commentary of Tso,* Duke Hsiang, IX (547 B.C.)

The *Spring and Autumn Annals* is a factual, yearly chronicle, from 722 to 481 B.C., of the state of Lu, then one of the most civilized parts of China. The philosopher Mencius said (though this now seems not to be the historical case) that Confucius, fearing for his times, worked on the *Spring and Autumn Annals.* Later, the great historian Ssŭ-ma Ch'ien stated that what Confucius was after was to set the record straight.

Then, utilizing the historical records, he composed the *Spring and Autumn Annals,* going back to Duke Yin of Lu (722–712 B.C.) and coming down to the fourteenth year of Duke Ai (481 B.C.), a total of twelve dukes. In his history he took the state of Lu as his basis, kept close to Chou, dealt with Yin as a time of the past, and circulated the principles of the Three Dynasties. His style was concise, but his meaning rich. Thus, when the rulers of Wu and Yüeh states style themselves Kings, the *Annals* reproves them by giving them their proper title of Viscount. And at the meeting of Chien-t'u (632 B.C.), when the Chou Emperor had actually been ordered to attend (by Duke Wên of Chin), the *Spring and Autumn Annals* avoids mentioning this fact by saying: "The celestial King went hunting at Ho-yang." Confucius offered examples of this sort to serve as rules for his own age. "And if later on there be kings who will arise and bring out the meaning of the censures and abasements, so that the meaning of the *Annals* becomes generally known, at that time rebellious subjects and criminals in the world will become seized with terror." *

* Translated from the Chinese by Derk Bodde in Fung Yu-lan, *A History of Chinese*

The *Commentary of Tso* or *Tso Chuan*—in part an explanatory elaboration of the *Spring and Autumn Annals* covering more or less the same span, 722–468 B.C.—reveals that the grand historians of other states of the time could also strike terror by recording evil deeds.

The title of this excellently written and exciting work is of uncertain meaning. The book seems to be the chronicles of a person named Tso. It is one of the greatest Chinese prose works.

The *Commentary of Tso* is invaluable generally for clarifying and expanding the brief, almost abrupt court entries in the *Annals*. Therefore, in the readings to follow, a selection from the *Annals* appears first (in italics), while the corresponding event in the *Commentary* immediately follows it (in roman type). The first entry records scandalous acts; the second, an assassination; the third, presumed revenge; the fourth, another assassination.

Philosophy, 2 vols. (Princeton: Princeton University Press, 1952), I, pp. 45–46. (Translation slightly modified.)

THE *SPRING AND AUTUMN ANNALS*

(Ch'un Ch'iu)

WITH THE
COMMENTARY OF TSO

(Tso Chuan)

Selections

(Year IX)[1] *Ch'ên put to death its great officer Hsieh Yeh. (Book 7)**

Duke Ling of Ch'ên, with [his two ministers] K'ung Ning and I Hang-fu all had an intrigue with Hsia Chi (a daughter of the House of Chêng,

From James Legge, tr., *The Ch'un Ts'ew with the Tso Chuen, The Chinese Classics*, 5 vols. (Hong Kong: Hong Kong University Press, 1960), vol. 5.

* Material in italics is from the *Spring and Autumn Annals*. Material in roman type is from the *Commentary of Tso*.

surnamed Chi, the widow of an officer of Ch'ên, surnamed or designated Hsia) and each of the three of them wore an article of her underclothing, with which they made game with one another in the court. Hsieh Yeh remonstrated with the duke, saying, "When ruler and ministers thus proclaim their lewdness, the people have nothing good to imitate. The report of such things is not good;—let your lordship put that article away." The duke said he would change his conduct, but he told the other two what Hsieh Yeh had said; and when they asked leave to kill him, he did not forbid them. Yeh thereon was killed.

(Year X)² On Kuei-chi, I Hang-fu of Ch'ên murdered his ruler, P'ing-kuo. (Book 7)

Duke Ling of Ch'ên, with K'ung Ning and I Hang-fu, was drinking in the house of the Hsia family, when the duke said to Hang-fu, "Chêng-shu (the son of Hsia Chi, and Head of the family, as his father was dead) is like you." "He is also like your lordship," was the reply. Chêng-shu (overheard these remarks, and) was indignant at them; and when the duke was (trying to) escape (from the house) by the stable, he shot, and killed him.

(Year XI)³ In winter, in the tenth month the people of Ch'u put to death Hsia Chêng-shu of Ch'ên. (Book 7)

In winter, the viscount of Ch'u, because of the deed perpetrated by the head of the Hsia family, invaded Ch'ên, publishing a notice to the people that they should make no movement, as he wished to punish only the head of the Shao-hsi. Forthwith he entered (the capital of) Ch'ên, and put to death Hsia Chêng-shu, having him torn in pieces by chariots.

(Year XXV)⁴ In summer, in the fifth month, on I-hai, Ts'ui Chu of Ch'i murdered his ruler Kuang. (Book 9)

The wife of the commandant of T'ang of Ch'i was an elder sister of Tung-kuo Yen, who was a minister of Ts'ui Wu-tzŭ. When the commandant died, Yen drove Wu-tzŭ (to his house) to offer his condolences. Wu-tzŭ then saw T'ang Chiang (the wife of the commandant), and, admiring her beauty, wished Yen to give her to him for his wife. Yen said, "Husband and wife should be of different surnames. You are descended from (duke) Ting, and I from (duke) Huan; the thing cannot be." Wu-tzŭ consulted the milfoil about it, and got the diagram K'un

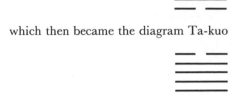

which then became the diagram Ta-kuo

which the diviners all said was fortunate. He showed it to Ch'ên Wên-tzŭ, but he said, "The (symbol for) a man (in K'un) is displaced by that for wind (in Ta-kuo). Wind overthrows things. The woman ought not to be married. And moreover, (upon K'un) it is said, 'Distressed by rocks; holding to brambles; he enters his palace and does not see his wife. It is evil (see the *I* [5] on the third line of K'un).' 'Distressed by rocks';—in vain does one attempt to go forward. 'Holding by brambles';—that in which trust is placed wounds. 'He enters his palace and does not see his wife; it is evil':—there is nowhere to turn to." Ts'ui-tzŭ replied, "She is a widow;—what does all this matter? Her former husband bore the brunt of it." So he married her. Afterward duke Chuang had an intrigue with her, and constantly went to Ts'ui's house. (On one occasion) he took Ts'ui's hat and gave it to another person; and when his attendants said that he should not do so, he remarked, "Although he be not Ts'ui-tzŭ should he therefore be without a hat?"

Ts'ui-tzŭ (was enraged) by these things and because the duke took occasion (of its troubles) to invade Chin, thinking that Chin would be sure to retaliate, he wished to murder the duke in order to please that State. He did not, however, find an opportunity, till the duke had whipt one of his attendants, called Chia Chü, whom notwithstanding he kept near him. This man then watched the duke for Ts'ui-tzŭ.

In summer, in the fifth month, on account of the affair at Ch'ieh Yü, the viscount of Chü came to the court of Ch'i and on Chia-shu the duke entertained him in the north suburbs. Ts'ui-tzŭ gave out that he was ill, and did not go to see the affair. Next day the duke went to ask for him, and went after the lady Chiang, who entered into a chamber, and passed out of it by a side door along with Ts'ui-tzŭ while the duke patted a pillar and sang. (In the meantime), his attendant Chia Chü stopped all the duke's followers, entered (the house himself), and shut the door. Men-at-arms made their appearance, and the duke, ascending a tower, begged them to let him off. They would not do so, and he then begged to make a covenant but neither would they agree to this. He begged (finally) to be allowed to kill himself in the ancestral temple; but they again declined, all saying, "Your lordship's servant Chu is very ill, and cannot receive your commands. And this is near the duke's palace. We are watchmen, (and have to take) an adulterer. We can know nothing of two commands." The duke then attempted to get over a wall, when they shot and wounded him in the thigh; and as he fell backwards, they murdered him. Chia Chü, Chou Ch'ao, Ping Shih, Kung-sun Ao, Fêng Chü, To Fu, Hsiang I, and Lü Yin all died at the same time.

The priest T'o Fu had been sacrificing in Kao T'ang, and when he came to report the execution of his commission, he was killed at Ts'ui's house, before he could take off his cap. Shên K'uai should have been superintending the fishermen, but he retired (from that duty), and said to his steward, "You can make your escape with your family. I will die (here)." The steward replied, "If I made my escape, I should be acting contrary to your righteous course." So he went with him, and they both died. Ts'ui-tzŭ also put to death Tsung Mieh in Ping-yin.

Yen-tzŭ stood outside the gate of Ts'ui's house. His people said to him, "Will you die?" "Was he my ruler only?" replied he. "Why should I die?" "Will you leave then?" "Is his death my crime? Why should I flee?" "Will you (now) go back to your house?" "Our ruler is dead. Where should I go back to? Is it the business of the ruler of the people to merely be above them? The altars of the State should be his chief care. Is it the business of the minister of a ruler merely to be concerned about his support? The nourishment of the altars should be his object. Therefore when a ruler dies or goes into exile for the altars, the minister should die or go into exile with him. If he die or go into exile for his seeking his own ends, who, excepting his private associates, would presume to bear the consequences with him? Moreover, when another man murders his ruler, how can I die with him? how can I go into exile with him? of what use would it be for me to return home?" When the gate was opened, he went into the house, pillowed the corpse upon his thigh, and wept. He then rose, gave three leaps up, and went out. People advised Ts'ui-tzŭ to put him to death, but he said, "The people look up to him. Let him alone, and it will conciliate them."

Lu p'u-kuei fled to Chin, and Wang Ho fled to Chü. After Shu-sun Hsüan Po took up his residence in Ch'i, Shu-sun Huan introduced his daughter to duke Ling, with whom she became a favorite, and she bore him a son, (who now became) duke Ching. On Ting-ch'ou, Ts'ui Chu raised him to the State, and became his chief minister, Ch'ing Fêng being minister of the Left. They made a covenant with the people of the State in the temple of T'ai-kung, which began, "If we do not adhere to Ts'ui and Ch'ing," when Yen-tzŭ looking up to heaven, sighed and broke in with, "If I do not adhere to those who are faithful to the ruler and seek the good of the altars, may God witness it!" With this he smeared his lips with the blood.

On Hsin-ssŭ, the (new) duke and the great officers made a covenant with the viscount of Chü.

The grand historiographer wrote (in his tablets)—"Ts'ui Chu murdered his ruler";—for which Ts'ui-tzŭ put him to death. Two of his brothers did the same after him, and were also put to death. A third wrote the same, and was let alone. The historiographer in the south, hearing that the grand historiographer and his brothers had died in this way, took his tablets and set out (for the court); but learning on his way that the record was made, he returned.

Lü-shih Ying wrapped up his wife in a curtain, put her into a carriage, and then got into it with Shên Hsien-yü, and quitted the capital. Hsien-yü pushed the lady out of the carriage, saying (to Ying), "You could not correct the ruler in his blindness, nor save him in his peril, nor die with him in his death, and yet you know how to conceal your wife here:—who will receive you?" Coming to a narrow pass, they thought of resting in it, but Ying said, "Ts'ui and Ch'ing will be pursuing us!" The other replied, "Here it will be one to one. Who can frighten us?" They rested accordingly, and (Shên) slept with his head upon the reins. (In the morning), he fed their horses and then ate, himself yoked their carriage, and issued from the pass. When they had done so, he said to Ying, "Now urge on the horses to their speed. The multitudes of Ts'ui and Ch'ing could not (here) be withstood." In this way they came flying to Lai.

Ts'ui-tzŭ placed the coffin of duke Chuang in the northern suburbs, and on Ting-hai he buried it in the village of Shih-sun. There were (only) four plumes to the carriage; travellers were not warned out of the way; and there were (but) seven inferior carriages in the procession, without any men-at-arms.

6

Book of Rites

Our unworthy Prince has some inferior wine, and, wishing your honours to spend a little time with him, he sends me to invite you.

—*Book of Rites*, 12:2

The *Book of Rites (I Li)* is the oldest existing book of Chinese ceremonial. The music that was played during the ancient rites must have accompanied them in formality. Unfortunately, the *Book of Music* has been lost. Surely it would have contained much of great interest, for the Chou seemed thoroughly to enjoy watching and performing ceremony with music and dance, and writing about them.

Two other books of ritual procedure exist—the *Chou Rites (Chou Li)* and the *Ritual Records (Li Chi)*. All three of these books of ceremony were probably written later than the Chou period, but the *Book of Rites (I Li)*, as confirmed through other sources, retains the spirit of an earlier day. It was first counted among the classics on its own; at some point (c. 100 B.C.) in the former Han Dynasty, the *Chou Rites* and *Ritual Records* were grouped with it and the three counted as one work in the classics.

In Chou China a formal archery contest had all the pomp and circumstance of a medieval tournament of knights. The *Book of Rites* describes the minutiae of manners to be observed on these festive occasions. An interesting political detail has been traced to a word used in ancient archery matches. The words *official* and *historian* are linked to a term that first signified *score-keeper of the archery contest.**

The *Book of Rites* was written for the kind of lesser aristocrats and officers, near and far in the realm, who participated in such contests. It

---

* Herrlee Glessner Creel, *The Birth of China* (New York: Unger Publishing Company, 1937), p. 144.

also details the ceremonies for their coming of age, death, mourning, and burial, the rites of sacrifice, the formalities of official visits and banquets, and the rules for embassies to foreign countries. An occasional striking phrase or moral appears in it too, but the *Ritual Records (Li Chi)* (in which Confucians of the First Empire and Han Dynasty made use of the materials in the *Book of Rites*, among others) surpasses it in importance for political thought. Hence, whereas the first four selections to follow— on appointments and archery—are from the *Book of Rites*, the others— chiefly on music and sacrifice—are all from the more elaborated and informative *Ritual Records*. Together with the selections from the *Ritual Records* (pp. 100–108), they show how the rites helped define the critical political roles in China of ruler and subject, king and minister, father and son, through ceremony and music.

BOOK OF RITES

(I Li)

Selections

The Visits of One Ordinary Officer to Another

The Mode of Speaking and the Direction of the Eyes.

(a) Whoever comes to speak with the Prince, first of all puts himself at his ease, thus settling his mind, and then speaks. This does not apply to one answering the Prince's questions.

(b) In speaking with the Prince, one talks of one's official business; with an official, of one's service of his Prince; with older men, of the control of children; with young people, of their filial and brotherly duties;

From E. R. Hughes, tr. *Chinese Philosophy in Classical Times* (New York: E. P. Dutton, Everyman's Library, 1942), pp. 277–286. Headings are those of the translator.

with the common man, of geniality and goodness; with those in minor offices, of loyalty and sincerity.

(c) In speaking to an official, one begins by looking him in the face to gauge one's chances of a favourable reception; towards the middle of the interview one looks at his breast as an indication of one's trust in him, and also respect, indicated by the lowering of the eyes; and at the end of the interview one's eyes are again directed to his face, to see how he is impressed. The order is never changed, and is used in all cases.

(d) In the case of a father, the son's eyes are allowed to wander, but not higher than the face, so as not to seem too proud, nor lower than the girdle.

(e) If one is not speaking, then, when the other is standing, one looks at his feet, and, if he sits, at his knees, in sign of humility.

The Banquet

The Duke Feasts with the Visitors

(a) Then the Duke feasts with the visitors from other States.

(b) The invitation is extended to them in the following form: "Our unworthy Prince has some inferior wine, and, wishing your honours to spend a little time with him, he sends me to invite you."

(c) To this they reply: "Our unworthy Prince is a feudatory of yours, so let your Prince not incur disgrace by conferring benefits on us mere messengers. Your servants venture to decline."

(d) The messenger replies: "My unworthy Prince insists on saying that the wine is of poor quality, and sends me to press the invitation on your honours." To which the guests reply: "Our unworthy Prince is the feudatory of yours, and your Prince should not demean himself by showing kindness to mere messengers. Your servants venture to persist in declining."

(e) The messenger again replies: "My unworthy Prince persists in saying the wine is of no quality, and he sends me to urge his invitation on you." They answer: "As we have failed to secure permission to decline, dare we do other than accept?"

(f) The words he uses in communicating his instructions are: "My unworthy Prince sends me to say that his wine is of no quality, and to invite your honours to spend a short time with him."

(g) They reply: "Your Prince confers many favours on our unworthy ruler, and demeans himself by giving presents to mere messengers such as we are. Your servants presume to bow in acknowledgment of his gracious commands."

The Archery Meeting

The Second Shooting

When the Duke has finished shooting, the head retainer takes the cloth and withdraws to his place. The captain of archers then receives the bow, and the lieutenant the finger-stall and armlet in the tray, and, withdrawing, places them on the cupboard and returns to his place. The captain of archers then withdraws to the place occupied by the overseer, and the head retainer assists the Duke to draw on his coat.

(aa) Then the Duke turns, and thereafter the guest goes down the steps, and, laying down his bow to the west of the hall, returns to his place at the west of the steps, where he stands, facing east.

(bb) The Duke then goes to his mat, and the overseer, in the name of the Duke, sends the guest up the stairs. He returns to his mat, and thereafter the ministers and great officers shoot in succession.

(cc) The ducal and ordinary ministers take their bows in the dressing-tent, bare the left arm, put on the finger-stall and armlet, grasp their bows, put three arrows in their belts, and fit one on the string. Then they come out, face west, and salute. Then they salute as the three couples did, and ascend to shoot. When their shooting is finished, they descend like the three couples, and, going to the dressing-tent, put away their bows, doff finger-stall and armlet, draw on their coats, and return to their places. The rest all shoot in succession, the score being taken, and all else conducted as before.

(dd) When the shooting is finished, the scorer takes the odd tally that he holds, and, going to the foot of the east steps, faces north, and announces to the Duke that both sides are finished. Thereafter he returns to his place, sits, and, laying out the odd tally to the west of the holder, rises, lifts his joined hands, and stands at attention.

o   o   o   o

Announcing the Score

The director of archery then goes to the west of the steps, lays down his bow, puts away his rod, draws on his coat, and, advancing by the east of the tally-holder, stands to the south of it, and, facing north, examines the score.

o   o   o   o

Then the director of archery returns to his place, and the scorer thereupon advances, and taking up a tally for the winning side, holds it, and, going to the foot of the east stairs, faces north and announces the score to the Duke. If the right side has won, he says: "The right side has excelled the left"; while if the left side has won, he says: "The left side has excelled the right." Then he announces the number of pairs of tallies, and if there be an odd one over, he says: "And the odd." If left and right be equal, then he takes one tally of each side, and says: "The two sides are equal." Then he turns and goes back to his place, sits and gathers up the tallies, places eight in the holder, and spreads the rest to the west of it. He then rises, lifts his joined hands, and stands to attention.

The Ceremonial of a Mission

Appointing the Commissioner and His Suite

(a) The Prince and his ministers deliberate on the matter.

(b) And then the commissioner is appointed.

(c) The commissioner kowtows twice, declining the honour;

(d) But accepts when the Prince refuses to allow him to decline, and withdraws.

(e) When all the deliberations are complete, the chief of the commissioner's suite is apprised of his appointment in the same manner.

(f) Then the court steward orders the master-at-arms to appoint the rest of the suite, and they all consent to the appointment, in accordance with the instructions of the Duke.

o   o   o   o

Receiving His Instructions

(a) The chief and the rest of the suite stand at attention outside the commissioner's door.

(b) And the commissioner, carrying the banner, leads them to the audience hall to receive his instructions.

(c) The Prince, in dress clothes, takes his place in the hall of audience, with his face to the south, the ministers and great officers facing west, and grading from the north. Then the Prince calls on a minister to bring forward the commissioner.

(d) The latter enters, followed by his suite, and they stand, facing north, and graded from the east. The Prince then calls the commissioner forward with a salute, and his chief of suite stands at his left hand to hear the instructions along with him.

(e) Then the appraiser sits, facing west, and, opening the case, takes out the jade symbol of authority, letting the wrapper hang down over his hands, and, without rising, hands it to the steward.

(f) The steward, sitting, takes the symbol, folds the wrapper over it, and, going from the left side of the Prince, hands it to the commissioner.

(g) The commissioner, facing north, as the steward does, receives the symbol, and allows the wrapper to hang down while he receives his instructions.

(h) When he has repeated the instructions, he hands the symbol to the chief of staff, who is facing in the same direction.

(i) He receives it, folds the wrapper over it, goes out, and hands it to the appraiser attached to the mission, the rest of the suite not following him.

(j) They receive the presents for the Prince of the State to be visited—silk, with a round jade symbol laid on it; and the half jade symbol for presentation to the Princess, and rolls of black and red silk, having a star-shaped symbol upon them, all with the ceremonial noted above.

o   o   o   o

The Send-Off

(a) Then they set off, and put up for the night in the suburbs.

(b) And the banner is furled. . . .

RITUAL RECORDS

(Li Chi)

Selections

Record of Music

Now there is no end of the things by which man is affected; and when his likings and dislikings are not subject to regulation from within, he is changed into the nature of things as they come before him; that is, he stifles the voice of T'ien's principle within, and gives the utmost indulgence to the desires by which men may be possessed. On this we have the rebellious and deceitful heart, with licentious and violent disorder. The strong press upon the weak; the many are cruel to the few; the knowing impose upon the dull; the bold make it bitter for the timid; the

From James Legge, tr., *Sacred Books of the East*, vol. 28, *The Lî Ki* (London: Oxford University Press, 1926).

diseased are not nursed; the old and young, orphans and solitaries are neglected: such is the great disorder that ensues.

Therefore the ancient kings, when they instituted their ceremonies and music, regulated them by consideration of the requirements of humanity. By the sackcloth worn for parents, the wailings, and the weepings, they defined the terms of the mourning rites. By the bells, drums, shields, and axes, they introduced harmony into their seasons of rest and enjoyment. By marriage, capping, and the assumption of the hair-pin, they maintained the separation that should exist between male and female. By the archery gatherings in the districts, and the feastings at the meetings of princes, they provided for the correct maintenance of friendly intercourse.

Ceremonies afforded the defined expression for the affections of the people's minds; music secured the harmonious utterance of their voices; the laws of government were designed to promote the performance of the ceremonies and music; and punishments, to guard against the violation of them. When ceremonies, music, laws, and punishments had everywhere full course, without irregularity or collision, the method of kingly rule was complete.

o   o   o   o

Through the perception of right produced by ceremony, came the degrees of the noble and the mean; through the union of culture arising from music, harmony between high and low. By the exhibition of what was to be liked and what was to be disliked, a distinction was made between the worthy and unworthy. When violence was prevented by punishments, and the worthy were raised to rank, the operation of government was made impartial. Then came benevolence in the love of the people, and righteousness in the correction of their errors; and in this way good government held its course.

o   o   o   o

Let music attain its full results, and there would be no dissatisfactions in the mind; let ceremony do so, and there would be no quarrels. When bowings and courtesies marked the government of the kingdom, there would be what might be described as music and ceremony indeed. Violent oppression of the people would not arise; the princes would appear submissively at court as guests; there would be no occasion for the weapons of war, and no employment of the five punishments; the common people would have no distresses, and the Son of T'ien no need to be angry: such a state of things would be a universal music.

o   o   o   o

Harmony is the thing principally sought in music: it therein follows T'ien, and manifests the spirit-like expansive influence characteristic of it. Normal distinction is the thing aimed at in ceremonies: they therein follow earth, and exhibit the spirit-like retractive influence characteristic of it. Hence the sages made music in response to T'ien, and framed ceremonies in correspondence with earth. In the wisdom and completeness of their ceremonies and music we see the directing power of T'ien and earth.

o   o   o   o

Music appeared in the Grand Beginning of all things, and ceremonies had their place on the completion of them. Their manifestation, being ceaseless, gives the idea of heaven; and again, being motionless, gives the idea of earth. Through the movement and repose of their interaction come all things between heaven and earth. Hence the sages simply spoke of ceremonies and music.

Law of Sacrifices

According to the law of sacrifices, Shun, the sovereign of the line of Yü, at the great associate sacrifice, gave the place of honour to Huang-ti, and at the border sacrifice made K'u the correlate of T'ien; he sacrificed also to Chuan hsü as his ancestor on the throne, and to Yao as his honoured predecessor.

o   o   o   o

Thus the king made for himself seven ancestral temples, with a raised altar and the surrounding area for each. The temples were—his father's; his grandfather's; his great-grandfather's; his great-great-grandfather's; and the temple of his high ancestor.

o   o   o   o

The king, for all the people, appointed seven altars for the seven sacrifices: one to the superintendent of the lot; one in the central court, for the admission of light and the rain from the roofs; one at the gates of the city wall; one in the roads leading from the city; one for the discontented ghosts of kings who had died without posterity; one for the guardian of the door; and one for the guardian of the furnace. He also had seven corresponding altars for himself.

A feudal prince, for his state, appointed five altars for the five sacrifices: one for the superintendent of the lot; one in the central court, for the admission of light and rain; one at the gates of the city wall; one in the roads leading from the city; one for the discontented ghosts of princes who had died without posterity. He also had five corresponding altars for himself.

o   o   o   o

An officer of the first grade appointed two altars for the two sacrifices: one at the gates, and one on the roads outside the gates.

Other officers and the common people had one altar and one sacrifice. Some raised one altar for the guardian of the door; and others, one for the guardian of the furnace.

o   o   o   o

According to the institutes of the sage kings about sacrifices, sacrifice should be offered to him who had given good laws to the people; to him who had laboured to the death in the discharge of his duties; to him who had strengthened the state by his laborious toil; to him who had boldly and successfully met great calamities; and to him who had warded off great evils.

o   o   o   o

The Meaning of Sacrifices. I

Sacrifices should not be frequently repeated. Such frequency is indicative of importunateness; and importunateness is inconsistent with reverence. Nor should they be at distant intervals. Such infrequency is indicative of indifference; and indifference leads to forgetting them altogether. Therefore the superior man, in harmony with the course of the heavens, offers the sacrifices of spring and autumn. When he treads on the dew which has descended as hoar-frost he cannot help a feeling of sadness, which arises in his mind, and cannot be ascribed to the cold. In spring, when he treads on the ground, wet with the rains and dews that have fallen heavily, he cannot avoid being moved by a feeling as if he were seeing his departed friends. We meet the approach of our friends with music, and escort them away with sadness, and hence at the sacrifice in spring we use music, but not at the sacrifice in autumn.

The severest vigil and purification is maintained and carried on inwardly; while a looser vigil is maintained externally. During the days of such vigil, the mourner thinks of his departed, how and where they sat, how they smiled and spoke, what were their aims and views, what they delighted in, and what things they desired and enjoyed. On the third day of such exercise he will see those for whom it is employed.

On the day of sacrifice, when he enters the apartment of the temple, he will seem to see the deceased in the place where his spirit-tablet is. After he has moved about and performed his operations, and is leaving at the door, he will seem to be arrested by hearing the sound of his movements, and will sigh as he seems to hear the sound of his sighing.

o   o   o   o

The superior man, while his parents are alive, reverently nourishes them; and, when they are dead, he reverently sacrifices to them; his chief thought is how to the end of life not to disgrace them. The saying that the superior man mourns all his life for his parents has reference to the recurrence of the day of their death. That he does not do his ordinary work on that day does not mean that it would be unpropitious to do so; it means that on that day his thoughts are occupied with them, and he does not dare to occupy himself as on other days with his private and personal affairs.

It is only the sage[1] who can sacrifice to Ti, and only the filial son who can sacrifice to his parents. Sacrificing means directing one's self to. The son directs his thoughts to his parents, and then he can offer his sacrifice so that they shall enjoy it. Hence the filial son approaches the personator of the departed [2] without having occasion to blush; the ruler leads the victim forward, while his wife puts down the bowls; the ruler presents the offerings to the personator, while his wife sets forth the various dishes; his ministers and Great officers assist the ruler, while their acknowledged wives assist his wife. How well sustained was their reverence! How complete was the expression of their loyal devotion! How earnest was their wish that the departed should enjoy the service!

o o o o

The Meaning of Sacrifices. II

o o o o

The Master said, ". . . All the living must die, and dying, return to the ground; this is what is called *k'uei*. The bones and flesh moulder below, and, hidden away, become the earth of the fields. But the spirit issues forth, and is displayed on high in a condition of glorious brightness. The vapours and odours which produce a feeling of sadness, and arise from the decay of their substance, are the subtle essences of all things, and also a manifestation of the *shên* nature.

"On the ground of these subtle essences of things, with an extreme decision and inventiveness, the sages framed distinctly the names of *k'uei* and *shên* to constitute a pattern for the black-haired race;[3] and all the multitudes were filled with awe, and the myriads of the people constrained to submission.

"The sages did not consider these names to be sufficient, and therefore they built temples with their different apartments, and framed their rules for ancestors who were always to be honoured, and those whose tablets should be removed—thus making a distinction for nearer and more distant kinship, and for ancestors the remote and the recent, and teaching the people to go back to their oldest fathers, and retrace their beginnings, not forgetting those to whom they owed their being. In consequence of this the multitude submitted to their lessons, and listened to them with a quicker readiness.

"These two elements of the human constitution having been established with the two names, two ceremonies were framed in accordance with them. They appointed the service of the morning, when the fat of the inwards was burned so as to bring out its fragrance, and this was mixed with the blaze of dried southern wood. This served as a tribute to the intelligent spirit, and taught all to go back to their originating ancestors. They also presented millet and rice, and offered the delicacies of the liver, lungs, head, and heart, along with two bowls of liquor and odoriferous spirits. This served as a tribute to the animal soul, and taught the people to love one another, and high and low to cultivate good feeling between them; such was the effect of those ceremonies."

o   o   o   o

Thus it was that anciently the Son of T'ien had his field of a thousand acres, in which he himself held the plough, wearing the square-topped cap with red ties. The feudal princes also had their field of a hundred acres, in which they did the same, wearing the same cap with green ties. They did this in the service of T'ien, Earth, the Spirits of the land and grain, and their ancient fathers, to supply the new wine, cream, and vessels of grain. In this way did they procure these things; it was a great expression of their reverence.

o   o   o   o

Anciently, the sovereigns of the line of Yü honoured virtue, and highly esteemed age; the sovereigns of Hsia honoured rank, and highly esteemed age; under Yin they honoured riches, and highly esteemed age;[4] under Chou, they honoured kinship, and highly esteemed age. Yü, Hsia, Yin, and Chou produced the greatest kings that have appeared under T'ien and there was not one of them who neglected age. For long has honour been paid to years under the sky; to pay it is next to the service of parents.

Therefore, at court among parties of the same rank, the highest place was given to the oldest. Men of seventy years carried their staffs at the court. When the ruler questioned one of them, he made him sit on a mat. One of eighty years did not wait out the audience, and when the ruler would question him he went to his house. Thus the submission of a younger brother and juniors generally was recognized at the court.

A junior walking with one older than himself, if they were walking shoulder to shoulder, yet it was not on the same line. If he did not keep transversely a little behind, he followed the other. When they saw an old man, people in carriages or walking got out of his way. Men, where the white were mingling with their black hairs, did not carry burdens on the roads. Thus the submission of juniors was recognized on the public ways.

Residents in the country took their places according to their age, and the old and poor were not neglected, nor did the strong come into collision with the weak, or members of a numerous clan do violence to those of a smaller. Thus the submission of juniors was recognized in the country districts and hamlets.

According to the ancient rule, men of fifty years were not required to serve in hunting expeditions; and in the distribution of the game, a larger share was given to the more aged. Thus the submission of juniors was recognized in the arrangements for the hunts. In the tens and fives of the army and its detachments, where the rank was the same, places were given according to age. Thus the submission of juniors was recognized in the army.

The display of filial and fraternal duty in the court; the practice of them on the road; their reaching to the districts and hamlets; their extension to the huntings; and the cultivation of them in the army, have thus been described. All would have died for them under the constraint of righteousness, and not dared to violate them.

o o o o

Anciently, the sages, having determined the phenomena of heaven and earth in their states of rest and activity, made them the basis of the *I* (and divining by it).[5] The diviner held the tortoise shell in his arms, with his face towards the south, while the son of T'ien, in his dragon-robe and square-topped cap, stood with his face to the north. The latter, however intelligent might be his mind, felt it necessary to set forth and obtain a decision on what his object was—showing that he did not dare to take his own way, and giving honour to T'ien as the supreme Decider. What was good in him or in his views he ascribed to others; what was wrong, to himself; thus teaching not to boast, and giving honour to men of talents and virtue.

o o o o

The Different Teachings of the Different Kings

o o o o

The ceremonies at the court audiences of the different seasons were intended to illustrate the righteous relations between ruler and subject; those of friendly messages and inquiries, to secure mutual honour and respect between the feudal princes; those of mourning and sacrifice, to illustrate the kindly feelings of ministers and sons; those of social meetings in the country districts, to show the order that should prevail between young and old; and those of marriage, to exhibit the separation that should be maintained between males and females. Those ceremonies prevent the rise of disorder and confusion, and are like the embankments which prevent the overflow of water.

o   o   o   o

Therefore the instructive and transforming power of ceremonies is subtile; they stop depravity before it has taken form, causing men daily to move towards what is good, and keep themselves farther apart from guilt, without being themselves conscious of it. It was on this account that the ancient kings set so high a value upon them.

o   o   o   o

7

The Age of
Contending Philosophies

It seems my lord is content to find his mounts and maidens in this age but must look to more ancient times for men of honor.

—*Intrigues of the Warring States*, 29:3

Out of the breakup of the Chou system varied men emerged as wandering experts and sages. Some settled in towns as tutors for aspirants to government office; others went from one prince or lord to another seeking to put their talents to work as specialists or advisers in courts large or small. Some gained high position, fame, and following; some resided in academies patronized by royalty; others became hermits living in mountain fastnesses; still others, disenchanted by the corruption around them or unable to win an audience, retreated to their homes with their disciples congregated around. A number became technocrats for the modern age of war and political consolidation.

An age of many states and many wars began, leading into what is called the Warring States Era (403–221 B.C.). It is also known as the time when all flowers bloomed and a hundred schools of thought contended. For there were not only technocrats and experts; there were philosophers too, in this age, men concerned with the not-so-apparent truth, with ethics, and with the good state. Having gained the perspective of many states, they could see the defects as well as the merits of any one. Their outlook was comparative and international. One world and one government was their aim—the unity of all under the sky—for only then could war be avoided. Most of them had no taste for war. It was visible evidence of the lack of harmony in the cosmos.

In this troubled, exciting, dangerous world, then, the philosophers also

TABLE 6. The Classical Philosophers and Their Schools

CHOU DYNASTY:		
EASTERN CHOU	770–256 B.C.	
Spring and Autumn Era	772–481 B.C.	
Confucius	551–479 B.C.	Confucianism
Lao Tzŭ	Sixth century B.C.?	Taoism
Warring States Era	403–221 B.C.	
Mo Tzŭ	c. 470–c. 391 B.C.	Mo-ism
Mencius	c. 372–c. 289 B.C.	Confucianism
Yang Chu	Fourth century B.C.?	Taoism
Sun Tzŭ	Fourth century B.C.?	Warring States Strategy
Shang Yang	d. 338 B.C.	Legalism
Chuang Tzŭ	c. 369–c. 286 B.C.	Taoism
Hsün Tzŭ	c. 312–c. 238 B.C.	Confucianism
Han Fei Tzŭ	d. 233 B.C.	Legalism
THE FIRST EMPIRE	221–206 B.C.	

walked. (See Table 6.) Of the great ones, Confucius perhaps came earliest. His span on earth fell in the latter days of the period called Spring and Autumn (722–481 B.C.), the times described in the annals of Lu, Confucius's native land and a repository of Chou ritual and tradition. For Lao Tzŭ, the Taoist, the only one who may antedate Confucius, the dates are most uncertain. Mo Tzŭ, another great philosopher, follows immediately in Confucius's footsteps, in time, but not in ideas. His stretch of years, however, crosses over into the period of Warring States, when the pace of warfare began to accelerate. Confucius does not talk much of war. For Mo Tzŭ it is a horror. The other great classical philosophers—Mencius and Hsün Tzŭ, the Confucians; Chuang Tzŭ, the Taoist; Shang Yang and Han Fei Tzŭ, the Legalists—all lived in this era of clashing states. Sun Tzŭ, that disarming general, wrote the treatise for the times on the art of war. His thirteen chapters give a clear picture of how the military man, one of the new class of specialists, looked on that violent world.

The philosophers describe it too. The bodies of the slain choked the countryside and the city walls. The rich plundered the poor, the old trudged the roads like beasts of burden. Thus Mencius bewails the times that lived off human flesh. Yet in those same days commerce thrived and contacts with foreigners and barbarians multiplied; problems came from every side and men sprang up like Cadmus's teeth to attack them with all the force and will of body and mind. New ideas were everywhere. Out of this conflict came creation.

8

Confucius

The Master said, I have never yet seen anyone whose desire to build up his moral power was as strong as sexual desire.

—*Analects,* 9:17

Many are the stories told of Confucius; few are the facts. He was born in 551 B.C. and died in 479 B.C. His days and years are entwined in the downspin of the Chou Dynasty. Lu was his native land, one of the states longest to hold on to Chou tradition. (These few data of his life are held to account for the feudalistic elements in Confucius's teachings.) His ancestry is uncertain: some say he was of noble birth, a scion of the ruling Sung house. He twice hints at possession of a rank equivalent to a *shih* or knight. He must have been married: he refers to a daughter whose marriage he arranged and a son who died in his lifetime. Much of his character shines through his sayings. They make clear, too, that his situation in life was humble.

According to a remark of Mencius (c. 372–c. 289 B.C.), the first great Confucian, Confucius once worked as a bookkeeper; at another time as caretaker of pasture land. Since no one offered him an important government post, one in which he could hope to build an ideal polity (although he later was consulted by a few rulers and probably offered a few minor posts, unacceptable for one reason or another), he dedicated the last years of his life—but not without disappointment—solely to teaching. He must have been one of the first in China to be master of the kind of school in which the one teacher has private, paying students who learn by living with him, and following him about, by listening and discussing his ideas.

Confucius's immediate success as a teacher was remarkable. He produced some able envoys, efficient administrators, respected counsellors, and influential teachers. Out of twenty-two students mentioned in the *Analects* nine attained important posts—ranging from diplomats to town managers and chief administrators of state—and a tenth turned one down. He never produced a Plato who produced an Aristotle who produced an Epicurus, but his long-range success as a teacher can hardly have been greater. To all China for two and one-half thousand years he is "the Master."

Confucius had no desire to found a religion. He could find nothing wrong with that of the Chou. Yet a religion was made out of Confucius himself, indeed a state religion. In December, 195 B.C., the first Han emperor, Kao-tsu, appears to have passed through Lu and sacrificed at the Kung family temple ("Confucius" is the Latinized version of "Kung Fu Tzŭ") to pay homage to the Master. In his first years on the throne, Emperor Wu (156–87 B.C.) established Confucianism as the state cult. In 37 A.D., all descendants of Confucius were made nobles. In 59 A.D., Han Ming Ti ordered official sacrifice to him in all schools. In time each city and town had its Confucian temple whose service was celebrated by local scholars and officials, in particular the mandarins, whose power and prestige the cult of Confucius symbolized. Music, solemn dances, and rites derived from the cult of ancestors and nature-spirits were part of the ceremonies. Not until 1928, by order of the Ministry of Education of the Chinese Republic, were official sacrifices at the temple of Confucius abolished.

Confucius is a philosopher of politics. His concern focuses on the good state. Toward this goal he offers a positive, constructive, decorous, and humanistic course. For him the ideal is the harmony of the perfect individual and a well-ordered society based on the mutual moral obligations of the five human relations between ruler and minister, father and son, elder brother and younger brother, husband and wife, and one friend and another, with filial piety and brotherly respect as the two fundamental virtues. Government is to be conducted through the ruler's moral example, and religious ceremonies are to express moral duties. Confucius sharply contrasted the superior man, whose standard is moral principle, with the inferior man whose standard is profit.

Yet Confucius nowhere presented his political or ethical thought in systematic form. For anyone else to try to do so would upset the balance of the *Analects*. To say, for example, that the important elements in Confucius's philosophy are one, two, three, four, etc., rites, benevolence, rightfulness, moral persuasion, the teacher, the gentleman, or the way of model Chou kings, while it may help readers today to remember certain points, invariably gives an order of precedence or at the very least a weighting to some sayings above others. Much of the force of the *Analects* lies in their brevity and randomness. They are so briefly put as to encourage multiple interpretations and are so randomly offered that on almost any one a monograph can be written.

Confucius's aim was to bring up a ruling class. Most of his teachings concern the thought and conduct not of kings themselves but of those who may become the counsellors of kings, royal families, or states. The counsellors, though, will know what a good king is, for they are superior men or gentlemen of noble minds and hearts. The good king may not be the one they are serving at any given moment; but if they find their ruler wicked and incapable of improvement, they are to leave him to go to a more promising ruler elsewhere. Confucius's own life is the story of such a counsellor, wandering to find a king or state to pay him, to listen to him, and to learn. At age fifty-six, finding the ruler no longer interested in his ideas, he left Chou and spent almost thirteen years traveling with some of his pupils through nine states. Unable to influence their rulers, he returned to Lu to continue teaching and perhaps to work on the documents and songs that eventually formed part of the Confucian classics.

He said he was only a transmitter and looked to ancient sage kings as models, but he was the first in China to become a professional teacher, to teach people literature and principles of conduct instead of vocational statecraft, and to open the doors of education to all.

Like proverbs, the *Analects* incorporate the wisdom of centuries. These sayings were selected and compiled long after the Master's death. They are short and simple, the whole collection amounting to about one hundred and fifty printed pages. Like proverbs they admit of few qualifications yet do not ring dogmatic. Instructive and sincere, they are never pedantic or maudlin. The reader is uplifted not because of a sentimental or exalted style; the *Analects* convince him by straightforwardness and by lack of any doubt that nobility of thought and action is the only way to virtue and happiness.

THE *ANALECTS*

(Lun Yü)

Selections

Book 1

1. The Master[1] said, To learn and at due times to repeat what one
has learnt, is that not after all a pleasure? That friends should come to
one from afar, is this not after all delightful? To remain unsoured even
though one's merits are unrecognized by others, is that not after all what
is expected of a gentleman?

From Arthur Waley, tr., *The Analects of Confucius* (London: George Allen and
Unwin, 1938).

Book 2

4. The Master said, At fifteen I set my heart upon learning. At thirty, I had planted my feet firm upon the ground. At forty, I no longer suffered from perplexities. At fifty, I knew what were the biddings of T'ien. At sixty, I heard them with docile ear. At seventy, I could follow the dictates of my own heart; for what I desired no longer overstepped the boundaries of right.

11. The Master said, He who by reanimating the Old can gain knowledge of the New is fit to be a teacher.

12. The Master said, A gentleman is not an implement.

20. Chi K'ang-tzŭ[2] asked whether there were any form of encouragement by which he could induce the common people to be respectful and loyal. The Master said, Approach them with dignity, and they will respect you. Show piety towards your parents and kindness towards your children, and they will be loyal to you. Promote those who are worthy, train those who are incompetent; that is the best form of encouragement.

21. Someone, when talking to Master K'ung,[3] said, How is it that you are not in the public service? The Master said, The Book[4] says: "Be filial, only be filial and friendly towards your brothers, and you will be contributing to government." There are other sorts of service quite different from what you mean by "service."

Book 3

3. The Master said, A man who is not Good, what can he have to do with ritual? A man who is not Good, what can he have to do with music?

5. The Master said, The barbarians of the East and North[5] have retained their princes. They are not in such a state of decay as we in China.

7. The Master said, Gentlemen never compete. You will say that in archery[6] they do so. But even then they bow and make way for one another when they are going up to the archery-ground, when they are coming down, and at the subsequent drinking-bout. Thus even when competing, they still remain gentlemen.

11. Someone asked for an explanation of the Ancestral Sacrifice. The Master said, I do not know. Anyone who knew the explanation could

deal with all things under Heaven as easily as I lay this here; and he laid his finger upon the palm of his hand.

14. The Master said, Chou could survey the two preceding dynasties. How great a wealth of culture! And we follow upon Chou.

17. Tzŭ-kung[7] wanted to do away with the presentation of a sacrificial sheep at the announcement of each new moon. The Master said, Ssŭ! You grudge sheep, but I grudge ritual.

18. The Master said, Were anyone today to serve his prince according to the full prescriptions of ritual, he would be thought a sycophant.

20. The Master said, The Ospreys![8] Pleasure not carried to the point of debauch; grief not carried to the point of self-injury.

25. The Master spoke of the Succession Dance as being perfect beauty and at the same time perfect goodness; but of the War Dance[9] as being perfect beauty, but not perfect goodness.

26. The Master said, High office filled by men of narrow views, ritual performed without reverence, the forms of mourning observed without grief—these are things I cannot bear to see!

Book 4

1. The Master said, It is Goodness that gives to a neighbourhood its beauty. One who is free to choose, yet does not prefer to dwell among the Good—how can he be accorded the name of wise?

2. The Master said, Without Goodness a man

> Cannot for long endure adversity,
> Cannot for long enjoy prosperity.[10]

The Good Man rests content with Goodness; he that is merely wise pursues Goodness in the belief that it pays to do so.

5. Wealth and rank are what every man desires; but if they can only be retained to the detriment of the Way he professes, he must relinquish them. Poverty and obscurity are what every man detests; but if they can only be avoided to the detriment of the Way he professes, he must accept them. The gentleman who ever parts company with Goodness does not fulfil that name. Never for a moment does a gentleman quit the way of Goodness. He is never so harried but that he cleaves to this; never so tottering but that he cleaves to this.

6. The Master said, I for my part have never yet seen one who really

cared for Goodness, nor one who really abhorred wickedness. One who really cared for Goodness would never let any other consideration come first. One who abhorred wickedness would be so constantly doing Good that wickedness would never have a chance to get at him. Has anyone ever managed to do Good with his whole might even as long as the space of a single day? I think not. Yet I for my part have never seen anyone give up such an attempt because he had not the *strength* to go on. It may well have happened, but I for my part have never seen it.

8. The Master said, In the morning, hear the Way; in the evening, die content!

9. The Master said, A Knight whose heart is set upon the Way, but who is ashamed of wearing shabby clothes and eating coarse food, is not worth calling into counsel.

10. The Master said, A gentleman in his dealings with the world has neither enmities nor affections; but wherever he sees Right he ranges himself beside it.

12. The Master said, Those whose measures are dictated by mere expediency will arouse continual discontent.

16. The Master said, A gentleman takes as much trouble to discover what is right as lesser men take to discover what will pay.

18. The Master said, In serving his father and mother a man may gently remonstrate with them. But if he sees that he has failed to change their opinion, he should resume an attitude of deference and not thwart them; may feel discouraged, but not resentful.

19. The Master said, While father and mother are alive, a good son does not wander far afield; or if he does so, goes only where he has said he was going.

23. The Master said, Those who err on the side of strictness are few indeed!

24. The Master said, A gentleman covets the reputation of being slow in word but prompt in deed.

25. The Master said, Moral force never dwells in solitude; it will always bring neighbours.

Book 5

5. The Master gave Ch'i-tiao K'ai[11] leave to take office, but he replied, "I have not yet sufficiently perfected myself in the virtue of good faith." The Master was delighted.

6. The Master said, The Way makes no progress. I shall get upon a raft and float out to sea. I am sure Yu would come with me. Tzǔ-lu[12] on hearing of this was in high spirits. The Master said, That is Yu indeed! He sets far too much store by feats of physical daring. It seems as though I should never get hold of the right sort of people.

7. Mêng Wu Po[13] asked whether Tzǔ-lu[14] was Good. The Master said, I do not know. On his repeating the question the Master said, In a country of a thousand war-chariots Yu could be trusted to carry out the recruiting. But whether he is Good I do not know. "What about Ch'iu?" [14] The Master said, In a city of a thousand families or a baronial family with a hundred chariots he might do well as Warden. But whether he is Good, I do not know. "What about Ch'ih?" [14] The Master said, Girt with his sash, standing in his place at Court he might well be charged to converse with strangers and guests. But whether he is Good, I do not know.

9. Tsai Yü[15] used to sleep during the day. The Master said, Rotten wood cannot be carved, nor a wall of dried dung be trowelled. What use is there in my scolding him any more?

The Master said, There was a time when I merely listened attentively to what people said, and took for granted that they would carry out their words. Now I am obliged not only to give ear to what they say, but also to keep an eye on what they do. It was my dealings with Tsai Yü that brought about the change.

11. Tzǔ-kung said, What I do not want others to do to me, I have no desire to do to others. The Master said, Oh Ssǔ! You have not quite got to that point yet.

12. Tzǔ-kung said, Our Master's views concerning culture and the outward insignia of goodness, we are permitted to hear; but about Man's nature and the ways of T'ien he will not tell us anything at all.

15. Of Tzǔ-ch'an[16] the Master said that in him were to be found four of the virtues that belong to the Way of the true gentleman. In his private conduct he was courteous, in serving his master he was punctilious, in providing for the needs of the people he gave them even more than their due; in exacting service from the people, he was just.

19. Chi Wên Tzǔ[17] used to think thrice before acting. The Master hearing of it said, Twice is quite enough.

26. The Master said, In vain have I looked for a single man capable of seeing his own faults and bringing the charge home against himself.

27. The Master said, In a hamlet of ten houses you may be sure of finding someone quite as loyal and true to his word as I. But I doubt if you would find anyone with such a love of learning.

Book 6

5. The Master said, Hui[18] is capable of occupying his whole mind for three months on end with no thought but that of Goodness. The others can do so, some for a day, some even for a month; but that is all.

6. Chi K'ang-tzŭ[19] asked whether Tzŭ-lu was the right sort of person to put into office. The Master said, Yu is efficient. It goes without saying that he is capable of holding office. Chi K'ang-tzŭ said, How about Tzŭ-kung? Would he be the right sort of person to put into office? The Master said, He can turn his merits to account. It goes without saying that he is capable of holding office. Chi K'ang-tzŭ said, How about Jan Ch'iu? Would he be the right sort of person to put into office? The Master said, He is versatile. It goes without saying that he is capable of holding office.

8. When Po Niu[20] was ill, the Master went to inquire after him, and grasping his hand through the window said, It is all over with him! Heaven [*ming*] has so ordained it— But that such a man should have such an illness! That such a man should have such an illness!

13. The Master said, Mêng Chih-fan[21] is no boaster. When his people were routed he was the last to flee; but when they neared the city-gate, he whipped up his horses, saying, It was not courage that kept me behind. My horses were slow.

15. The Master said, Who expects to be able to go out of a house except by the door? How is it then that no one follows this Way of ours?

16. The Master said, When natural substance prevails over ornamentation, you get the boorishness of the rustic. When ornamentation prevails over natural substance, you get the pedantry of the scribe. Only when ornament and substance are duly blended do you get the true gentleman.

18. The Master said, To prefer it[22] is better than only to know it. To delight in it is better than merely to prefer it.

19. The Master said, To men who have risen at all above the middling sort, one may talk of things higher yet. But to men who are at all

below the middling sort it is useless to talk of things that are above them.

20. Fan Ch'ih[23] asked about wisdom. The Master said, He who devotes himself to securing for his subjects what it is right they should have, who by respect for the Spirits keeps them at a distance, may be termed wise. He asked about Goodness. The Master said, Goodness cannot be obtained till what is difficult has been duly done. He who has done this may be called Good.

25. The Master said, A gentleman who is widely versed in letters and at the same time knows how to submit his learning to the restraints of ritual is not likely, I think, to go far wrong.

27. The Master said, How transcendent is the moral power of the Middle Use! [24] That it is but rarely found among the common people is a fact long admitted.

28. Tzŭ-kung said, If a ruler not only conferred wide benefits upon the common people, but also compassed the salvation of the whole State, what would you say of him? Surely, you would call him Good? The Master said, It would no longer be a matter of "Good." He would without doubt be a Divine Sage. Even Yao and Shun could hardly criticize him.[25] As for Goodness—you yourself desire rank and standing; then help others to get rank and standing. You want to turn your own merits to account; then help others to turn theirs to account—in fact, the ability to take one's own feelings as a guide—that is the sort of thing that lies in the direction of Goodness.

Book 7

1, 2, 3. The Master said, I have "transmitted what was taught to me without making up anything of my own." I have been faithful to and loved the Ancients. In these respects, I make bold to think, not even our old P'êng[26] can have excelled me. The Master said, I have listened in silence and noted what was said, I have never grown tired of learning nor wearied of teaching others what I have learnt. These at least are merits which I can confidently claim. The Master said, The thought that "I have left my moral power untended, my learning unperfected, that I have heard of righteous men, but been unable to go to them; have heard of evil men, but been unable to reform them"—it is these thoughts that disquiet me.

4. In his leisure hours the Master's manner was very free and easy, and his expression alert and cheerful.

6. The Master said, Set your heart upon the Way, support yourself by its power, lean upon Goodness, seek distraction in the arts.

7. The Master said, From the very poorest upwards—beginning even with the man who could bring no better present than a bundle of dried flesh—none has ever come to me without receiving instruction.

8. The Master said, Only one who bursts with eagerness do I instruct; only one who bubbles with excitement, do I enlighten. If I hold up one corner and a man cannot come back to me with the other three, I do not continue the lesson.

9. If at a meal the Master found himself seated next to someone who was in mourning, he did not eat his fill. When he had wailed at a funeral, during the rest of the day he did not sing.[27]

10. The Master said to Yen Hui, The maxim

> *When wanted, then go;*
> *When set aside; then hide.*

is one that you and I could certainly fulfil. Tzŭ-lu said, Supposing you had command of the Three Hosts,[28] whom would you take to help you? The Master said, The man who was ready to "beard a tiger or rush a river" without caring whether he lived or died—that sort of man I should not take. I should certainly take someone who approached difficulties with due caution and who preferred to succeed by strategy.

12. The rites to which the Master gave the greatest attention were those connected with purification before sacrifice, with war, and with sickness.

13. When he was in Ch'i the Master heard the Succession,[29] and for three months did not know the taste of meat. He said, I did not picture to myself that any music existed which could reach such perfection as this.

15. The Master said, He who seeks only coarse food to eat, water to drink, and a bent arm for pillow, will without looking for it find happiness to boot. Any thought of accepting wealth and rank by means that I know to be wrong is as remote from me as the clouds that float above.

16. The Master said, Give me a few more years, so that I may have spent a whole fifty in study, and I believe that after all I should be fairly free from error.

18. The Duke of Shê[30] asked Tzǔ-lu about Master K'ung. Tzǔ-lu did not reply. The Master said, Why did you not say "This is the character of the man: so intent upon enlightening the eager that he forgets his hunger, and so happy in doing so, that he forgets the bitterness of his lot and does not realize that old age is at hand. That is what he is."

19. The Master said, I for my part am not one of those who have innate knowledge. I am simply one who loves the past and who is diligent in investigating it.

20. The Master never talked of prodigies, feats of strength, disorders, or spirits.

22. The Master said, T'ien begat the power that is in me. What have I to fear from such a one as Huan T'ui? [31]

24. The Master took four subjects for his teaching: culture, conduct of affairs, loyalty to superiors, and the keeping of promises.

25. The Master said, A Divine Sage I cannot hope ever to meet; the most I can hope for is to meet a true gentleman. The Master said, A faultless man I cannot hope ever to meet; the most I can hope for is to meet a man of fixed principles. Yet where all around I see Nothing pretending to be Something, Emptiness pretending to be Fulness, Penury pretending to be Affluence, even a man of fixed principles will be none too easy to find.

26. The Master fished with a line but not with a net; when fowling he did not aim at a roosting bird.

31. When in the Master's presence anyone sang a song that he liked, he did not join in at once, but asked for it to be repeated and then joined in.

Book 8

1. The Master said, Of T'ai Po[32] it may indeed be said that he attained to the very highest pitch of moral power. No less than three times he renounced the sovereignty of all things under Heaven, without the people getting a chance to praise him for it.

8. The Master said, Let a man be first incited by the *Songs*,[33] then given a firm footing by the study of ritual, and finally perfected by music.

9. The Master said, The common people can be made to follow it; they cannot be made to understand it.[34]

10. The Master said, One who is by nature daring and is suffering from poverty will not long be law-abiding. Indeed, any men, save those that are truly Good, if their sufferings are very great, will be likely to rebel.[35]

13. The Master said, Be of unwavering good faith, love learning, if attacked be ready to die for the good Way. Do not enter a State that pursues dangerous courses, nor stay in one where the people have rebelled. When the Way prevails under Heaven, then show yourself; when it does not prevail, then hide. When the Way prevails in your own land, count it a disgrace to be needy and obscure; when the Way does not prevail in your land, then count it a disgrace to be rich and honoured.

14. The Master said, He who holds no rank in a State does not discuss its policies.

18. The Master said, Sublime were Shun and Yü! All that is under Heaven was theirs, yet they remained aloof from it.

19. The Master said, Greatest, as lord and ruler, was Yao. Sublime, indeed, was he. "There is no greatness like the greatness of T'ien," yet Yao could copy it. So boundless was it that the people could find no name for it; yet sublime were his achievements, dazzling the insignia of his culture!

21. The Master said, In Yü I can find no semblance of a flaw. Abstemious in his own food and drink, he displayed the utmost devotion in his offerings to spirits and divinities. Content with the plainest clothes for common wear, he saw to it that his sacrificial apron and ceremonial head-dress were of the utmost magnificence. His place of habitation was of the humblest, and all his energy went into draining and ditching. In him I can find no semblance of a flaw.

Book 9

2. A villager from Ta-hsiang[36] said, Master K'ung is no doubt a very great man and vastly learned. But he does nothing to bear out this reputation. The Master, hearing of it, said to his disciples, What shall I take up? Shall I take up chariot-driving? Or shall it be archery? I think I will take up driving!

3. The Master said, The hemp-thread crown is prescribed by ritual. Nowadays people wear black silk, which is economical; and I follow the general practice. Obeisance below the daïs is prescribed by ritual.

Nowadays people make obeisance after mounting the daïs. This is presumptuous, and though to do so is contrary to the general practice, I make a point of bowing while still down below.

5. When the Master was trapped in K'uang,[37] he said, When King Wên perished, did that mean that culture ceased to exist? If T'ien had really intended that such culture as his should disappear, a latter-day mortal would never have been able to link himself to it as I have done. And if T'ien does not intend to destroy such culture, what have I to fear from the people of K'uang?

6. The Grand Minister[38] asked Tzŭ-kung, saying, Is your Master a Divine Sage? If so, how comes it that he has many practical accomplishments? Tzŭ-kung said, T'ien certainly intended him to become a Sage; it is also true that he has many accomplishments. When the Master heard of it he said, The Grand Minister is quite right about me. When I was young I was in humble circumstances; that is why I have many practical accomplishments in regard to simple, everyday matters. Does it befit a gentleman to have many accomplishments? No, he is in no need of them at all.

Lao[39] says that the Master said, It is because I have not been given a chance that I have become so handy.

7. The Master said, Do I regard myself as a possessor of wisdom? Far from it. But if even a simple peasant comes in all sincerity and asks me a question, I am ready to thrash the matter out, with all its pros and cons, to the very end.

8. The Master said, The phoenix does not come; the river gives forth no chart.[40] It is all over with me!

11. When the Master was very ill, Tzŭ-lu caused some of the disciples to get themselves up as official retainers. Coming to himself for a short while, the Master said, How like Yu, to go in for this sort of imposture! In pretending to have retainers when I have none, whom do I deceive? Do I deceive T'ien? Not only would I far rather die in the arms of you disciples than in the arms of retainers, but also as regards my funeral— even if I am not accorded a State Burial, it is not as though I were dying by the roadside.

12. Tzŭ-kung said, Suppose one had a lovely jewel, should one wrap it up, put it in a box, and keep it, or try to get the best price one can for it? The Master said, Sell it! Most certainly sell it! I myself am one who is waiting for an offer.

13. The Master wanted to settle among the Nine Wild Tribes of the East.[41] Someone said, I am afraid you would find it hard to put up with their lack of refinement. The Master said, Were a true gentleman to settle among them there would soon be no trouble about lack of refinement.

15. The Master said, I can claim that at Court[42] I have duly served the Duke and his officers; at home, my father and elder brother. As regards matters of mourning, I am conscious of no neglect, nor have I ever been overcome with wine. Concerning these things at any rate my mind is quite at rest.

22. The Master said, Respect the young. How do you know that they will not one day be all that you are now? But if a man has reached forty or fifty and nothing has been heard of him, then I grant there is no need to respect him.

25. The Master said, You may rob the Three Armies[43] of their commander-in-chief, but you cannot deprive the humblest peasant of his opinion.

26. The Master said, "Wearing a shabby hemp-quilted gown, yet capable of standing unabashed with those who wore fox and badger." That would apply quite well to Yu, would it not?

> Who harmed none, was foe to none,
> Did nothing that was not right.[44]

Afterwards Tzŭ-lu kept on continually chanting those lines to himself. The Master said, Come now, the wisdom contained in them is not worth treasuring to that extent!

27. The Master said, Only when the year grows cold do we see that the pine and cypress are the last to fade.

Book 11

1. The Master said, "Only common people wait till they are advanced in ritual and music [before taking office]. A gentleman can afford to get up his ritual and music later on." Even if I accepted this saying, I should still be on the side of those who get on with their studies first.

3. The Master said, Hui was not any help to me; he accepted everything I said.

11. Tzŭ-lu asked how one should serve ghosts and spirits. The Master said, Till you have learnt to serve men, how can you serve ghosts? Tzŭ-lu then ventured upon a question about the dead. The Master said, Till you know about the living, how are you to know about the dead?

9

Mencius

No man is devoid of a heart sensitive to the sufferings of others.

—*Mencius*, 2A.6

Mencius (c. 372–c. 289 B.C.) is known as Confucius's successor. He was born in the kingdom of Chou about a century after Confucius, and his adult life spanned most of the harsh, warlike fourth century B.C. After finishing his study under a disciple of Tzǔ-Ssǔ, grandson of Confucius, he traveled to various feudal states—Liang, Ch'i, Chou, and Lu—and called on their respective kings. When he found that no ruler would take him into confidence, he devoted himself to writing. Mencius's philosophy was first recognized by Emperor Wên Ti of the Former Han Dynasty (reigned 179–157 B.C.), who also founded a professorial chair for the study of Mencius's works.

His work *The Book of Mencius* consists of seven books with 261 chapters. Whether this voluminous work was written by Mencius himself or by his pupils or others is still a question, but the style of the language does show the imprint of Mencius's strong character. It may be safely assumed that most of the dialogues in the book are derived from Mencius's own notes at least, and are probably the organized expression of his mature views, the distillation of a lifetime of thinking and teaching.

The dialogues Mencius writes of make longer and more contrived literary statements than the *Analects* of Confucius. The one consists of anecdotes; the other of sayings. Furthermore, while the *Analects* essentially record Confucius's remarks to his students, the *Mencius* brings the reader in to listen to a philosopher during his exchanges with kings and ministers as well. Thus, while Confucius spoke often and forcefully to students of court employment, its benefits and dangers, Mencius at court tells the king to his face where he has gone wrong, making the reader glance about warily for the nearest exit.

Mencius and Confucius both were convinced that all men desire wealth and detest poverty, but in general on questions of man's nature, Confucius was brief, whereas Mencius can truly be said to have sketched not only an original nature but a psychology of man. Mencius believed that there is a beginning of goodness in human nature. The senses of humanity and justice are based on innate feelings, or men's natural ways of reacting to events. One feeling is that of compassion, or distress at seeing others suffer—*any* others, not just kin or countrymen. An appeal to these innate qualities, even if they are not fully developed in the mass of mankind, will gain people's hearts. Force will eventually go against their nature. So it is that virtue invariably subverts and conquers force. The ruler has only to be humane to be a good ruler. His nature and his people's and T'ien's sympathy run in parallel lines.

Mencius's political philosophy rests on the concept of T'ien. He has absolutely no doubt that the ruler is granted the Mandate by T'ien for the benefit of all people. Whether a ruler deserves to remain a ruler depends on his carrying out his charge. If he fails to do so, he not only should be, but inevitably will be, removed.

It is no exaggeration to say that what is called Confucianism in subsequent times contains as much of the thought of Mencius as of Confucius. From the Sung Dynasty onward, the doctrines of Mencius formed part of the orthodoxy. The *Great Learning*, the *Doctrine of the Mean* (see Chapter 11), the *Analects* of Confucius, together with *The Book of Mencius*, became known as the Four Books (see Table 3). Until the present century, they were read and memorized by every schoolboy in his first years at school. Thus the position and influence of Mencius were assured.

THE *MENCIUS*

(*Mêng Tzŭ*)

Selections

Book I

Part A

1. Mencius went to see King Hui of Liang.[1] "Sir," said the King.
"You have come all this distance, thinking nothing of a thousand *li*. You
must surely have some way of profiting my state?"

"Your Majesty," answered Mencius. "What is the point of mentioning the word 'profit'? All that matters is that there should be benevolence and rightness. If Your Majesty says, 'How can I profit my state?'
and the Counsellors say, 'How can I profit my family?' and the Gentle-

From D. C. Lau, tr., *Mencius* (London: Penguin Books, 1970).

men and Commoners say, 'How can I profit my person?' then those above and those below will be trying to profit at the expense of one another and the state will be imperilled. When regicide is committed in a state of ten thousand chariots,[2] it is certain to be by a vassal with a thousand chariots, and when it is committed in a state of a thousand chariots, it is certain to be by a vassal with a hundred chariots. A share of a thousand in ten thousand or a hundred in a thousand is by no means insignificant, yet if profit is put before rightness, there is no satisfaction short of total usurpation. No benevolent man ever abandons his parents, and no dutiful man ever puts his prince last. Perhaps you will now endorse what I have said, 'All that matters is that there should be benevolence and rightness. What is the point of mentioning the word "profit"?' "

5. King Hui of Liang said, "As you know, the state of Chin[3] was second to none in power in the Empire. But when it came to my own time we suffered defeat in the east by Ch'i when my eldest son died, and we lost territory to the extent of seven hundred *li* to Ch'in in the west, while to the south we were humiliated by Ch'u. I am deeply ashamed of this and wish, in what little time I have left in this life, to wash away all this shame. How can this be done?"

"A territory of a hundred *li* square," answered Mencius, "is sufficient to enable its ruler to become a true King. If Your Majesty practises benevolent government towards the people, reduces punishment and taxation, gets the people to plough deeply and weed promptly, and if the able-bodied men learn, in their spare time, to be good sons and good younger brothers, loyal to their prince and true to their word, so that they will, in the family, serve their fathers and elder brothers, and, outside the family, serve their elders and superiors, then they can be made to inflict defeat on the strong armour and sharp weapons of Ch'in and Ch'u, armed with nothing but staves.

"These other princes take the people away from their work during the busy seasons, making it impossible for them to till the land and so minister to the needs of their parents. Thus parents suffer cold and hunger while brothers, wives, and children are separated and scattered. These princes push their people into pits and into water. If you should go and punish such princes, who is there to oppose you? Hence it is said, 'The benevolent man has no match.' I beg of you not to have any doubts."

7. King Hsüan of Ch'i[4] asked, "Can you tell me about the history of Duke Huan of Ch'i and Duke Wên of Chin?"[5]

"None of the followers of Confucius," answered Mencius, "spoke of the history of Duke Huan and Duke Wên. It is for this reason that no one in after ages passed on any accounts, and I have no knowledge of them. If you insist, perhaps I may be permitted to tell you about becoming a true King."

"How virtuous must a man be before he can become a true King?"

"He becomes a true King by bringing peace to the people. This is something no one can stop."

"Can someone like myself bring peace to the people?"

"Yes."

"How do you know that I can?"

"I heard the following from Hu Ho:

The King was sitting in the upper part of the hall and someone led an ox through the lower part. The King noticed this and said, 'Where is the ox going?' 'The blood of the ox is to be used for consecrating a new bell.' [6] 'Spare it. I cannot bear to see it shrinking with fear, like an innocent man going to the place of execution.' 'In that case, should the ceremony be abandoned?' 'That is out of the question. Use a lamb instead.'

"I wonder if this is true?"

"It is."

"The heart behind your action is sufficient to enable you to become a true King. The people all thought that you grudged the expense, but, for my part, I have no doubt that you were moved by pity for the animal."

"You are right," said the King. "How could there be such people? Ch'i may be a small state, but I am not quite so miserly as to grudge the use of an ox. It was simply because I could not bear to see it shrink with fear, like an innocent man going to the place of execution, that I used a lamb instead."

"You must not be surprised that the people thought you miserly. You used a small animal in place of a big one. How were they to know? If you were pained by the animal going innocently to its death, what was there to choose between an ox and a lamb?"

The King laughed and said, "What was really in my mind, I wonder? It is not true that I grudged the expense, but I *did* use a lamb instead of the ox. I suppose it was only natural that the people should have thought me miserly."

"There is no harm in this. It is the way of a benevolent man. You saw the ox but not the lamb. The attitude of a gentleman towards animals is this: once having seen them alive, he cannot bear to see them die, and once having heard their cry, he cannot bear to eat their flesh. That is why the gentleman keeps his distance from the kitchen."

The King said, "The *Book of Odes* says,

> The heart is another man's,
> But it is I who have surmised it[7]

This describes you perfectly. For though the deed was mine, when I looked into myself I failed to understand my own heart. You described it for me and your words struck a chord in me. What made you think that my heart accorded with the way of a true King?"

"Should someone say to you, 'I am strong enough to lift a hundred *chün* but not a feather; I have eyes that can see the tip of a fine hair but not a cartload of firewood,' would you accept the truth of such a statement?"

"No."

"Why should it be different in your own case? Your bounty is sufficient to reach the animals, yet the benefits of your government fail to reach the people. That a feather is not lifted is because one fails to make the effort; that a cartload of firewood is not seen is because one fails to use one's eyes. Similarly, that peace is not brought to the people is because you fail to practise kindness. Hence your failure to become a true King is due to a refusal to act, not to an inability to act."

"What is the difference in form between refusal to act and inability to act?"

"If you say to someone, 'I am unable to do it,' when the task is one of striding over the North Sea with Mount T'ai under your arm, then this is a genuine case of inability to act. But if you say, 'I am unable to do it,' when it is one of massaging an elder's joints for him, then this is a case of refusal to act, not of inability. Hence your failure to become a true King is not the same in kind as 'striding over the North Sea with Mount T'ai under your arm', but the same as 'massaging an elder's joints for him.'

"Treat the aged of your own family in a manner befitting their venerable age and extend this treatment to the aged of other families; treat your own young in a manner befitting their tender age and extend this to the young of other families, and you can roll the Empire on your palm.

"The *Book of Odes* says,

> He set an example for his consort
> And also for his brothers,
> And so ruled over the family and the state[8]

In other words, all you have to do is take this very heart here and apply it to what is over there. Hence one who extends his bounty can bring peace to the Four Seas; one who does not cannot bring peace even to his own family. There is just one thing in which the ancients greatly surpassed others, and that is the way they extended what they did. Why is it then that your bounty is sufficient to reach animals yet the benefits of your government fail to reach the people?

"It is by weighing a thing that its weight can be known and by measuring it that its length can be ascertained. It is so with all things, but particularly so with the heart. Your Majesty should measure his own heart.

"Perhaps you find satisfaction only in starting a war, imperilling your subjects, and incurring the enmity of other feudal lords?"

"No. Why should I find satisfaction in such acts? I only wish to realize my supreme ambition."

"May I be told what this is?"

The King smiled, offering no reply.

"Is it because your food is not good enough to gratify your palate, and your clothes not good enough to gratify your body? Or perhaps the sights and sounds are not good enough to gratify your eyes and ears and your close servants not good enough to serve you? Any of your various officials surely could make good these deficiencies. It cannot be because of these things."

"No. It is not because of these things."

"In that case one can guess what your supreme ambition is. You wish to extend your territory, to enjoy the homage of Ch'in and Ch'u, to rule over the Central Kingdoms, and to bring peace to the barbarian tribes on the four borders. Seeking the fulfilment of such an ambition by such means as you employ is like looking for fish by climbing a tree."

"Is it as bad as that?" asked the King.

"It is likely to be worse. If you look for fish by climbing a tree, though you will not find it, there is no danger of this bringing disasters in its train. But if you seek the fulfilment of an ambition like yours by such means as you employ, after putting all your heart and might into the pursuit, you are certain to reap disaster in the end."

"Can I hear about this?"

"If the men of Tsou[9] and the men of Ch'u were to go to war, who do you think would win?"

"The men of Ch'u."

"That means that the small is no match for the big, the few no match for the many, and the weak no match for the strong. Within the Seas there are nine areas of ten thousand *li* square, and the territory of Ch'i makes up one of these. For one to try to overcome the other eight is no different from Tsou going to war with Ch'u. Why not go back to fundamentals?

"Now if you should practise benevolence in the government of your state, then all those in the Empire who seek office would wish to find a place at your court, all tillers of land to till the land in outlying parts of your realm, all merchants to enjoy the refuge of your market-place, all travellers to go by way of your roads, and all those who hate their rulers to lay their complaints before you. This being so, who can stop you from becoming a true King?"

"I am dull-witted," said the King, "and cannot see my way beyond this point. I hope you will help me towards my goal and instruct me plainly. Though I am slow, I shall make an attempt to follow your advice."

"Only a Gentleman can have a constant heart in spite of a lack of constant means of support. The people, on the other hand, will not have constant hearts if they are without constant means. Lacking constant hearts, they will go astray and fall into excesses, stopping at nothing. To punish them after they have fallen foul of the law is to set a trap for the people. How can a benevolent man in authority allow himself to set a trap for the people? Hence when determining what means of support the people should have, a clear-sighted ruler ensures that these are sufficient, on the one hand, for the care of parents, and, on the other, for the support of wife and children, so that the people always have sufficient food in good years and escape starvation in bad; only then does he drive them towards goodness; in this way the people find it easy to follow him.

"Nowadays, the means laid down for the people are sufficient neither for the care of parents nor for the support of wife and children. In good years life is always hard, while in bad years there is no way of escaping death. Thus simply to survive takes more energy than the people have. What time can they spare for learning about rites[10] and duty?

"If you wish to put this into practice, why not go back to fundamentals? If the mulberry is planted in every homestead of five *mu*[11] of land, then those who are fifty can wear silk; if chickens, pigs, and dogs do not miss their breeding season, then those who are seventy can eat meat; if each lot of a hundred *mu* is not deprived of labour during the busy seasons, then families with several mouths to feed will not go hungry. Exercise due care over the education provided by village schools, and discipline the people by teaching them duties proper to sons and younger brothers, and those whose heads have turned grey will not be carrying loads on the roads. When the aged wear silk and eat meat[12] and the masses are neither cold nor hungry, it is impossible for their prince not to be a true King."

Part B

7. Mencius went to see King Hsüan of Ch'i. "A 'state of established traditions,' " said he, "is so called not because it has tall trees but because it has ministers whose families have served it for generations. You no longer have trusted ministers. Those you promoted yesterday have all disappeared today without your even being aware of it."

"How could I have known," said the King, "that they lacked ability and so avoided making the appointments in the first instance?"

"When there is no choice, the ruler of a state, in advancing good and wise men,[13] may have to promote those of low position over the heads of those of exalted rank and distant relatives over near ones. Hence such a decision should not be taken lightly. When your close attendants all say of a man that he is good and wise, that is not enough; when the Counsellors all say the same, that is not enough; when everyone says so, then have the case investigated. If the man turns out to be good and wise, then and only then should he be given office. When your close attendants all say of a man that he is unsuitable, do not listen to them; when the Counsellors all say the same, do not listen to them; when everyone says so, then have the case investigated. If the man turns out to be unsuitable, then and only then should he be removed from office. When your close attendants all say of a man that he deserves death, do not listen to them; when the Counsellors all say the same, do not listen to them; when everyone says so, then have the case investigated. If the man turns out to deserve death, then and only then should he be put to death. In this way, it will be said, 'He was put to death by the whole country.' [14] Only by acting in this manner can one be father and mother to the people."

13. Duke Wên of T'êng[15] asked, "T'êng is a small state, wedged between Ch'i and Ch'u. Should I be subservient to Ch'i or should I be subservient to Ch'u?"

"This is a question that is beyond me," answered Mencius. "If you insist, there is only one course of action I can suggest. Dig deeper moats and build higher walls and defend them shoulder to shoulder with the people. If they would rather die than desert you, then all is not lost."

Book II

Part A

5. Mencius said, "If you honour the good and wise and employ the able so that outstanding men are in high position, then Gentlemen throughout the Empire will be only too pleased to serve at your court. In the market-place, if goods are exempted when premises are taxed, and premises exempted when the ground is taxed, then the traders throughout the Empire will be only too pleased to store their goods in your market-place. If there is inspection but no duty at the border stations, then the travellers throughout the Empire will be only too pleased to go by way of your roads. If tillers help in the public fields but pay no tax on the land, then farmers throughout the Empire will be only too pleased to till the land in your realm. If you abolish the levy in lieu of corvée and the levy in lieu of the planting of the mulberry, then all the people of the Empire will be only too pleased to come and settle in your state. If you can truly execute these five measures, the people of your neighbouring states will look up to you as to their father and mother; and since man came into this world no one has succeeded in inciting children against their parents. In this way, you will have no match in the Empire. He who has no match in the Empire is a T'ien-appointed officer, and it has never happened that such a man failed to become a true King."

6. Mencius said, "No man is devoid of a heart sensitive to the suffering of others. Such a sensitive heart was possessed by the Former Kings[16] and this manifested itself in compassionate government. With such a sensitive heart behind compassionate government, it was as easy to rule the Empire as rolling it on your palm.

"My reason for saying that no man is devoid of a heart sensitive to the suffering of others is this. Suppose a man were, all of a sudden, to see a young child on the verge of falling into a well. He would certainly be moved to compassion, not because he wanted to get in the good graces of the parents, nor because he wished to win the praise of his fellow villagers or friends, nor yet because he disliked the cry of the child. From this it can be seen that whoever is devoid of the heart of compassion is not human, whoever is devoid of the heart of shame is not human, whoever is devoid of the heart of courtesy and modesty is not human, and whoever is devoid of the heart of right and wrong is not human. The heart of compassion is the germ of benevolence; the heart of shame, of dutifulness; the heart of courtesy and modesty, of observance of the rites; the heart of right and wrong, of wisdom. Man has these four germs just as he has four limbs. For a man possessing these four germs to deny his own potentialities is for him to cripple himself; for him to deny the potentialities of his prince is for him to cripple his prince. If a man is able to develop all these four germs that he possesses, it will be like a fire starting up or a spring coming through. When these are fully developed, he can take under his protection the whole realm within the Four Seas, but if he fails to develop them, he will not be able even to serve his parents."

Book IV

Part A

3. Mencius said, "The Three Dynasties won the Empire through benevolence and lost it through cruelty. This is true of the rise and fall, survival and collapse, of states as well. An Emperor cannot keep the Empire within the Four Seas unless he is benevolent; a feudal lord cannot preserve the altars to the gods of earth and grain unless he is benevolent;[17] a Minister or a Counsellor cannot preserve his ancestral temple

unless he is benevolent; a Gentleman or a Commoner cannot preserve his four limbs unless he is benevolent. To dislike death yet revel in cruelty is no different from drinking beyond your capacity despite your dislike of drunkenness."

5. Mencius said, "There is a common expression, 'The Empire, the state, the family.' The Empire has its basis in the state, the state in the family, and the family in one's own self."

6. Mencius said, "It is not difficult to govern. All one has to do is not to offend the noble families. Whatever commands the admiration of the noble families will command the admiration of the whole state; whatever commands the admiration of a state will command the admiration of the Empire. Thus moral influence irresistibly fills to overflowing the whole Empire within the Four Seas."

14. Mencius said, "While he was steward to the Chi family, Jan Ch'iu[18] doubled the yield of taxation without being able to improve their virtue. Confucius said, 'Ch'iu is not my disciple. You, little ones, may attack him to the beating of drums.' From this it can be seen that Confucius rejected those who enriched rulers not given to the practice of benevolent government. How much more would he reject those who do their best to wage war on their behalf. In wars to gain land, the dead fill the plains; in wars to gain cities, the dead fill the cities. This is known as showing the land the way to devour human flesh. Death is too light a punishment for such men. Hence those skilled in war should suffer the most severe punishments; those who secure alliances with other feudal lords come next, and then come those who open up waste lands and increase the yield of the soil."

23. Mencius said, "The trouble with people is that they are too eager to assume the role of teacher."

Part B

8. Mencius said, "Only when a man will not do some things is he capable of doing great things."

11. Mencius said, "A great man need not keep his word nor does he necessarily see his action through to the end. He aims only at what is right."

12. Mencius said, "A great man is one who retains the heart of a newborn babe."

Book V

Part B

9. King Hsüan of Ch'i asked about ministers. "What kind of ministers," said Mencius, "is Your Majesty asking about?"

"Are there different kinds of ministers?"

"Yes. There are ministers of royal blood and those of families other than the royal house."

"What about ministers of royal blood?"

"If the prince made serious mistakes, they would remonstrate with him, but if repeated remonstrations fell on deaf ears, they would depose him."

The King blenched at this.

"Your Majesty should not be surprised by my answer. Since you asked me, I dared not give you anything but the proper answer."

Only after he had regained his composure[19] did the King ask about ministers of families other than the royal house.

"If the prince made mistakes, they would remonstrate with him, but if repeated remonstrations fell on deaf ears, they would leave him."

Book VI

Part A

2. Kao Tzŭ said,[20] "Human nature is like whirling water. Give it an outlet in the east and it will flow east; give it an outlet in the west and it will flow west. Human nature does not show any preference for either good or bad just as water does not show any preference for either east or west."

"It certainly is the case," said Mencius, "that water does not show any preference for either east or west, but does it show the same indifference to high and low? Human nature is good just as water seeks low ground. There is no man who is not good; there is no water that does not flow downwards.

"Now in the case of water, by splashing it one can make it shoot up higher than one's forehead, and by forcing it one can make it stay on a hill. How can that be the nature of water? It is the circumstances being what they are. That man can be made bad shows that his nature is no different from that of water in this respect."

6. Kung-tu Tzŭ²¹ said, "Kao Tzŭ said, 'There is neither good nor bad in human nature,' but others say, 'Human nature can become good or it can become bad, and that is why with the rise of King Wên and King Wu, the people were given to goodness, while with the rise of King Yu and King Li,²² they were given to cruelty.' Then there are others who say, 'There are those who are good by nature, and there are those who are bad by nature. For this reason, Hsiang could have Yao as prince, and Shun could have the Blind Man as father, and Ch'i, Viscount of Wei and Prince Pi Kan could have Chou as nephew as well as sovereign.'²³ Now you say human nature is good. Does this mean that all the others are mistaken?"

"As far as what is genuinely in him is concerned, a man is capable of becoming good," said Mencius. "That is what I mean by good. As for his becoming bad, that is not the fault of his native endowment. The heart of compassion is possessed by all men alike; likewise the heart of shame, the heart of respect, and the heart of right and wrong. The heart of compassion pertains to benevolence, the heart of shame to dutifulness, the heart of respect to the observance of the rites, and the heart of right and wrong to wisdom. Benevolence, dutifulness, observance of the rites, and wisdom are not welded on to me from the outside; they are in me originally. Only this has never dawned on me. That is why it is said, 'Seek and you will find it; let go and you will lose it.' There are cases where one man is twice, five times, or countless times better than another man, but this is only because there are people who fail to make the best of their native endowment. The *Book of Odes* says,

> T'ien produces the teeming masses,
> And where there is a thing there is a norm.
> If the people held on to their constant nature,
> They would be drawn to superior virtue.²⁴

Confucius commented, 'The author of this poem must have had knowledge of the Way.' Thus where there is a thing there is a norm, and because the people hold on to their constant nature they are drawn to superior virtue."

7. Mencius said, "In good years the young men are mostly lazy, while in bad years they are mostly violent. T'ien has not sent down men whose endowment differs so greatly. The difference is due to what ensnares

their hearts. Take the barley for example. Sow the seeds and cover them with soil. The place is the same and the time of sowing is also the same. The plants shoot up and by the summer solstice they all ripen. If there is any unevenness, it is because the soil varies in richness and there is no uniformity in the fall of rain and dew and the amount of human effort devoted to tending it. Now things of the same kind are all alike. Why should we have doubts when it comes to man? The sage and I are of the same kind. Thus Lung Tzŭ[25] said, 'When someone makes a shoe for a foot he has not seen, I am sure he will not produce a basket.' All shoes are alike because all feet are alike. All palates show the same preferences in taste. I Ya[26] was simply the man first to discover what would be pleasing to my palate. Were the nature of taste to vary from man to man in the same way as horses and hounds differ from me in kind, then how does it come about that all palates in the world follow the preferences of I Ya? The fact that in taste the whole world looks to I Ya shows that all palates are alike. It is the same also with the ear. The whole world looks to Shih K'uang, and this shows that all ears are alike. It is the same also with the eye. The whole world appreciates the good looks of Tzŭ-tu; whoever does not is blind. Hence it is said: all palates have the same preference in taste; all ears in sound; all eyes in beauty. Should hearts prove to be an exception by possessing nothing in common? What is common to all hearts? Reason and rightness. The sage is simply the man first to discover this common element in my heart. Thus reason and rightness please my heart in the same way as meat pleases my palate."

8. Mencius said, "There was a time when the trees were luxuriant on the Ox Mountain. As it is on the outskirts of a great metropolis, the trees are constantly lopped by axes. Is it any wonder that they are no longer fine? With the respite they get in the day and in the night, and the moistening by the rain and dew, there is certainly no lack of new shoots coming out, but then the cattle and sheep come to graze upon the mountain. That is why it is as bald as it is. People, seeing only its baldness, tend to think that it never had any trees. But can this possibly be the nature of a mountain? Can what is in man be completely lacking in moral inclinations? A man's letting go of his true heart is like the case of the trees and the axes. When the trees are lopped day after day, is it any wonder that they are no longer fine? If, in spite of the respite a man gets in the day and in the night and of the effect of the morning air on him, scarcely any of his likes and dislikes resemble those of other men, it is be-

cause what he does in the course of the day once again dissipates what he has gained. If this dissipation happens repeatedly, then the influence of the air in the night will no longer be able to preserve what was originally in him, and when that happens, the man is not far removed from an animal. Others, seeing his resemblance to an animal, will be led to think that he never had any native endowment. But can that be what a man is genuinely like? Hence, given the right nourishment there is nothing that will not grow, and deprived of it there is nothing that will not wither away. Confucius said, 'Hold on to it and it will remain; let go of it and it will disappear. One never knows the time it comes or goes, neither does one know the direction.' It is perhaps to the heart this refers."

10. Mencius said, "Fish is what I want; bear's palm is also what I want. If I cannot have both, I would rather take bear's palm than fish. Life is what I want; dutifulness is also what I want. If I cannot have both, I would rather take dutifulness than life. On the one hand, though life is what I want, there is something I want more than life. That is why I do not cling to life at all costs. On the other hand, though death is what I loathe, there is something I loathe more than death. That is why there are troubles I do not avoid. If there is nothing a man wants more than life, then why should he have scruples about any means, so long as it will serve to keep him alive? If there is nothing a man loathes more than death, then why should he have scruples about any means, so long as it helps him to avoid trouble? Yet there are ways of remaining alive and ways of avoiding death to which a man will not resort. In other words, there are things a man wants more than life and there are also things he loathes more than death. This is an attitude not confined to the moral man but common to all men. The moral man simply never loses it.

"Here is a basketful of rice and a bowlful of soup. Getting them will mean life; not getting them will mean death. When these are given with abuse, even a wayfarer would not accept them; when these are given after being trampled upon, even a beggar would not accept them. Yet when it comes to ten thousand bushels of grain one is supposed to accept without asking if it is in accordance with the rites or if it is right to do so. What benefit are ten thousand bushels of grain to me? [Do I accept them] for the sake of beautiful houses, the enjoyment of wives and concubines, or for the sake of the gratitude my needy acquaintances will show me? What I would not accept in the first instance when it was a matter of life and death I now accept for the sake of beautiful houses; what I would not accept when it was a matter of life and death I now accept for the enjoyment of wives and concubines; what I would not accept when it was a matter of life and death I now accept for the sake of the gratitude my needy acquaintances will show me. Is there no way of putting a stop to this? This way of thinking is known as losing one's original heart."

18. Mencius said, "Benevolence overcomes cruelty just as water overcomes fire. Those who practise benevolence today are comparable to someone trying to put out a cartload of burning firewood with a cupful of water. When the fire fails to be extinguished, they say water cannot overcome fire. For a man to do this is for him to place himself on the side of those who are cruel to the extreme, and in the end he is sure only to perish."

Part B

9. Mencius said, "Those who are in the service of princes today all say, 'I am able to extend the territory of my prince, and fill his coffers for him.' The good subject of today would have been looked upon in antiquity as a pest on the people. To enrich a prince who is neither attracted to the Way nor bent upon benevolence is to enrich a Chieh.[27]

"Again, they say, 'I am able to gain allies and ensure victory in war for my prince.' The good subject of today would have been looked upon in antiquity as a pest on the people. To try to make a prince strong in war who is neither attracted to the Way nor bent upon benevolence is to aid a Chieh.

"Following the practice of the present day, unless there is a change in the ways of the people, a man could not hold the Empire for the duration of one morning, even if it were given to him."

15. Mencius said, "Shun[28] rose from the fields: Fu Yüeh was raised to office from amongst the builders; Chiao Chi from amidst the fish and salt; Kuan I-wu from the hands of the prison officer; Sun-shu Ao from the sea, and Po-li Hsi from the market. That is why T'ien, when it is about to place a great burden on a man, always first tests his resolution, exhausts his frame and makes him suffer starvation and hardship, frustrates his efforts so as to shake him from his mental lassitude, toughen his nature, and make good his deficiencies. As a rule, a man can mend his ways only after he has made mistakes. It is only when a man is frustrated

in mind and in his deliberations that he is able to innovate. It is only when his intentions become visible on his countenance and audible in his tone of voice that others can understand him. As a rule, a state without law-abiding families and reliable Gentlemen on the one hand, and, on the other, without the threat of foreign invasion, will perish. Only then do we learn the lesson that we survive in adversity and perish in ease and comfort.ʺ

16. Mencius said, ʺThere are more ways than one of instructing others. My disdain to instruct a man is itself one way of instructing him.ʺ

Book VII

Part A

2. Mencius said, ʺThough nothing happens that is not due to destiny, one accepts willingly only what is one's proper destiny. That is why he who understands destiny does not stand under a wall on the verge of collapse. He who dies after having done his best in following the Way dies according to his proper destiny. It is never anyone's proper destiny to die in fetters.ʺ

10. Mencius said, ʺThose who make the effort only when there is a King Wên are ordinary men. Outstanding men make the effort even without a King Wên.ʺ

11. Mencius said, ʺTo look upon oneself as deficient even though the possessions of the families of Han and Wei[29] be added to one's own is to surpass other men by a long way.ʺ

20. Mencius said, ʺA gentleman delights in three things, and being ruler over the Empire is not amongst them. His parents are alive and his brothers are well. This is the first delight. Above, he is not ashamed to face T'ien; below, he is not ashamed to face man. This is the second delight. He has the good fortune of having the most talented pupils in the Empire. This is the third delight. A gentleman delights in three things and being ruler over the Empire is not amongst them.ʺ

21. Mencius said, ʺAn extensive territory and a vast population are things a gentleman desires, but what he delights in lies elsewhere. To stand in the centre of the Empire and bring peace to the people within the Four Seas is what a gentleman delights in, but that which he follows as his nature lies elsewhere. That which a gentleman follows as his na-

ture is not added to when he holds sway over the Empire, nor is it detracted from when he is reduced to straitened circumstances. This is because he knows his allotted station. That which a gentleman follows as his nature, that is to say, benevolence, rightness, the rites, and wisdom, is rooted in his heart, and manifests itself in his face, giving it a sleek appearance. It also shows in his back and extends to his limbs, rendering their message intelligible without words."

22. Mencius said, "Po I [30] fled from Chou and settled on the edge of the North Sea. When he heard of the rise of King Wên he stirred and said, 'Why not go back? I hear that Hsi Po takes good care of the aged.' T'ai Kung fled from Chou and settled on the edge of the East Sea. When he heard of the rise of King Wên he stirred and said, 'Why not go back? I hear that Hsi Po takes good care of the aged.' When there is someone in the Empire who takes good care of the aged, benevolent men will look upon him as their refuge.

"If the mulberry is planted at the foot of the walls in every homestead of five *mu* of land and the woman of the house keeps silkworms, then the aged can wear silk. If there are five hens and two sows, and these do not miss their breeding season, then the aged will not be deprived of meat. If a man tills a hundred *mu* of land, there will be enough for his family of eight mouths not to go hungry.

"When Hsi Po was said to 'take good care of the aged,' what was meant is this. He laid down the pattern for the distribution of land, taught the men the way to plant trees and keep animals, and showed their womenfolk the way to care for the aged. A man needs silk for warmth at fifty and meat for sustenance at seventy. To have neither warm clothes nor a full belly is to be cold and hungry. The people under King Wên had no old folk who were cold and hungry."

23. Mencius said, "Put in order the fields of the people, lighten their taxes, and the people can be made affluent. If one's consumption of food is confined to what is in season and one's use of other commodities is in accordance with the rites,[31] then one's resources will be more than sufficient. The common people cannot live without water and fire, yet one never meets with a refusal when knocking on another's door in the evening to beg for water or fire. This is because these are in such abundance. In governing the Empire, the sage tries to make food as plentiful as water and fire. When that happens, how can there be any amongst his people who are not benevolent?"

35. T'ao Ying[32] asked, "When Shun was Son of T'ien and Kao Yao was the judge, if the Blind Man killed a man, what was to be done?"

"The only thing to do was to apprehend him."

"In that case, would Shun not try to stop it?"   ·

"How could Shun stop it? Kao Yao had his authority from which he received the law."

"Then what would Shun have done?"

"Shun looked upon casting aside the Empire as no more than discarding a worn shoe. He would have secretly carried the old man on his back and fled to the edge of the Sea and lived there happily, never giving a thought to the Empire."

45. Mencius said, "A gentleman is sparing with things but shows no benevolence towards them; he shows benevolence towards the people but is not attached to them. He is attached to his parents but is merely benevolent towards the people; he is benevolent towards the people but is merely sparing with things."

Part B

2. Mencius said, "In the Spring and Autumn period there were no just wars. There were only cases of one war not being quite as bad as another. A punitive expedition is a war waged by one in authority against his subordinates. It is not for peers to punish one another by war."

12. Mencius said, "If the benevolent and the good and wise are not trusted, the state will only be a shell; if the rites and rightness are absent, the distinction between superior and inferior will not be observed; if government is not properly regulated, the state will not have enough resources to meet expenditure."

14. Mencius said, "The people are of supreme importance; the altars to the gods of earth and grain come next; last comes the ruler. That is why he who gains the confidence of the multitudinous people will be Son of T'ien; he who gains the confidence of the Son of T'ien will be a feudal lord; he who gains the confidence of a feudal lord will be a Counsellor. When a feudal lord endangers the altars to the gods of earth and grain he should be replaced. When the sacrificial animals are sleek, the offerings are clean and the sacrifices are observed at due times, and yet floods and droughts come, then the altars should be replaced."

20. Mencius said, "A good and wise man helps others to understand

clearly by his own clear understanding. Nowadays, men try to help others understand by their own benighted ignorance."

28. Mencius said, "The feudal lords have three treasures: land, people, and government. Those who treasure pearls and jade are sure to suffer the consequences in their own lifetime."

34. Mencius said, "When speaking to men of consequence it is necessary to look on them with contempt and not be impressed by their lofty position. Their hall is tens of feet high; the capitals are several feet broad. Were I to meet with success, I would not indulge in such things. Their tables, laden with food, measure ten feet across, and their female attendants are counted in the hundreds. Were I to meet with success, I would not indulge in such things. They have a great time drinking, driving, and hunting, with a retinue of a thousand chariots. Were I to meet with success I would not indulge in such things. All the things they do I would not do, and everything I do is in accordance with ancient institutions. Why, then, should I cower before them?"

10

Hsün Tzŭ

The true way of the man who knows how to rule by force
is not to be anxious to use force.

—Hsün Tzŭ, 21

The trio of great Confucians consists of Confucius himself (551–479
B.C.), the philosopher Mencius (c. 372–c. 289 B.C.), and Hsü Tzŭ
(c. 312–c. 238 B.C.), the farthest-ranging and also the most uncertain
thinker of the group.

The opening of Book 23 of the *Hsün Tzŭ* is startling. "The nature of
man is evil; his goodness is only acquired training." As it turns out,
Hsün Tzŭ's bark is worse than his bite. He nowhere paints a fearful,
brutal, or repulsive portrait of this nature. Moreover, the remedy one
should apply to evil-natured man in order to bring him to good government differs little from that provided by Mencius for good-natured man.
Few men are so perverse by nature that nurture cannot straighten them
out.

Hsün Tzŭ declares that since man is born bad by nature, only a cultural and moral teaching based on the Confucian classics can change
him into something good.

Hsün Tzŭ had a fairly long and apparently uneventful life. The first
news we have of him is at age fifty: he is staying at the court of the state
of Ch'i, for half a century a well-known rallying point for scholars and
philosophers. Mencius in his time had journeyed there and argued with
King Hsüan. Hsün Tzŭ, at the time of his own visit, around 264 B.C.,
had apparently attained the reputation of a distinguished elder scholar
and was fittingly welcomed. Some backbiting or other, that perennial of
academic society, moved him to leave the court and go south to Ch'u,
where he was appointed magistrate of the district of Lan-ling, a job with
both judicial and administrative duties. Many years later, when his pa-

tron, the Lord of Ch'un-shên, was assassinated, Hsün Tzŭ lost the post but stayed on in Lan-ling for the rest of his days. The exact year of his death is unknown.

Hsün Tzŭ called himself a Confucian and on the whole he remained one. He accords with Mencius in holding the ruler to be a teacher whose scripture is the literature about the ancient kings, and in raising the ideal in politics of the gentleman whose gentleness abhors force and who takes the welfare of the common people to be the end of good government. Hsün Tzŭ's ruler wields authority by the Mandate of T'ien, and should he prove an evil man, let it be recalled: tyrannicide is not regicide. Along with Mencius, too, Hsün Tzŭ values above weapons and generals the support that people can give their ruler's force of arms. He would protect commoners by rules of warfare. Going further here than Mencius, Hsün Tzŭ condemns hereditary titles and would promote a good and learned commoner right up to the rank of prime minister.

Hsün Tzŭ was also a pioneer secularist. He may have been trying to modernize Confucian and Mencian doctrine for an increasingly secular age. He discussed religion and rites in utilitarian and anthropological terms, insisting that Heaven helps those who help themselves. He may also have been trying to prepare for an age of empire. He discussed not only how a good king rules, but also how a dictator, military man, or overlord should govern to give the state security and stability. Alongside virtue and example in the ruling of men he added law and force. This addition seems to follow as a logical consequence of his doctrine that man's disposition is bad. Although human nature is corrigible, through cultural and moral teaching based on the Confucian classics, apparently force is sometimes needed, not for swinging it over to the side of goodness but for keeping its wayward impulses in check. Later governments discarded his secularism but took his stress on the exact carrying out of ritual; they paid lip service to the use of virtue and example in the governing of men but leaned more heavily on force and fear. Confucianism in imperial practice, though it remained with Mencius in theory, took its ruling guidelines from Hsün Tzŭ.

Hsün Tzŭ's prose—though sometimes self-contradicting—is direct, orderly, and cool. He left a work of thirty-two chapters covering the gamut of man and nature, semantics, education, psychology, music, and ritual.

THE *HSÜN TZŬ*

Selections

Book 1. An Encouragement to Study

What should one study? How should one begin? The art begins by reciting the Classics and ends in learning the rites. Its purpose begins with making the scholar, and ends in making the sage. Sincerely put forth your efforts, and finally you will progress. Study until death and do not

From Homer H. Dubs, tr., *The Works of Hsüntze* (London: Probsthain, 1928). In the selections from Hsün Tzŭ, whenever *t'ien* occurs as a separate character in the original Chinese, it will—no matter what its sense—be reproduced as *"t'ien."* The lower case (as contrasted with the upper-case "T'ien" used elsewhere herein) will serve to indicate that the import of the term in these writings fluctuates too often and subtly for nice, ready distinctions of meaning. See notes p. 10 above and p. 283 below, and note 16, p. 393 below.

stop before. For the art of study occupies the whole of life; to arrive at its purpose, you cannot stop for an instant. To do that is to be a man; to stop is to be a bird or beast. The *Book of Documents*[1] records political events. The *Book of Songs* regulates sounds so that they should attain the normal and not go beyond it. The *Book of Rites* deals with the great distinctions of society through rules; it is the unifying principle of general classes of action. Study advances to the *Book of Rites* and stops there. This is what is meant by the extreme of virtue. The reverence and love of elegance of the *Book of Rites*, the harmony of the *Book of Music*, the broad knowledge of the *Book of Songs* and *Book of Documents*, the subtleties of the *Spring and Autumn* are the completion of all creation.

This is the manner of the superior man's learning; it goes into his ears, it is taken into his heart, it spreads through his entire body, it shows itself in every movement. Speaking in low tones and moving gently are his ways of action.

Book 8. The Merit of the Confucian

The Model of the Great Confucians

Thus there are common men, there are common Confucians, there are correct Confucians, and there are great Confucians. They have no scholarship; they are without correct moral feeling; and they consider riches and profit to be the *summum bonum*—such are common men.

They have large clothes, wide girdles, and high hats;[2] they sketchily follow the early Kings, but are satisfied with the teaching of a confused age; they have erroneous learning and confused actions; they do not know that they should imitate the later Kings and unify their purposes; they do not know that they should exalt the rules of proper conduct and justice and regard the *Book of Songs* and the *Book of Documents* as important; their clothes, hat, and deportment are quite like that fashionable and common, yet they do not know enough to dislike it; their speech and talk has quite no difference from that of Mo Tzŭ[3] yet they cannot clearly distinguish it: they invoke the early Kings in order to cheat stupid people and seek for a living; if they get fed and accumulate enough to fill their mouths they are satisfied; they follow their master, and they serve their talkative favourites and their upper-class retainers, they are quite like life-long prisoners, not daring to have any other purposes—such are common Confucians.

Therefore if a man is without a teacher or precepts, then if he is intelligent, he will certainly become a robber; if he is brave, he will certainly become a murderer; if he has ability he will certainly cause disorder; if he is an investigator he will certainly become bizarre; if he is a dialectician, he will certainly go far from the truth. If he has a teacher and precepts, then if he is intelligent, he will quickly become learned; if he is brave, he will quickly become awe-inspiring; if he has ability, he will quickly become perfect; if he is an investigator, he will quickly arrive at all truth; if he is a dialectician, he will quickly be able to determine the truth or falsity of all things. Therefore the possession of a teacher and of precepts is the greatest treasure a man can have; the lack of a teacher and of precepts is the greatest calamity a man can have.

If a man is without a teacher or precepts, he will exalt his original nature; if he has a teacher and precepts, he will exalt self-cultivation. Now a teacher and precepts are what is gained by self-cultivation, not what is obtained from original nature.

Book 9. Kingly Government

Please Tell about the Art of Government

Do not regard seniority but advance the worthy and able; dismiss the incompetent and incapable without delay; put incorrigible ringleaders to death without trying to reform them; develop the common people without waiting to compel them by laws. When men's rank is uncertain, then there is the order of seniority of their families. Yet although a man is the descendant of a king, duke, prefect, or officer, if he does not observe the rules of proper conduct and justice, he must be relegated to the common ranks; although he is the descendant of a commoner, if he have acquired learning, developed a good character, and is able to observe the rules of proper conduct and justice, then elevate him to be minister, prime minister, officer, or prefect. But lewd people, scandal-mongers, evil-doers, people of perverted abilities, shirkers, and unreliable people, should be trained, given employment, and time for reformation. Stimulate them by rewards; warn them by punishments; if they are satisfied with employment, then keep them; if they are not satisfied to work, then deport them. Defectives[4] should be received and cared for; if they have ability, they should be given positions. The authorities should employ them and clothe and feed them; they should all be cared for without exception. Those who are incorrigible should be put to death without mercy. For this is what is called virtue of *t'ien;* this is the government of a king.

o   o   o   o

The Great Distinctions to Be Made in Holding Court

He who when there is a law, acts according to the law, but when there is no law, decides according to the analogies of the case, is doing the utmost possible in holding court. He who is prejudiced, shows a partisan spirit, and has no principles of action is the basest of all in holding court. For there has been bad government under good laws; but from ancient times to the present there has never been known to be a bad government under a superior man. It is said: "Good government springs from the superior man; bad government springs from the small-minded man"—this expresses what I mean.

If the classes are equal, there will not be enough for everybody; when everyone's powers are equal, there is no unity in the state; when everyone is equal, there is no one to employ the people on public services. As soon as there was heaven and earth, there was the distinction of above and below; when the first wise king arose, the country he occupied had the division of classes. For two nobles[5] cannot serve each other; two commoners cannot employ each other—this is a law of *t'ien*. Were people's power and position equal, and their likes and dislikes the same, there would not be sufficient goods to satisfy everybody, and hence there would inevitably be strife. If there were strife, there would inevitably result general disorder; if general disorder, then general poverty. The ancient kings hated any disorder, and hence established the rules of proper conduct and justice to divide the people, to cause them to have the classes of poor and rich, of noble and inferior, so that everyone would be under someone's control—this is the fundamental thing in caring for the whole country. The *Book of Documents* says: "They are only uniform in that they are not uniform"—this expresses what I mean.

When a horse hitched to a carriage is restless, a gentleman is not secure in the carriage. When the common people are restless under the government, then a prince is not secure in his position. When a horse hitched to a carriage is restless, there is nothing better than quieting him; when the people are restless under the government, there is nothing better than treating them generously. If he chooses the worthy and the good, advances the sincere and the reverent, stimulates filial piety and respectfulness for elders, shelters the orphan and the widow, and helps the poor and the needy—if he does this, the common people will be satisfied with his government. When the common people are satisfied with his government, then only is a prince secure in his position. It is said: The prince is the boat; the common people are the water. The water can support the boat, or the water can capsize the boat—this expresses my meaning.

o   o   o   o

The true *Tao* of the man who knows how to rule by force is not to be anxious to use force. He ponders over the edicts of the emperor; he conserves his strength; he consolidates his power. When his strength is conserved, the feudal nobles cannot weaken him; when his power is consolidated, they cannot despoil him. If the empire is without a righteous king or lord protector in control, such a man will always prevail. This is the true *Tao* of the man who knows how to rule by force.

But the lord protector acts differently. He opens up new lands; he fills granaries and storehouses; he provides good implements; he carefully prepares officers of ability and talent. Then he gives them rewards in order to encourage them to progress; he severely punishes in order to restrain them. He preserves those who have lost their country and sustains those whose line of succession has run out; he protects the weak and restrains the oppressive. Yet he has no intention of acquiring territory; then the feudal nobles will be friends with him. His way is to treat enemies as friends; he respectfully meets the feudal nobles, and then the feudal nobles will be pleased with him. They make friends with him because he does not seek territory; if he appears to want territory, the feudal princes would be distant to him. They are pleased with him because he treats enemies as friends; if he appears to want to make them his subordinates, then the feudal nobles will leave him. Hence he makes it plain that his motives are not to gain territory; he makes them believe in his way of treating enemies as friends. If the empire is without a righteous King in control, such a man will always prevail. This is the true *Tao* of the man who knows how to be a Lord Protector.

o   o   o   o

The Methods of a Righteous King

He grades taxation and rectifies the amount of service[6] to be given; he regulates everything in order to nourish all his people. He levies a tithe on the land. At the customs houses and market places he inspects travellers[7] but does not levy duties. He prohibits or permits forestry and fishing, according to the season; but he does not tax it. He appraises the land and assesses its tax. He regulates tribute according to the distance of the place. There should be a circulation of valuables[8] and grain without restriction or hindrance, enabling foodstuffs to be freely transported, and all within the four seas[9] to be like one family. Then those who are near will not hide their ability, and those who are distant will not grumble at their toil. There will be no unenlightened or secluded country which will fail to fly to serve him and be satisfied and rejoice in him. This is what is called being a leader and teacher of men. These are the methods of a righteous King.

On the north sea there are swift horses and great dogs; if this policy were carried out, then China could obtain, raise, and use them. On the south sea there are fine feathers, ivory, rhinoceros hides, copper, cinnabar, and cornelian,[10] then China could get them, and be enriched thereby. On the eastern sea there is purple, coarse linen, fish, and salt; then China could get them and wear and eat them. On the western sea there are felt rugs, furs, dyed yak-tails; then China could get them and use them. Then people who live on the borders of the sea would have a sufficiency of wood; people who live in the mountains would have plenty of fish; farmers would have a sufficiency of implements without chopping, scraping, making pottery, or smelting; the workman and the merchant would have sufficient pulse and millet without ploughing the fields. For the tiger and leopard are fierce, yet the gentleman could have them skinned and use them. For nothing which *t'ien* covers or the earth sustains would fail to yield up all its goodness and be brought for his use. On the one hand they would adorn the worthy and good, and on the other they would nourish the people and give them happiness. This is what it means to be a great ruler.

o   o   o   o

T'ien and earth are the source of life. The rules of proper conduct and justice are the source of good government; the superior man is the source of the rules of proper conduct and justice. To carry them out, to practise them, to study them much, and to love them greatly is the source of being a superior man. For *t'ien* and earth give birth to the superior man; the superior man brings *t'ien* and earth into order; the superior man forms a triad with *t'ien* and earth; he is the controller of all things, the father and mother of the people. Without the superior man, *t'ien* and earth are not ordered, the rules of proper conduct and justice have no control. When on the one hand there is no prince and leader, on the other hand there cannot be the distinction of father and son—this is what is called extreme disorder. The prince and minister, the father and son, the older and younger brother, husband and wife—here we have a beginning and end, an end and a beginning; this social structure exhibits the same principles as *t'ien* and earth; it is of equal permanence with the universe —this is called the great foundation.

o   o   o   o

Water and fire have essences, but not life; herbs and trees have life, but no knowledge; birds and beasts have knowledge but no sense of what are rights. Man has an essence, life, knowledge, and in addition has a sense of human rights; hence he is the highest being on earth. His strength is not equal to that of the bull; his running is not equal to that of the horse; yet the bull and horse are used by him. How is that? Men are able to form social organizations, the former are not able to form social organizations. How is it that men are able to form social organizations? Because of their distinctions. How is it that distinctions can be carried out? Through rights. For class rights are harmonized through social distinctions. When people are harmonious, they can unite; when united, they have greater strength; when they have great strength, they become strong; when strong, they can dominate nature. Hence they can have palaces and houses for habitation. Hence they can order their actions according to the four seasons and control all things. Hence they can enjoy the goodness of the whole world. They gain this for no other reason than that they have social distinctions and class rights. Hence, if men are to live, they cannot get along without forming a social organization. If they form a social organization, but have no social distinctions, then they will quarrel; if they quarrel, there will be disorder; if there is disorder, people will fail to cooperate; if they fail to cooperate, then they will be weak; if they are weak, then they will not be able to dominate nature. Hence they could not have palaces or houses for habitation. All of which means that people cannot abandon the rules of proper conduct or class rights for an instant. He who is able thereby to serve his parents, is said to have filial piety; he who is able thereby to serve his older brother is said to have brotherly respect; he who is able thereby to serve his superior is said to be obedient; he who is able thereby to utilize his inferiors is said to have the virtues of a prince. A prince is one who is good at social organization.

o   o   o   o

Book 10. A Rich Country

People desire and hate the same things. Their desires are many but things are few. Since they are few, there will inevitably be strife. For what a hundred workmen accomplish goes for the nourishment of one individual; yet an able person cannot be skilled in more than one line; one man cannot govern two departments. If people leave their positions and do not serve each other, there will be poverty; if the masses are without social divisions, there will be strife. He who is impoverished is in trouble; he who strives will suffer calamity. For the purpose of rescuing people from trouble and eliminating calamity there is no method as good as that of making social distinctions plain, and forming a social organization. If the strong coerce the weak and the wise terrorize the stupid and the people who should be subjects rebel against their rulers and the young insult the aged and the government is not guided by virtue, if these are the circumstances, then the aged and the weak will suffer the trouble of losing their support and the strong will suffer the calamity of division and strife.

Work is what people dislike; gain and profit is what they like. If there is no distinction of occupation, then people will have difficulty in getting work done and the calamity of striving in order to obtain any desired result. If the union of male and female, the separation from other males and females inherent in the relation of husband and wife, the making of engagements by the relatives of the groom and bride to be, the sending of betrothal presents and the going to get the bride, are not according to the rules of proper conduct; if this is the case, then men will have the trouble of losing their mates and the calamity of having to struggle to gain any sex relation. Hence for this reason wise men have introduced social distinctions.

o   o   o   o

A Paragraph from Book 11. Kings and Lords Protector

For the superior there is nothing as good as loving his inferior and ruling according to the rules of proper conduct. The relation of the superior to the inferior should be that of protecting infants. In treating people who are inferior to oneself, if a subject has committed a petty wrong, although he be an orphan, childless, a widower, or widow,[11] do not apply the government regulations to him. Then the inferiors will love their superior, and rejoice in him as in a father and mother; they can be killed rather than disobey him; the prince and the ministers, the rulers and the ruled, the noble and the base, the old and the young, even to the common people, all will make this their greatest standard of conduct. Then they will all examine themselves within, and be careful of their duties. In this respect all the Kings were alike, and it is the central and indispensable thing in the rules of proper conduct and laws.

Book 15. A Debate on Military Affairs

Lin-wu-chün[12] debated military affairs with the master, Hsün Ch'ing, before King Hsiao-ch'êng[13] of Chao.

The King said, "I should like to ask what are the important points of military art."

Lin-wu-chün replied: "On the one hand observe the seasons, on the other take an advantageous position; observe the movements of the enemy; when following the enemy attack them; when preceding them, reach the goal first. These are the important points in managing an army."

The master, Hsün Ch'ing, said, "No. What I have heard of the ancient methods is that in managing an army or a war, everything depends on uniting the people. If the bow and arrow did not fit each other, *I* could not hit the bulls-eye with it. If the six horses did not team together, Ts'ao-fu[14] could not go far with them. If the officers and people had not been attached and accordant with their prince, T'ang and Wu[15] could not have conquered. Hence the man who can get the accord of the people is the best man at managing an army. Hence the only important point in military affairs is in getting the accord of the people."

Lin-wu-chün said, "No. What is valuable in military affairs is strength and advantage; what is done is sudden alteration of troop movements and deceitful stratagems. He who knows best how to manage an army is sudden in his movements; his plans are very deep laid; and no one knows whence he may attack. When Sun Wu and Wu Ch'i[16] led armies, they had no enemies in the whole country; why should it be necessary to wait for the accord of the people?"

The master,[17] Hsün Ch'ing, said, "No. What I am speaking of are the armies of the benevolent man, the purposes of righteous Kings. What you value is planning on the instant, strength, and advantage; what you do is attacking, capturing, sudden alterations of troop movements, and deceit—the deeds of the nobles. The armies of the benevolent man cannot use deceit. The former can be deceitful, disrespectful, and exhaust the people. Between the prince and the subject, the ruler and the ruled, there is a separation, since there are deviations from virtue. For a Chieh to deceive a Chieh, is like the wise deceiving the stupid—some success may be looked for. For a Chieh to deceive a Yao, is like using an egg instead of a stone in throwing, or using a finger to stir boiling water, or like going into water or fire; if you go into it you will be burned or drowned. For with the benevolent man, the commanders and commanded, all the generals, are of one mind; the three armies are of like strength; the subject serves his prince, and the inferior serves his superior as the son serves his father or the younger brother serves his older brother, or as the hand and arm defend the head and eyes and cover the breast and abdomen. To deceive and surprise the enemy has just the same effect as first to alarm and then attack him. Moreover, when a benevolent man controls a state of ten *li*,[18] he will have intelligence from a hundred *li;* when he controls a state of a hundred *li*, he will have intelligence from a thousand *li;* when he controls a country of a thousand *li*, he will have intelligence from the whole continent. His wisdom and his admonitions will certainly strike the people harmoniously and unite them. For when the soldiers of a benevolent man are gathered together, they form files; when scattered, they form ranks. His army reaches as far as the long blade of Mo-yeh;[19] whoever runs against it is cut in two. It is as keen as the sharp point of

Mo-yeh; whoever meets it is destroyed. When inactive it is like a rock; whoever butts against it will be gored and broken like a drooping deer, dripping and wet, and will retreat. Moreover, whom would the prince of an aggressive country send against me? Those whom he would send must be his people. But his people would be attached to me; and they would rejoice in me as in their father and mother; they would love me as the fragrance of an epidendrum. On the other hand, they would regard their superior as a branding iron or a tattooing needle, as an enemy. Although a man's passions be those of Chieh or Chih,[20] how could he be willing to do what he hates and injure him whom he loves? This would be like trying to get a man's sons and grandsons to injure their own father and mother; instead they would certainly come and inform him; then how could he be deceived?

o   o   o   o

Book 17. *Concerning* T'ien

One ought not to grumble at *t'ien* that things happen according to its Way. Hence to know the Way of *t'ien* is man's duty; he who does this is a great Sage. To produce without acting and to obtain without seeking, this is what is meant by the office of *t'ien*. Therefore although the Way of *t'ien* is deep, this man will not put deep thought on it; although it is great, he will not use his ability for its investigation; although it is mysterious, he will not scrutinize it—this is what is meant by refraining from contesting with *t'ien*. T'ien has its seasons, earth has its wealth, man has his government. The foregoing is what is meant by being able to form a triad with *t'ien* and earth. To give up that wherewith one can form such a triad and to desire to know those with whom he forms a triad is to be led into error.

The fixed stars make their round; the sun and moon alternately shine; the four seasons come in succession; the *yin* and *yang*[21] go through their great mutations; the wind and rain widely affect things; all things acquire their germinating principle, and are brought into existence; each gets its nourishing principle and develops to its completed state. We do not see the cause of these occurrences, but we do see their effects—this is what is meant by the influence of the spirits.

o   o   o   o

What is known about *t'ien* is that we see its phenomena have their regular sequences; what is known about earth is that it is seen that it meets the conditions of life and can produce; what is known about the four seasons is that it is seen that they have a definite number, and can be used to serve humanity; what is known about the *yin* and *yang* is that it is seen that they interact and can be used in ruling a country. If the man who has a responsible post attends to what belongs to *t'ien* the people of themselves will keep to the right Way of life.

Are good and bad government, prosperity and calamity, from *t'ien?* I reply: The sun, the moon, the heavenly bodies, the auspicious times, the astrological calculations of the calendar were the same in the time of Yü[22] as in that of Chieh. In the time of Yü there was good government and prosperity; in the time of Chieh there was ill-government and calamity; prosperity and calamity do not come from *t'ien.*

Do they come from the seasons? I answer: The myriad plants spring up, flourish, and grow in spring and summer; they are nourished, the grain develops, is reaped and gathered in in the fall and winter. In this also the times of Yü and Chieh were the same. Yü had prosperity and Chieh had disaster; prosperity and disaster do not come from the seasons.

Do they come from the earth? I answer: When a plant or a state obtains a place on the earth, it lives; when its place on the earth is lost, it dies; in this too Yü and Chieh were the same. Yü had prosperity, Chieh had misfortune. Prosperity and misfortune, good and bad government, are not from the earth.

o   o   o   o

How can exalting *t'ien* and wishing for its gifts be as good as heaping up wealth and using it advantageously? How can obeying *t'ien* and praising it be as good as adapting oneself to the appointments of *t'ien* and using them? How can hoping for the proper time and waiting for it be as good as seizing the opportunity and acting? How can relying on things increasing of themselves be as good as putting forth one's energy and developing things? How can thinking of things and comparing them be as good as looking after things and not losing them? How can wishing that things may come to pass be as good as taking what one has and bringing things to pass? Therefore if a person neglects what men can do and seeks for what *t'ien* does, he fails to understand the nature of things.

o   o   o   o

Book 18. On the Correction of Errors

The sophists[23] common today say: "It is best for a lord to be secretive." This is not so. The lord is the singing-leader of the people; the ruler is the model of the subject. When they hear the singing-leader, they respond; when they see the model, they act accordingly. But when the singing-leader is silent, the people are without response; when the model is inaccessible, then the subjects do not act according to it. If they do not respond nor act according to the model, then the ruler and ruled cannot help each other. If things are thus, then it is the same as if there were no ruler, than which no misfortune is greater. For the ruler is the foundation of the subjects. When the ruler makes known clearly what is to be done, then the subjects are governed well. When the ruler is upright and sincere, then the subjects are honest and guileless; when the ruler is just and right, then the subjects are easily straight. When they are governed well, then they are easily united; when they are honest and guileless, they are easily employed. When they are easily straight, then they are easily understood. When they are easily united, then the state is strong; when they are easily employed, then the ruler gains glory; when they are easily understood, then the ruler is illustrious. This is the source of good government.

But when the ruler is secretive, then the subjects are confused; when the ruler is inaccessible and difficult to fathom, then the subjects are embued with falseness; when the ruler is partial and crooked, then the subjects form cliques. When the subjects are confused, they are united with difficulty; when they are imbued with falseness, then they are difficult to employ; when they form cliques, they are difficult to understand. When they are united with difficulty, the state is not strong; when they are difficult to employ, the ruler has no glory; when they are difficult to understand, then the ruler is not illustrious. This is the source of bad government.

o   o   o   o

When the country has no real prince, if there is a feudal noble who has ability, and if his virtue is illustrious and his majesty is great, none of the people of the country will be unwilling to take him for prince and leader; then if he should seek out and kill this isolated and wasteful tyrant, he would not injure anyone, he would be a blameless subject. If he put to death the prince of a tyrannous state, it would be the same as killing an ordinary individual. A person like this can be said to be able to wield the empire. He who is able to wield the empire can be called a King.

o   o   o   o

The sophists of the day say: "The ancient beneficent rulers had no corporal punishments, but instead had punishments by altering the clothing. Instead of kneeling on a line, there was wearing an inky turban; instead of cutting off the nose, there was wearing straw fringes; instead of castration, there was cutting off the leather knee-pads; instead of cutting off the feet, there was wearing hemp sandals; instead of execution, there was wearing ochre-coloured clothes without any hems—the ancient beneficent government was like this."

This is not so. Do you think that that government was beneficent? If so, men certainly did commit crime, and not only did they not use corporal punishments, but also they did not use punishments by altering the clothing. There is no greater confusion than thinking that if a man has committed a crime, his punishments should be directly lightened, so that a murderer should not die, a man who has assaulted another should not be punished, so that for an extremely great crime the punishment should be extremely light—the ordinary man does not know that there is anything to dislike in such punishment!

The origin of all punishment is the restraint of violence, the hatred of evil, and the warning against its future occurrence. That a murderer should not die, or a man who injures another should not be punished, is favouring violence and being liberal to robbers, not hatred of evil. For punishments by altering the clothing are dangerous; they are not born of the ancient beneficent government, but come from the confused and evil present.

The ancient beneficent government was not thus. All the ranks of nobility and the different grades of officials have rewards and punishments to repay them for their deeds; as their deeds, so their reward. That one thing should lose its appropriate recompense is the beginning of confusion. That a man's virtue should not correspond to his rank; that his ability should not correspond to his official grade; that rewards should not fit merit; that punishments should not fit the crime—there is no misfortune greater than this! In ancient times King Wu chastised the monarch of the Shang dynasty; he killed Chou;[24] he cut off his head and hung it on a crimson banner. Now chastising the violent and punishing the overbearing is the summit of good government. All the Kings agreed that a murderer should die, and that whoever injures another should be punished. We do not know the origin of this idea. When punishment fits the crime there is good government; when it does not fit the crime, there is bad government. Hence in good government the punishments are severe; in bad government the punishments are light. Therefore the crimes committed against a good government are severe; the crimes committed against a bad government are light. The *Book of Documents* says: "Punishments at times are light and at times are severe"—this expresses what I mean.

o   o   o   o

Book 19. On the Rules of Proper Conduct

Thus the rules of proper conduct are to educate and nourish. Meat, grain, the blending of the five flavours,[25] are that whereby the mouth is educated and nourished. The pepper, the orchid, fragrance, and perfume are that whereby the nose is educated and nourished. Engraving, cut gems, engraved metal, elegant compositions are that whereby the eye is educated and nourished. Bells, drums, pipes, stone chimes, lutes, lyres, reed organs are that whereby the ear is educated and nourished. Large houses, deep temples, fine rush mats, elevated beds, bedrooms, low tables, and bamboo mats are that whereby the body is nourished. Hence the rules of proper conduct are to educate and nourish. When the superior man has gotten its education and nourishment, he also esteems its distinctions.

What are meant by its distinctions? There are the classes of the noble and the base; there are the inequalities of the senior and the younger; there is what is appropriate to those who are poor and those who are rich, to those who are unimportant and those who are important. Hence the imperial chariot has a fine rush mat wherewith to take care of the emperor's body; by his side is carried a fragrant flower wherewith to take care of his sense of smell; in front it has ornamented yokes to care for his sense of sight; the harmonious sound of little bells, when going slow the Wu and Hsiang, when going fast the Shao and Hu[26] are to care for his sense of hearing; the dragon flag with nine scallops on the lower border to refresh his spirits; a sleeping rhinoceros, a male tiger, alligator adorned harness, a silken canopy, dragon yoke-ends, to care for his majesty. Hence the horses of the imperial chariot must be very trustworthy and well trained, and then only driven—thus caring for his safety. He has very capable braves, willing to die, who have agreed to be temperate, in order to care for his life. Very prudent men expend his money and use it in order to care for his wealth. He has very sagacious men who are respectful and courteous in order to preserve his calmness. He has very discreet men who observe the rules of proper conduct, justice, and all principles of refinement, in order to care for his emotions.

o   o   o   o

Rites are that whereby *t'ien* and earth unite, whereby the sun and moon are bright, whereby the four seasons are ordered, whereby the stars move in the courses, whereby rivers flow, whereby all things prosper, whereby love and hatred are tempered, whereby joy and anger keep their proper place. It causes the lower orders to obey, and the upper orders to be illustrious; through a myriad changes it prevents going astray. But if one departs from it, he will be destroyed. Are not rites the greatest of all principles? When it is established grandly, it becomes the centre of all, and the whole world will not be able to subtract from or add to it. Its source and aim accord with one another. Its end and beginning reach each other. It is most beautiful, but preserves the distinctions. It can be most closely scrutinized, and will be found to be explicable. When the country follows it, there is good government and prosperity; when it is not followed there is anarchy and calamity. He who follows it is safe; he who does not follow it is in danger. He who follows it will be preserved; he who does not follow it will be destroyed. The small-minded man cannot fathom this.

o   o   o   o

The Regular Principle of Funeral Rites

At every turn beautify it;[27] in every move, remove it farther away; with the lapse of time return to the ordinary course of life. For the way of death is thus; if it is not made beautiful, it becomes ugly; if it is ugly, there is no mourning; if it is near, it becomes wearisome; if wearisome, then it becomes distasteful; if distasteful, then it becomes neglected; if neglected, then it is not done reverently. Suppose on one morning I should lose both parents, and the mourners in the funeral should not mourn nor be respectful, then I should be loathed by the birds and beasts. The superior man would feel shame at that, hence at every turn he beautifies death, thereby to lessen its ugliness; at every move, he removes it farther away, thereby reverence continues to be felt; with the lapse of time he returns to the ordinary course of life, thereby to tranquillize life. The rules of proper conduct cut off that which is too long and stretch out that which is too short; they diminish that which is too much and increase that which is insufficient; they attain to the beauty of love and reverence, and they strengthen the excellence of character and right moral feeling. For beautiful adornment and ugliness, music and weeping, contentment and sorrow are opposites; yet the rites unite them and use them, at the right time they arouse them and in turn bring them forward. For beautiful adornment, music, and contentment, are that whereby a tranquil life is supported, and that which brings good fortune. Ugliness, weeping, sorrow are that whereby anxiety is nourished, and that which brings ill-fortune. For the rites provide for beautiful adornment, but do not go so far as to be fascinating; they provide for coarse mourning clothes, but do not go so far as to be stingy and neglectful; they provide for music and contentment, but do not go so far as licentiousness or laziness; they provide for weeping and sorrow, but do not go so far as an undue degree of distress and self-injury. This is the middle path of the rites.

o   o   o   o

All rites, if for the service of the living, are to beautify joy; or if to send off the dead, they are to beautify sorrow; or if for sacrifice, they are to beautify reverence; or if they are military, they are to beautify majesty. In this all the Kings were alike, the ancient times and the present are the same. But we do not know whence they came. Hence the appearance of a tomb and its tumulus is like a house. The appearance of the coffin is like the carriage screen and cover; it is like the carriage screen. The appearance of the coverings for the hearse and the feathery ornaments on it are like a door curtain or a bed curtain. The matting and framework for keeping the dirt off the coffin is like the plaster on the thatch and the screen in front of the door. Hence funeral ceremonies are for nothing else than to make plain the meaning of death and life, to send off the dead with sorrow and reverence, and at his end to provide for storing his body away; for burial is reverently storing his body away. Sacrifice is reverently serving his spirit; engraving his eulogy to hand it on to posterity is reverently passing on his fame. Service of the living is beautifying their life; sending off the dead is beautifying their end; when the end and the previous life are both attended to, the way of the Sage is completed. Slighting the dead and overemphasizing the living is obscurantism; slighting the living and overemphasizing the dead is to be misled; killing the living to send off the dead is murder. The method and manner of the rules of proper conduct and justice is to send off the dead very similarly to in their life; to cause death and life, the end and the present existence both to be suitably treated, and to love goodness—the Confucian does this.

o   o   o   o

Book 20. On Music

Now "music is the expression of joy." [28] Men's feelings make this inevitable. For man must needs be joyous; if joyous, his feelings must needs be expressed in sound, and bodied forth in movement and rest, and the fact that man directs sound together with movement and rest to express the changes in his disposition is completely expressed in that statement. Hence man must needs be joyous; if joyous, then he must needs embody his feelings; if they are embodied, but without conforming to any principles, then they cannot avoid being disordered. The early Kings hated this disorder, hence established the music of the "Ya" and "Sung" [29] to conform it to principle so as to cause its music to produce joy and not to degenerate, so as to cause its beauty to change but not stop, so as to cause its indirect and direct appeals, its manifoldness and simplicity, its frugality and richness, its rests and notes, to stir up the goodness in men's minds, and to prevent evil feelings from gaining any foothold. This is the manner in which the early Kings established music. But Mo Tzŭ attacks it; what is to be done now?

For when music is performed in the ancestral temple, the prince and minister, the ruler and ruled hear it together, and they cannot fail to be harmonious and reverent; when it is performed in the inner apartments of the house, father and son, older and younger brothers hear it together, and cannot fail to be harmonious and affectionate; when it is performed before the elders of the village or clan, old and young hear it together, and cannot fail to be harmonious and obedient. For music discriminates and unites in order to establish harmony; it compares and distinguishes in order to beautify its measures; it is performed in harmony in order to create beauty, so that it leads everything in one direction so that it controls all changes—this is the manner in which the early Kings established music. But Mo Tzŭ attacks it; what is to be done now?

For when I hear the music of the "Ya" and "Sung," my purposes are broadened. When I see the dancers grasp their shields and pole-axes, practise the lowering and raising of their heads, the bending and straightening of their bodies, my deportment becomes dignified. From the way in which they move in groups and adapt themselves to the music, the arrangement of the ranks is made correct, and their advancing and retreating are together. For music, when the dancers step forward, is of attacking and dealing death; when they step back it is of courtesy. The meaning of attacking, dealing death, and of courtesy are the same; when the dancers step forward to attack and deal death, none fail to obey; when they step back and act courteously, none fail to accord. Hence music is the greatest unifier in the world, the bond of inner harmony, the inevitable consequence of human emotion. This is the manner in which the early Kings established music. But Mo Tzŭ attacks it: what is to be done now?

o   o   o   o

Now sound and music enter deeply into people; their influence is rapid. For the early Kings carefully made it beautiful. When music is moderate and even, the people are harmonious and do not degenerate; when music is reverent and dignified, the people are tranquil and not in turmoil. When the people are harmonious and tranquil, the armies are strong, cities are secure, and enemy countries dare not attack. Then the people will all be safe in their dwellings, and happy in their villages, to the point of being satisfied with their rulers. Therefore their fame will be bright; therefore their glory will be great; in the whole empire none of the people will be unwilling to have this prince for their leader. This was the beginning made by the Kings.

When music is pretty and fascinating, it is dangerous; then the people degenerate, are negligent, mean, and low. If they lose self-restraint and are negligent, turmoil will begin; if they are mean and low, they will wrangle. If they are in turmoil and wrangle among themselves, then the armies will be weak, cities will be attacked, and enemy states will be dangerous. In this situation the people will not be safe in their dwellings nor happy in their villages, and they will not be satisfied with their rulers. Hence the casting aside of the rules of proper conduct and music, and the arising of unorthodox ditties, are the source of anger, loss of territory, insult, and disgrace. Therefore the early Kings honoured the rules of proper conduct and music, and despised unorthodox ditties. In the "Arrangement of Officials" [30] it is said: "The preparation of the laws and edicts, the examination of odes and essays, the elimination of licentious music, and obediently to do each at its proper time, so that barbarian or popular ditties do not confuse the *Songs*—this is the business of the Chief Instructor."

o   o   o   o

Moreover "music is unchanging" [31] concord. "The rules of proper conduct are unvarying principles." Music unites; the rules of proper conduct distinguish. The "union" of the rules of proper conduct and music embraces the whole "heart" of man. To exhaust the source and extreme of change is the nature of music. To display sincerity and take away falseness is the law of the rules of proper conduct; Mo Tzŭ attacked it; he almost met with punishment, but the wise Kings had already passed away, and no one corrected him. Stupid people learn his doctrines and endanger themselves. The superior man is clear about music, but he is born in an evil generation which hates goodness and will not listen to him. Alas! It cannot be done! Students avoid studying music and there is no way to attend to it.

o   o   o   o

Book 21. The Removal of Prejudices

Everything that men suffer is from being prejudiced by one false thing: and so the great principles are hidden from them. Good government consists in returning to the principles of the Classics; other doubtful principles lead into error. In the world there are not two Ways; the Sages had not two minds. But now the dukes have a strange government; the hundred schools of philosophy have strange doctrines; so that right and wrong are uncertain, good and bad government are uncertain.

o   o   o   o

What brings prejudice? Desire can bring prejudice; hate can bring prejudice; the beginning can bring prejudice; the end can bring prejudice; distance can bring prejudice; nearness can bring prejudice; the profound can bring prejudice; the superficial can bring prejudice; the ancient can bring prejudice; the present can bring prejudice. Everything that is unorthodox cannot help from bringing prejudice—this is the universal affliction of the mind.

o   o   o   o

For if we consider life from the standpoint of utility, it will merely be seeking for profit. If we consider life from the standpoint of desire, it will merely be seeking for satisfaction. If we consider life from the standpoint of law, it will merely be an art. If we consider life from the standpoint of power, it will merely be convenience. If we consider life from the standpoint of words, it will merely be dialectic. If we consider life from the standpoint of Nature, it will merely be cause and effect. These different presentations are all one aspect of life. Now the right Way of life is constant and includes all changes; one aspect is insufficient to express the whole. Those who have partial knowledge perceive one aspect of the Way, but they cannot know its totality. So they think it sufficient, and gloss things over. On the one hand they confuse themselves, and on the other they mislead others. The rulers prejudice their inferiors; the inferiors prejudice their superiors. This is the calamity which comes from being prejudiced and hindered from knowing the truth.

o   o   o   o

How can a person know the right *Tao?* By the mind. How does the mind know? By emptiness, unity or concentration, and unperturbedness.

The mind never ceases to store away impressions, yet there is that which may be called emptiness. The mind has always a multiplicity, yet there is that which may be called a unity. The mind is always in motion, yet there is that which may be called quiescence or unperturbedness.

A man from birth has the capacity to know things; this capacity to know things has its collected data; these collected data are what are meant by stored away impressions. Moreover he has that which may be called emptiness. That which does not allow what is already stored away to injure that which is about to be received is called the mind's emptiness. The mind from birth has the capacity for knowledge; this knowledge contains distinctions; these distinctions consist of at the same time perceiving more than one thing. To perceive more than one thing at the same time is plurality. Yet the mind has that which may be called a unity. That which does not allow that impression to harm this impression is called the mind's unity. When the mind sleeps, it dreams; when it takes its ease, it indulges in reverie; when it is used, it reflects. Hence the mind is always in motion. Yet it has that which may be called unperturbedness. That which does not permit dreams to disturb one's knowledge is called the mind's unperturbedness.

o   o   o   o

Whenever in observing things there is doubt and the mind is uncertain, then things are not apprehended clearly. When my thoughts are unclear, then I cannot decide whether a thing is so or is not so. When a person walks in the dark, he sees a stone lying down and takes it to be a crouching tiger; he sees a clump of trees standing upright and takes them to be standing men. The darkness has perverted his clear-sightedness. The drunken man crosses a hundred-pace-wide aqueduct and takes it to be a half-step-wide ditch; he bends down his head when going out of a city gate, taking it to be a small private door—the wine has confused his spirit.

o   o   o   o

Book 22. On the Rectification of Terms

When the later Kings formed the terminology, in the names of punishments they followed the Shang dynasty, in the titles of nobility they followed the designations of the Chou dynasty, and in ceremonial terms they followed the Ritual. In the case of miscellaneous names given to things they followed the established customary designations of the Chinese people. Because of them, when people of distant districts with different customs indirectly meet, they can communicate.

o   o   o   o

For when the Kings had regulated names, when they had fixed terms and so distinguished realities, and when this principle was carried out and hence their will was everywhere known, they were careful to lead the people and so the people were unified. Therefore distinguishing words, and making unauthorized distinctions, thus confusing the correct nomenclature, causing the people to be in doubt, and bringing about much litigation was called great wickedness. It was a crime like that of using false credentials or false measures. For their people did not dare to make strange terms a pretext for confusing the correct nomenclature, hence their people were guileless. Since they were guileless, they could easily be moved to action; since they were easily moved to action, they produced achievements. Since their people did not care to make strange terms a pretext for confusing the correct nomenclature, they were united in virtue and law-abidingness, and respectful in following orders. In this way their example spread. Their example spread and they produced achievements—this was the extreme of good government. This was the benefit of being careful in preserving the terms which had been agreed upon.

Now the Sage-Kings are dead, terms are carelessly preserved, strange nomenclature arises, terms and realities are confused, and what is right and wrong is not clear, so that even an official who guards the laws or a scholar who chants the Classics is all confused. Should a King arise, he would certainly follow the ancient terms and reform the new terms. Then he could not but investigate the reason for having terms, together with the means through which similarities and differences are found, and the fundamental principles in applying terms to things.

o   o   o   o

Then by what means are similarities and differences found? The means are the senses given by *t'ien*. Whenever anything is judged to be the same sort or the same emotion, it is because the perception of the senses given by *t'ien* is that the thing is the same. Hence for example, the reason that similarities are universally recognized to be such everywhere is because their agreed upon names have become universal, and so they can be recognized. Form and colour are distinctions made by the eyes. "Clear" and "confused" sound, harmony, musical time, and other sounds are distinctions made by the ear. Sweet and bitter, salty and fresh, peppery and sour, and other flavours are distinctions made by the mouth. Perfumes and smells, fragrant and putrid, the smell of fresh meat and fetid smells, the smell of the mole-cricket and the smell of decayed wood, and other smells are distinctions made by the nose. Pain and itching, cold and heat, smooth and rough, light and heavy, are distinctions made by the body. Doing things from a liking to do them and forcing oneself to do things; joy and anger, sorrow and pleasure, love, hatred, and desire are distinctions made by the mind.

The mind also gives meaning to impressions. It gives meaning to impressions, and only then, by means of the ear, sound can be known; by means of the eye, forms can be known. But the giving of meaning to impressions must depend on the senses given by *t'ien,* each noting its particular kind of sensations, and then only can knowledge be had. When the five senses[32] note something but do not comprehend it, and the mind tries to give it a meaning but has no explanation; nobody would differ, everyone would call this ignorance. These are the means by which similarities and differences are found.

Then in accordance with that, names are given to things. When things are alike, they are named alike; when different, they are named differently. When a simple term would be sufficient to convey the meaning, a simple term is used; when a simple term is insufficient, then a compound term is used. When simple and compound concepts do not conflict, then the general term may be used; although it is a general term, there is no harm in using it. The person who apprehends different realities uses different terms for them; hence he who refers to different realities should never use other than different terms; thus there could not be any confusion. Likewise he who refers to the same reality should never use other than the same term.

For although all things are manifold, there are times when we wish to speak of them all, so we call them "things." "Things" is the most general term.

o   o   o   o

"To receive an insult is no disgrace"; "a Sage does not love himself"; "to kill robbers is not to kill men"; these are fallacies in the use of terms with the result of confusing the terms.[33] Investigate the reason for having terms, observe of what sort the terms are, and then you will be able to stop this confusion. "Mountains and abysses are on the same level," "the desires seek to be few," "the flesh of domestic animals is not included in what is considered good tasting; the great bell is not included in music"— these are fallacies in the use of realities with the result of confusing the terms. Investigate the means through which similarities and differences are found, and see what fits the reality, and then you will be able to stop this confusion. "Even if you do not go and see, the centre pillar exists," "an ox-horse is not a horse"—these are fallacies in the use of terms with the result of confusing the realities.

o   o   o   o

Moreover the person who has tried to see into man's hidden parts, and put himself hard at work to investigate it, knows that there is no one who in their purpose despises moral principles, who does not value material things; and that there is no one who does not externally value material things and is not inwardly anxious; and that there is no one whose actions deviate from moral principles who is not in dangerous circumstances; and that there is no one who is in dangerous circumstances who is not inwardly fearful. When the mind is anxious and fearful, though the mouth be holding meat, it will not recognize the flavour thereof; though the ears hear bells and drums, they will not recognize the sound thereof; though the eyes behold fine embroidery, they will not know the pattern thereof; though the clothes be light and warm, and he be sitting on a rush or fine bamboo mat, the body will not recognize the comfort thereof; for he may enjoy the goodness of all things, yet he cannot be contented. If he gains a respite and contentment, his anxiety and fear nevertheless do not leave him. For though he be enjoying the goodness of all things, yet he is greatly anxious; though he be absorbing the benefit of all things, yet he gains great injury. Thus fares he who seeks material things. Is food life? Is porridge old age? For he desires to foster his desires, but indulges his emotions; he desires to foster his nature, but he endangers his body; he desires to foster his enjoyment, but he attacks his mind; he desires to foster his fame, but he disorders his actions. Although this sort of man be made a marquis and called a prince, he would be no whit different from a common man or a robber; although he were to ride in a nobleman's coach or wear a crown, he would be no whit different from a footless cripple. Then he could well be called one who makes himself the servant of material things.

If the heart is tranquil and contented, though the colours be below the ordinary, they can nourish the eyes; though sounds be below the ordinary, they can nourish the ears; coarse food and vegetable soup can nourish the taste; coarse cotton clothes and coarse hemp sandals can nourish the body; a straw hut for a house, reed screens for doors, straw beds, ancient plain stands and mats can nourish the form.

o   o   o   o

Book 23. The Nature of Man Is Evil

The nature of man is evil; his goodness is only acquired training. The original nature of man today is to seek for gain. If this desire is followed, strife and rapacity results, and courtesy dies. Man originally is envious and naturally hates others. If these tendencies are followed, injury and destruction follows; loyalty and faithfulness are destroyed. Man originally possesses the desires of the ear and eye; he likes praise and is lustful. If these are followed, impurity and disorder results, and the rules of proper conduct and justice and etiquette are destroyed. Therefore to give rein to man's original nature, to follow man's feelings, inevitably results in strife and rapacity, together with violations of etiquette and confusion in the proper way of doing things, and reverts to a state of violence. Therefore the civilizing influence of teachers and laws, the guidance of the rules of proper conduct and justice are absolutely necessary. Thereupon courtesy results; public and private etiquette is observed; and good government is the consequence. By this line of reasoning it is evident that the nature of man is evil and his goodness is acquired.

Crooked wood needs to undergo steaming and bending to conform to the carpenter's rule; then only is it straight. Blunt metal needs to undergo grinding and whetting; then only is it sharp. The original nature of man today is evil, so he needs to undergo the instruction of teachers and laws, then only will he be upright. He needs the rules of proper conduct and justice, then only will there be good government. But man today is without good teachers and laws; so he is selfish, vicious, and un-righteous. He is without the rules of proper conduct and justice, so there is rebellion, disorder, and no good government. In ancient times the Sage-Kings knew that man's nature was evil, selfish, vicious, unright-eous, rebellious, and of itself did not bring about good government. For this reason they created the rules of proper conduct and justice; they es-tablished laws and ordinances to force and beautify the natural feelings of man, thus rectifying them. They trained to obedience and civilized men's natural feelings, thus guiding them. Then good government arose and men followed the right Way. Now the people who are influenced by good teachers and laws, who accumulate literature and knowledge, who are led by the rules of proper conduct and justice become superior men. Those who give rein to their natural feelings, who take joy in haughti-ness, and break the rules of proper conduct and justice become small-minded men. By this line of reasoning it is evident that the original na-ture of man is evil and his goodness is acquired.

Mencius says, "The fact that men are teachable shows that their origi-nal nature is good." I reply: This is not so. This is not understanding the nature of man, nor examining the original nature of man, nor the part played by acquired elements. Whatever belongs to original nature is the gift of Nature. It cannot be learned. It cannot be worked for. The Sage-Kings brought forth the rules of proper conduct and justice. Men learn them and gain ability; they work for them and obtain results in the de-velopment of character. What cannot be learned and cannot be worked for, what is in the power of Nature only is what is meant by original na-ture. That which can be learned and which gives men ability, which can be worked for and which brings results in the development of character, whatever is in the power of man is what is meant by acquired charac-ter. This is the distinction between original nature and acquired charac-ter. Now according to the nature of man, the eye has the power of seeing and the ear has the power of hearing. However, when a person sees a thing, his quickness of sight is not outside of his eye; when he hears, his quickness of hearing is not outside of his ear. It is evident that quickness of sight and quickness of hearing cannot be learned. Mencius says: Now the original nature of man is good; all have lost and destroyed their orig-inal nature, hence it is evil. I reply: When he says this, he is greatly mis-taken. Now considering the nature of man, as soon as he is born, he would already have grown away from his first estate, he would already have grown from his natural disposition. He would already have lost and destroyed it. By this line of reasoning it is evident that the original nature of man is evil and his goodness is acquired.

The doctrine that man's original nature is good implies that without growing away from his first estate, he becomes admirable; without growing away from his natural disposition, he becomes beneficial. To say that man's original nature is admirable, his heart and thoughts are good, is the same as to say that the power of seeing is not apart from the eye and the power of hearing is not apart from the ear. So we say, if there is an eye, there is the power of seeing; if there is an ear, there is the power of hearing. Now the nature of man is that when he is hungry, he desires repletion; when he is cold, he desires warmth; when he labours, he seeks rest. This is man's natural feeling. But now when a man is hungry and sees food, he dares not rush in ahead of others; instead the eater yields to others. When working, he dares not seek rest, instead he works for others. The son yielding precedence to his father, the younger brother yielding to his older brother; the son working for his father, the younger brother working for his older brother—these two kinds of actions are contrary to original nature and antagonistic to natural feeling. Nevertheless there is the doctrine of filial piety, the etiquette of the rules of proper conduct and justice. If a person follows his natural feelings, he has no courtesy; if he has courtesy, then it is antagonistic to his natural feelings. By this line of reasoning it is evident that man's original nature is evil and his goodness is acquired.

A questioner may say: If man's original nature is evil, then whence come the rules of proper conduct and justice? In answer I say: All rules of proper conduct and justice come from the acquired training of the Sage, not from man's original nature. The potter pounds and moulds the clay and makes the vessel—but the vessel comes from the potter's acquired skill, not from the potter's innate character. The workman hews a piece of wood and makes a vessel; but the vessel comes from the workman's acquired training, not from his innate character. The Sage gathers together ideas and thoughts, and becomes skilled by his acquired training, so as to bring forth the rules of proper conduct and justice, and originate laws and regulations. So the rules of proper conduct, justice, laws and regulations come from the acquired knowledge of the Sage, not from man's original nature.

o   o   o   o

The Sage has his original nature in common with ordinary people; he is not different from ordinary people in this respect. He is different and superior to ordinary people in his acquired training.

It is the original nature and tendency of man to desire gain and to seek to obtain it. If brothers have property and are to divide it, if they follow their original nature and feelings of desiring gain and seeking to obtain it, thus they will mutually thwart each other and endeavour to seize the property. But reform them by the etiquette of the rules of proper conduct and justice, and they will be willing to yield to outsiders. So by following the original nature and feelings, brothers will quarrel; influence them by the rules of proper conduct and justice, and they will yield to strangers. Every man's desire to be good is because his nature is evil. So if he is mean, he wants to be generous; if he is in circumscribed circumstances he wants unhampered circumstances; if he is poor, he wants to be rich; if he is in a low social position, he wishes to be in an honourable position; if he has it not within himself, he inevitably seeks it from without. For if he were rich, he would not desire wealth; if he were in a high position, he would not want more power. If he has it within his power, he would certainly not seek it from without. By this line of reasoning we see that man's desire to be good comes from his original nature being evil.

o   o   o   o

Mencius says, "The nature of man is good." I reply: This is not so. In whatever age or place on earth, in ancient times or in the present, men have meant by goodness true principles and just government. They have meant by evil partiality, a course bent on evil, rebellion, and disorder. This is the distinction between goodness and evil. Now if we sincerely consider the nature of man, is it firmly established in true principles and just government? If so, then what use are the Sage-Kings? What use are the rules of proper conduct and justice? Although there were Sage-Kings, the rules of proper conduct, and justice, what could they add to true principles and just government?

Now that is not the situation. Man's nature is evil. Anciently the Sage-Kings knew that man's nature was evil, that it was partial, bent on evil, and corrupt, rebellious, disorderly, without good government, hence they established the authority of the prince to govern man; they set forth clearly the rules of proper conduct and justice to reform him; they established laws and government to rule him; they made punishments severe to warn him; and so they caused the whole country to come to a state of good government and prosperity, and to accord with goodness. This is the government of the Sage-Kings, the reforming influence of the rules of proper conduct and justice.

Now suppose we try to remove the authority of the prince, and be without the reforming influence of the rules of proper conduct and justice; suppose we try to remove the beneficent control of the laws and the government, and be without the restraining influence of punishments. Let us stand and see how the people of the whole country would behave. If this were the situation, then the strong would injure the weak and rob him; the many would treat cruelly the few and rend them. The whole country would be in a state of rebellion and disorder. It would not take an instant to get into this condition. By this line of reasoning, it is evident that the nature of man is evil and that his goodness is acquired.

o   o   o   o

"The man on the street can become a Yü"—how about that? What gave Yü the qualities of Yü was that he carried into practice benevolence, justice, obedience to the laws, and uprightness. If so, then there is the means of knowing and practising benevolence, justice, obedience to law, and uprightness. Moreover, every man on the street has the nascent ability of knowing the principles of benevolence, justice, obedience to law, and uprightness, and the means whereby he can carry out the principles of benevolence, justice, obedience to law, and uprightness. Thus it is evident that he can become a Yü.

Now are the qualities of benevolence, justice, obedience to law, and uprightness definitely without the possibility of being known or of being carried out? If so, then even Yü could not have known benevolence, justice, obedience to law and uprightness, nor could he have been able to be benevolent, just, law-abiding, or upright. Then is the man on the street definitely without the power of knowing benevolence, justice, obedience to law, and uprightness, and definitely without the ability to be benevolent, just, law-abiding, and upright? Then the man on the street, on the one hand, could not know the righteous relation between father and son, nor on the other hand could he know the standard of correctness of prince and minister. Now that is not so. Every man on the street can on the one hand know the righteous relation between father and son, and on the other hand he can know the standard of uprightness of prince and minister. Thus it is evident that the man on the street possesses the power of knowing and the ability to practise these virtues. Now if the man on the street uses his power of knowledge and his ability of acting on the nascent ability of knowing benevolence and justice and the means of becoming so, then it is clear that he can become a Yü; if he concentrates his mind on one purpose, if he thinks and studies and investigates thoroughly, daily adding to his knowledge and retaining it long, if he accumulates goodness and does not stop, then he will become as wise as the gods, a third with *t'ien* and earth. For the Sage is the man who has attained to that state by accumulative effort.

A person may say: The Sage attains to that stage by accumulative effort, but not everyone can accumulate his efforts: why is that? I reply: He has the capability, but he does not use it. For the small-minded man can become a superior man, but he is not willing to become a superior man; the superior man can become a small-minded man, but he is not willing to become a small-minded man. It is not impossible for the small-minded man and the superior man to exchange places; nevertheless they do not exchange places.

ᴏ　　ᴏ　　ᴜ　　ᴏ

It is said: "If you do not know a person, look at his friends. If you do not know the prince of a state, look at those to the right and left of him." Follow that and it will be sufficient! Follow that and it will be sufficient!

11

The Classic of Filial Piety and Ritual Texts

It commences with the service of parents;
it proceeds to the service of the ruler.
—*Filial Piety,* 1

Confucius believed in the supreme importance of high court ritual. The rites had sacred significance for him. If the ruler does not perform them right, he sounds a jarring note into the harmony of heaven and earth. "If [a ruler] could for one day himself submit to ritual, everyone under heaven would respond to his Goodness" (*Analects,* 12:1). To explain this satisfactorily to an increasingly skeptical age, Confucius had to start, at least, on a theory of ritual.

Later scholars found the remarks he made about rites pregnant with meaning. The emperor had simply to be a symphonist. Keeping harmony in the rites, he would keep harmony among his subjects; keeping harmony among his subjects, he would keep harmony in nature.

In the Sung Dynasty (960–1279 A.D.), Chu Hsi (1130–1200 A.D.), the great synthesizer of the Neo-Confucians, established the canon of "Four Books," turning them thus to use as children's schoolbooks. (See Table 3.) As two of them he took the *Analects* and the *Mencius*; the other two he extracted from the *Ritual Records (Li Chi)*, the collection of short works on ritual written by the immediate followers of Confucius and by ritualists of the early Han Dynasty. The *Records* was compiled about 100 B.C. Those works in it that Chu Hsi chose for the "Four Books" were two of the more philosophical chapters: the *Mean-in-Action* (Chapter 28) and the *Great Learning* (Chapter 39). The first reveals the influence of Confucius and Mencius; the second shows affinities also with the ideas of Hsün Tzŭ.

In these texts no longer do the model kings hold the center of attention. A new actor appears on stage—a Confucius who is not the Confucius of the *Analects* but rather a new Master who speaks with authority on difficult questions of ritual and history. He is still not the divine sage he was later to become; already, though, he is an object of veneration. In the *Mean-in-Action* he is likened "to the four seasons in their alternating progress, and to the Sun and Moon in their successive shining." Confucius's emphasis on ritual was to prove useful to an emerging imperial age; useful also was to be his stress on the relationship of political and filial piety, and the loyalty of the gentleman and scholar.

These last views appear most authoritatively in a short text of doubtful authorship, the *Classic of Filial Piety*, that might easily have been lumped with the forty-nine sections compiled in the *Ritual Records*. Instead, it came down through history from about 200 B.C. as a small, separate work. Already in late Han times it had acquired canonical status. Henceforth it was to be numbered among most groupings of the classics and made a necessary part of an accredited education, beginning as every schoolboy's primer. In briefest form, it shows Confucius explaining to a disciple that at the base of all morality lies filial piety.

The selections in this chapter include the larger part of the *Classic of Filial Piety* and the *Mean-in-Action* and the whole of the *Great Learning*. The last selection consists of another chapter (38), definitive and lofty on its subject, from the *Ritual Records*—the "Conduct of the Scholar."

Together with the Confucian classics already selected, these texts have been recited and memorized at school and in later adult life by all civil servants and political writers, indeed by all literate Chinese, if not from the Han Dynasty then from the Sung Dynasty until the Chinese Republic.

THE CLASSIC OF FILIAL PIETY

(Hsiao Ching)

Selections

The Scope and Meaning of the Treatise

1. Once, when Chung-ni[1] was unoccupied, and his disciple Tsêng Tzŭ[2] was sitting by in attendance on him, the Master said, "Shên, the ancient kings had a perfect virtue and all-embracing rule of conduct, through which they were in accord with all under heaven. By the practice of it the people were brought to live in peace and harmony, and there was no ill-will between superiors and inferiors. Do you know what

From James Legge, tr., *Classic of Filial Piety*, in *Sacred Books of China* (Oxford: Clarendon Press, 1879).

it was?" Tsêng Tzŭ rose from his mat, and said, "How should I, Shên, who am so devoid of intelligence, be able to know this?" The Master said, "It was filial piety. Now filial piety is the root of all virtue, and the stem out of which grows all moral teaching. Sit down again, and I will explain the subject to you. Our bodies—to every hair and bit of skin— are received by us from our parents, and we must not presume to injure or wound them: this is the beginning of filial piety. When we have established our character by the practice of the filial course, so as to make our name famous in future ages, and thereby glorify our parents: this is the end of filial piety. It commences with the service of parents; it proceeds to the service of the ruler; it is completed by the establishment of the character.

"It is said in the Major Odes of the Kingdom,[3]

> Ever think of your ancestor,
> Cultivating your virtue."

Filial Piety in the Son of T'ien

2. He who loves his parents will not dare to incur the risk of being hated by any man, and he who reveres his parents will not dare to incur the risk of being contemned by any man. When the love and reverence of the Son of T'ien are thus carried to the utmost in the service of his parents, the lessons of his virtue affect all the people, and he becomes a pattern to all within the four seas: this is the filial piety of the Son of T'ien.

It is said in the Marquis of Fu on Punishments,[4] "The One man will have felicity, and the millions of the people will depend on what ensures his happiness."

Filial Piety in the Princes of States

3. Above others, and yet free from pride, they dwell on high, without peril; adhering to economy, and carefully observant of the rules and laws, they are full, without overflowing. To dwell on high without peril is the way long to preserve nobility; to be full without overflowing is the way long to preserve riches. When their riches and nobility do not leave their persons, then they are able to preserve the altars of their land and

grain, and to secure the harmony of their people and men in office: this is the filial piety of the princes of states.

It is said in the *Book of Songs,*

> Be apprehensive, be cautious,
> As if on the brink of a deep abyss,
> As if treading on thin ice.

Filial Piety in High Ministers and Great Officers

4. They do not presume to wear robes other than those appointed by the laws of the ancient kings; nor to speak words other than those sanctioned by their speech; nor to exhibit conduct other than that exemplified by their virtuous ways. Thus none of their words being contrary to those sanctions, and none of their actions contrary to the right way, from their mouths there comes no exceptionable speech, and in their conduct there are found no exceptionable actions. Their words may fill all under heaven, and no error of speech will be found in them. Their actions may fill all under heaven, and no dissatisfaction or dislike will be awakened by them. When these three things—their robes, their words, and their conduct—are all complete as they should be, they can then preserve their ancestral temples: this is the filial piety of high ministers and great officers.

It is said in the *Book of Songs,*

> He is never idle, day or night,
> In the service of the One man.

Filial Piety in Inferior Officers

5. As they serve their fathers, so they serve their mothers, and they love them equally. As they serve their fathers, so they serve their rulers, and they reverence them equally. Hence love is what is chiefly rendered to the mother, and reverence is what is chiefly rendered to the ruler, while both of these things are given to the father. Therefore when they serve their ruler with filial piety they are loyal; when they serve their superiors with reverence they are obedient. Not failing in this loyalty and obedience in serving those above them, they are then able to preserve

their emoluments and positions, and to maintain their sacrifices: this is the filial piety of inferior officers.

It is said in the *Book of Songs,*

> Rising early and going to sleep late,
> Do not disgrace those who gave you birth.

Filial Piety in the Common People

6. They follow the course of heaven in the revolving seasons; they distinguish the advantages afforded by different soils; they are careful of their conduct and economical in their expenditure, in order to nourish their parents: this is the filial piety of the common people.

Therefore from the Son of T'ien down to the common people, there never has been one whose filial piety was without its beginning and end on whom calamity did not come.

THE DOCTRINE OF THE MEAN

(Chung Yung)

Selections

An Appreciation of Tzŭ Ssŭ's[1]
Mean-in-Action *by a Later Scholar*

That which T'ien entrusts to man is to be called his nature. The following out of this nature is to be called the Way. The cultivation of the Way is to be called instruction in systematic truth. The Way, it may not be abandoned for a moment. If it might be abandoned, it would not be the Way. Because this is so, the man of principle holds himself restrained

From E. R. Hughes, tr., *The Great Learning and the Mean-in-Action* (New York: E. P. Dutton, 1943). Copyright 1943, 1971 by E. R. Hughes. Reprinted by permission of E. P. Dutton & Co., Inc., and J. M. Dent & Sons Ltd. Headings are those of the translator.

and keyed up in relation to the unseen world [*lit.* what he cannot see or hear]. Since there is nothing more manifest than what is hidden, nothing more visible than what is minute, therefore the man of principle is on guard when he is alone with himself.

To have no emotions of pleasure and anger and sorrow and joy surging up, this is to be described as being in a state of equilibrium. To have these emotions surging up but all in tune, this is to be described as a state of harmony. This state of equilibrium is the supreme foundation, this state of harmony the highway, of the Great Society [? civilization]. Once equilibrium and harmony are achieved, heaven and earth maintain their proper positions, and all living things are nourished.

Tzŭ Ssŭ invokes Confucius's Authority for the Idea of the Mean-in-Action.

Chung-ni[2] said: "This man of true breeding is the mean-in-action. The man of no breeding is the reverse. The relation of the man of true breeding to the mean-in-action is that, being a man of true breeding, he consistently holds to the Mean. The reverse relationship of the man of no breeding is that, being what he is, he has no sense of moral caution."

The Master said: "Perfect is the mean-in-action, and for a long time now very few people have had the capacity for it."

The Master said: "I know why the Way is not pursued. (It is because) the learned run to excess and the ignorant fall short. I know why the Way is not understood. The good run to excess and the bad fall short. Amongst men there are none who do not eat and drink, but there are few who can really appreciate flavours."

The Master said: "Alas, this failure to pursue the Way!"

The Master said: "Consider Shun,[3] the man of great wisdom. He loved to ask advice and to examine plain speech. He never referred to what was evil, and publicly praised what was good. By grasping these two extremes he put into effect the Mean among his people. In this way he was Shun, was he not?"

The Master said: "All men say 'I know,' but they are driven into nets, caughts in traps, fall into pitfalls, and not one knows how to avoid this. All men say 'I know,' but, should they choose the mean-in-action, they could not persist in it for a round month."

The Master said: "Hui,[4] a real man! He chose the mean-in-action, and, if he succeeded in one element of good, he grasped it firmly, cherished it in his bosom, and never let it go."

The Master said: "The states and families of the Great Society might have equal divisions of land. Men might refuse noble station, and the wealth that goes with it. They might trample the naked sword under foot. But the mean-in-action, it is impossible for them to achieve that."

Tzŭ-lu[5] inquired about strong men, and the Master said: "Is it strong men of the southern kind that you have in mind? The strong man of the south is magnanimous and gentle in instructing people, and he takes no revenge for being treated vilely; it is the habit of a man of true breeding to be like this. The strong man of the north lives under arms and dies without a murmur: it is the habit of a man of true force to be like this. Hence the man of true breeding, how steadfast he is in his strength, having a spirit of concord and not giving way to pressure. He takes up a central position and does not waver one way or another. How steadfast his strength, for, when there is good government, he does not change his original principles, and, when there is vile government, he does not change, even though his life be at stake."

The Master said: "To unravel mysteries and work miracles, that I will not do, even though my name should be recorded for ages to come. The man of true breeding follows the Way in all his acts, and it is impossible for me, therefore, to abandon the course half-way. The man of true breeding has faith in the mean-in-action. Although he live the life of a recluse, unknown to his age, he has no regrets. A man must be a sage to have this capacity."

The Material World is Limited,
the Way Unlimited

The way of the true man is widely apparent and yet hidden. Thus the ordinary man and woman, ignorant though they are, can yet have some knowledge of it; and yet in its perfection even a sage finds that there is something there which he does not know. Take the vast size of heaven-and-earth; men can still find room for criticism of it. Hence, when the enlightened man speaks of supreme bigness, it cannot be contained within the world of our experience. Nor, when he speaks of supreme smallness, can it be split up in the world of our experience into nothing. As is said in the *Book of Songs,* "The hawk beats its way up to the height of heaven, the fish dives down into the abyss." That refers to things being examined from above and from below. Thus the Way of the man of principle: its early shoots coming into existence in the ordinary man and woman, but in its ultimate extent to be examined in the light of heaven-and-earth.

Confucius's Authority Invoked to show that the Way of the Mean is one which involves an Unlimited Demand on every Sort of Individual, and also is mixed up with Religion

The Master said: "The Way is not far removed from men. If a man pursues a way which removes him from men, he cannot be in the Way. In the *Book of Songs* there is the word, 'When hewing an axe-handle, hew an axe-handle. The pattern of it is close at hand.' You grasp an axe-handle to hew an axe-handle, although, when you look from the one to the other they are very different. Therefore the right kind of ruler uses men to control men and attempts nothing beyond their correction; and fidelity and mutual service, these two human qualities, cannot be outside the scope of the Way. The treatment which you do not like for yourself you must not hand out to others. And this Way for the man of true breeding has four sides to it, in not one of which have I succeeded. To serve my father as I would have a son serve me as a father, in this I, Ch'iu, have failed. To serve my prince as I would have a minister serve me as a prince, in this I, Ch'iu, have failed. To serve my elder brother as I would have a younger brother serve me as an older brother, in this I, Ch'iu, have failed. To be beforehand in treating a friend as I would have him treat me as a friend, in this I, Ch'iu, have failed."

The acts of the true man agree with the station in life in which he finds himself, and he is not concerned with matters outside that station. If he is a man of wealth and high position, he acts as such. If he is a poor man and low in the social scale, he acts accordingly. So also, if he is among barbarians, or if he meets trouble. In fact, there is no situation into which he comes in which he is not himself. In a high station he does not disdain those beneath him. In a low station he does not cling round those above him. He puts himself in the right and seeks no favours. Thus he is free from ill will, having no resentment against either T'ien or men. He preserves an easy mind as he awaits the Will of T'ien: in contrast to the man who is not true, who walks in perilous paths and hopes for good luck. As the Master said: "In archery there is a resemblance to the man of true breeding. If a man misses the target, he looks for the cause in himself."

The Way of the true man is like a long journey, since it must begin with the near at hand. It is like the ascent of a high mountain, since it must begin with the low ground. In the *Book of Songs* there is:

> The happy union with wife and child
> Is like the music of lutes and harps.
> When concord grows between brother and brother,
> The harmony is sweet and intimate.
> The ordering of your household,
> Your joy in wife and child!

The Master said: "How greatly parents are served in this!"

The Master said: "How irrepressible is the spiritual power in the manes! [6] Look for them and they are not to be seen. Listen for them, and they are not to be heard. They are in things, and there is nothing without them. They stir all the people in the Great Society to fast and purify themselves and wear their ritual robes, in order that they may sacrifice to them. They fill the air, as if above, as if on the left, as if on the right. As the *Book of Songs* has it, 'The coming of the Spirits! Incalculable. And yet they cannot be disregarded.'" Even so is the manifestation of the minute and the impossibility of hiding the real.

Outstanding Personality cannot but have Wide and Continuing Influence, as is proved by the Hero-Saints of Tradition

The Master said: Consider Shun, the man of superb filial piety. By the virtue in him he was a sage. In his dignity he was Son of T'ien. In his wealth he owned all within the four seas. Temple sacrifices were made to him, and his memory was cherished by his descendants. Thus it is that outstanding personality is bound to obtain its position of authority, its wealth, its fame, and its lasting life. For thus it is that T'ien, as it gives life to all creatures, can be surely trusted to give to each what is due to its basic capacity. And thus it is that the well-planted is nourished and the ill-planted falls prostrate.

The *Book of Songs* has the word:

> Hail to our sovereign prince!
> How gracious is his personality!
> He has put the people to right: he has put his men to right.
> T'ien has vouchsafed its bounty to him.
> T'ien has protected him and appointed him king;
> T'ien's blessing is his, not once but again and yet again.

Thus it is that the man of superb personality is bound to receive the Mandate of T'ien.

The Master said: "The only man who has been without sorrow is King Wên.[7] He had Wang Chi for father and King Wu for son. The father laid the foundation, and the son built on it. King Wu thus inherited from a line of kingly men, T'ai Wang, Wang Chi, and King Wên. Once he had buckled on his armour, the world was his, for (although he rebelled) he suffered no loss to his world-wide reputation. In dignity he became the Son of T'ien, in wealth he owned all within the four seas. Temple sacrifices were made to him, and his memory was cherished by his descendants."

It was in his old age that King Wu received the Mandate, and it was Duke Chou who carried to completion the virtue of King Wên and King Wu. The rite reserved for sacrificing to a Son of T'ien he used for sacrificing to his (non-royal) forebears. And this rule in ritual was extended to the feudatories and great officers and was applied in every rank of society down to the minor officials and the common people. If the father was a great officer and the son a minor official, then the father was buried with the rite of a great officer, but afterwards was sacrificed to with the rite of a minor official. If the father was a minor official and the son a great officer, then the father was buried with the rite of a minor official, but afterwards was sacrificed to with the rite of a great officer. The practice of mourning for one year was extended to a great officer, of mourning for three years to a Son of T'ien. In the case of mourning for a father or a mother, there was no difference for the noble or the commoner. The practice was the same.

The Master said: "How wide an influence King Wu's and Duke

Chou's filial piety had." Filial men are those who are well able to follow up what the men before have willed, and preserve what they have undertaken. In the spring and the autumn they repair their ancestral temples, arrange the sacrificial vessels, set in order the ceremonial robes, and offer the seasonal meats. The ritual of the temple is the means by which the line on the male side and the line on the female side are kept distinct. The gradation of titles is the means by which higher and lower ranks are defined. The distinctions of office are the means by which the worth of men is marked. In the pledging rite those of low station present the cup to those of high, and thus a place is made for the common man. At the festal board white-haired old men have their places, and by this means differences of age are observed. To maintain one's ancestors in their proper shrines, to carry out their rites, to play their music, to reverence those whom they honoured, to love those closely related to them, to serve the dead as they were served alive, to serve those who are no more as they were served when they were here: this is the height of filial piety. Let (a ruler) only grasp the significance of the rites at the altars of T'ien and Earth and those in the ancestral temple, and government will become (as easy) as pointing to the palm of the hand. For the rites to T'ien and Earth are means by which service is rendered to Shang Ti,[8] the rites in the temple are the means by which (grateful) offerings are made to those from whom we have sprung.

The Governing of Men

The Primary Need for Men who can Govern

The Duke Ai[9] asked advice as to governing, and the Master said: "King Wên's and King Wu's system of government is revealed in the historical records. It is this: with their kind of men the system worked: without their kind of men it came to an end. Man's right way is to be prompt in good government as the earth's way is to be prompt in making things grow. Thus, good government is like the speed with which some reeds grow. For this reason good government depends on the men (who govern). Such men are obtainable on the basis of their personality. The cultivation of personality is on the basis of the Way. The cultivation of the Way is on the basis of human-heartedness. To be human-hearted is to be a man, and the chief element in human-heartedness is loving one's relations. So it is with justice: it is to put things right, and the chief element in it is employing worthy men in public service, whilst the degrees in kinship and the grades of offices are the product of the established order of procedure. (Unless those in the high ranks of society can capture the confidence of those in the lower ranks, they cannot gain the support of the people for their administrative measures.) Thus it is that the true ruler must not fail to cultivate his self; and, having it in mind to do this, he must not fail to serve his parents; and having it in mind to do this, he must not fail to have knowledge of men; and, having it in mind to have this knowledge, he must not fail to have knowledge of T'ien."

Those Aspects of Government which concern Everybody

There are five things which concern everybody in the Great Society, as also do the three means by which these five things are accomplished. To explain, the relationship between sovereign and subject, between father and son, between husband and wife, between elder and younger brother, and the equal intercourse of friend and friend, these five relationships concern everybody in the Great Society. Knowledge, human-heartedness, and fortitude, these three are the means; for these qualities are the spiritual power in society as a whole. The means by which this power is made effective is unity.

Some people know these relationships by the light of nature. Others know them by learning about them from a teacher. Others, again, know them through hard experience. But once they all do know them, there is unity. Some people practise these relationships with a natural ease. Others derive worldly advantage from their practice of them. Others, again, have no force themselves to practise them. But once they all have achieved success in practising them, there is unity.

The Master said: "To love to learn is to be near to having knowledge. To put into practice vigorously is to be near to being human-hearted. To know the stings of shame is to be near to fortitude. So we may infer that the man who knows these three things, knows how to cultivate his self. When he knows how to do that, it may be inferred that he knows how to rule other individuals. And, when he knows how to do that, it may be inferred that he knows how to rule the whole of the Great Society with its states and families."

The Basic Duties of Rulers

For those whose function covers the whole Great Society or any one of its constituent states, there are nine basic duties: cultivation of one's self, honouring men of worth, affectionate treatment of the royal family, high respect towards ministers of state, courtesy towards all the other officers, fatherly care of the common people, promotion of the hundred crafts, kindly treatment of strangers, enlistment of the fervent loyalty of the fief-holders. Let the self be cultivated, then the Way is established in the country. Let the right men be put into the right posts, then mistakes will not occur. Let the royal family be treated affectionately, then the royal uncles and cousins will bear no ill will. Let the ministers of state be held in high respect, then there will be no vacillation in policy. Let courtesy be extended to all the other officers, then the lower ranks will doubly repay that courtesy. Let fatherly care be bestowed on the common people, then they will gladly obey. Let the hundred crafts be promoted, then the resources for expenditure will be ample. Let strangers be treated with kindness, then men from all parts will be attracted. Let the loyalty of the fief-holders be enlisted, then the whole Great Society will stand in awe of the Throne.

(At the times of solemn sacrifice) when purification is to be made and ritual robes to be worn, if nothing be done in contravention of the established order of procedure this is the means by which the individual self is cultivated. If intriguers be expelled from court and seductive beauties kept well away, if riches be regarded lightly and the virtue in men be prized, men of worth are thereby encouraged. If high titles together with generous allowances be given to the members of the royal family, if sympathy be shown with their natural likes and dislikes, they are thereby encouraged to family affection. If their departments be enlarged, and they be given full responsibility, ministers of state are thereby encouraged. If an honest confidence be given to them and allowances be on a generous scale, lower ranks of officers are thereby encouraged. If the corvée be used only at the farmer's slack time and the taxes be lightened, the common people are thereby encouraged. If daily and monthly trials of skill be held, and grants of better rations be given on the merit of the work done, the hundred crafts are thereby encouraged. If they be escorted on their return and welcomed on their arrival, if those who are men of merit be entertained and those who are not be given charity, kindness is thereby shown to strangers. If arrangements be made for sacrifices in great families whose line of succession has been broken, and fiefs which have been extinguished be restored, if order be made where anarchy prevails and support be given where there is danger from attack, and if courts be held at stated intervals and a generous bounty be dispensed at their close with a moderate tribute required at their opening, the fervent loyalty of the fief-holders is thereby enlisted. These are the nine basic duties for the men whose function covers the whole Great Society or one of its states. By the practice of these duties and the way in which they work, there is unity.

The Necessity for Unremitting Effort and for Truth and Reality in the Self

In the transaction of business success depends on preparation beforehand: without preparation there will be failure. If you decide beforehand what you are going to say, when the time comes, you will not stutter and stammer; and if you are decided on what you are setting out to do, you will fall into no quandaries. Decide therefore beforehand what conduct should be, and then there will be no regrets: decide beforehand what the Way is, and then there will be no limit to the result. Thus unless those in the higher ranks of society can capture the confidence of those in the lower ranks it is impossible for them to gain the support of the people for their administrative measures. But there is only one way by which this confidence may be captured; for, if friends cannot trust each other, there can be no confidence in the men in the higher ranks. But there is only one way by which friends can come to trust each other; for, if men are not dutiful to their parents, there can be no trust between them as friends. But there is only one way for men to be dutiful to their parents; for, if in rounding in on themselves, they are not true, they cannot be dutiful to their parents. But there is only one way for a man to have a true and real self; for, if he does not understand the good, he cannot be true and real in himself.

Reality in T'ien and Realness in Man

It is the characteristic of T'ien to be the real. It is the characteristic of man to be coming-to-be-real. For a man to be real [i.e. to have achieved realness] is to hit the Mean without effort, to have it without thinking of it, entirely naturally to be centred in the Way. This is to be a sage. To be coming-to-be-real is to choose the good and to hold fast to it. This involves learning all about the good, asking about it, thinking it over carefully, getting it clear by contrast, and faithfully putting it into practice. If there is any part about which he has not learnt or asked questions, which he has not thought over and got clear by contrast, or which he has not put into practice, he sets to work to learn and ask and think and get clear and put into practice. If he does not get the required result, he still does not give up working. When he sees other men succeeding by one effort, or it may be a hundred, he is prepared to add a hundredfold to his own efforts. The man who can last this course, although he is stupid, will come to understand: although he is weak, will become strong.

To be able to proceed from the capacity for realness to understanding is to be ascribed to the nature of man. To proceed from understanding to realness is to be ascribed to instruction in truth. Logically, realness involves understanding and understanding involves realness.

Human Realness in Action: its Power to bring Completion in Development

It is only the man who is entirely real in this world of experience who has the power to give full development to his own nature. If he has that power, it follows that he has the power to give full development to other men's nature. If he has that power, it follows that he has the power to give full development to the natures of the creatures. Thus it is possible for him to be assisting the transforming, nourishing work of T'ien and Earth. That being so, it is possible for him to be part of a trinity of power: T'ien, Earth, and himself.

For, in the second place, with regard to the lopsided man, he can have realness. Assuming there is realness, the inference is that it takes on form. If it takes on form, then it is conspicuous. If conspicuous, then full of light: if full of light, then stirring things: if stirring things, then changing them: if changing them, then transforming them. Thus it is only the man who is entirely real in the world of experience who has the capacity to transform.

Human Realness in Action: the Ability to Foreknow

A characteristic of the entirely real man is that he is able to foreknow. When a country is about to flourish, there are bound to be omens of good. When it is about to perish, there are bound to be omens of evil fortune. These are revealed in the milfoil and the lines on the shell of the tortoise.[10] They affect the four limbs. When disasters or blessings are on the way, the morally good and the morally evil elements in a country are bound to be known first of all. Thus the entirely real man has a likeness to the divine.

Realness again in relation to Completion of Things

Realness is self-completing, and the way of it is to be self-directing. Realness is the end as well as the beginning of things, for without realness there would be no things at all: which is the reason why the true man prizes above everything coming-to-be-real. Realness is not merely a matter of an individual completing himself. It is also that by which things in general are completed. The completing of the individual self involves man-to-man-ness. The completing of things in general involves knowledge. Man-to-man-ness and knowledge are spiritual powers inherent in man, and they are the bridge bringing together the outer and the inner. Hence it is self-evidently right that realness should function continuously.

Realness Transcends the Material

The result is that entire realness never ceases for a moment. Now if that be so, then it must be extended in time: if extended in time, then capable of proof: if capable of proof, then extended in space-length: if extended in length, then extended in area: if extended in area, then extended in height-visibility. And this quality of extension in area is what makes material things supportable from below: this quality of extension in height-visibility is what makes things coverable from above: whilst the extension in time is what makes them capable of completion. Thus area pairs with earth, height-visibility with heaven, and space plus time makes limitlessness. This being its nature, it is not visible and yet clearly visible, does not (deliberately) stir things and yet changes them, takes no action and yet completes them.

o   o   o   o

Tzŭ Ssŭ Links Human Realness to the Spiritual Power of T'ien

It is only the man who is entirely real in his world of men who can make the warp and woof of the great fabric of civilized life, who can establish the great foundations of civilized society, and who can understand the nourishing processes of T'ien and Earth. Can there be any variableness in him? His human-heartedness how insistent! His depth how unfathomable! His superhumanness how overwhelming! Who is there who can comprehend this unless he possess acute intelligence and sagelike wisdom, unless he reach out to the spiritual power of T'ien!

THE GREAT LEARNING

(Ta Hsüeh)

Selections

Theme of the Book

The Way of learning to be great consists in shining with the illustrious power of moral personality, in making a new people, in abiding in the highest goodness. To know one's abiding place leads to fixity of purpose, fixity of purpose to calmness of mind, calmness of mind to serenity of life, serenity of life to careful consideration of means, careful consideration of means to the achievement of the end.

From E. R. Hughes, tr., *The Great Learning and the Mean-in-Action* (New York: E. P. Dutton, 1943). Copyright 1943, 1971 by E. R. Hughes. Reprinted by permission of E. P. Dutton & Co., Inc., and J. M. Dent & Sons Ltd. Headings are those of the translator.

Things have their roots and branches, human affairs their endings as well as beginnings. So to know what comes first and what comes afterwards leads one near to the Way. The men of old who wished to shine with the illustrious power of personality throughout the Great Society, first had to govern their own states efficiently. Wishing to do this, they first had to make an ordered harmony in their own families. Wishing to do this, they first had to cultivate their individual selves. Wishing to do this, they first had to put their minds right. Wishing to do this, they first had to make their purposes genuine. Wishing to do this, they first had to extend their knowledge to the utmost. Such extension of knowledge consists in appreciating the nature of things. For with the appreciation of the nature of things knowledge reaches its height. With the completion of knowledge purposes become genuine. With purposes genuine the mind becomes right. With the mind right the individual self comes into flower. With the self in flower the family becomes an ordered harmony. With the families ordered harmonies the State is efficiently governed. With states efficiently governed the Great Society is at peace.

Thus from the Son of T'ien down to the common people there is unity in this; that for everybody the bringing of the individual self to flower is to be taken as the root. (Since that is so), for the root to be out of order and the branches to be in order is an impossibility. For a man to despise what he should respect and then be respected for having what he despises, is contrary to human experience. This is to be described as knowing the root.

On Knowing the Root

As for what is described as knowing the root, this means the height of knowledge. For in the *Book of Songs* are the words:

> See there, the Ch'i river with its winding course,
> Its bamboos all lush and green!
> Even so our accomplished prince!
> The bone is carved and the ivory polished;
> The jade is cut and granite ground smooth.
> So he, like the music of strings yet with a martial air,
> Stern yet debonair.
> So accomplished a prince,
> Ever to be held in memory.

That "carving and polishing" means learning. That "cutting and grinding" means the cultivation of the self. "Like the music of strings," so he trembles within himself. "Stern yet debonair," so he is the very pattern of majesty. "Ever to be held in memory," so abounding power of personality and the height of goodness are what the common people can never forget. As the *Book of Songs* has it: "How the kings of old are borne in mind." The true man deems worthy those whom they deemed worthy: the common people take pleasure in the pleasures and gain profit from the profits which they made. Thus it is that although he is gone from the world he is not forgotten.

In the *K'ang Kao*[1] it is said: "He has the gifts of illustrious power of personality." In the *T'ai Chia* it is said: "He guards this illustrious charge from T'ien." In the *Ti Tien* it is said: "He has the gifts for shedding lustre on his outstanding power of personality." These three are cases of the self giving lustre.

On King T'ang's[2] bath-tub there was an inscription: "If on one day there may be a renovation, then every day there may be, indeed, daily there must be." So in the *K'ang Kao* it is said: "Making a new people" and in the *Book of Songs* is the saying: "The fief which Chou held was an ancient one, but the mandate from T'ien was new." The true man, therefore, in everything uses his supreme endeavours.

In the *Book of Songs* it is said: "The royal demesne of a thousand *li* is where the people are really at rest." In the *Book of Songs* it is said: "*Mingmang*[3] goes the oriole's song, as it rests on a corner of a mound"; and the Master said: "As to resting, the bird knows where it can rest—is it right for a man to be less than a bird?"

In the *Book of Songs* it is said:

> Hail to King Wên
> And the glorious homage he paid to abiding!
> As a monarch he abode in human-heartedness,
> As a minister he abode in reverence,
> As a son he abode in filial piety,
> As a father he abode in kindness,
> With his fellow countrymen he abode in good faith.

The Master said: "As an arbitrator in men's quarrels I am no better than other men. Inevitably so! If only there could be no cases for arbitration." Then inhuman men would be barred from acting out their (inhuman) contentions, and people's private-mindedness would be greatly checked.

All this means knowing the root.

On Making Purposes Genuine

What is described as "making one's purposes genuine" is as follows. Beware of self-deception. It is to be compared to hating a bad smell and loving a lovely sight; this is what is called self-fulfillment. Thus it is that the true man is sure to be on guard when he is alone. The man who is not true in his privacy has the habit of setting no limit to the badness of his actions. Then when he comes into the presence of a true man he is abashed. He conceals his bad qualities and displays his good. But he gains nothing by doing so, for under these conditions a man sees himself as if he saw his own liver and reins. This means that what is really within will take on form without. That is why the true man is sure to be on guard when he is alone. As Master Tsêng[4] said: "How awe-inspiring must be what many eyes gaze at and many hands point to!" As riches adorn a house, so moral power adorns a man. The mind is enlarged, the limbs are at ease. This is why a true man is sure to make his purposes genuine.

On the Relation of the Rectification of the Mind to Cultivation of the Self

As for the meaning of "the cultivation of the self consists in the recti-fication of the mind," if the self is angry about anything, or frightened, or delighted over anything, or unhappily perturbed about anything, in each case it follows that it cannot get itself right. When the mind is away, we gaze at things and do not see them, sounds come to our ears and we do not hear them, we eat and do not discern the flavours. This is what is meant by "the cultivation of the self consists in the rectification of the mind."

On the Relation of the Cultivation of
the Self to the Bringing of an Ordered Harmony
in the Family

As for the meaning of "the bringing of the members of the family into an ordered harmony consists in cultivating the self," men are prejudiced about those whom they love, prejudiced about those whom they hate, prejudiced about those whom they revere, prejudiced about those whom they pity, prejudiced about those whom they despise. There are very few people in the world who are awake to the evil in the object of their liking and awake to the attractiveness in the object of their dislike. Hence, as the proverb puts it: "Men are not aware of the evil of their sons or of the fertility of their field." This means that there can be no bringing of the members of the family into an ordered harmony unless there is cultivation of the self.

On the Relation between Bringing the
Family into an Ordered Harmony and
the Efficient Ruling of the State

As for the meaning of "the efficient ruling of a State of necessity consists in bringing its families into an ordered harmony," it is not the case that a man can fail in instilling good principles into his own family and, at the same time, succeed in instilling those principles into men outside it. Thus it is that a true man without going outside his family brings good principles into being throughout the country. Filial piety is the means by which the prince is served. Deference to an elder brother is the means by which the elder generation is served. The exercise of parental kindness is the means by which a whole population is influenced. In the *K'ang Kao* it is said: "Act as if you were watching over an infant." If your mind is truly set on your action, although you may miss your mark, you will not go far astray. A young woman has never had to learn to suckle an infant before she gets married.

If one family be human-hearted, human-heartedness will grow in the whole country. If the members of one family give way to each other, the spirit of giving way will grow in the whole country. If one man be incontinently wicked, he will cause anarchy in the whole country. The mechanism of the situation is like that. This means that one remark may throw public business into disorder, or one man may consolidate a country.

It was through being human-hearted that Yao and Shun were the leaders in the Great Society. The people followed their example. It was through being oppressors that Chieh and Chou[5] were the leaders in the Great Society: the people obeyed them. But since the actions they commanded were contrary to what they liked to do themselves, there was no real obedience. Thus it is that what the true man has in himself, that he can require from others: what he has not in himself, that he cannot require from others: there never has been a man who had no store of reciprocity in himself and yet was able to communicate it to other men. Hence the ruling of a state consists in ordered harmony in the family.

In the *Book of Songs* is the saying:

> How charming the peach-tree
> Its leaves thickly massed!
> The bride is coming to her home:
> The bride will rightly order her household.

True! Order your household and then you can teach good principles to influence the nation. In the *Book of Songs* is the saying: "With elder brother's duty done, with younger brother's duty done." True. Fulfil your duties as elder and younger brother, and then you can teach good principles to the nation. In the *Book of Songs* is the saying: "His ways are faultless. He puts the four fiefs to rights." True! The ruler as a father, as a son, as a younger brother, as an elder brother, first rises to the level of being a model, then the people come to be modelled on him. This is the meaning of "the ruling of a state consists in ordered harmony in the family."

On the Relation between the Government of States and Universal Peace

The Way of the Measuring Square

As to the meaning of "the attainment of peace in the Great Society consists in the efficient government of the States," if those in high places treat old age as old age should be treated, the people develop the filial spirit. If those in high places treat their seniors as seniors should be treated, the people develop the younger-brotherly spirit. If they have pity on orphans, the people will not go counter to them. Thus there is for the true man the Way of the Measuring Square. What a man dislikes in those above him, he must not bring to bear on those beneath him. What he dislikes in those beneath him, he must not bring to the service of those above him. What he dislikes in his forebears, he must not do in advance for his descendants. What he would dislike in his descendants, he must not do as following his forebears. The treatment which he dislikes from his neighbours on the right, he must not give to those on the left. The treatment which he dislikes from his neighbours on the left, he must not give to those on the right. This is what is meant by the Way of the Measuring Square.

What Being Father and Mother to the People Entails

In the *Book of Songs* is the saying: "Blessings on our true man, father and mother to his people." To like what the people like and to hate what the people hate, this is the meaning of being father and mother. As in the *Book of Songs*:

> That South Mountain with its beetling crags!
> The height of it before our eyes!
> So the Grand Master
> In his overwhelming might!
> Not one can take his eyes from him.

True! The man with a country in his charge cannot afford not to be cautious. If he leaves that true path, he becomes the world's criminal. Again, as the *Book of Songs* says:

> Before they lost their people's (hearts)
> The Yin[6] kings stood at God's *[Shang Ti]* right hand,
> The Yin kings stand before our eyes (as proof):
> God's high commission is hard to keep.

It is that: win the people, and the country is won: lose the people, and the country is lost. This is why the true man is first concerned with the power of moral personality. Possessing the power in himself, he possesses men. Possessing men, he possesses the soil. Possessing the soil, he possesses wealth. Possessing wealth, he possesses the means of governing.

Power of Personality Is the Root, Wealth Is the Branch

This moral power is the root: wealth is but a branch. If the root be discounted and the branch be prized, there will be quarrelling, and the people will be incited to steal. This is why the people will disperse if the wealth be amassed in the ruler's hands, and why the people will mass round the ruler if the wealth be dispersed among them. And if the ruler's words go forth in injustice it is the reason why injustice will come home to roost. If injustice enters the palace with the produce of the country, injustice will take that produce away. It is said in the *K'ang Kao*: "The mandate of T'ien itself is not irremovable." This means that goodness brings it to a man, and evil takes it away from him.

Human-Heartedness Essential

It is said in the *Book of Ch'u*:[7] "The State of Ch'u has nothing it considers precious except its good men. Them it holds precious." Uncle Fan said: "As exiles there is nothing we count precious, only to be human-hearted to our kin." In the *Ch'in Shih*[8] it is said: "If I have but one minister, a man with no guile in him, having no special skill, but open-hearted and showing this in his demeanour, welcoming another man's skill as if it were his own, in his heart no less than in his speech hailing genius in other men, and thus able to make way for them so that they can protect my descendants and my people—if I have this, how great is the gain. If, however, my minister be jealous of another's skill and go on to hate him: if he thwart the man of genius and block his way to advancement so that he is unable to guard my descendants and my people, how great is the peril." The human-hearted man, he alone can send such a man packing, driving him out among the barbarian tribes, refusing to have him living alongside in the Middle Kingdom.[9] This is the meaning of "only the human-hearted man can love men, only he can hate men." You may discover a man of worth and be unable to employ him, that is fate. But to discover a bad man to be in office and be unable to remove and banish him; that is your own fault. For to love what men hate and to hate what men love, this is an outrage on human nature, and disaster inevitably falls on such an individual. Thus it is that the true man has a supremely right Way. With devotion and good faith he is sure to succeed in it. With arrogance and dissipation, he is sure to fail.

On the National Scale Justice is Gain

For the creation of wealth there is a supremely right Way. If those who create the wealth be many, those who consume it few, and if the accumulating departments be zealous, the spending departments economical, then there will be a permanent sufficiency of wealth.

For the human-hearted man wealth is the means by which the individual self is expanded. For the non-human-hearted man the individual is a tool for the expansion of wealth. There never has been a case in which those in high places were devoted to human-heartedness and those beneath them were not devoted to justice. There never has been a case in which there was devotion to justice and state affairs failed of completion. There never has been a case in which in these circumstances there was opposition to the wealth being in the Government's storehouses.

Mêng Hsien Tzŭ[10] said: "If you have the status of keeping a horse and carriage, you do not keep a check on fowls and pigs. The great family with its stores of ice does not tend sheep and cattle." So also the great house of a hundred chariots does not keep a special officer for collecting taxes. With such an officer, in what way is it better than employing a robbing expert? This means that on the national scale it is not gain that is gain, but justice. The man at the head of a country's administration who is only concerned with wealth and expenditure is himself a base fellow. He may think he is doing good, but his ways of getting things done are those of a base fellow. Calamity from T'ien and injury from men both ensue, and although there may be good men in the country, they can do nothing to stop this. This means that on the national scale gain is not gain: justice is gain.

THE CONDUCT OF
THE SCHOLAR

(Li Chi: Ju Hsing P'ien)

Selections

The Conduct of the Scholar (Ju[1])

1. Duke Ai of Lu[2] asked Confucius, saying, "Is not the dress, Master, which you wear that of the scholar?"[3] Confucius replied, "When I was little, I lived in Lu, and wore the garment with large sleeves; when I was grown up, I lived in Sung, and was then capped with the *kang-fu* cap. I have heard that the studies of the scholar are extensive, but his dress is

From James Legge, tr., *Ju hsing, Conduct of the Scholar*, in *Sacred Books of the East*, vol. 28, *The Lî Kî*.

that of the state from which he sprang. I do not know any dress of the scholar."

2. The duke said, "Allow me to ask what is the conduct of the scholar." Confucius replied, "If I were to enumerate the points in it summarily, I could not touch upon them all; if I were to go into details on each, it would take a long time. You would have changed all your attendants-in-waiting before I had concluded." The duke ordered a mat to be placed for him,[4] and Confucius took his place by his side.

3. He then said, "The scholar has a precious gem[5] placed upon its mat, with which he is waiting to receive an invitation from some ruler; early and late he studies with energy, waiting to be questioned. He carries in his bosom loyal-heartedness and good faith, waiting to be raised to office; he is vigorous in all his doings, waiting to be chosen to employment: so does he establish his character and prepare himself for the future.

4. "The scholar's garments and cap are all fitting and becoming; he is careful in his undertakings and doings: in declining great compliments he might seem to be rude, and in regard to small compliments, hypocritical; in great matters he has an air of dignity, and in small matters, of modesty; he seems to have a difficulty in advancing, but retires with ease and readiness; and he has a shrinking appearance, as if wanting in power: such is he in his external appearance.

5. "The scholar, wherever he resides, ordinarily or only for a time, is grave as if he were apprehensive of difficulties; when seated or on foot, he is courteous and respectful; in speaking, his object is, first of all, to be sincere; in acting, he wishes to be exact and correct; on the road, he does not strive about the most difficult or easiest places; in winter and summer, he does not strive about the temperature, the light and shade; he guards against death that he may be in waiting for whatever he may be called to; he attends well to his person that he may be ready for action: such are his preparations and precautions for the future.

6. "The scholar does not consider gold and jade to be precious treasures, but loyal-heartedness and good faith; he does not desire lands and territory, but considers the establishment of righteousness as his domain; he does not desire a great accumulation of wealth, but looks on many accomplishments as his riches; it is difficult to win him, but easy to pay him; it is easy to pay him, but difficult to retain him. As he will not show himself when the time is not proper for him to do so, is it not dif-

ficult to win him? As he will have no fellowship with what is not right-eous, is it not difficult to retain him? As he must first do the work, and then take the pay, is it not easy to pay him? Such are the conditions of his close association with others.

7. "Though there may be offered to the scholar valuable articles and wealth, and though it be tried to enervate him with delights and pleas-ures, he sees those advantages without doing anything contrary to his sense of righteousness; though a multitude may attempt to force him from his standpoint, and his way be stopped by force of arms, he will look death in the face without changing the principles which he main-tains; he would face birds and beasts of prey with their talons and wings, without regard to their fierceness; he would undertake to raise the heavi-est tripod, without regard to his strength; he has no occasion to regret what he has done in the past, nor to make preparations for what may come to him in the future; he does not repeat any error of speech; any rumours against him he does not pursue up to their source; he does not allow his dignity to be interrupted; he does not dread to practise before-hand the counsels which he gives: such are the things in which he stands out and apart from other men.

8. "With the scholar friendly relations may be cultivated, but no at-tempt must be made to constrain him; near association with him can be sought, but cannot be forced on him; he may be killed, but he cannot be disgraced; in his dwelling he will not be extravagant; in his eating and drinking he will not be luxurious; he may be gently admonished of his errors and failings, but he should not have them enumerated to him to his face: such is his boldness and determination.

9. "The scholar considers loyal-heartedness and good faith to be his coat-of-mail and helmet; propriety and righteousness to be his shield and buckler; he walks along, bearing aloft over his head benevolence; he dwells, holding righteousness in his arms before him; the government may be violently oppressive, but he does not change his course: such is the way in which he maintains himself.

10. "The scholar may have a house in only [a small plot] of ground— a poor dwelling each of whose surrounding walls is only ten paces long, with an outer door of thorns and bamboos, and openings in the wall, long and pointed; within, the inner door stopped up by brushwood, and little round windows[6] like the mouth of a jar; the inmates may have to exchange garments when they go out; they may have to make one day's

food serve for two days; if the ruler respond to him, he does not dare to have any hesitation in accepting office; if he do not respond, he does not have recourse to flattery: such is he in the matter of taking office, however small.

11. "The scholar lives and has his associations with men of the present day, but the men of antiquity are the subjects of his study. Following their principles and example in the present age, he will become a pattern in future ages. If it should be that his own age does not understand and encourage him, that those above him do not bring him, and those below him do not push him, forward, or even that calumniators and flatterers band together to put him in danger, his person may be placed in peril, but his aim cannot be taken from him. Though danger may threaten him in his undertakings and wherever he is, he will still pursue his aim, and never forget the afflictions of the people, which he would relieve: such is the anxiety which he cherishes.

12. "The scholar learns extensively, but never allows his researches to come to an end; he does what he does with all his might, but is never weary; he may be living unnoticed, but does not give way to licentiousness; he may be having free course in his acknowledged position, but is not hampered by it; in his practice of ceremonial usages he shows the value which he sets on a natural ease; in the excellence of his loyalheartedness and good faith, he acts under the law of a benignant playfulness; he shows his fond regard for men of virtue and ability, and yet is forbearing and kind to all; he is like a potter who breaks his square mould, and his tiles are found to fit together: such is the largeness and generosity of his spirit.

13. "The scholar recommends members of his own family to public employment, without shrinking from doing so, because of their kinship, and proposes others beyond it, without regard to their being at enmity with him; he estimates men's merits, and takes into consideration all their services, selecting those of virtue and ability, and putting them forward, without expecting any recompense from them; the ruler thus gets what he wishes, and if benefit results to the state, the scholar does not seek riches or honours for himself: such is he in promoting the employment of the worthy and bringing forward the able.

14. "The scholar when he hears what is good, tells it to his friends, and when he sees what is good, shows it to them; in the view of rank and position, he gives the precedence to them over himself; if they encounter

calamities and hardships, he is prepared to die with them; if they are long in getting advancement, he waits for them; if they are far off, he brings them together with himself: such is he in the employment and promotion of his friends.

15. "The scholar keeps his person free from stain, and continually bathes and refreshes his virtue; he sets forth what he has to say to his superior by way of admonition, but remains himself in the background, trying thus quietly to correct him; if his superior do not acknowledge his advice, he more proudly and clearly makes his views known, but still does not press them urgently; he does not go among those who are low to make himself out to be high, nor place himself among those who have little wisdom to make himself out to have much; in a time of good government, he does not think little of what he himself can do; in a time of disorder, he does not allow his course to be obstructed; he does not hastily agree with those who think like himself, nor condemn those who think differently: so does he stand out alone among others and take his own solitary course.

16. "The scholar sometimes will not take the high office of being a minister of the Son of T'ien, nor the lower office of serving the prince of a state; he is watchful over himself in his retirement, and values a generous enlargement of mind, while at the same time he is bold and resolute in his intercourse with others; he learns extensively that he may know whatever should be done; he makes himself acquainted with elegant accomplishments, and thus smoothes and polishes all his corners and angles; although the offer were made to share a state with him, it would be no more to him than the small weights of a balance; he will not take a ministry, he will not take an office: such are the rules and conduct he prescribes to himself.

17. "The scholar has those with whom he agrees in aim, and pursues the same objects, with whom he cultivates the same course, and that by the same methods; when they stand on the same level with him, he rejoices in them; if their standing be below his, he does not tire of them; if for long he has not seen them, and hears rumours to their prejudice, he does not believe them; his actions are rooted in correctness, and his standing is in what is right; if they proceed in the same direction with him, he goes forward with them, if not in the same direction, he withdraws from them: so is he in his intercourse with his friends.

18. "Gentleness and goodness are the roots of humanity; respect and

attention are the ground on which it stands; generosity and large-mind-edness are the manifestation of it; humility and courtesy are the ability of it; the rules of ceremony are the demonstration of it; speech is the or-nament of it; singing and music are the harmony of it; sharing and dis-tribution are the giving of it. The scholar possesses all these qualities in union and has them, and still he will not venture to claim a perfect hu-manity on account of them: such is the honour he feels for its ideal, and the humility with which he declines it for himself.

19. "The scholar is not cast down, or cut from his root, by poverty and mean condition; he is not elated or exhausted by riches and noble condi-tion; he feels no disgrace that rulers and kings may try to inflict; he is above the bonds that elders and superiors may try to impose; and supe-rior officers cannot distress him. Hence he is styled a scholar. Those to whom the multitude nowadays give that name have no title to it, and they constantly employ it to one another as a term of reproach."

When Confucius came from his wanderings to Lu to his own house, Duke Ai gave him a public lodging. When the duke heard these words, he became more sincere in his speech, and more righteous in his con-duct. He said, "To the end of my days I will not presume to make a jest of the name of scholar."

12

Mo Tzǔ

I pull with love and push with respect.
—*Mo Tzǔ*, 13:49

Mo Tzǔ (c. 470–c. 391 B.C.) was born shortly after Confucius's death and died not long before Mencius's birth. In that interim he mounted a full-scale ideological attack against Confucianism. Up to the beginning of the Han Empire, the two greatest philosophical contenders were not Confucianism and Taoism but Confucianism and Mo-ism. Mo Tzǔ's three hundred or so followers had the reputation of ascetics; they wore coarse garments and walked in sandals, and would go through a wall of fire to help their cause. Their master, Mencius said, would wear his head and heels off to help the world. So strong was the movement and so zealous its followers that Mencius was afraid Mo-ism was to be the wave of the future. Instead, after the third century B.C. the important Mo-ist doctrines seemed to have fallen by the wayside, not to be helped to their feet until some twentieth-century European writers thought they saw in Mo Tzǔ's T'ien of universal love a resemblance to the New Testament God of Love.

Many have wondered why Mo-ism all but disappeared. Perhaps Mencius's merciless attacks on the man and the movement took a fatal toll. It is more plausible that Mencius's vigorous and positive Confucianist position contributed to the downfall of rival doctrines. The turning of Confucianism into a state cult by the Han emperors may also have discouraged the remnants of Mo Tzǔ's following. More likely, Mo-ist doctrine had less support in popular religious belief and practice of the time than did the religiously more conservative Confucianism. It is also possible that many of Mo Tzǔ's students lost their lives in the wars that led to the domination of the state of Chin and its rise to become the First Empire. Mo Tzŭ's condemnation of war was the most uncompromising among all Chinese philosophies. Neither he nor his followers stopped at mere verbal condemnation: they became experts in defensive warfare and carried their doctrine with them when, as military engineers, they entered the thick of the fray.

Like other philosophers of the times, Mo Tzŭ spent a number of years as a roaming political counselor. Never given the opportunity to put his teachings into practice or the world in order, he eventually had to rest content with conducting a school and preparing his disciples for public office.

Universal love is the keystone of Mo Tzŭ's teaching. He exhorted everyone to regard the welfare of others as one regarded one's own. He was convinced that the practice of universal love would bring peace to the world and happiness to man, and he took pains to demonstrate that the principle of universal love was grounded simultaneously in its practicability on earth and its divine sanction from T'ien. Universal love for Mo Tzŭ was at once the way of man and the way of T'ien.

The will of T'ien was to be obeyed by man and held as the standard of human thought and action. T'ien loved all men, and it was the will of T'ien that men should love one another.

Another distinctive characteristic of Mo Tzŭ's thought was its stress on methodology. "Some standard of judgment must be established," he declared. "To make a proposition without regard for standard is like determining the directions of sunrise and sunset on a revolving potter's wheel." He attached great importance to the tests of evidence and standards he had devised and which he would apply to all propositions, the political included.

He left a work consisting supposedly of seventy-one chapters, of which eighteen are now lost. Parts of the work seem to be versions written and reworked by members of the later Mo-ist school.

From his words themselves, from his writing style, he starts as an originator. He offers not sayings but essays, each built around a theme. Expository, orderly prose takes over from sayings and anecdotes. Humor, sarcasm, caricature are all part of his freer style. There is much repetition, but there also is great tenseness and a staccato logic. One feels the force of an iconoclast.

THE *MO TZŬ*

Selections

Book *1*

Chapter 5. The Seven Causes of Anxiety

o   o   o   o

The history of Hsia[1] says that the Deluge lasted seven years in the time of Yü and the history of Yin tells that a drought visited T'ang for five years. These are the extremes of disasters. Yet the people were not frozen or starved. Why was this so? The reason lies in diligent produc-

From Yi-pao Mei, tr., *The Ethical and Political Works of Motse* (London: Probsthain, 1934).

tion and thrifty consumption. Therefore, famine and dearth cannot be prepared against unless there are stored grains in the granaries, and justice cannot be maintained against the unjust unless there are ready weapons in the armoury. One cannot defend himself unless the inner and the outer city walls are in repair, and one cannot meet emergencies unless his ideas are well thought out. Thus Ch'ing Chi[2] was unprepared, and he should not have set out on the journey. Chieh[3] made no preparations against T'ang and he was sent to exile. And Chou made no preparations against Wu and he was executed. Now, Chieh and Chou were both emperors in rank and possessed the whole empire, yet they both perished at the hands of rulers of states of only a hundred *li* square. What is the reason for this? Because they depended on their rank and wealth and made no preparations. Therefore, preparation is what a country should emphasize. Supply is the treasure of a country, armament its claws, and the city walls are the stronghold of its self-defence. And these three items are the essentials to the existence of a state.

The present rulers squander great amounts of wealth to reward the undeserving, empty the treasury to acquire carriages and horses, exhaust the labourers to build palaces and furnish amusements. Upon their death, again, thick coffins and many coats and fur coats are to be furnished. Porches and pavilions are built for them while they are living, and tombs when they are dead. By this the people are embittered and the treasury is left lean. While the amusements are not yet satisfying to the superiors, the hardship already becomes unbearable for the subjects. Such a state will fall under any attack and such people will perish by famine. And all this is due to the absence of preparation. Moreover, food is what the sages treasured. The history of Chou says: "Without three years' food in store a state cannot be a state as it is in danger of losing its sovereignty. A family being without food in store to be sufficient for three years its children cannot be its children who are in danger of being abandoned or sold to others." Such, then, is the preparation of a country.

o o o o

Book 2

Chapter 8. Exaltation of the Virtuous (1)

o   o   o   o

Therefore in administering the government, the ancient sage-kings ranked the morally excellent high and exalted the virtuous. If capable, even a farmer or an artisan would be employed—commissioned with high rank, remunerated with liberal emoluments, trusted with important charges, and empowered to issue final orders. For, if his rank were not high, people would not respect him; if his emoluments were not liberal, people would not have confidence in him; if his orders were not final, people would not stand in awe before him. To place these three honours upon the virtuous is not so much to reward virtue, as to bring about the success of the enterprise of government. Therefore ranks should be standardized according to virtue, tasks assigned according to office, and rewards given according to labour spent. When emoluments are distributed in proportion to achievements, officials cannot be in constant honour, and people in eternal humility. If a person is capable promote him, if incapable, lower his rank. Give prominence to public approval and keep back private grudges in the matter of selecting men. Here, then, is the principle.

o   o   o   o

Chapter 9. Exaltation of the Virtuous (2)

o   o   o   o

Now, who were those that, possessing wealth and position, still strove after virtues and were rewarded? They were the sage-kings of the Three Dynasties,[4] namely, Yao, Shun, Yü, T'ang, Wên, and Wu. How were they rewarded? When they governed the empire, they loved all the people universally and benefited them, and led them in doing honour to T'ien and service to the spirits. As they loved and benefited the people, T'ien and the spirits rewarded them, appointing them to be Sons of T'ien, and parents of the people. And, thereupon people praised them, calling them sage-kings even unto this day. These then were those that, possessing wealth and position, still strove after virtues and were rewarded. Now, who were those that, possessing wealth and position, yet practised evil and were punished? They were the wicked kings of the Three Dynasties, namely, Chieh, Chou Yu, and Li.[5] How do we know they were those? When they governed the empire they disliked all the people inclusively and oppressed them and led them to curse T'ien and the spirits. Oppressing and destroying the people, they were punished by T'ien and the spirits; their corpses were mangled and lacerated, their children and grandchildren were scattered and dispersed, their family hearths were extinguished and descendants exterminated. And, thereupon the people railed at them, calling them wicked kings even unto this day. These, then, are those that, possessing wealth and position, yet practised evil and were punished.

o   o   o   o

Chapter 10. Exaltation of the Virtuous (3)

o   o   o   o

The gentlemen of today all exalt the virtuous in their private speech and conduct. But when it comes to the administration of the government for the public, they fail to exalt the virtuous and employ the capable. Then I know the gentlemen understand only trifles and not things of significance.

How do I know it is so?

Suppose the ruler had a cow or a sheep which he could not have killed, he would surely look for a skilful butcher. Or if he wanted a garment which he could not have made, he would surely look for a skilful tailor. For these, the ruler would not employ his relatives, the rich without merit, and the good-looking, because he knew clearly they were incapable. He was afraid they would spoil the things to be attended to. So, in these, the rulers do not fail to exalt the virtuous and employ the capable. Again, if the ruler had a sick horse that he would not have cured, he would surely look for an experienced veterinary doctor. Of if he had a tight bow which he could not draw, he would surely look for a skilful workman. For these, the ruler would not employ his relatives, the rich without merit, and the good-looking, because he knew clearly they were incapable. He was afraid they would spoil the things to be attended to. So, in these matters the rulers do not fail to exalt the virtuous and employ the capable. But when it comes to the affairs of the state all is different. The relations of the rulers, the rich without merit, and the good-looking are all promoted. Then does it not seem that the rulers love their states not even as much as they love a tight bow, a sick horse, a garment, or a cow or a sheep? Therefore I know the gentlemen of the world understand only trifles and not things of significance. This is like trying to make messengers of the dumb and musical directors of the deaf.

To the contrary, in governing the empire the sage-kings of old enriched and honoured those who were not necessarily their relatives, the rich without merit, or the good-looking.

o   o   o   o

Book 3

Chapter 11. Identification with the Superior (1)

o   o   o   o

Mo Tzŭ said: In the beginning of human life, when there was yet no law and government, the custom was "everybody according to his own idea." Accordingly each man had his own idea, two men had two different ideas, and ten men had ten different ideas—the more people the more different notions. And everybody approved of his own view and disapproved the views of others, and so arose mutual disapproval among men. As a result, father and son and elder and younger brothers became enemies and were estranged from each other, since they were unable to reach any agreement. Everybody worked for the disadvantage of the others with water, fire, and poison. Surplus energy was not spent for mutual aid; surplus goods were allowed to rot without sharing; excellent teachings were kept secret and not revealed. The disorder in the human world could be compared to that among birds and beasts. Yet all this disorder was due to the want of a ruler.

Therefore [T'ien] ⁶ chose the virtuous in the world and crowned him the Son of T'ien. Feeling the insufficiency of his capacity, the Son of T'ien chose the virtuous in the world and installed them as the three ministers. Seeing the vastness of the empire and the difficulty of attending to matters of right and wrong and profit and harm among peoples of far countries, the three ministers divided the empire into feudal states and assigned them to feudal lords. Feeling the insufficiency of their capacity, the feudal lords, in turn, chose the virtuous of their states and appointed them as their officials. When the rulers were all installed, the Son of T'ien issued a mandate to all the people, saying: "Upon hearing good or evil one shall report it to a superior. What the superior thinks to be right all shall think to be right; what the superior thinks to be wrong all shall think to be wrong. When the superior is at fault there shall be good counsel, when the subordinates show virtue there shall be popular recommendation. To identify one's self with the superior and not to unite one's self with the subordinates—this is what deserves encouragement from above and praise from below. On the other hand, if upon hearing good or evil one should not report to a superior; if what the superior thought to be right one should not think to be right; if what the superior thought to be wrong one should not think to be wrong; if when the superior was at fault there should be no good counsel; if when the subordinates showed virtue there should be no popular recommendation; if there should be common cause with subordinates and no identification with the superior—this is what deserves punishment from above and condemnation from below." The superior made this the basis of reward and punishment. He was clear-sighted and won his people's confidence.

Now, how is order brought about in the empire? There was order in the empire because the Son of T'ien could unify the standards in the empire. If, however, the people all identify themselves with the Son of T'ien but not with T'ien itself, then the jungle is still unremoved. Now, the frequent visitations of hurricanes and torrents are just the punishments from T'ien upon the people for their not identifying their standards with the Will of T'ien. Therefore, Mo Tzŭ said: The sage-kings of old devised the five punishments to rule the people in order to be able to lay hands on those who did not identify themselves with their superiors—a device of the same nature as threads are tied into skeins and a net is controlled by a main rope.

o   o   o   o

Chapter 12. Identification with the Superior (2)

o   o   o   o

But to carry the process of identification with the superior up to the Son of T'ien and not further up to T'ien itself—then the jungle from

T'ien is yet removed. Thereupon T'ien would send down cold and heat without moderation, and snow, frost, rain, and dew untimely. As a result, the five grains[7] could not ripen and the six animals[8] could not mature; and there would be disease, epidemics, and pestilence. Now the repeated visitations of hurricanes and torrents are just punishments from T'ien—punishments to the people below for not identifying themselves with it. Therefore the sage-kings of old appreciated what T'ien and the spirits desire and avoided what they abominate, in order to increase benefits and to avoid calamities in the world. With purification and baths and clean wine and cakes they led the people to make sacrifice and libation to T'ien and the spirits. In such services to the spirits they dared not use wine and cakes that were unclean, sacrificial animals that were not fat, or jade and silk that did not satisfy the standard requirements[9] The proper time for the spring and autumn sacrifices they dared not miss. Judging lawsuits, they dared not be unjust. Distributing properties, they dared not be unfair. Even when at leisure they dared not be disrespectful. When the sage-kings made such good rulers, T'ien and the spirits commended their leadership from above, and the people cherished it from below. To work under the hearty approval of the T'ien and the spirits is to obtain their blessings. To work under the appreciation of the people is to obtain their confidence. Administering the government like this, consequently they would succeed in planning, accomplish their ends in executing, be strong in defence and victorious in attack. And the reason for all this lies in their employing the principle of Identification with the Superior in government. And this is how the sage-kings of old administered their government.

o   o   o   o

Hence the installing of the ruler in the ancient days was intended to govern the people. Just as there is one thread to hold together the others in a skein and a main rope to a fishing net, so the ruler is to hold together all the evil and wicked in the empire and bring their purposes into harmony with their superiors. Thus "Hsang Nien," [10] among the books of the ancient kings, says: "Now the empire is established and the capital is located: [T'ien] installed the Son of T'ien, kings, and lords not in order to make them proud, and [T'ien] appointed the ministers and the officials not in order to make them idle—it was to apportion duties among them and charge them with the maintenance of the justice of T'ien." This is to say that when Shang Ti and the spirits in the past established the capital and installed the rulers, it was not to make their ranks high, and their emoluments substantial, and to give them wealth and honour, and let them live in comfort and free of care. It was really to procure benefits and eliminate adversities for the people, and to enrich the poor and increase the few, and to bring safety where there is danger and to restore order where there is confusion—it was for this that the political leaders were appointed. And so the ancient sage-kings administered their government accordingly.

The lords at the present, however, do just the reverse. Administration is carried on to court flattery. Fathers and brothers and other relatives and friends are placed at the right and left and appointed rulers of the people. Knowing that the superior appointed the rulers not for the welfare of the people, the people all kept aloof and would not identify themselves with the superior. Therefore purposes of the superior and the subordinates are not unified. This being so, rewards and commendations would not encourage the people to do good, and punishments and fines would not restrain them from doing evil.

How do we know this would be so?

In governing the country, the ruler proclaims: "Whoever deserves reward I will reward." Suppose the purposes of the superior and the subordinates are different, whoever is rewarded by the superior would be condemned by the public. And in community life the condemnation of the public is supreme. Though there is reward from the superior, it will not be an encouragement. In governing the country, again, the ruler proclaims: "Whoever deserves punishment I will punish." Suppose the purposes of the superior and the subordinates are different, whoever is punished by the superior would be applauded by the public. And in community life the approval of the public is supreme. Though there is punishment from the superior, it will not be an obstruction. Now, in governing the country and ruling the people, if rewards cannot encourage the people to do good and punishments cannot restrain them from doing evil, is this not just the same as in the beginning of human life when there were no rulers? If it is the same with rulers or without them, it is not the way to govern the people and unify the multitude.

o   o   o   o

Therefore, if there was a virtuous man thousands of *li* away, though his clansmen did not all know it and people in the same district did not all know it, the Son of T'ien could reward him. And if there was an evil man thousands of *li* away, though his clansmen did not all know it and people in the same village did not all know it, the Son of T'ien could punish him. Thereupon all the people in the world were astonished, and carefully avoided doing evil, saying: "The Son of T'ien is like a spirit in his hearing and sight." But the ancient kings said: "It was no spirit but only the ability to make use of others' ears and eyes to help one's own hearing and sight, to make use of others' lips to help one's own speech, to make use of others' minds to help one's own thought, to make use of others' limbs to help one's own actions." When there are many to help one's hearing and sight then of course one can hear and see far; when there are many to help one's speech then one's good counsel can comfort many; when there are many to help one's thought then one's plans can be shaped speedily; when there are many to help one's actions then one can accomplish one's undertaking quickly. So there was no other reason for the success and great fame of the ancient sages than that they could carry out the principle of Identification with the Superior in their administration.

o   o   o   o

Chapter 13. Identification with the Superior (3)

Mo Tzŭ said: The interest of the wise ruler lies in carrying out what makes for order among the people and avoiding what makes for confusion.

But what is it that makes for order among the people?

When the administration of the ruler answers to the desires of the people there will be order, otherwise there will be confusion.

How do we know it is so?

When the administration of the ruler answers to the desires of the subjects, it manifests an understanding of the approvals and disapprovals of the people. When there is such an understanding, the good will be discovered and rewarded and the bad will be discovered and punished, and the country will surely have order. When the administration of the ruler does not answer to the desires of the subjects, it shows a lack of understanding of the approvals and disapprovals of the subjects. When there is no such understanding then the good will not be discovered and rewarded and the bad will not be discovered and punished. With the good unrewarded and the evil unpunished, such a government will surely put the country into disorder. Therefore when rewards and punishments do not answer to the desires of the people, the matter has to be carefully looked into.

But how can the desires of the people (being so many and various) be met?

Therefore Mo Tzŭ said: It can be done only by adopting the principle of Identification with the Superior in government.

o   o   o   o

Therefore Identification with the Superior as a principle can govern the empire when used by the Son of T'ien, it can govern the state when used by the feudal lord, and it can govern the clan when used by the clan patriarch. To be found not wanting when used on a large scale to govern the empire, and not useless when employed on a small scale to govern a clan—this is said of such a principle. Hence the proverb: "To govern the world-empire is the same as to rule a single family clan; to command all the people in the world is the same as to order a single individual."

o   o   o   o

Therefore Mo Tzŭ said: Whoever orders his people to identify themselves with their superior must love them dearly. For the people will not obey orders except when they are ordered with love and held in confidence. Lead them with wealth and honour ahead, and push them with just punishments from behind. When government is carried on like this, even though I wanted to have someone not to identify himself with me, it would be impossible.

o   o   o   o

Book 4

Chapter 16. Universal Love (3)

Mo Tzŭ said: The purpose of the magnanimous lies in procuring benefits for the world and eliminating its calamities. Now among all the current calamities, which are the most important? The attack on the small states by the large ones, disturbances of the small houses by the large ones, oppression of the weak by the strong, misuse of the few by the many, deception of the simple by the cunning, disdain towards the humble by the honoured—these are the misfortunes in the empire. Again, the lack of grace on the part of the ruler, the lack of loyalty on the part of the ruled, the lack of affection on the part of the father, the lack of filial piety on the part of the son—these are further calamities in the empire. Also, the mutual injury and harm which the unscrupulous do to one another with weapons, poison, water, and fire is still another calamity in the empire.

When we come to think about the cause of all these calamities, how have they arisen? Have they arisen out of love of others and benefiting others? Of course we should say no. We should say they have arisen out of hate of others and injuring others. If we should classify one by one all those who hate others and injure others, should we find them to be universal in love or partial? Of course we should say they are partial. Now, since partiality against one another is the cause of the major calamities in the empire, then partiality is wrong.

Mo Tzŭ continued: Whoever criticizes others must have something to replace them. Criticism without suggestion is like trying to stop flood with flood and put out fire with fire. It will surely be without worth.

Mo Tzŭ said: Partiality is to be replaced by universality. But how is it that partiality can be replaced by universality? Now, when everyone regards the states of others as he regards his own, who would attack the others' states? Others are regarded like self. When everyone regards the capitals of others as he regards his own, who would seize the others' capitals? Others are regarded like self. When everyone regards the houses of others as he regards his own, who would disturb the others' houses? Others are regarded like self. Now, when the states and cities do not attack and seize each other and when the clans and individuals do not disturb and harm one another—is this a calamity or a benfit to the world? Of course it is a benefit. When we come to think about the several benefits in regard to their cause, how have they arisen? Have they arisen out of hate of others and injuring others? Of course we should say no. We should say they have arisen out of love of others and benefiting others. If we should classify one by one all those who love others and benefit others, should we find them to be partial or universal? Of course we should say they are universal. Now, since universal love is the cause of the major benefits in the world, therefore Mo Tzŭ proclaims universal love is right.

And, as has already been said, the interest of the magnanimous lies in procuring benefits for the world and eliminating its calamities. Now that we have found out the consequences of universal love to be the major benefits of the world and the consequences of partiality to be the major calamities in the world; this is the reason why Mo Tzŭ said partiality is wrong and universality is right. When we try to develop and procure benefits for the world with universal love as our standard, then attentive ears and keen eyes will respond in service to one another, then limbs will be strengthened to work for one another, and those who know the *Tao*[11] will untiringly instruct others. Thus the old and those who have neither wife nor children will have the support and supply to spend their old age with, and the young and weak and orphans will have the care and admonition to grow up in. When universal love is adopted as the standard, then such are the consequent benefits. It is incomprehensible, then, why people should object to universal love when they hear it.

Yet the objection is not all exhausted. It is asked: "It may be a good thing, but can it be of any use?"

Mo Tzŭ replied: If it were not useful then even I would disapprove of it. But how can there be anything that is good but not useful? Let us consider the matter from both sides. Suppose there are two men. Let one of them hold to partiality and the other to universality. Then the advocate of partiality would say to himself, how can I take care of my friend as I do of myself, how can I take care of his parents as my own? Therefore when he finds his friend hungry he would not feed him, and when he finds him cold he would not clothe him. In his illness he would not minister to him, and when he is dead he would not bury him. Such is the word and such is the deed of the advocate of partiality. The advocate of universality is quite unlike this both in word and in deed. He would say to himself, I have heard that to be a superior man one should take care of his friend as he does of himself, and take care of his friend's parents as his own. Therefore when he finds his friend hungry he would feed him, and when he finds him cold he would clothe him. In his sickness he would serve him, and when he is dead he would bury him. Such is the word and such is the deed of the advocate of universality.

These two persons then are opposed to each other in word and also in deed. Suppose they are sincere in word and decisive in deed so that their word and deed are made to agree like the two parts of a tally, and that there is no word but what is realized in deed, then let us consider further: Suppose a war is on, and one is in armour and helmet ready to join the force, life and death are not predictable. Or suppose one is commissioned a deputy by the ruler to such far countries like Pa, Yüeh, Ch'i, and Ching,[12] and the arrival and return are quite uncertain. Now under such circumstances, let us inquire upon whom would one lay the trust of one's family and parents. Would it be upon the universal friend or upon the partial friend? It seems to me, on occasions like these, there are no fools in the world. Even if he is a person who objects to universal love, he will lay the trust upon the universal friend all the same. This is verbal objection to the principle but actual selection by it—this is self-contradiction between one's word and deed. It is incomprehensible, then, why people should object to universal love when they hear it.

Yet the objection is not all exhausted. It is objected:

Maybe it is a good criterion to choose among ordinary men, but it may not apply to the rulers.

Let us again consider the matter from both sides. Suppose there are two rulers. Let one of them hold partiality and the other universality. Then the partial ruler would say to himself, How can I take care of the people as I do of myself? This would be quite contrary to common sense. A man's life on earth is of short duration, it is like a galloping horse passing by. Therefore when he finds his people hungry he would not feed them, and when he finds them cold he would not clothe them. When they are sick he would not minister to them, and upon their death he would not bury them. Such is the word and such is the deed of the partial ruler. The universal ruler is quite unlike this both in word and in deed. He would say to himself, I have heard that to be an upright ruler of the world one should first attend to his people and then to himself. Therefore when he finds his people hungry he would feed them, and when he finds them cold he would clothe them. In their sickness he would minister to them, and upon their death he would bury them. Such is the word and such is the deed of the universal ruler.

These two rulers, then, are opposed to each other in word and also in deed. Suppose they are sincere in word and decisive in deed so that their word and deed are made to agree like the two parts of a tally, and that there is no word but what is realized in deed, then let us consider further: Suppose, now, that there is a disastrous pestilence, that most people are in misery and privation, and that many lie dead in ditches. Under such circumstances, let us inquire, if a person could choose one of the two rulers, which would he prefer? It seems to me on such occasions there are no fools in the world. Even if he is a person who objects to universal love, he will choose the universal ruler. This is verbal objection to the principle but actual selection by it—this is self-contradiction between one's word and deed. It is incomprehensible, then, why people should object to universal love when they hear it.

Yet the objection is still not exhausted. It points out that universal love may be magnanimous and righteous, but how can it be realized? Universal love is impracticable just as carrying Mount T'ai[13] and leaping over rivers. So, then, universal love is but a pious wish, how can it be actualized?

Mo Tzŭ replied: To carry Mount T'ai and leap over rivers is something that has never been accomplished since the existence of man. But universal love and mutual aid has been personally practised by six ancient sage-kings.

How do we know they have done it?

Mo Tzŭ said: I am no contemporary of theirs, neither have I heard their voice or seen their faces. The sources of our knowledge lie in what is written on the bamboos and silk, what is engraved in metal and stones, and what is cut in the vessels to be handed down to posterity.[14]

o   o   o   o

Yet the objection is still not exhausted. It raises the question, when one does not think in terms of benefits and harm to one's parents would it be filial piety?

Mo Tzŭ replied: Now let us inquire about the plans of the filial sons for their parents. I may ask, when they plan for their parents, whether they desire to have others love or hate them. Judging from the whole doctrine of filial piety, it is certain that they desire to have others love their parents. Now, what should I do first in order to attain this? Should I first love others' parents in order that they would love my parents in return, or should I first hate others' parents in order that they would love my parents in return? Of course I should first love others' parents in order that they would love my parents in return. Hence those who desire to be filial to one another's parents, if they have to choose between whether they should love or hate others' parents, had best first love and benefit others' parents. Would anyone suspect that all the filial sons are stupid and incorrigible in loving their own parents? We may again inquire about it. It is said in the "Ta Ya" [15] among the books of the ancient kings: "No idea is not given its due value; no virtue is not rewarded. When a peach is thrown to us, we would return with a prune." This is to say whoever loves others will be loved and whoever hates others will be hated. It is then quite incomprehensible why people should object to universal love when they hear it.

o   o   o   o

Now to endure limited diet, to be burnt alive, and to wear coarse clothing are the hardest things in the world, yet when the superiors encouraged them the people could be changed within a generation. Why was this so? It was due to the desire to conform to the superior. Now, as to universal love and mutual aid, they are beneficial and easy beyond a doubt. It seems to me that the only trouble is that there is no superior who encourages it. If there is a superior who encourages it, promoting it with rewards and commendations, threatening its reverse with punishments, I feel people will tend toward universal love and mutual aid like fire tending upward and water downwards—it will be unpreventable in the world.

Therefore, universal love is really the way of the sage-kings. It is what gives peace to the rulers and sustenance to the people. The gentleman would do well to understand and practise universal love; then he would be gracious as a ruler, loyal as a minister, affectionate as a father, filial as a son, courteous as an elder brother, and respectful as a younger brother. So, if the gentleman desires to be a gracious ruler, a loyal minister, an affectionate father, a filial son, a courteous elder brother, and a respectful younger brother, universal love must be practised. It is the way of the sage-kings and the great blessing of the people.

o   o   o   o

Book 5

Chapter 18. Condemnation of Offensive War (2)

o   o   o   o

Now, about a country going to war. If it is in winter it will be too cold; if it is in summer it will be too hot. So it should be neither in winter nor in summer. If it is in spring it will take people away from sowing and planting; if it is in autumn it will take people away from reaping and harvesting. Should they be taken away in either of these seasons, innumerable people would die of hunger and cold. And, when the army sets out, the bamboo arrows, the feather flags, the house tents, the armour, the shields, the sword hilts—innumerable quantities of these will break and rot and never come back. The spears, the lances, the swords, the poniards, the chariots, the carts—innumerable quantities of these will break and rot and never come back. Then innumerable horses and oxen will start out fat and come back lean or will not return at all. And innumerable people will die because their food will be cut off and cannot be supplied on account of the great distances of the roads. And innumerable people will be sick and die of the constant danger and the irregularity of eating and drinking and the extremes of hunger and over-eating. Then, the army will be lost in large numbers or entirely; in either case the number will be innumerable. And this means the spirits will lose their worshippers, and the number of these will also be innumerable.

Why then does the government deprive the people of their opportunities and benefits to such a great extent? It has been answered: "I covet the fame of the victor and the possessions obtainable through the conquest. So I do it."

Mo Tzŭ said: But when we consider the victory as such, there is nothing useful about it. When we consider the possessions obtained through it, it does not even make up for the loss. Now about the siege of a city of three *li* or a *kuo*[16] of seven *li*—if these could be obtained without the use of weapons or the killing of lives, it would be all right. But (as a matter of fact) those killed must be counted by the ten thousand, those widowed or left solitary must be counted by the thousand, before a city of three *li* or a *kuo* of seven *li* could be captured. Moreover the states of ten thousand chariots now have empty towns to be counted by the thousand, which can be entered without conquest; and their extensive lands to be counted by the ten thousand of *mu*,[17] which can be cultivated without conquest. So, land is abundant but people are few. Now to pursue the people to death and aggravate the danger feared by both superiors and subordinates in order to obtain an empty city—this is to give up what is needed and to treasure what is already in abundance. Such an undertaking is not in accordance with the interest of the country.

o   o   o   o

Chapter 19. Condemnation of Offensive War (3)

o   o   o   o

The rulers and lords of today are quite different. They all rank their warriors and arrange their boat and chariot forces; they make their armour strong and weapons sharp in order to attack some innocent state. Entering the state they cut down the grain fields and fell the trees and woods; they tear down the inner and outer walls of the city and fill up the ditches and ponds; they seize and kill the sacrificial animals and burn down the ancestral temple; they kill and murder the people and exterminate the aged and weak; they move away the treasures and valuables. The soldiers are encouraged to advance by being told: "To suffer death is the highest service you can render, to kill many is the next, to be wounded is the lowest. But if you should drop out from your rank and attempt to sneak away, the penalty will be death without moderation." Thus the soldiers are put to fear.

Now to capture a state and to destroy an army, to disturb and torture the people, and to set at naught the aspirations of the sages by confusion —is this intended to bless T'ien? But the people of T'ien are gathered together to besiege the towns belonging to T'ien. This is to murder men of T'ien and dispossess the spirits of their altars and to ruin the state and to kill the sacrificial animals. It is then not a blessing to T'ien on high. Is it intended to bless the spirits? But men of T'ien are murdered, spirits are deprived of their sacrifices, the earlier kings are neglected, the multitude are tortured and the people are scattered; it is then not a blessing to the spirits in the middle. Is it intended to bless the people? But the blessing of the people by killing them off must be very meagre. And when we calculate the expense, which is the root of the calamities to living, we find the property of innumerable people is exhausted. It is, then, not a blessing to the people below either.

Now that the armies are intended for mutual destruction, it is evident: If the general be not courageous, if soldiers be not brave, if weapons be not sharp, if drills be not frequent, if the force be not large, if generals be not harmonious, if power be not august, if a siege be not enduring, if an assault be not speedy, if people be not strongly bound together, if determination be not firm—if this be so, the other feudal lords will suspect. When feudal lords entertain suspicion, enemies will be stirred up and cause anxiety, and the morale will be weakened. On the other hand, if every preparation is in good shape and the state goes out to engage in war, then the state will lose its men and the people will neglect their vocations. Have we not heard it said that, when a warring state goes on an expedition, of the officers there must be several hundred, of the common people there must be several thousand, and of the soldiers and prisoners there must be ten thousand, before the army can set out? It may last for several years, or, at the shortest, several months. So, the superior will have no time to attend to government, the officials will have no time to attend to their offices, the farmers will have no time to sow or reap, the women will have no time to weave or spin: that is, the state will lose its men and the people will neglect their vocations. Besides, the chariots will break and horses will be exhausted. As to tents, army supplies, and soldiers' equipment—if one-fifth of these can remain after the war it would already be beyond expectation. Moreover, innumerable men will be missing and lost on the way, and will become sick from the long distances, meagre rations, hunger, and cold, and die in the ditches. Now the calamity to the people and the world is tremendous. Yet the rulers enjoy doing it. This means they enjoy injuring and exterminating the people; is this not perversity?

The most warring states in the empire today are Ch'i, Chin, Ch'u, and Yüeh. These four states are all successful in the world. Even if their people be increased tenfold, still they could not consume all that their land could produce. That is, they are in need of men while they have a surplus of land. Still they strove against each other to possess more land. This is to neglect what is needed and to value what is already in plenty.

The warring lords would gloss over their conduct with arguments to confute Mo Tzŭ saying: "Do you condemn attack and assault as unrighteous and not beneficial? But, anciently, Yü made war on the Prince of Miao,[18] T'ang on Chieh, and King Wu on Chou. Yet these are regarded as sages. What is your explanation for this?" Mo Tzŭ said: You have not examined the terminology of my teaching and you do not understand its motive. What they did is not to be called "attack" but "punishment."

o   o   o   o

Book 6

Chapter 21. Economy of Expenditures (2)

o   o   o   o

And the ancient sage-kings authorized the code of laws of economy, saying: "All you artisans and workers, carpenters and tanners, potters and smiths, do what you can do. Stop when the needs of the people are satisfied." What causes extra expense but adds no benefit to the people the sage-kings would not undertake.

The ancient sage-kings authorized the code of laws regarding food and drink, saying: "Stop when hunger is satiated, breathing becomes strong, limbs are strengthened, and ears and eyes become sharp. There is no need of combining the five tastes extremely well or harmonizing the different sweet odours. And efforts should not be made to procure rare delicacies from far countries." How do we know such were the laws? In ancient times, when Yao was governing the empire he consolidated Chiao Chih[19] on the south, reached Yu Tu on the north, expanded from where the sun rises to where the sun sets on the east and west, and none was unsubmissive or disrespectful. Yet, even when he was served with what he much liked, he did not take a double cereal or both soup and meat. He ate out of an earthen dish and drank out of an earthen cup, and took wine out of a spoon. With the ceremonies of bowing and stretching and courtesies and decorum the sage-king had nothing to do.

o   o   o   o

Chapter 25. Simplicity in Funeral (3)

o   o   o   o

Mo Tzŭ said: I have examined the sayings of those who uphold elaborate funeral and extended mourning. If they should be taken seriously in the country, it would mean: when a lord dies, there would be several inner and outer coffins. He would be buried deep. There would be many shrouds. Embroidery would be elaborate. The grave mound would be massive. So, then, the death of a common man would exhaust the wealth of a family. And the death of a feudal lord would empty the state treasury before his body would be surrounded with gold, jade, and pearls, and the grave filled with carts and horses and bundles of silk. Further, there should be plenty of canopies and hangings, tripods,[20] drums, tables, pots, and ice receptacles, spears, swords, feather banners, and hides all to be carried along and buried. Not till then are the requirements considered fulfilled. And, regarding those who were to die to accompany their lord,[21] for the Son of T'ien or a feudal lord there should be from several hundred to several tens, and for a minister or secretary there should be from several tens to several.

What are the rules to be observed by the mourner? He must weep without restraint and sound as if he is choking. Sackcloth is worn on the breast and hat of flax on the head. His tears and snivel are not to be wiped away. The mourner is to live in a mourning hut, sleep on a coarse mat of straw, and lay his head on a lump of earth. Then, he would be obliged to abstain from food in order to look hungry, and to wear little in order to look cold. The face and eyes are to look sunken and as if in fear, and the complexion is to appear dark. Ears and eyes are to become dull, and hands and feet to become weak and unusable. And, also, if the mourner is a high official, he has to be supported to rise, and lean on a cane to walk. And all this is to last three years.[22]

Adopting such a doctrine and practising such a principle: rulers cannot come to court early and retire late; the officials cannot attend to the five offices and six posts[23] and encourage farming and forestry and fill the granaries; the farmers cannot start out early and come in late to cultivate the land and plant trees; the artisans cannot build boats and vehicles and make vessels and utensils; and the women cannot rise early and retire late to weave and spin. So, then, in elaborate funerals much wealth is buried, and in extended mourning abstention from work is prolonged. Wealth already produced is carried away into the grave. Childbearing is postponed. To seek wealth in this way is like seeking a harvest by prohibiting farming. The way to wealth then is not here found.

Now that the practice of elaborate funerals and extended mourning has failed to enrich the country perhaps it can yet increase the population? Again it is powerless. For if elaborate funeral and extended mourning are adopted as the rule, then upon the death of the Son of T'ien there will be three years' mourning, upon the death of a parent there will be three years' mourning, upon the death of the wife or the eldest son there will be three years' mourning. There will be three years' mourning for all five relations. Besides, there will be one year for uncles, brothers, and the other sons; and five months for the near relatives, and also several months for aunts, sisters, nephews, and uncles on the mother's side. Further, there are set rules to emaciate one's health: the face and eyes are to look sunken and as if in fear, and the complexion is to appear dark. Ears and eyes are to become dull, and hands and feet are to become weak and unusable. And, also, if the mourner is a high official, he has to be supported to rise and lean on a cane to walk. And this is to last three years if such a doctrine is adopted and such a principle is practised. Being so hungry and weak, the people cannot stand the cold in winter and the heat in summer. And countless numbers will become sick and die. Sexual relations between husband and wife are prevented. To seek to increase the population by this way is like seeking longevity by thrusting one's self upon a sword. The way to dense population is not here found.

o   o   o   o

For, adopting elaborate funeral and extended mourning as a principle in government, the state will become poor, the people few, and the jurisdiction disorderly. When the state is poor the cakes and wine will be unclean.[24] When the people are few the worshippers of Shang Ti and the spirits will be reduced in number. And when jurisdiction is in disorder the sacrifice will not be made according to season. Moreover, the worship of Shang Ti and the spirits is now even prohibited. When the government is run like this, Shang Ti and the spirits would deliberate from on high, saying: "Which is better, to have these people exist or not to have them exist? It really makes no difference whether they exist or not." Therefore Shang Ti and spirits will send judgment upon them and visit them with calamities and punish and desert them. Is not this quite in place?

o   o   o   o

Book 7

Chapter 26. Will of T'ien (1)

o   o   o   o

Now, what does T'ien desire and what does it abominate? T'ien desires righteousness and abominates unrighteousness. Therefore, in leading the people in the world to engage in doing righteousness I should be doing what T'ien desires. When I do what T'ien desires, T'ien will also do what I desire. Now, what do I desire and what do I abominate? I desire blessings and emoluments, and abominate calamities and misfortunes. When I do not do what T'ien desires, neither will T'ien do what I desire. Then I should be leading the people into calamities and misfortunes. But how do we know T'ien desires righteousness and abominates unrighteousness? For, with righteousness the world lives and without it the world dies; with it the world becomes rich and without it the world becomes poor; with it the world becomes orderly and without it the world becomes chaotic. And T'ien likes to have the world live and dislikes to have it die, likes to have it rich and dislikes to have it poor, and likes to have it orderly and dislikes to have it disorderly. Therefore we know T'ien desires righteousness and abominates unrighteousness.

Moreover, righteousness is the standard. A standard is not to be given by the subordinates to the superior but by the superior to the subordinates. Therefore, while the common people should spare no pains at work they may not make the standard at will. There are the scholars to give them the standard. While the scholars should spare no pains at work, they may not make the standard at will. There are the ministers and secretaries to give them the standard. While the ministers and secretaries should spare no pains at work, they may not make the standard at will. There are the high duke and feudal lords to give them the standard. While the high duke and the feudal lords should spare no pains at work, they may not make the standard at will. There is the Son of T'ien to give them the standard. The Son of T'ien may not make the standard at will either. There is T'ien to give him the standard. That the Son of T'ien gives the standard to the high duke, to the feudal lords, to the scholars, and to the common people, the gentlemen in the world clearly understand. But that T'ien gives the standard to the Son of

T'ien, the people do not know well. Therefore the ancient sage-kings of the Three Dynasties, Yü, T'ang, Wên, and Wu, desiring to make it clear to the people that T'ien gives the standard to the Son of T'ien, fed oxen and sheep with grass, and pigs and dogs with grain, and cleanly prepared the cakes and wine to do sacrifice to Shang Ti and the spirits, and invoked T'ien's blessing. But I have not yet heard of T'ien invoking the Son of T'ien for blessing. So I know T'ien gives the standard to the Son of T'ien.

o   o   o   o

How do we know T'ien loves the people? Because it teaches them all. How do we know it teaches them all? Because it claims them all. How do we know it claims them all? Because it accepts sacrifices from them all. How do we know it accepts sacrifices from all? Because within the four seas all who live on grains, feed oxen and sheep with grass, and dogs and pigs with grains, and prepare clean cakes and wine to do sacrifice to Shang Ti and the spirits. Claiming all the people, why will T'ien not love them? Moreover, as I have said, for the murder of one innocent individual there will be one calamity. Who is it that murders the innocent? It is man. Who is it that sends down the calamity? It is T'ien. If T'ien should be thought of as not loving the people, why should it send down calamities for the murder of man by man? So, I know T'ien loves the people.

o   o   o   o

Mo Tzŭ said: The will of T'ien to me is like the compasses to the wheelwright and the square to the carpenter. The wheelwright and the carpenter measure all the square and circular objects with their square and compasses and accept those that fit as correct and reject those that do not fit as incorrect. The writings of the gentlemen of the world of the present day cannot be all loaded in a cart, and their doctrines cannot be exhaustively enumerated. They endeavour to convince the feudal lords on the one hand and the scholars on the other. But from magnanimity and righteousness they are far off. How do we know? Because I have the most competent standard in the world to measure them with.

o   o   o   o

Chapter 28. Will of T'ien (3)

o   o   o   o

To obey the will of T'ien is to be universal and to oppose the will of T'ien is to be partial in love. According to the doctrine of universality righteousness is the standard; in the doctrine of partiality force is the basis of government. What is it like to have righteousness as the basis of government? The great will not attack the small, the strong will not plunder the weak, the many will not oppress the few, the clever will not deceive the ignorant, the honoured will not disdain the humble, the rich will not mock the poor, and the young will not rob the old. And the states in the empire will not ruin each other with water, fire, poison, and weapons. Such a regime will be beneficial to T'ien above, to the spirits in the middle sphere, to the people below.

o   o   o   o

Book 8

Chapter 31. On Ghosts (3)

o   o   o   o

And so the world falls into chaos.

Now what is the reason for this confusion? It is all because of the doubt of the existence of the ghosts and spirits, and the ignorance of their being able to reward virtue and punish vice. If all the people in the world believed that the spirits are able to reward virtue and punish vice, how could the world be in chaos? Those who deny the existence of spirits proclaim: "Of course there are no spirits." And from morning till evening they teach this doctrine to the people of the empire. They bewilder the people, causing them all to doubt the existence of ghosts and spirits. In this way the empire becomes disorderly. Therefore Mo Tzǔ said: If the rulers and the gentlemen of the world really desire to procure benefits for the empire and remove its calamities they must understand whether ghosts and spirits exist or not.

Since we must understand whether ghosts and spirits exist or not, how can we find out? Mo Tzǔ said: The way to find out whether anything exists or not is to depend on the testimony of the ears and eyes of the multitude. If some have heard it or some have seen it then we have to say it exists. If no one has heard it and no one has seen it then we have to say it does not exist. So, then, why not go to some village or some district and inquire? If from antiquity to the present, and since the beginning of man, there are men who have seen the bodies of ghosts and spirits and heard their voice, how can we say that they do not exist? If none have heard them and none have seen them, then how can we say they do? But those who deny the existence of the spirits say: "Many in the world have heard and seen something of ghosts and spirits. Since they vary in their testimony, who are to be accepted as really having heard and seen them?" Mo Tzǔ said: As we are to rely on what many have jointly seen and what many have jointly heard, the case of Tu Po[25] is to be accepted.

o   o   o   o

Mo Tzǔ said: If the senses of hearing and sight of the multitude are thought to be not trustworthy, we may ask if such men like the sage-kings of the Three Dynasties, Yao, Shun, Yü, T'ang, Wên, and Wu, are trustworthy?

o   o   o   o

Mo Tzǔ said: As to the fact that ghosts and spirits can reward virtue as well as punish vice, if it could be proclaimed to the whole country and to all the people it would really be a source of orderliness in the country and blessing to the people. The corruption of the officials in their public charges and the immorality among men and women will all be seen by ghosts and spirits. The vice of those who, with weapons, poisons, and water and fire, waylay innocent travellers and rob them of their carts and horses, coats and fur coats to enrich themselves will be seen by ghosts and spirits. Thereupon the officials will not dare be corrupt in office, withholding reward when they find the virtuous or withholding punishment when they find the wicked. And those among the people who commit vice and cruelties and with weapons, poisons, and water and fire waylay the innocent travellers, robbing them of their carts and horses, coats and fur coats to enrich themselves—all these will be no more. And the world will have order. Really the intelligence of the ghosts and spirits cannot be combated. Even in solitary caves, big ponds, woods and valleys, the ghosts and spirits are watching. And the punishments from ghosts and spirits cannot be evaded. Even wealth and great numbers, daring and strength, strong armour and sharp weapons, the punishment of ghosts and spirits will frustrate.

o   o   o   o

At any rate, we should prepare clean cakes and wine reverently to do sacrifice. If ghosts and spirits do exist, then it is to serve father and mother, elder sisters and elder brothers with food and drink. Is not this a great blessing? If ghosts and spirits did not exist it would seem to be a waste of the material for the cakes and wine. But such use is not just to throw it into the ditch or gully. For the relatives from the clan and friends from the village and district can yet eat and drink them. So, even if there were really no ghosts and spirits, a sacrifice will yet gather together a party and the participants can enjoy themselves and befriend the neighbours.

o   o   o   o

Chapter 32. Anti-Music (1)

o   o   o   o

There are three things that the people worry about, namely, that the hungry cannot be fed, that the cold cannot be clothed, and that the tired cannot get rest. These three are the great worries of the people. Now suppose we strike the big bell, beat the sounding drum, play the *ch'in* and the *shê*, and blow the *yü* and the *shêng*,[26] can the material for food and clothing then be procured for the people? Even I do not think this is possible. Again, every large state now attacks small states and every large house molests small houses. The strong plunder the weak, the many oppress the few, the clever deceive the stupid and the honoured disdain the humble. And bandits and thieves rise all together and cannot be suppressed. But can the chaos in the world be put in order by striking the big bell, beating the sounding drum, playing the *ch'in* and the *shê*, and blowing the *yü* and the *shêng*? Even I do not think it is possible.

o   o   o   o

Also, man is different from birds and beasts and insects. The birds, beasts, and insects have their feathers and furs for coats and fur coats, have their hoofs and claws for sandals and shoes, and have water and grass for drink and food. Therefore the male do not sow seeds or plant trees, neither do the female weave or spin, yet food and clothing are provided. Now, man is different from these. Those who exert themselves will live. Those who do not exert themselves cannot live. When the gentlemen do not attend to government diligently, the jurisdiction will be in chaos. When the common men do not attend to work, supply will not be sufficient.

If the gentlemen of the world should doubt my word, let us enumerate the several duties in the world and see the harm music does: For the rulers to go to court early and retire late to listen to lawsuits and attend to government is their duty. For the gentlemen to exhaust the energy of their limbs and employ fully the wisdom of their minds to attend to the court within and to collect taxes without from passes, markets, and products from mountains, woods, and water and fields in order to fill up the granaries and the treasury is their duty. For the farmers to set out early and come back late, to sow seeds and plant trees in order to produce a large quantity of soy beans and millet is their duty. For the women to rise up at dawn and retire in the night to weave and spin in order to produce much silk, flax linen, and cloth is their duty. Now if the rulers should love music and listen to it, they would not be able to go to court early and retire late to listen to lawsuits and attend to government. Then the country would be in chaos and the state would be in danger. If the gentlemen should love music and listen to it, they would not be able to exhaust the energy in their limbs and employ fully the wisdom in the mind to attend to court within and collect taxes without from passes and markets and products from mountains, woods, water, and fields to fill up the granaries and the treasury. Then the granaries and the treasury would not be filled. If the farmers should love music and listen to it, they would not be able to set out early and come back late to sow seeds and plant trees and produce a large quantity of soy beans and millet. Then the soy beans and millet would not be sufficient. If the women should love music and listen to it, they would not be able to rise up at dawn and retire in the night to weave and spin and produce much silk, flax linen, and cloth. Then cloth and linen will not be sufficient. If it is asked what is it that interfered with the rulers' attending to government and the common man's attending to work? it must be answered, music. Therefore Mo Tzǔ said: To have music is wrong.

o   o   o   o

Book 9

Chapter 35. Anti-Fatalism (1)

o   o   o   o

Now, the fatalists say: "Whoever is rewarded by the superior is destined to be rewarded. It is not because of his virtue that he is rewarded." Under these conditions the people would not be filial to their parents at home, and respectful to the elders in the village or the district. They would not observe propriety in conduct, moderation in going out and coming in, or decency between men and women. And, if they were made to look after the court they would steal, if they were made to defend a city they would raise an insurrection. If the lord met with death they would not commit suicide, and if the lord were banished they would not accompany him. This is what the superior will punish, and what the people will condemn. The fatalists say: "Whoever is punished by the superior is destined to be punished. It is not because of his vice that he is punished." Believing in this, the ruler would not be righteous, the minister would not be loyal, the father would not be affectionate, the son would not be filial, the elder brother would not be brotherly, and the younger brother would not be respectful. The unnatural adherence to this doctrine is responsible for pernicious ideas and is the way of the wicked.

o   o   o   o

Book 12

Chapter 47. Esteem for Righteousness

o   o   o   o

Mo Tzǔ said: As the gentlemen in the world cannot be butchers of dogs and pigs, they would refuse when asked to be such. Yet, though they are not capable of being ministers in a state, they would accept it when asked to be such. Isn't this perverse?

○ ○ ○ ○

Chapter 48. Kung Mêng

○ ○ ○ ○

Kung Mêng Tzǔ[27] said to Mo Tzǔ: "You think mourning for three years is wrong. Your mourning for three days is also wrong." Mo Tzǔ replied: You hold mourning for three years and condemn mourning for three days. This is similar to the naked person condemning the person who lifted up his garments for indecency.

○ ○ ○ ○

Book 13

Chapter 49. Lu's Question

○ ○ ○ ○

Mo Tzǔ was visiting Wei Yüeh.[29] The latter asked: "Now that you have seen the gentlemen of the four quarters, what would you say is the most urgent enterprise?" Mo Tzǔ replied: Upon entering a country one should locate the need and work on that. If the country is upset in confusion, teach them with the doctrines of Exaltation of the Virtuous and Identification with the Superior. If the country is in poverty, teach them with Economy of Expenditures and Simplicity in Funeral. If the country is indulging in music and wine, teach them with Condemnation of Music and Anti-fatalism. If the country is insolent and without propriety, teach them to reverence T'ien and worship the spirits. If the country is engaged in conquest and oppression, teach them with Universal Love and Condemnation of Offensive War. Hence we say, one should locate the need and work on that.

13

Tao-tê-ching
and the Taoists

The best rulers are those whose existence is hardly known
to people.

—Tao-tê-ching, 17

There is nothing else like the *Tao-tê-ching* in political philosophy. This
little work of poetry—for poetry it is, not analects or prose—has had an
effect on China comparable to Homer's on Greece or Dante's on Italy.
The author (the name usually given is Lao Tzŭ) is even more mysterious
to history than the author of the *Iliad* and *Odyssey*. Historians are not yet
sure who he was or just when he lived—some think the sixth century B.C.
To attribute authorship to Lao Tzŭ is a convention. The book as we
know it seems to have been written in the fourth or third century B.C.,
but it may well have been written in the sixth century and been the contemporary of the *Analects*. The title, *Tao-tê-ching*, can best be translated as
the *Book (ching) of the Way (tao) and the Power (tê)*. The word *tao* is familiar to Chinese philosophy in its elastic meaning of a road or way, the
path of the model kings, the course of nature, the cosmic order or principle, the absolute, and, by extension, truth, reality, and right conduct.

Taoism and Confucianism should not be regarded as poles apart at
every point of the philosophical compass. The one remained true to the
way of nature, the other to the way of ancestors, and the two schools encounter each other in the common key concept—the *tao*. For both, the
life to lead is one that follows the *tao*, which for the Confucian is to be
good to ancestors and family and to perform the appropriate rites; for
the Taoist, to emulate nature in its indifference to men, to take the example of the heavenly bodies, the plants and trees, the streams, to do just

what is necessary to get along, to let others be, and so to shy from all uniquely man-contrived institutions such as language, civilization, and government.

Of all Taoist books, indeed of all Chinese books, the *Tao-tê-ching* has garnered the most translations. It is by far the most influential Taoist book outside of China. This should not be taken to imply that the *Tao-tê-ching* is the one masterpiece of all Taoism: there is a prose work that rivals it—the *Chuang Tzŭ*. Nor does it mean that the *Tao-tê-ching* is fully representative of Taoism; with at least two truly great works, no one work could be that. There is even a third thinker of classical times whose ideas can be grouped with the Taoists'—Yang Chu (c. 350 B.C.). Unfortunately, the writings that seem to incorporate his ideas are so few as to confine his greatness (though not to diminish his originality). To skirt such difficulties, perhaps the philosophy of the one great Taoist should be modified as Chuangtzian, and that of the other as Laoist. The difference between Lao Tzŭ and Chuang Tzŭ is as great as that within the great Confucian trio, whose philosophies can, when the need arises, be distinguished as Confucian, Mencian, and Hsüntzian.

There are at least thirty to forty versions of the *Tao-tê-ching* in English alone—which fact is to the credit of the English-speaking world, for it has been said, and by Chinese, that there is no one book that can better claim to interpret Chinese traits or the Asian spirit. This is to be expected, considering the extent to which the book itself has shaped Chinese character, language, and spirit.

If one may risk a guess, the influence of Taoism may have been all the greater because of the dominance of Confucianism. The aim of the state in Confucian political thought is to enable everyone to lead an orderly, peaceful existence. The means to it, generally speaking, is a kingship or empire over which the ruler rules through learned officials dedicated to the same aim. Every law and custom, every instance of conduct, is judged by its utility in this political sense. The question of what is to be done once the state has achieved its reason for existing is nowhere clearly answered.

Taoism offered as a model something other than a serious and high-minded officialdom. Unable to confront the government official in the public world it seduced him in his private life. The ideal of simplicity of life and politics was entertained by gentlemen after their hours of public employment. An outright hedonist philosophy could never have come to terms with a Confucian, whereas the simple pleasures of Taoism—the love of nature, the quiet of meditation, the unhurriedness of nothing-to-do—infiltrated the gentleman's home.

Among the phenomena Taoists often remarked is the natural strength of things or beings commonly thought of as weak. The infant, the female, water, become important symbols, water that seeks lowly places but benefits everythings; soft in itself, in the quiet of time it reduces the hardest things to nothing.

The central Taoist thesis is quietism. It is not quietism for survival alone, but he who is quiet does survive. It is not passive resistance to bureaucracy, but the problems that a hierarchy of functionaries can solve do not interest the quietist. It is not a fable of fraud versus force, the fox versus the lion. It is not a plea for a return to an anarchic state of nature, but better the quiet, rural, little country than the big, efficient, warlike state.

14

Tao-tê-ching

The empire is a spiritual thing, and should not be acted on.

—*Tao-tê-ching,* 29

Of the Taoist trio, Lao Tzǔ, Yang Chu, and Chuang Tzǔ, only Chuang Tzǔ holds claim to actual existence, and then he doubted whether he was really himself or a butterfly dreaming it was a philosopher. "Such men as they," Confucius is said (fictitiously) to have remarked, "wander beyond the realm; men like me wander within it. Beyond and within can never meet." (*Chuang Tzǔ,* 6)

The three major Taoists are known by the works that bear their names, but the dating of the works differs widely from that of their supposed lifetimes. If the *Tao-tê-ching* dates from the sixth century B.C. (as its author is today supposed to do), it would have been roughly contemporaneous with Confucius. If the *Tao-tê-ching* dates instead from the late fourth century B.C., it would have coexisted with the first seven chapters of the *Chuang Tzǔ,* while both would have been more or less contemporaneous with the *Mencius.* The *Chuang Tzǔ* gives no clue; it never refers to the *Tao-tê-ching* by name.

The *Tao-tê-ching* contains only somewhat more than five thousand words and is divided into two parts of altogether eighty-one chapters, mostly rhymed.

TAO-TÊ-CHING

Selections

I

The Tao that can be told of is not the eternal Tao;
The name that can be named is not the eternal name.
The Nameless is the origin of heaven and earth;
The Named is the mother of all things.
Therefore let there always be non-being so we may see their sub-
tlety,
And let there always be being so we may see their outcome.
The two are the same,

From Wing-tsit Chan, tr., *A Source Book in Chinese Philosophy* (Princeton: Princeton University Press, 1963), pp. 139–175, translation slightly modified.

But after they are produced, they have different names.
They both may be called deep and profound.
Deeper and more profound,
The door of all subtleties!

2

When the people of the world all know beauty as beauty,
   There arises the recognition of ugliness.
When they all know the good as good
   There arises the recognition of evil.
Therefore:
   Being and non-being produce each other;
   Difficult and easy complete each other;
   Long and short contrast each other;
   High and low distinguish each other;
   Sound and voice harmonize with each other;
   Front and back follow each other.
   Therefore the sage manages affairs without action
   And spreads doctrines without words.
   All things arise, and he does not turn away from them.
   He produces them, but does not take possession of them.
   He acts, but does not rely on his own ability.
   He accomplishes his task, but does not claim credit for it.
   It is precisely because he does not claim credit that his accom-
      plishment remains with him.

3

Do not exalt the worthy, so that the people shall not compete.
Do not value rare treasures, so that the people shall not steal.
Do not display objects of desire, so that the people's hearts shall
      not be disturbed.
Therefore in the government of the sage,
   He keeps their hearts vacuous,
   Fills their bellies,
   Weakens their ambitions,
   And strengthens their bones,
He always causes his people to be without knowledge or desire,
And the crafty to be afraid to act.
By acting without action, all things will be in order.

4

Tao is empty [like a bowl],[1]
It may be used but its capacity is never exhausted.
It is bottomless, perhaps the ancestor of all things.
It blunts its sharpness,
It unties its tangles.
It softens its light.
It becomes one with the dusty world.
Deep and still, it appears to exist forever.
I do not know whose son it is.
It seems to have existed before the Lord.

5

T'ien and earth are not humane.
They regard all things as straw dogs.[2]
The sage is not humane.
He regards all people as straw dogs.
How the sky and earth are like a bellows!
While vacuous, it is never exhausted.
When active, it produces even more.
Much talk will of course come to a dead end.
It is better to keep to the center.

8

The best [man] is like water.
Water is good; it benefits all things and does not compete with
  them.
It dwells in [lowly] places that all disdain.
This is why it is so near to Tao.
[The best man] in his dwelling loves the earth.
  In his heart, he loves what is profound.
  In his associations, he loves humanity.
  In his words, he loves faithfulness.
  In government, he loves order.
  In handling affairs, he loves competence.
  In his activities, he loves timeliness.
  It is because he does not compete that he is without reproach.

9

To hold and fill to overflowing
  Is not as good as to stop in time.
Sharpen a sword-edge to its very sharpest,
  And the edge will not last long.
When gold and jade fill your hall,
  You will not be able to keep them.
To be proud with honor and wealth
  Is to cause one's own downfall.
Withdraw as soon as your work is done.
Such is the Tao of T'ien.

10

Can you keep the spirit and embrace the One without departing
  from them?
Can you concentrate your vital force and achieve the highest de-
  gree of weakness like an infant?
Can you clean and purify your profound insight so it will be spot-
  less?
Can you love the people and govern the state without knowledge
  [cunning]?
Can you play the role of the female in the opening and closing
  of the gates of T'ien?
Can you understand all and penetrate all without taking any ac-
  tion?
  To produce things and to rear them,
To produce, but not to take possession of them,
  To act, but not to rely on one's own ability,
  To lead them, but not to master them—
  This is called profound and secret virtue.

11

Thirty spokes are united around the hub to make a wheel,
  But it is on the non-being [the area of the circle] that the util-
  ity of the wheel depends.
Clay is molded to form a utensil,
  But it is on the non-being [its hollowness] that the utility of
  the utensil depends.

Doors and windows are cut to make a room,
But it is on the non-being [its empty space] that the utility of
the room depends.
Therefore turn being into advantage, and turn non-being into
utility.

13

Be apprehensive when receiving favor or disgrace.
Regard great trouble as seriously as you regard your body.
What is meant by being apprehensive when receiving favor or dis-
grace?
Favor is considered inferior.
Be apprehensive when you receive them and also be apprehen-
sive when you lose them.
This is what is meant by being apprehensive when receiving
favor or disgrace.
What does it mean to regard great trouble as seriously as you re-
gard the body?
The reason why I have great trouble is that I have a body [and
am attached to it].
If I have no body,
What trouble could I have?
Therefore he who values the world as his body may be entrusted
with the empire.
He who loves the world as his body may be entrusted with the em-
pire.

14

We look at it and do not see it;
Its name is The Invisible.
We listen to it and do not hear it;
Its name is The Inaudible.
We touch it and do not find it;
Its name is The Subtle [formless].
These three cannot be further inquired into,
And hence merge into one.
Going up high, it is not bright, and coming down low, it is not
dark.

Infinite and boundless, it cannot be given any name;
It reverts to nothingness.
This is called shape without shape,
Form without object.
It is The Vague and Elusive.
Meet it and you will not see its head.
Follow it and you will not see its back.
Hold on to the Tao of old in order to master the things of the
    present.
From this one may know the primeval beginning [of the universe].
This is called the bond of Tao.

15

Of old those who were the best rulers were subtly mysterious and
    profoundly penetrating;
    Too deep to comprehend.
And because they cannot be comprehended,
    I can only describe them arbitrarily:
    Cautious, like crossing a frozen stream in the winter,
    Being at a loss, like one fearing danger on all sides,
Reserved, like one visiting,
    Supple and pliant, like ice about to melt,
    Genuine, like a piece of uncarved wood,
    Open and broad, like a valley,
    Merged and undifferentiated, like muddy water.

    Who can make muddy water gradually clear through tranquil-
        lity?
    Who can make the still gradually come to life through activity?
    He who embraces this Tao does not want to fill himself to
        overflowing.
    It is precisely because there is no overflowing that he is
        beyond wearing out and renewal.

16

Attain complete vacuity,
Maintain steadfast quiet.
All things come into being,

And I see thereby their return.
All things flourish,
But each one returns to its root.
This return to its root means tranquillity.
It is called returning to its destiny.
To return to destiny is called the eternal.
To know the eternal is called enlightenment.
Not to know the eternal is to act blindly to result in disaster.
He who knows the eternal is all-embracing.
Being all-embracing, he is impartial.
Being impartial, he is kingly.
Being kingly, he is of T'ien.
Being of T'ien, he is in accord with Tao.
Being in accord with Tao, he is everlasting,
And though his body decay, is free from danger.

17

The best [rulers] are those whose existence is hardly known to
    the people.
The next best are those who are loved and praised.
The next are those who are feared.
And the next are those who are despised.
It is only when one does not have enough faith in others that oth-
    ers will have no faith in him.
They [the great rulers] value their words highly.
They accomplish their tasks; they complete their work.
Yet their people say: Things just happen naturally.

18

When the great Tao declined,
The doctrines of humanity and righteousness arose.
When knowledge and wisdom appeared,
There emerged great hypocrisy.
When the six family relationships[3] are not in harmony,
There will be the advocacy of filial piety and deep love to chil-
    dren.
When a country is in disorder,
There will be praise of loyal ministers.

20

Abandon learning and there will be no sorrow.
How much difference is there between "Yes, sir," and "Of course
    not"?
How much difference is there between "good" and "evil"?
What people dread, do not fail to dread.
But, alas, how confused, and the end is not yet.
The multitude are merry, as though feasting on a day of sacrifice,
Or like ascending a tower at springtime.
I alone am inert, showing no sign,
Like an infant that has not yet smiled.
Wearied, indeed, I seem to be without a home.
The multitude all possess more than enough,
I alone seem to have lost all.
Mine is indeed the mind of an ignorant man,
Indiscriminate and dull!
Common folks are indeed brilliant;
I alone seem to be in the dark.
Common folk see differences and are clear-cut;
I alone make no distinctions.
I seem drifting as the sea;
Like the wind blowing about, seemingly without destination.
The multitude all have a purpose;
I alone seem to be stubborn and rustic.
I alone differ from others,
And value drawing sustenance from Mother.[4]

21

The all-embracing quality of the great virtue follows alone from
    the Tao.
The thing that is called Tao is eluding and vague.
    Vague and eluding, there is in it the form.
    Eluding and vague, in it are things.
Deep and obscure, in it is the essence.
The essence is very real; in it are evidences.
From the time of old until now, its name [manifestations] ever re-
    mains,
By which we may see the beginning of all things.

How do I know that the beginnings of all things are so?
Through this.

25

There was something undifferentiated and yet complete,
Which existed before heaven and earth.
Soundless and formless, it depends on nothing and does not
    change.
It operates everywhere and is free from danger.
It may be considered the mother of the universe.
I do not know its name; I call it Tao.
If forced to give it a name, I shall call it Great.
Now being great means functioning everywhere.
Functioning everywhere means far-reaching.
Being far-reaching means returning to the original point.
Therefore Tao is great.
T'ien is great.
Earth is great.
And the king is also great.
There are four great things in the universe, and the king is one
    of them.
Man models himself after earth.
Earth models itself after T'ien.
T'ien models itself after Tao.
And Tao models itself after the spontaneous.

27

A good traveler leaves no track or trace.
A good speech leaves no flaws.
A good reckoner uses no counters.
A well-shut door needs no bolts, and yet it cannot be opened.
A well-tied knot needs no rope and yet none can untie it.
Therefore the sage is always good in saving men and conse-
    quently no man is rejected.
He is always good in saving things and consequently nothing is re-
    jected.
This is called following the light [of Nature].
Therefore the good man is the teacher of the bad,

And the bad is the material from which the good may learn.
He who does not value the teacher,
Or greatly care for the material,
Is greatly deluded although he may be learned.
Such is the essential mystery.

28

He who knows the male [active force] and keeps to the female
  [the passive force or receptive element]
Becomes the ravine of the world.
Being the ravine of the world,
He will never depart from eternal virtue,
But returns to the state of infancy.
He who knows the white [glory] and yet keeps to the black [humil-
  ity],
Becomes the model for the world.
Being the model for the world,
He will never deviate from eternal virtue,
But returns to the state of the Ultimate of Non-being.
He who knows glory but keeps to humility,
Becomes the valley of the world.
Being the valley of the world,
He will be proficient in eternal virtue,
And returns to the state of simplicity [like uncarved wood].
When the uncarved wood is broken up, it is turned into concrete
  things [as Tao is transformed into the myriad things].
But when the sage uses it, he becomes the leading official.
Therefore the great ruler does not cut up.

29

When one desires to take over the empire and act on it [interfere
  with it],
I see that he will not succeed.
The empire is a spiritual thing, and should not be acted on.
He who acts on it harms it.
He who holds on to it loses it.
Among creatures some lead and some follow.
Some blow hot and some blow cold.

Some are strong and some are weak.
Some may break and some may fall.
Therefore the sage discards the extremes, the extravagant, and
the excessive.

30

He who assists the ruler with Tao does not dominate the world
with force.
The use of force usually brings requital.
Wherever armies are stationed, briers and thorns grow.
Great wars are always followed by famines.
A good [general] achieves his purpose and stops,
But dares not seek to dominate the world.
He achieves his purpose but does not brag about it.
He achieves his purpose but does not boast about it.
He achieves his purpose but is not proud of it.
He achieves his purpose but only as an unavoidable step.
He achieves his purpose but does not aim to dominate.
[For] after things reach their prime, they begin to grow old,
Which means being contrary to Tao.
Whatever is contrary to Tao will soon perish.

31

Fine weapons are instruments of evil.
They are hated by men.
Therefore those who possess Tao turn away from them.
The good ruler when at home honors the left.
When at war he honors the right.[5]
Weapons are instruments of evil, not the instruments of a good
ruler.
When he uses them unavoidably, he regards calm restraint as
the best principle.
Even when he is victorious, he does not regard it as praiseworthy,
For to praise victory is to delight in the slaughter of men.
He who delights in the slaughter of men will not succeed in the
empire.
In auspicious affairs, the left is honored.
In inauspicious affairs, the right is honored.

The lieutenant-general stands on the left.
The senior general stands on the right.
That is to say that the arrangement follows that of funeral ceremonies.
For the slaughter of the multitude, let us weep with sorrow and grief.
For a victory, let us observe the occasion with funeral ceremonies.

32

Tao is eternal and has no name.
Though its simplicity seems insignificant, none in the world can master it.
If kings and barons would hold on to it, all things would submit to them spontaneously.
Heaven and earth unite to drip sweet dew.
Without the command of men, it drips evenly over all.
As soon as there were regulations and institutions, there were names [differentiation of things].
As soon as there are names, know that it is time to stop.
It is by knowing when to stop that one can be free from danger.
In likeness, Tao in the world,
    may be compared to
    the sea into which the rivers and streams run.

35

Hold fast to the Great Form [Tao],
And all the world will come.
They come and will encounter no harm;
But enjoy comfort, peace, and health.
When there are music and dainties,
Passing strangers will stay.
But the words uttered by Tao,
How insipid and tasteless!
We look at Tao; it is imperceptible.
We listen to it; it is inaudible.
We use it; it is inexhaustible.

36

In order to contract,
    It is necessary first to expand.

In order to weaken,
  It is necessary first to strengthen.
In order to destroy,
  It is necessary first to promote.
In order to grasp,
  It is necessary first to give.
This is called subtle light.
The weak and the tender overcome the hard and the strong.
Fish should not be taken away from water.
And sharp weapons of the state should not be displayed to the people.

37

Tao invariably takes no action, and yet there is nothing left undone.
If kings and barons can keep it, all things will transform spontaneously.
If, after transformation, they should desire to be active,
I would restrain them with simplicity, which has no name.
Simplicity, which has no name, is free of desires.
Being free of desires, it is tranquil.
And the world will be at peace of its own accord.

38

The man of superior virtue is not [conscious of] his virtue,
And in this way he really possesses virtue.
The man of inferior virtue never loses [sight of] his virtue,
And in this way he loses his virtue.
The man of superior virtue takes no action, but has no ulterior motive to do so.
The man of inferior virtue takes action, and has an ulterior motive to do so.
The man of superior humanity takes action, but has no ulterior motive to do so.
The man of superior righteousness takes action, and has an ulterior motive to do so.
The man of superior propriety takes action,
And when people do not respond to it, he will stretch his arms and force it on them.

Therefore, only when Tao is lost does the doctrine of virtue arise.

When virtue is lost, only then does the doctrine of humanity arise.

When humanity is lost, only then does the doctrine of righteousness arise.

When righteousness is lost, only then does the doctrine of ritual arise.

Now, ritual is a superficial expression of loyalty and faithfulness, and the beginning of disorder.

Those who are the first to know have the flowers [appearance] of Tao but also the beginning of ignorance.

For this reason the great man dwells in the thick [substantial], and does not rest with the thin [superficial].

He dwells in the fruit [reality], and does not rest with the flower [appearance].

Therefore he rejects that, and accepts this.

39

Of old those that obtained the One:[6]

Heaven obtained the One and became clear.

Earth obtained the One and become tranquil.

The spiritual beings obtained the One and became divine.

The valley obtained the One and became full.

The myriad things obtained the One and lived and grew.

Kings and barons obtained the One and became rulers of the empire.

What made them so is the One.

If heaven had not thus become clear,

It would soon crack.

If the earth had not thus become tranquil,

It would soon be shaken.

If the spiritual beings had not thus become divine,

They would soon wither away.

If the valley had not thus become full,

It would soon become exhausted.

If the myriad things had not thus lived and grown,

They would soon become extinct.

If kings and barons had not thus become honorable and high in position,

They would soon fall.
Therefore humble station is the basis of honor.
The low is the foundation of the high.
For this reason kings and barons call themselves the orphaned,
the lonely ones, the unworthy.
Is this not regarding humble station as the basis of honor?
Is it not?
Therefore enumerate all the parts of a chariot as you may, and
you still have no chariot.
Rather than jingle like jade,
Resound like rocks.

42

Tao produced the One.
The One produced the two.
The two produced the three.
And the three produced the ten thousand things.
The ten thousand things carry the yin and embrace the yang,[7]
and through the blending of the material force they achieve
harmony.
People hate to be the orphaned, lonely, unworthy.
Yet kings and lords call themselves by these names.
Therefore it is often the case that things gain by losing and lose
by gaining.
What others have taught, I teach also:
"Violent and fierce people do not die a natural death."
I shall make this the father [basis or starting point] of my teaching.

44

Which does one love more, fame or one's own life?
Which is more valuable, one's own life or wealth?
Which is worse, gain or loss?
Therefore he who has lavish desires will spend extravagantly.
He who hoards most will lose heavily.
He who is contented suffers no disgrace.
He who knows when to stop is free from danger.
Therefore he can long endure.

47

One may know the world without going out of doors.
One may see the Tao of T'ien without looking through the windows.
The further one goes, the less one knows.
Therefore the sage knows without going about,
Understands without seeing,
And accomplishes without action.

49

The sage makes no personal judgments.
He regards the people's judgments as his own.
Those who are good I treat with goodness,
And those who are bad I also treat with goodness.
Thus goodness is attained.
I am honest to those who are honest,
And I am also honest to the dishonest.
Thus honesty is attained.
The sage, in the government of his empire, has no subjective viewpoint.
His mind forms a harmonious whole with that of his people.
They all lend their eyes and ears, and he treats them all as infants.

52

There was a beginning of the universe
Which may be called the Mother of the Universe.
He who has found the Mother
And thereby understands her sons
And having understood the sons,
Still keeps to its Mother,
Will be free from danger throughout his lifetime.
Close the mouth.
Shut the doors [of cunning and desire].
And to the end of life there will be [peace] without toil.
Open the mouth.
Meddle with affairs,
And to the end of life there will be no salvation.
Seeing what is small is called enlightenment.

Keeping to weakness is called strength.
Use the light.
Revert to enlightenment,
And thereby avoid danger to one's life—
This is called practicing the eternal.

53
If I had but little knowledge
I should, in walking on a broad way,
Fear getting off the road.
Broad ways are extremely even,
But people are fond of by-paths.
The courts are exceedingly splendid,
While the fields are exceedingly weedy,
And the granaries are exceedingly empty.
Elegant clothes are worn,
Sharp weapons are carried,
Foods and drinks are enjoyed beyond limit,
And wealth and treasures are accumulated in excess.
This is robbery and extravagance.
This is indeed not Tao.

55
He who possesses virtue in abundance
May be compared to an infant.
Poisonous insects will not sting him.
Fierce beasts will not seize him.
Birds of prey will not strike him.
His bones are weak, his sinews tender, but his grasp is firm.
He does not yet know the union of male and female,
But his virility is aroused.
This means that his essence is at its height.
He may cry all day without becoming hoarse,
This means that his harmony is perfect.
To know harmony means to be in accord with the eternal.
To be in accord with the eternal means to be enlightened.
To force the growth of life means ill omen.
For the mind to employ the vital force without restraint means vi-
    olence.

After things reach their prime, they begin to grow old,
Which means being contrary to Tao.
Whatever is contrary to Tao will soon perish.

57

Govern the state with correctness.
Operate the army with surprise tactics.
Administer the empire by engaging in no activity.
How do I know that this should be so?
By this:
> The more taboos and prohibitions there are in the world,
>> The poorer the people will be.
> The more sharp weapons the people have,
>> The more troubled the state will be.
> The more cunning and skill man possesses,
>> The more vicious things will appear.
> The more laws and orders are made prominent,
>> The more thieves and robbers there will be.
Therefore the sage says:
> I take no action and the people of themselves are transformed.
> I love tranquillity and the people of themselves become correct.
> I engage in no activity and the people of themselves become prosperous.
> I have no desires and the people of themselves become simple.

58

When the government is non-discriminative and dull,
The people are contented and generous.
When the government is searching and discriminative,
The people are disappointed and contentious.
Calamity is that upon which happiness depends;
Happiness is that in which calamity is latent.
Who knows when the limit will be reached?
Is there no correctness [used to govern the world]?
Then the correct again becomes the perverse
And the good will again become evil.
The people have been deluded for a long time.
Therefore the sage is as pointed as a square but does not pierce.

He is as acute as a knife but does not cut.
He is as straight as an unbent line but does not extend.
He is as bright as light but does not dazzle.

59

To rule people and to serve T'ien there is nothing better than to
    be sparing.
Only by being sparing can one recover quickly.
To recover quickly means to amass virtue.
By the massing of virtue one can overcome everything.
If one can overcome everything, then one's capacity is beyond
    anyone's conception.
When his capacity is beyond conception, he is fit to rule a state.
He who possesses the Mother of the state will last long.
This means that the roots are deep and the stalks are firm,
    which is the way of long life and everlasting existence.

61

A great state may be compared to the lower part of a river.
It is the converging point of the world;
    It is the female of the world.
The female always overcomes the male by quiescence,
    And by quiescence she gets underneath.
A big state can take over a small state if it places itself under the
    small state;
And the small state can take over a big state if it places itself under
    the big state.
Thus some, by placing themselves underneath, take over [others],
And some, by being [naturally] low, take over [other states].
After all, what a big state wants is but to annex and herd others,
And what a small state wants is merely to join and serve others.
For both big and small states to get what they want,
The big state should place itself low.

62

Tao is the storehouse of all things.
It is the good man's treasure and the bad man's refuge.
Fine words can buy honor,

And fine deeds can gain respect from others.
Even if a man is bad, why should he be rejected?
Therefore on the occasion of crowning an emperor or installing
    the three ministers,
Rather than present large pieces of jade preceded by teams of
    four horses,
It is better to kneel and offer this Tao.
Why did the ancients highly value this Tao?
Did they not say, "Those who seek shall have it and those who
    sin shall be freed"?
For this reason it is valued by the world.

64

What remains still is easy to hold.
What is not yet manifest is easy to plan for.
What is brittle is easy to crack.
What is minute is easy to scatter.
Deal with things before they appear.
Put things in order before disorder arises.
A tree as big as a man's embrace grows from a tiny shoot.
A tower of nine storeys begins with a heap of earth.
The journey of a thousand *li* starts from where one stands.
He who takes an action fails.
He who grasps things loses them.
For this reason the sage takes no action and therefore does not fail.
He grasps nothing and therefore he does not lose anything.
People in their handling of affairs often fail when they are about
    to succeed.
If one remains as careful at the end as he was at the beginning,
    there will be no failure.
Therefore the sage desires to have no desire.
He does not value rare treasures.
He learns to be unlearned, and returns to what the multitude
    has missed.
Thus he supports all things in their natural state but does not
    take any action.

65

In ancient times those who practiced Tao well
Did not seek to enlighten the people, but to make them ignorant.

People are difficult to govern because they have too much knowledge.

Therefore he who rules the state through knowledge is a robber of the state;

He who rules a state not through knowledge is a blessing to the state.

One who knows these two things also [knows] the standard.

Always to know the standard is called profound and secret virtue.

Virtue becomes deep and far-reaching,

And with it all things return to their original natural state.

Then complete harmony will be reached.

66

The great rivers and seas are kings of all mountain streams

Because they skillfully stay below them.

That is why they can be their kings.

Therefore, in order to be the superior of the people,

One must, in the use of words, place himself below them.

And in order to be ahead of the people,

One must, in one's own person, follow them.

Therefore the sage places himself above the people and they do not feel his weight.

He places himself in front of them and the people do not harm him.

Therefore the world rejoices in praising him without getting tired of it.

It is precisely because he does not compete that the world cannot compete with him.

67

All the world says that my Tao is great and does not seem to resemble the ordinary.

It is precisely because it is great that it does not resemble the ordinary.

If it did resemble, it would have been small for a long time.

I have three treasures. Guard and keep them:

The first is compassion,

The second is frugality,

And the third is not to dare to be ahead of the world.
Because of deep love, one is courageous.
Because of frugality, one is generous.
Because of not daring to be ahead of the world, one becomes the
    leader of the world.
Now, to be courageous by forsaking compassion,
To be generous by forsaking frugality,
And to be ahead of the world by forsaking following behind—
    This is fatal.
For deep love helps one to win in the case of attack,
    And to be firm in the case of defense.
When T'ien is to save a person,
    T'ien will protect him through compassion.

68

A skillful leader of troops is not oppressive with his military
    strength.
A skillful fighter does not become angry.
A skillful conqueror does not compete with people.
One who is skillful in using men puts himself below them.
This is called the virtue of not-competing.
This is called the strength to use men.
This is called linking with T'ien, the highest principle of old.

69

The strategists say:
    "I dare not take the offensive but I take the defensive;
    I dare not advance an inch but I retreat a foot."
This means:
    To march without formation,
    To stretch one's arm without showing it,
    To confront enemies without seeming to meet them,
    To hold weapons without seeming to have them.
There is no greater disaster than to make light of the enemy.
Making light of the enemy will destroy my treasures.
Therefore when armies are mobilized and issues joined,
The man who is sorry over the fact will win.

70

My doctrines are very easy to understand and very easy to prac-
tice,
But none in the world can understand or practice them.
My doctrines have a source; my deeds have a master.
It is because people do not understand this that they do not under-
stand me.
Few people know me, and therefore I am highly valued.
Therefore the sage wears coarse cloth[8] on top and carries jade in-
side his bosom.

71

To know that you do not know is the best.
To pretend to know when you do not know is a disease.
Only when one recognizes this disease as a disease can one be
frcc from the disease.
The sage is free from the disease.
Because he recognizes this disease to be disease, he is free from it.

72

When the people do not fear what is dreadful,
Then what is greatly dreadful will descend on them.
Do not reduce the size of their dwellings.
Do not oppress their lives.
It is because you do not oppress them that they are not oppressed.
Therefore the sage knows himself but does not show himself.
He loves himself but does not exalt himself.
Therefore he rejects the one but accepts the other.

73

He who is brave in daring will be killed.
He who is brave in not daring will live.
Of these two, one is advantageous and one is harmful.
Who knows why T'ien dislikes what it dislikes?
Even the sage considers it a difficult question.
The Tao of T'ien does not compete, and yet it skillfully achieves
victory.
It does not speak, and yet it skillfully responds to things.

It comes to you without your invitation.
It is not anxious about things and yet it plans well.
T'ien's net is indeed vast.
Though its meshes are wide, nothing slips through.

74

The people are not afraid of death.
Why, then, threaten them with death?
Suppose the people are always afraid of death and we can seize those who are vicious and kill them,
Who would dare to do so?
There is always the master executioner who kills.
To undertake executions for the master executioner is like hewing wood for the master carpenter.
Whoever undertakes to hew wood for the master carpenter rarely escapes injuring his own hands.

76

When man is born, he is tender and weak.
At death, he is stiff and hard.
All things, the grass as well as trees, are tender and supple while alive.
When dead, they are withered and dried.
Therefore the stiff and the hard are companions of death.
The tender and the weak are companions of life.
Therefore if the army is strong, it will not win.
If a tree is stiff, it will break.
The strong and the great are inferior, while the tender and the weak are superior.

80

Let there be a small country with few people.
Let there be ten times and a hundred times as many utensils
But let them not be used.
Let the people value their lives highly and not migrate far.
Even if there are ships and carriages, none will ride in them.
Even if there are armor and weapons, none will display them.
Let the people knot cords[9] once more and use them [in place of writing].

Let them relish their food, be pleased with their clothing, be content with their homes, and delight in their customs.

Though neighboring communities overlook one another and the crowing of cocks and barking of dogs can be heard,

Yet the people there may grow old and die without ever visiting one another.

15

The Historical Yang Chu, from the *Book of Lieh Tzŭ*

Ch'in Ku-li asked Yang Chu: "If you could help the whole world by sacrificing one hair of your body, would you do it?" [Yang Chu replied:] "The world certainly will not be helped by one hair."

—*Book of Lieh Tzŭ*, 7

Whether the *Tao-tê-ching* or the *Chuang Tzŭ* comes first, the *Book of Lieh Tzŭ* almost certainly comes third. The book appears to be a compilation by one or more anonymous authors living in the fourth century A.D. who worked with materials dating from the fourth to third centuries B.C. The extracts to follow come from Chapter 7 of the *Book of Lieh Tzŭ*, which contains material believed to originate in older sources. They concern one Yang Chu.

There are three Yang Chus in Chinese philosophy. First is the historical Yang Chu, the pre-Taoist or proto-Taoist thinker of c. 350 B.C. Second comes the Yang Chu of Taoist fiction and parable, whose interlocutors range anywhere between 600 and 300 B.C. Third is the Yang of the third or early fourth centuries A.D. through whom hedonist and anarchist ideas are expressed. It is the first, the forerunner of Taoist thought, a philosopher living in the fourth century, with whose ideas the present section is concerned.

Yang Chu is a conscientious objector to public service. Out of tune with the conviction among early Chinese thinkers that the true man must involve himself in government, he offers a philosophy for the individual who elects to stay out of politics. Mencius and others satirically distorted his concern for individual integrity with a jibe: Yang Chu would not give up even one hair of his body to save the Empire. True, but, according to Yang Chu, that is not the way to save the Empire. Instead, do not harm a hair of anyone, do not even try to benefit the Empire, neither give to others nor take from them, mind your own business, enjoy your own pleasures, and lo, you will see how well the Empire runs itself.

THE HISTORICAL YANG CHU, FROM THE *BOOK OF LIEH TZŬ*

Selections

I

Yang Chu said:

"Po-ch'êng Tzŭ-kao[1] would not benefit others at the cost of one hair; he renounced his state and retired to plough the fields. The Great Yü did not keep even his body for his own benefit; he worked to drain the Flood until one side of him was paralyzed.[2] A man of ancient times, if he could have benefited the Empire by the loss of one hair, would not have given it; and if everything in the Empire had been offered to him alone,

From A. C. Graham, tr., *The Book of Lieh Tzŭ* (London: John Murray, 1960). Reprinted with the kind permission of the translator.

would not have taken it. When no one would lose a hair, and no one would benefit the Empire, the Empire was in good order."

Ch'in Ku-li[3] asked Yang Chu:

"If you could help the whole world by sacrificing one hair of your body, would you do it?"

"The world certainly will not be helped by one hair."

"But supposing it did help, would you do it?"

Yang Chu did not answer him. When Ch'in Ku-li came out he told Mêng Sun-yang,[4] who said:

"You do not understand what is in my Master's mind. Let me explain. If you could win ten thousand pieces of gold by injuring your skin and flesh, would you do it?"

"I would."

"If you could gain a kingdom by cutting off one limb at the joint, would you do it?"

Ch'in Ku-li was silent for a while. Mêng Sun-yang continued:

"It is clear that one hair is a trifle compared with skin and flesh, and skin and flesh compared with one joint. However, enough hairs are worth as much as skin and flesh, enough skin and flesh as much as one joint. You cannot deny that one hair has its place among the myriad parts of the body; how can one treat it lightly?"

Ch'in Ku-li said:

"I do not know how to answer you. I can only say that if you were to question Lao Tzŭ and Kuan Yin[5] about your opinion they would agree with you, and if I were to question the Great Yü and Mo Tzŭ about mine they would agree with me."

Mêng Sun-yang thereupon turned to his disciples and changed the subject.

2

Yang Chu visited the King of Liang,[6] and told him that ruling the Empire was like rolling it in the palm of your hand. The King said:

"You have one wife and one concubine, whom you cannot control, and a garden of three acres, which you cannot weed. Are you the person to tell me that it is so easy to rule the Empire?"

"Have you seen a shepherd with his flock? Send a boy four foot high with a stick on his shoulder to follow a flock of a hundred sheep, and it will go East or West as he wishes. Make Yao lead one sheep, with Shun following behind with a stick on his shoulder, and they couldn't make the sheep budge. Besides, I have heard that the fish which can swallow a boat does not swim in side streams, the high-flying hawk and swan do not settle in ponds and puddles. Why? Because their aims are set very high. The *Huang-chung* and *Ta-lü* [7] music cannot accompany the dance in common entertainments. Why? Because its sound is too far above the ordinary. It is this that is meant by the saying: 'One who sets out on a great enterprise does not concern himself with trifles; one who achieves great success does not achieve small ones.' "

3

Yang Chu said:

"Man resembles the other species between heaven and earth, and like them owes his nature to the Five Elements.[8] He is the most intelligent of living things. But in man, nails and teeth are not strong enough to provide defence, skin and flesh are too soft for protection; he cannot run fast enough to escape danger, and he lacks fur and feathers to ward off heat and cold. He must depend on other things in order to tend his nature, must trust in knowledge and not rely on force. Hence the most valuable use of knowledge is for self-preservation, while the most ignoble use of force is to attack others.

"However, my body is not my possession; yet once born, I have no choice but to keep it intact. Other things are not my possessions; yet once I exist, I cannot dispense with them. Certainly, it is by the body that we live; but it is by means of other things that we tend it.

"Although I keep life and body intact, I cannot possess this body; although I may not dispense with things, I cannot possess these things. To possess these things, possess this body, would be violently to reserve for oneself body and things which belong to the world. Is it not only the sage, only the highest man, who treats as common possessions the body and the things which belong to the world? It is this which is meant by 'highest of the highest.' "

16

Chuang Tzŭ

Please may I ask how to rule the world?
—*Chuang Tzŭ,* 7

In the *Historical Records* of Ssŭ-ma Ch'ien where the few facts of Chuang Tzŭ's life (c. 369–c. 286 B.C.) are preserved, his personal name appears as Chou. He was born in a place called Mêng, probably in Honan, south of the Yellow River, and lived about the same time as Mencius (although neither one ever referred to the other). Chuang Tzŭ once served as a minor official in Mêng but declined an offer to the premiership (by King Wei of Ch'u) lest he lose his freedom.

The works of Chuang Tzŭ as they stand today consist of thirty-three chapters wherein stories, parables, and philosophic discourse all blend happily together. The first seven chapters, supposedly those of Chuang Tzŭ's own hand, are called the "inner chapters." Of the rest, fifteen are called the "outer," and eleven, the "miscellaneous chapters," to indicate that they are more likely to contain the insertions of pupils or others. Some excellent writing appears in these latter chapters, however, and while there have undoubtedly been many interpolations, especially here and there among the anecdotes, the question of wholesale forgery is complicated: if Chuang Tzŭ himself did not write the good passages, who did? Nowhere near as great a writer can be found around to fit the bill.

Chuang Tzŭ's influence has been tremendous. Even among Confucians, whose master and ideas he so soundly spoofed, he finds admirers. His writings have invigorated Buddhism in the growth of Zen, inspired Chinese art, particularly landscape painting and poetry, and furthered the transformation of Confucianism into Neo-Confucianism from the eleventh century A.D. onward.

While most of the classical philosophers of China had good imaginations, none showed true fantasy. They were too engrossed in the seriousness of statecraft to rollick with words; too impressed by the historian's presence at the king's right hand.

Chuang Tzŭ had fantasy. He thought statecraft a waste of time. He invented names of people and places; he parodied improbable stories in phony technical lingo, and had them acted out by pompous types. He feared no historian. What was the historian but a sermonizing scribbler, a mite on a piece of flotsam bobbing on the vast ocean?

Chuang Tzŭ knew how to put his own mind through dialectic paces and how to pour fantasy into paradox and prose. What he has to say, he knows how to say, and will tell you.

THE *CHUANG TZŬ*

Selections

Free and Easy Wandering (1)

o   o   o   o

Yao wanted to cede the empire to Hsü Yu.[1] "When the sun and moon have already come out," he said, "it's a waste of light to go on burning the torches, isn't it? When the seasonal rains are falling, it's a waste of

From Burton Watson, tr., *The Complete Works of Chuang Tzŭ* (New York: Columbia University Press, 1968). In the selections from the *Chuang Tzŭ*, whenever *t'ien* occurs as a separate character in the original Chinese, it will—no matter what its sense—be reproduced as *"t'ien."* The lower case (as contrasted with the upper-case "T'ien" used elsewhere herein) will serve to indicate that the import of the term in these writings fluctuates too often and subtly for nice, ready distinctions of meaning. See footnotes pp. 10 and 151 above and note 16, p. 393 below.

water to go on irrigating the fields. If you took the throne, the world would be well ordered. I go on occupying it, but all I can see are my failings. I beg to turn over the world to you."

Hsü Yu said, "You govern the world and the world is already well governed. Now if I take your place, will I be doing it for a name? But name is only the guest of reality—will I be doing it so I can play the part of a guest? When the tailor-bird builds her nest in the deep wood, she uses no more than one branch. When the mole drinks at the river, he takes no more than a bellyful. Go home and forget the matter, my lord. I have no use for the rulership of the world! Though the cook may not run his kitchen properly, the priest and the impersonator of the dead at the sacrifice do not leap over the wine casks and sacrificial stands and go take his place."

o   o   o   o

Discussion on Making All Things Equal (2)

Tzŭ-ch'i[2] of South Wall sat leaning on his armrest, staring up at the sky and breathing—vacant and far away, as though he'd lost his companion. Yen Ch'êng Tzŭ-yu, who was standing by his side in attendance, said, "What is this? Can you really make the body like a withered tree and the mind like dead ashes? The man leaning on the armrest now is not the one who leaned on it before!"

Tzŭ-ch'i said, "You do well to ask the question, Yen. Now I have lost myself. Do you understand that? You hear the piping of men, but you haven't heard the piping of earth. Or if you've heard the piping of earth, you haven't heard the piping of *t'ien!*"

Tzŭ-yu said, "May I venture to ask what this means?"

Tzŭ-ch'i said, "The Great Clod[3] belches out breath and its name is wind. So long as it doesn't come forth, nothing happens. But when it does, then ten thousand hollows begin crying wildly. Can't you hear them, long drawn out? In the mountain forests that lash and sway, there are huge trees a hundred spans around with hollows and openings like noses, like mouths, like ears, like jugs, like cups, like mortars, like rifts, like ruts. They roar like waves, whistle like arrows, screech, gasp, cry, wail, moan, and howl, those in the lead calling out yeee! those behind calling out yüüü! In a gentle breeze they answer faintly, but in a full gale the chorus is gigantic. And when the fierce wind has passed on, then all the hollows are empty again. Have you never seen the tossing and trembling that goes on?"

Tzŭ-yu said, "By the piping of earth, then, you mean simply the sound of these hollows, and by the piping of man the sound of flutes and whistles. But may I ask about the piping of *t'ien?*"

Tzŭ-ch'i said, "Blowing on the ten thousand things in a different way, so that each can be itself—all take what they want for themselves, but who does the sounding?"

Great understanding is broad and unhurried; little understanding is cramped and busy. Great words are clear and limpid; little words are shrill and quarrelsome. In sleep, men's spirits go visiting; in waking hours, their bodies hustle. With everything they meet they become entangled. Day after day they use their minds in strife, sometimes grandiose, sometimes sly, sometimes petty. Their little fears are mean and trembly; their great fears are stunned and overwhelming. They bound off like an arrow or a crossbow pellet, certain that they are the arbiters of right and wrong. They cling to their position as though they had sworn before the gods, sure that they are holding on to victory. They fade like fall and winter—such is the way they dwindle day by day. They drown in what they do—you cannot make them turn back. They grow dark, as though sealed with seals—such are the excesses of their old age. And when their minds draw near to death, nothing can restore them to the light.

Joy, anger, grief, delight, worry, regret, fickleness, inflexibility, modesty, willfulness, candor, insolence—music from empty holes, mushrooms springing up in dampness, day and night replacing each other before us, and no one knows where they sprout from. Let it be! Let it be! It is enough that morning and evening we have them, and they are the means by which we live. Without them we would not exist; without us they would have nothing to take hold of. This comes close to the matter. But I do not know what makes them the way they are. It would seem as though they have some True Master, and yet I find no trace of him. He can act—that is certain. Yet I cannot see his form. He has identity but no form.

The hundred joints, the nine openings, the six organs, all come together and exist here as my body. But which part should I feel closest to? I should delight in all parts, you say? But there must be one I ought to favor more. If not, are they all of them mere servants? But if they are all servants, then how can they keep order among themselves? Or do they take turns being lord and servant? It would seem as though there must be some True Lord among them. But whether I succeed in discovering his identity or not, it neither adds to nor detracts from his Truth.

Once a man receives this fixed bodily form, he holds on to it, waiting for the end. Sometimes clashing with things, sometimes bending before them, he runs his course like a galloping steed, and nothing can stop him. Is he not pathetic? Sweating and laboring to the end of his days and never seeing his accomplishment, utterly exhausting himself and never knowing where to look for rest—can you help pitying him? I'm not dead yet! he says, but what good is that? His body decays, his mind follows it—can you deny that this is a great sorrow? Man's life has always been a muddle like this. How could I be the only muddled one, and other men not muddled?

So it is that long ago Yao said to Shun, "I want to attack the rulers of Tsung, Kuei, and Hsü-ao.[4] Even as I sit on my throne, this thought nags at me. Why is this?"

Shun replied, "These three rulers are only little dwellers in the weeds and brush. Why this nagging desire? Long ago, ten suns came out all at once and the ten thousand things were all lighted up. And how much greater is virtue than these suns!"

o   o   o   o

Men eat the flesh of grass-fed and grain-fed animals, deer eat grass, centipedes find snakes tasty, and hawks and falcons relish mice. Of these four, which knows how food ought to taste? Monkeys pair with monkeys, deer go out with deer, and fish play around with fish. Men claim that Mao-ch'iang and Lady Li were beautiful, but if fish saw them they would dive to the bottom of the stream, if birds saw them they would fly away, and if deer saw them they would break into a run. Of these four, which knows how to fix the standard of beauty for the world? The way I see it, the rules of benevolence and righteousness and the paths of right and wrong are all hopelessly snarled and jumbled. How could I know anything about such discriminations?

o   o   o   o

I'm going to try speaking some reckless words and I want you to listen to them recklessly.[5] How will that be? The sage leans on the sun and moon, tucks the universe under his arm, merges himself with things, leaves the confusion and muddle as it is, and looks on slaves as exalted. Ordinary men strain and struggle; the sage is stupid and blockish. He takes part in ten thousand ages and achieves simplicity in oneness. For him, all the ten thousand things are what they are, and thus they enfold each other.

How do I know that loving life is not a delusion? How do I know that in hating death I am not like a man who, having left home in his youth, has forgotten the way back?

Lady Li was the daughter of the border guard of Ai. When she was first taken captive and brought to the state of Chin, she wept until her tears drenched the collar of her robe. But later, when she went to live in the palace of the ruler, shared his couch with him, and ate the delicious meats of his table, she wondered why she had ever wept. How do I know that the dead do not wonder why they ever longed for life?

He who dreams of drinking wine may weep when morning comes; he who dreams of weeping may in the morning go off to hunt. While he is dreaming he does not know it is a dream, and in his dream he may even try to interpret a dream. Only after he wakes does he know it was a dream. And someday there will be a great awakening when we know that this is all a great dream. Yet the stupid believe they are awake, busily and brightly assuming they understand things, calling this man ruler, that one herdsman—how dense! Confucius and you are both dreaming! And when I say you are dreaming, I am dreaming, too. Words like these will be labeled the Supreme Swindle. Yet, after ten thousand generations, a great sage may appear who will know their meaning, and it will still be as though he appeared with astonishing speed.

Suppose you and I have had an argument. If you have beaten me instead of my beating you, then are you necessarily right and am I necessarily wrong? If I have beaten you instead of your beating me, then am I necessarily right and are you necessarily wrong? Is one of us right and the other wrong? Are both of us right or are both of us wrong? If you and I don't know the answer, then other people are bound to be even more in the dark. Whom shall we get to decide what is right? Shall we get someone who agrees with you to decide? But if he already agrees with you, how can he decide fairly? Shall we get someone who agrees with me? But if he already agrees with me, how can he decide? Shall we get someone who disagrees with both of us? But if he already disagrees with both of us, how can he decide? Shall we get someone who agrees with both of us? But if he already agrees with both of us, how can he decide? Obviously, then, neither you nor I nor anyone else can know the answer. Shall we wait for still another person?

But waiting for one shifting voice to pass judgment on another is the same as waiting for none of them. Harmonize them all with the Equality of *t'ien*, leave them to their endless changes, and so live out your years. What do I mean by harmonizing them with the Equality of *t'ien?* Right is not right; so is not so. If right were really right, it would differ so clearly from not right that there would be no need for argument. If so were really so, it would differ so clearly from not so that there would be no need for argument. Forget the years; forget distinctions. Leap into the boundless and make it your home!

o   o   o   o

Once Chuang Chou dreamt he was a butterfly, a butterfly flitting and fluttering around, happy with himself and doing as he pleased. He didn't know he was Chuang Chou. Suddenly he woke up and there he was, solid and unmistakable Chuang Chou. But he didn't know if he was Chuang Chou who had dreamt he was a butterfly, or a butterfly dreaming he was Chuang Chou. Between Chuang Chou and a butterfly there must be *some* distinction! This is called the Transformation of Things.

The Secret of Caring for Life (3)

Your life has a limit but knowledge has none. If you use what is limited to pursue what has no limit, you will be in danger. If you understand this and still strive for knowledge, you will be in danger for certain! If you do good, stay away from fame. If you do evil, stay away from punishments. Follow the middle; go by what is constant, and you can stay in one piece, keep yourself alive, look after your parents, and live out your years.

Cook Ting was cutting up an ox for Lord Wên-hui. At every touch of his hand, every heave of his shoulder, every move of his feet, every thrust of his knee—zip! zoop! He slithered the knife along with a zing, and all was in perfect rhythm, as though he were performing the dance of the Mulberry Grove or keeping time to the *Ching-shou* music.

"Ah, this is marvelous!" said Lord Wên-hui. "Imagine skill reaching such heights!"

Cook Ting laid down his knife and replied, "What I care about is the Way, which goes beyond skill. When I first began cutting up oxen, all I could see was the ox itself. After three years I no longer saw the whole ox. And now—now I go at it by spirit and don't look with my eyes. Perception and understanding have come to a stop and spirit moves where it wants. I go along with the natural makeup, strike in the big hollows, guide the knife through the big openings, and follow things as they are. So I never touch the smallest ligament or tendon, much less a main joint.

"A good cook changes his knife once a year—because he cuts. A mediocre cook changes his knife once a month—because he hacks. I've had this knife of mine for nineteen years and I've cut up thousands of oxen with it, and yet the blade is as good as though it had just come from the grindstone. There are spaces between the joints, and the blade of the knife has really no thickness. If you insert what has no thickness into such spaces, then there's plenty of room—more than enough for the blade to play about in. That's why after nineteen years the blade of my knife is still as good as when it first came from the grindstone.

"However, whenever I come to a complicated place, I size up the difficulties, tell myself to watch out and be careful, keep my eyes on what I'm doing, work very slowly, and move the knife with the greatest subtlety, until—flop! the whole thing comes apart like a clod of earth crumbling to the ground. I stand there holding the knife and look all around me, completely satisfied and reluctant to move on, and then I wipe off the knife and put it away."

"Excellent!" said Lord Wên-hui. "I have heard the words of Cook Ting and learned how to care for life!"

o   o   o   o

In the World of Men (4)

Yen Hui[6] went to see Confucius and asked permission to take a trip.

"Where are you going?"

"I'm going to Wei."

"What will you do there?"

"I have heard that the ruler of Wei is very young. He acts in an independent manner, thinks little of how he rules his state, and fails to see his faults. It is nothing to him to lead his people into peril, and his dead are reckoned by swampfuls like so much grass. His people have nowhere to turn. I have heard you say, Master, 'Leave the state that is well ordered and go to the state in chaos! At the doctor's gate are many sick men.' I want to use these words as my standard, in hopes that I can restore his state to health."

"Ah," said Confucius, "you will probably go and get yourself executed, that's all. The Way [*Tao*] doesn't want things mixed in with it. When it becomes a mixture, it becomes many ways; with many ways, there is a lot of bustle; and where there is a lot of bustle, there is trouble —trouble that has no remedy! The Perfect Man of ancient times made sure that he had it in himself before he tried to give it to others. When you're not even sure what you've got in yourself, how do you have time to bother about what some tyrant is doing?"

o   o   o   o

Yen Hui said, "If I am grave and empty-hearted, diligent and of one mind, won't that do?"

"Goodness, how could *that* do? You may put on a fine outward show and seem very impressive, but you can't avoid having an uncertain look on your face, any more than an ordinary man can. And then you try to gauge this man's feelings and seek to influence his mind. But with him, what is called 'the virtue that advances a little each day' would not succeed, much less a great display of virtue! He will stick fast to his position and never be converted. Though he may make outward signs of agreement, inwardly he will not give it a thought! How could such an approach succeed?"

o   o   o   o

Yen Hui said, "I have nothing more to offer. May I ask the proper way?"

"You must fast!" said Confucius. "I will tell you what that means. Do you think it is easy to do anything while you have a mind? If you do, Bright *t'ien* will not sanction you."

Yen Hui said, "My family is poor. I haven't drunk wine or eaten any strong foods for several months. So can I be considered as having fasted?"

"That is the fasting one does before a sacrifice, not the fasting of the mind."

"May I ask what the fasting of the mind is?"

Confucius said, "Make your will one! Don't listen with your ears, listen with your mind. No, don't listen with your mind, but listen with your spirit. Listening stops with the ears, the mind stops with recognition, but spirit is empty and waits on all things. The Way gathers in emptiness alone. Emptiness is the fasting of the mind."

Yen Hui said, "Before I heard this, I was certain that I was Hui. But now that I have heard it, there is no more Hui. Can this be called emptiness?"

"That's all there is to it," said Confucius. "Now I will tell you. You may go and play in his bird cage, but never be moved by fame. If he listens, then sing; if not, keep still. Have no gate, no opening, but make oneness your house and live with what cannot be avoided. Then you will be close to success. . . ."

o   o   o   o

Tzŭ-kao, duke of Shê, who was being sent on a mission to Ch'i, consulted Confucius. "The king is sending me on a very important mission. Ch'i will probably treat me with great honor but will be in no hurry to do anything more. Even a commoner cannot be forced to act, much less one of the feudal lords. I am very worried about it.

o   o   o   o

As a minister, I am not capable of carrying out this mission. But perhaps you have some advice you can give me. . . ."

Confucius said, "In the world, there are two great decrees: one is fate and the other is duty. That a son should love his parents is fate—you cannot erase this from his heart. That a subject should serve his ruler is duty—there is no place he can go and be without his ruler, no place he can escape to between the sky and earth. These are called the great decrees. Therefore, to serve your parents and be content to follow them anywhere—this is the perfection of filial piety. To serve your ruler and be content to do anything for him—this is the peak of loyalty. And to serve your own mind so that sadness or joy do not sway or move it; to understand what you can do nothing about and to be content with it as with fate—this is the perfection of virtue. As a subject and a son, you are bound to find things you cannot avoid. If you act in accordance with the state of affairs and forget about yourself, then what leisure will you have to love life and hate death? Act in this way and you will be all right.

"I want to tell you something else I have learned. In all human relations, if the two parties are living close to each other, they may form a bond through personal trust. But if they are far apart, they must use words to communicate their loyalty, and words must be transmitted by someone. To transmit words that are either pleasing to both parties or infuriating to both parties is one of the most difficult things in the world. Where both parties are pleased, there must be some exaggeration of the good points; and where both parties are angered, there must be some exaggeration of the bad points. Anything that smacks of exaggeration is irresponsible. Where there is irresponsibility, no one will trust what is said, and when that happens, the man who is transmitting the words will be in danger. Therefore the aphorism says, 'Transmit the established facts; do not transmit words of exaggeration.' If you do that, you will probably come out all right.

"When men get together to pit their strength in games of skill, they start off in a light and friendly mood, but usually end up in a dark and angry one, and if they go on too long they start resorting to various underhanded tricks. When men meet at some ceremony to drink, they start off in an orderly manner, but usually end up in disorder, and if they go on too long they start indulging in various irregular amusements. It is the same with all things. What starts out being sincere usually ends up being deceitful. What was simple in the beginning acquires monstrous proportions in the end.

"Words are like wind and waves; actions are a matter of gain and loss. Wind and waves are easily moved; questions of gain and loss easily lead to danger. Hence anger arises from no other cause than clever words and one-sided speeches. When animals face death, they do not care what cries they make; their breath comes in gasps and a wild fierceness is born in their hearts. [Men, too,] if you press them too hard, are bound to answer you with ill-natured hearts, though they do not know why they do so. If they themselves do not understand why they behave like this, then who knows where it will end?

"Therefore the aphorism says, 'Do not deviate from your orders; do not press for completion.' To go beyond the limit is excess; to deviate from orders or press for completion is a dangerous thing. A good completion takes a long time; a bad completion cannot be changed later. Can you afford to be careless?

"Just go along with things and let your mind move freely. Resign yourself to what cannot be avoided and nourish what is within you—this is best. What more do you have to do to fulfill your mission? Nothing is as good as following orders—that's how difficult it is!"

o   o   o   o

There's Crippled Shu—chin stuck down in his navel, shoulders up above his head, pigtail pointing at the sky, his five organs on the top, his two thighs pressing his ribs. By sewing and washing, he gets enough to fill his mouth; by handling a winnow and sifting out the good grain, he makes enough to feed ten people. When the authorities call out the troops, he stands in the crowd waving good-by; when they get up a big work party, they pass him over because he's a chronic invalid. And when they are doling out grain to the ailing, he gets three big measures and ten bundles of firewood. With a crippled body, he's still able to look after himself and finish out the years *t'ien* gave him. How much better, then, if he had crippled virtue!

o   o   o   o

When Confucius visited Ch'u, Chieh Yü, the madman of Ch'u, wandered by his gate crying, "Phoenix, phoenix, how has virtue failed! The future you cannot wait for; the past you cannot pursue. When the world has the Way, the sage succeeds; when the world is without the Way, the sage survives. In times like the present, we do well to escape penalty. Good fortune is light as a feather, but nobody' knows enough to pick it up. Misfortune is heavy as the earth, but nobody knows how to stay out of its way. Leave off, leave off—this teaching men virtue! Dangerous, dangerous—to mark off the ground and run! Fool, fool—don't spoil my walking! I walk a crooked way—don't step on my feet. The mountain trees do themselves harm; the grease in the torch burns itself up. The cinnamon can be eaten and so it gets cut down; the lacquer tree can be used and so it gets hacked apart. All men know the use of the useful, but nobody knows the use of the useless!"

o   o   o   o

The Sign of Virtue Complete (5)

o   o   o   o

Hui Tzŭ[7] said to Chuang Tzŭ, "Can a man really be without feelings?"

Chuang Tzŭ: "Yes."

Hui Tzŭ: "But a man who has no feelings—how can you call him a man?"

Chuang Tzŭ: "The Way gave him a face; *t'ien* gave him a form—why can't you call him a man?"

Hui Tzŭ: "But if you've already called him a man, how can he be without feelings?"

Chuang Tzŭ: "That's not what I mean by feelings. When I talk about having no feelings, I mean that a man doesn't allow good or bad to get in and do him harm. He just lets things be the way they are and doesn't try to help life along."

Hui Tzŭ: "If he doesn't try to help life along, then how can he keep himself alive?"

Chuang Tzŭ: "The Way gave him a face; *t'ien* gave him a form. He doesn't let good or bad get in and do him harm. You, now—you treat your spirit like an outsider. You wear out your energy, leaning on a tree and moaning, slumping at your desk and dozing—*t'ien* picked out a body for you and you use it to gibber about 'hard' and 'white'!" [8]

The Great and Venerable Teacher (6)

He who knows what it is that *t'ien* does, and knows what it is that man does, has reached the peak. Knowing what it is that *t'ien* does, he lives with *t'ien*. Knowing what it is that man does, he uses the knowledge of what he knows to help out the knowledge of what he doesn't know, and lives out the years that *t'ien* gave him without being cut off midway—this is the perfection of knowledge.

However, there is a difficulty. Knowledge must wait for something to fix on to, and that which it waits for is never certain. How, then, can I know that what I call *t'ien* is not really man, and what I call man is not really *t'ien?* There must first be a True Man[9] before there can be true knowledge.

What do I mean by a True Man? The True Man of ancient times did not rebel against want, did not grow proud in plenty, and did not plan his affairs. Being like this, he could commit an error and not regret it, could meet with success and not make a show. Being like this, he could climb the high places and not be frightened, could enter the water and not get wet, could enter the fire and not get burned. His knowledge was able to climb all the way up to the Way like this.

The True Man of ancient times slept without dreaming and woke without care; he ate without savoring and his breath came from deep inside. The True Man breathes with his heels; the mass of men breathe with their throats. Crushed and bound down, they gasp out their words as though they were retching. Deep in their passions and desires, they are shallow in the workings of *t'ien*.

The True Man of ancient times knew nothing of loving life, knew nothing of hating death. He emerged without delight; he went back in without a fuss. He came briskly, he went briskly, and that was all. He didn't forget where he began; he didn't try to find out where he would end. He received something and took pleasure in it; he forgot about it and handed it back again. This is what I call not using the mind to repel the Way, not using man to help out *t'ien*. This is what I call the True Man.

Since he is like this, his mind forgets, his face is calm; his forehead is broad. He is chilly like autumn, balmy like spring, and his joy and anger prevail through the four seasons. He goes along with what is right for things and no one knows his limit. Therefore, when the sage calls out the troops, he may overthrow nations but he will not lose the hearts of the people. His bounty enriches ten thousand ages but he has no love for men. Therefore he who delights in bringing success to things is not a sage; he who has affections is not benevolent; he who looks for the right time is not a worthy man; he who cannot encompass both profit and loss is not a gentleman; he who thinks of conduct and fame and misleads himself is not a man of breeding; and he who destroys himself and is without truth is not a user of men. Those like Hu Pu-hsieh, Wu Kuang, Po I, Shu Ch'i, Chi Tzŭ, Hsü Yü, Chi To, and Shên-t'u Ti[10]—all of them slaved in the service of other men, took joy in bringing other men joy, but could not find joy in any joy of their own.

This was the True Man of old: his bearing was lofty and did not crumble; he appeared to lack but accepted nothing; he was dignified in his correctness but not insistent; he was vast in his emptiness but not ostentatious. Mild and cheerful, he seemed to be happy; reluctant, he could not help doing certain things; annoyed, he let it show in his face; relaxed, he rested in his virtue. Tolerant, he seemed to be part of the world; towering alone, he could be checked by nothing; withdrawn, he seemed to prefer to cut himself off; bemused, he forgot what he was going to say.

He regarded penalties as the body, rites as the wings, wisdom as what is timely, virtue as what is reasonable. Because he regarded penalties as the body, he was benign in his killing. Because he regarded rites as the wings, he got along in the world. Because he regarded wisdom as what is timely, there were things that he could not keep from doing. Because he regarded virtue as what is reasonable, he was like a man with two feet who gets to the top of the hill. And yet people really believed that he worked hard to get there.

Therefore his liking was one and his not liking was one. His being one was one and his not being one was one. In being one, he was acting as a companion of *t'ien*. In not being one, he was acting as a companion of man. When man and *t'ien* do not defeat each other, then he may be said to have the True Man.

Life and death are fated—constant as the succession of dark and dawn, a matter of *t'ien*. There are some things which man can do nothing about—all are a matter of the nature of creatures. If a man is willing to regard *t'ien* as a father and to love it, then how much more should he be willing to do for that which is even greater! If he is willing to regard the ruler as superior to himself and to die for him, then how much more should he be willing to do for the Truth!

When the springs dry up and the fish are left stranded on the ground, they spew each other with moisture and wet each other down with spit —but it would be much better if they could forget each other in the rivers and lakes. Instead of praising Yao and condemning Chieh,[11] it would be better to forget both of them and transform yourself with the Way. . . .

      o   o   o   o

Master Ssŭ, Master Yü, Master Li, and Master Lai were all four talking together. "Who can look upon inaction as his head, on life as his back, and on death as his rump?" they said. "Who knows that life and death, existence and annihilation, are all a single body? I will be his friend!"

The four men looked at each other and smiled. There was no disagreement in their hearts and so the four of them became friends.

All at once Master Yü fell ill. Master Ssŭ went to ask how he was. "Amazing!" said Master Yü. "The Creator[12] is making me all crookedy like this! My back sticks up like a hunchback and my vital organs are on top of me. My chin is hidden in my navel, my shoulders are up above my head, and my pigtail points at the sky. It must be some dislocation of the *yin* and *yang!*"[13]

Yet he seemed calm at heart and unconcerned. Dragging himself haltingly to the well, he looked at his reflection and said, "My, my! So the Creator is making me all crookedy like this!"

"Do you resent it?" asked Master Ssŭ.

"Why no, what would I resent? If the process continues, perhaps in time he'll transform my left arm into a rooster. In that case I'll keep watch on the night. Or perhaps in time he'll transform my right arm into a crossbow pellet and I'll shoot down an owl for roasting. Or perhaps in time he'll transform my buttocks into cartwheels. Then, with my spirit for a horse, I'll climb up and go for a ride. What need will I ever have for a carriage again?

"I received life because the time had come; I will lose it because the order of things passes on. Be content with this time and dwell in this order and then neither sorrow nor joy can touch you. In ancient times this was called the 'freeing of the bound.' There are those who cannot free themselves, because they are bound by things. But nothing can ever win against *t'ien*—that's the way it's always been. What would I have to resent?"

Suddenly Master Lai grew ill. Gasping and wheezing, he lay at the point of death. His wife and children gathered round in a circle and began to cry. Master Li, who had come to ask how he was, said, "Shoo! Get back! Don't disturb the process of change!"

Then he leaned against the doorway and talked to Master Lai. "How marvelous the Creator is! What is he going to make out of you next? Where is he going to send you? Will he make you into a rat's liver? Will he make you into a bug's arm?"

Master Lai said, "A child, obeying his father and mother, goes wherever he is told, east or west, south or north. And the yin and yang—how much more are they to a man than father or mother! Now that they have brought me to the verge of death, if I should refuse to obey them, how perverse I would be! What fault is it of theirs? The Great Clod burdens me with form, labors me with life, eases me in old age, and rests me in death. So if I think well of my life, for the same reason I must think well of my death. When a skilled smith is casting metal, if the metal should leap up and say, 'I insist upon being made into a Mo-yeh!' [14] he would surely regard it as very inauspicious metal indeed. Now, having had the audacity to take on human form once, if I should say, 'I don't want to be anything but a man! Nothing but a man!' the Creator would surely regard me as a most inauspicious sort of person. So now I think of *t'ien* and earth as a great furnace, and the Creator as a skilled smith. Where could he send me that would not be all right? I will go off to sleep peacefully, and then with a start I will wake up.

o   o   o   o

"What's more, we go around telling each other,[15] I do this, I do that— but how do we know that this 'I' we talk about has any 'I' to it? You dream you're a bird and soar up into the sky; you dream you're a fish and dive down in the pool. But now when you tell me about it, I don't know whether you are awake or whether you are dreaming. Running around accusing others is not as good as laughing, and enjoying a good laugh is not as good as going along with things. Be content to go along and forget about change and then you can enter the mysterious oneness of *t'ien*."

o   o   o   o

Yi Erh-tzŭ went to see Hsü Yu.[16] Hsü Yu said, "What kind of assistance has Yao been giving you?"

Yi Erh-tzŭ said, "Yao told me, 'You must learn to practice benevolence and righteousness and to speak clearly about right and wrong!' "

"Then why come to see *me?*" said Hsü Yu. "Yao has already tattooed you with benevolence and righteousness and cut off your nose with right and wrong. Now how do you expect to go wandering in any far-away, carefree, and as-you-like-it paths?"

o   o   o   o

Yen Hui said, "I'm improving!"

Confucius said, "What do you mean by that?"

"I've forgotten benevolence and righteousness!"

"That's good. But you still haven't got it."

Another day, the two met again and Yen Hui said, "I'm improving!"

"What do you mean by that?"

"I've forgotten rites and music!"

"That's good. But you still haven't got it."

Another day, the two met again and Yen Hui said, "I'm improving!"

"What do you mean by that?"

"I can sit down and forget everything!"

Confucius looked very startled and said, "What do you mean, sit down and forget everything?"

Yen Hui said, "I smash up my limbs and body, drive out perception and intellect, cast off form, do away with understanding, and make myself identical with the Great Thoroughfare.[17] This is what I mean by sitting down and forgetting everything."

Confucius said, "If you're identical with it, you must have no more likes! If you've been transformed, you must have no more constancy! So you really are a worthy man after all! With your permission, I'd like to become your follower."

o   o   o   o

Master Yü and Master Sang were friends. Once it rained incessantly for ten days. Master Yü said to himself, Master Sang is probably having a bad time, and he wrapped up some rice and took it for his friend to eat. When he got to Master Sang's gate, he heard something like singing or crying, and someone striking a lute and saying:

> Father?
> Mother?
> T'ien?
> Man?

It was as though the voice would not hold out and the singer were rushing to get through the words.

Master Yü went inside and said, "What do you mean—singing a song like that!"

"I was pondering what it is that has brought me to this extremity, but I couldn't find the answer. My father and mother surely wouldn't wish this poverty on me. *T'ien* covers all without partiality; earth bears up all without partiality—*t'ien* and earth surely wouldn't single me out to make me poor. I try to discover who is doing it, but I can't get the answer. Still, here I am—at the very extreme. It must be fate."

Fit for Emperors and Kings (7)

o   o   o   o

Chien Wu went to see the madman Chieh Yü. Chieh Yü said, "What was Chung Shih telling you the other day?"

Chien Wu said, "He told me that the ruler of men should devise his own principles, standards, ceremonies, and regulations, and then there will be no one who will fail to obey him and be transformed by them."

The madman Chieh Yü said, "This is bogus virtue! To try to govern the world like this is like trying to walk the ocean, to drill through a river, or to make a mosquito shoulder a mountain! When the sage governs, does he govern what is on the *outside?* He makes sure of himself first, and then he acts. He makes absolutely certain that things can do what they are supposed to do, that is all. . . ."

o   o   o   o

T'ien Ken was wandering on the sunny side of Yin Mountain. When he reached the banks of the Liao River, he happened to meet a Nameless Man. He questioned the man, saying, "Please may I ask how to rule the world?"

The Nameless Man said, "Get away from me, you peasant! What kind of a dreary question is that! I'm just about to set off with the Creator. And if I get bored with that, then I'll ride on the Light-and-Lissome Bird out beyond the six directions, wandering in the village of Not-Even-Anything and living in the Broad-and-Borderless field. What business do you have coming with this talk of governing the world and disturbing my mind?"

But T'ien Ken repeated his question. The Nameless Man said, "Let your mind wander in simplicity, blend your spirit with the vastness, follow along with things the way they are, and make no room for personal views—then the world will be governed."

Yang-tzǔ Chü[18] went to see Lao Tan[19] and said, "Here is a man swift as an echo, strong as a beam, with a wonderfully clear understanding of the principles of things, studying the Way without ever letting up—a man like this could compare with an enlightened king, couldn't he?"

Lao Tan said, "In comparison to the sage, a man like this is a drudging slave, a craftsman bound to his calling, wearing out his body, grieving his mind. They say it is the beautiful markings of the tiger and the leopard that call out the hunters, the nimbleness of the monkey and the ability of the dog to catch rats that make them end up chained. A man like this—how could he compare to an enlightened king?"

Yang-tzǔ Chü, much taken aback, said, "May I venture to ask about the government of the enlightened king?"

Lao Tan said, "The government of the enlightened king? His achievements blanket the world but appear not to be his own doing. His transforming influence touches the ten thousand things but the people do not depend on him. With him there is no promotion or praise—he lets everything find its own enjoyment. He takes his stand on what cannot be fathomed and wanders where there is nothing at all."

o   o   o   o

Do not be an embodier of fame; do not be a storehouse of schemes; do not be an undertaker of projects; do not be a proprietor of wisdom. Embody to the fullest what has no end and wander where there is no trail. Hold on to all that you have received from *t'ien* but do not think you have gotten anything. Be empty, that is all. The Perfect Man uses his mind like a mirror—going after nothing, welcoming nothing, responding but not storing. Therefore he can win out over things and not hurt himself.

The emperor of the South Sea was called Shu [Brief], the emperor of the North Sea was called Hu [Sudden], and the emperor of the central region was called Hun-tun [Chaos]. Shu and Hu from time to time came together for a meeting in the territory of Hun-tun, and Hun-tun treated them very generously. Shu and Hu discussed how they could repay his kindness. "All men," they said, "have seven openings so they can see, hear, eat, and breathe. But Hun-tun alone doesn't have any. Let's try boring him some!"

Every day they bored another hole, and on the seventh day Hun-tun died.

Webbed Toes (8)

Two toes webbed together, a sixth finger forking off—these come from the inborn nature but are excretions as far as Virtue is concerned. Swelling tumors and protruding wens—these come from the body but are excretions as far as the inborn nature is concerned. Men overnice in the ways of benevolence and righteousness try to put these into practice, even to line them up with the five vital organs! This is not the right approach to the Way and its Virtue. Therefore he who has two toes webbed together has grown a flap of useless flesh; he who has a sixth finger forking out of his hand has sprouted a useless digit; and he who imposes overnice ways, webs, and forked fingers upon the original form of the five vital organs will become deluded and perverse in the practice of benevolence and righteousness and overnice in the use of his hearing and sight. Thus he who is web-toed in eyesight will be confused by the five colors, bewitched by patterns and designs, by the dazzling hues of blue and yellow, of embroidery and brocade—am I wrong? So we have Li Chu. He who is overnice in hearing will be confused by the five notes, bewitched by the six tones, by the sounds of metal and stone, strings and woodwinds, the *huang-chung* and *ta-lü*[20] pitch pipes—am I wrong? So we have Music Master K'uang. He who is fork-fingered with benevolence will tear out the Virtue given him and stifle his inborn nature in order to seize fame and reputation, leading the world on with pipe and drum in the service of an unattainable ideal—am I wrong? So we have Tsêng and Shih.[21] He who is web-toed in argumentation will pile up bricks, knot the plumb line, apply the curve, letting his mind wander in the realm of "hard" and "white," "likeness" and "difference," huffing and puffing away, lauding his useless words—am I wrong? So we have Yang and Mo.[22] All these men walk a way that is overnice, web-toed, wide of the mark, fork-fingered, not that which is the True Rightness of the world.

He who holds to True Rightness does not lose the original form of his inborn nature. So for him joined things are not webbed toes, things forking off are not superfluous fingers, the long is never too much, the short is never too little. The duck's legs are short, but to stretch them out would worry him; the crane's legs are long, but to cut them down would make him sad. What is long by nature needs no cutting off; what is short by nature needs no stretching. That would be no way to get rid of worry. I wonder, then, if benevolence and righteousness are part of man's true form? Those benevolent men—how much worrying they do!

The man with two toes webbed together would weep if he tried to tear them apart; the man with a sixth finger on his hand would howl if he tried to gnaw it off. Of these two, one has more than the usual number, the other has less, but in worrying about it they are identical. Nowadays the benevolent men of the age lift up weary eyes, worrying over the ills of the world, while the men of no benevolence tear apart the original form of their inborn nature in their greed for eminence and wealth. Therefore I wonder if benevolence and righteousness are really part of man's true form? From the Three Dynasties on down, what a lot of fuss and hubbub they have made in the world!

If we must use curve and plumb line, compass and square to make something right, this means cutting away its inborn nature; if we must use cords and knots, glue and lacquer to make something firm, this means violating its natural Virtue. So the crouchings and bendings of rites and music, the smiles and beaming looks of benevolence and righteousness, which are intended to comfort the hearts of the world, in fact destroy their constant naturalness.

For in the world there can be constant naturalness. Where there is constant naturalness, things are arced not by the use of the curve, straight not by the use of the plumb line, rounded not by compasses, squared not by T-squares, joined not by glue and lacquer, bound not by ropes and lines. Then all things in the world, simple and compliant, live and never know how they happen to live; all things, rude and unwitting, get what they need and never know how they happen to get it. Past and present it has been the same; nothing can do injury to this [principle]. Why then come with benevolence and righteousness, that tangle and train of glue and lacquer, ropes and lines, and try to wander in the realm of the Way and its Virtue? You will only confuse the world!

A little confusion can alter the sense of direction; a great confusion can alter the inborn nature. How do I know this is so? Ever since that man of the Yü[23] clan began preaching benevolence and righteousness and stirring up the world, all the men in the world have dashed headlong for benevolence and righteousness. This is because benevolence and righteousness have altered their inborn nature, is it not?

o   o   o   o

Horses' Hoofs (9)

Horses' hoofs are made for treading frost and snow, their coats for keeping out wind and cold. To munch grass, drink from the stream, lift up their feet and gallop—this is the true nature of horses. Though they might possess great terraces and fine halls, they would have no use for them.

Then along comes Po Lo. "I'm good at handling horses!" he announces, and proceeds to singe them, shave them, pare them, brand them, bind them with martingale and crupper, tie them up in stable and stall. By this time two or three out of ten horses have died. He goes on to starve them, make them go thirsty, race them, prance them, pull them into line, force them to run side by side, in front of them the worry of bit and rein, behind them the terror of whip and crop. By this time over half the horses have died.

The potter says, "I'm good at handling clay! To round it, I apply the compass; to square it, I apply the T-square." The carpenter says, "I'm good at handling wood! To arc it, I apply the curve; to make it straight, I apply the plumb line." But as far as inborn nature is concerned, the clay and the wood surely have no wish to be subjected to compass and square, curve and plumb line. Yet generation after generation sings out in praise, saying, "Po Lo is good at handling horses! The potter and the carpenter are good at handling clay and wood!" And the same fault is committed by the men who handle the affairs of the world!

In my opinion someone who was really good at handling the affairs of the world would not go about it like this. The people have their constant inborn nature. To weave for their clothing, to till for their food—this is the Virtue they share. They are one in it and not partisan, and it is called the Emancipation of *t'ien*. Therefore in a time of Perfect Virtue the gait of men is slow and ambling; their gaze is steady and mild. In such an age mountains have no paths or trails, lakes no boats or bridges. The ten thousand things live species by species, one group settled close to another. Birds and beasts form their flocks and herds, grass and trees grow to fullest height. So it happens that you can tie a cord to the birds and beasts and lead them about, or bend down the limb and peer into the nest of the crow and the magpie. In this age of Perfect Virtue men live the same as birds and beasts, group themselves side by side with the ten thousand things. Who then knows anything about "gentleman" or "petty man"? Dull and unwitting, men have no wisdom; thus their Virtue does not depart from them. Dull and unwitting, they have no desire; this is called uncarved simplicity. In uncarved simplicity the people attain their true nature.

Then along comes the sage, huffing and puffing after benevolence, reaching on tiptoe for righteousness, and the world for the first time has doubts; mooning and mouthing over his music, snipping and stitching away at his rites, and the world for the first time is divided. Thus, if the plain unwrought substance had not been blighted, how would there be any sacrificial goblets? If the white jade had not been shattered, how would there be any scepters and batons? If the Way and its Virtue had not been cast aside, how would there be any call for benevolence and righteousness? If the true form of the inborn nature had not been abandoned, how would there be any use for rites and music? If the five colors had not confused men, who would fashion patterns and hues? If the five notes had not confused them, who would try to tune things by the six tones? That the unwrought substance was blighted in order to fashion implements—this was the crime of the artisan. That the Way and its Virtue were destroyed in order to create benevolence and righteousness —this was the fault of the sage.

When horses live on the plain, they eat grass and drink from the streams. Pleased, they twine their necks together and rub; angry, they turn back to back and kick. This is all horses know how to do. But if you pile poles and yokes on them and line them up in crossbars and shafts, then they will learn to snap the crossbars, break the yoke, rip the carriage top, champ the bit, and chew the reins. Thus horses learn how to commit the worst kinds of mischief. This is the crime of Po Lo.

In the days of Ho Hsü,[24] people stayed home but didn't know what they were doing, walked around but didn't know where they were going. Their mouths crammed with food, they were merry; drumming on their bellies, they passed the time. This was as much as they were able to do. Then the sage came along with the crouchings and bendings of rites and music, which were intended to reform the bodies of the world; with the reaching-for-a-dangled-prize of benevolence and righteousness, which was intended to comfort the hearts of the world. Then for the first time people learned to stand on tiptoe and covet knowledge, to fight to the death over profit, and there was no stopping them. This in the end was the fault of the sage.

Rifling Trunks (10)

o   o   o   o

Have you alone never heard of that age of Perfect Virtue? Long ago, in the time of [the kings of antiquity], the people knotted cords and used them. They relished their food, admired their clothing, enjoyed their customs, and were content with their houses. Though neighboring states were within sight of each other, and could hear the cries of each other's dogs and chickens, the people grew old and died without ever traveling beyond their own borders. At a time such as this, there was nothing but the most perfect order.

But now something has happened to make people crane their necks and stand on tiptoe. "There's a worthy man in such and such a place!" they cry and, bundling up their provisions, they dash off. At home, they abandon their parents; abroad, they shirk the service of their ruler. Their footprints form an unending trail to the borders of the other feudal lords, their carriage tracks weave back and forth a thousand *li* and more. This is the fault of men in high places who covet knowledge.

As long as men in high places covet knowledge and are without the Way, the world will be in great confusion. How do I know this is so? Knowledge enables men to fashion bows, crossbows, nets, stringed arrows, and like contraptions, but when this happens the birds flee in confusion to the sky. Knowledge enables men to fashion fishhooks, lures, seines, dragnets, trawls, and weirs, but when this happens the fish flee in confusion to the depths of the water. Knowledge enables men to fashion pitfalls, snares, cages, traps, and gins, but when this happens the beasts flee in confusion to the swamps. And the flood of rhetoric that enables men to invent wily schemes and poisonous slanders, the glib gabble of "hard" and "white," the foul-fustian of "same" and "different" bewilder the understanding of common men. So the world is dulled and darkened by great confusion. The blame lies in this coveting of knowledge.

In the world everyone knows enough to pursue what he does not know, but no one knows enough to pursue what he already knows. Everyone knows enough to condemn what he takes to be no good, but no one knows enough to condemn what he has already taken to be good. This is how the great confusion comes about, blotting out the brightness of sun and moon above, searing the vigor of hills and streams below, overturning the round of the four seasons in between. There is no insect that creeps and crawls, no creature that flutters and flies that has not lost its inborn nature. So great is the confusion of the world that comes from coveting knowledge!

From the Three Dynasties on down, it has been this and nothing else —shoving aside the pure and artless people and delighting in busy, bustling flatterers; abandoning the limpidity and calm of inaction and delighting in jumbled and jangling ideas. And this jumble and jangle has for long confused the world.

Let It Be, Leave It Alone (11)

I have heard of letting the world be, of leaving it alone; I have never heard of governing the world. You let it be for fear of corrupting the inborn nature of the world; you leave it alone for fear of distracting the Virtue of the world. If the nature of the world is not corrupted, if the Virtue of the world is not distracted, why should there be any governing of the world?

o   o   o   o

If the gentleman finds he has no other choice than to direct and look after the world, then the best course for him is inaction. As long as there is inaction, he may rest in the true form of his nature and fate. If he values his own body more than the management of the world, then he can be entrusted with the world. If he is more careful of his own body than of the management of the world, then the world can be handed over to him. If the gentleman can in truth keep from rending apart his five vital organs, from tearing out his eyesight and hearing, then he will command corpse-like stillness and dragon vision, the silence of deep pools and the voice of thunder. His spirit will move in the train of *t'ien*, gentle and easy in inaction, and the ten thousand things will be dust in the wind. "What leisure have I now for governing the world?" he will say.

Ts'ui Chu was questioning Lao Tan.[25] "If you do not govern the world, then how can you improve men's minds?"

Lao Tan said, "Be careful—don't meddle with men's minds! Men's minds can be forced down or boosted up, but this downing and upping imprisons and brings death to the mind. Gentle and shy, the mind can bend the hard and strong; it can chisel and cut away, carve and polish. Its heat is that of burning fire, its coldness that of solid ice, its swiftness such that, in the time it takes to lift and lower the head, it has twice swept over the four seas and beyond. At rest, it is deep-fathomed and still; in movement, it is far-flung as the heavens, racing and galloping out of reach of all bonds. This indeed is the mind of man!"

In ancient times the Yellow Emperor[26] first used benevolence and righteousness to meddle with the minds of men. Yao and Shun followed him and worked till there was no more down on their thighs, no more hair on their shins, trying to nourish the bodies of the men of the world. They grieved their five vital organs in the practice of benevolence and righteousness, taxed their blood and breath in the establishment of laws and standards. But still some men would not submit to their rule, and so they had to exile Huan Tou to Mount Ch'ung, drive away the San-miao tribes to the region of San-wei, and banish Kung to the Dark City.[27] This shows that they could not make the world submit.

By the time the kings of the Three Dynasties appeared, the world was in great consternation indeed. On the lowest level there were men like the tyrant Chieh and Robber Chih, on the highest, men like Tseng and Shih, and the Confucianists and Mo-ists[28] rose up all around. Then joy and anger eyed each other with suspicion, stupidity and wisdom duped each other, good and bad called one another names, falsehood and truth slandered one another, and the world sank into a decline. There was no more unity to the Great Virtue, and the inborn nature and fate shattered and fell apart. The world coveted knowledge and the hundred clans were thrown into turmoil. Then there were axes and saws to shape things, ink and plumb lines to trim them, mallets and gouges to poke holes in them, and the world, muddled and deranged, was in great confusion. The crime lay in this meddling with men's minds. So it was that worthy men crouched in hiding below the great mountains and yawning cliffs, and the lords of ten thousand chariots fretted and trembled above in their ancestral halls.

In the world today, the victims of the death penalty lie heaped together, the bearers of cangues[29] tread on each other's heels, the sufferers of punishment are never out of each other's sight. And now come the Confucianists and Mo-ists, waving their arms, striding into the very midst of the fettered and manacled men. Ah, that they should go this far, that they should be so brazen, so lacking in any sense of shame! Who can convince me that sagely wisdom is not in fact the wedge that fastens the cangue, that benevolence and righteousness are not in fact the loop and lock of these fetters and manacles? How do I know that Tseng and Shih are not the whistling arrows that signal the approach of Chieh and Chih? Therefore I say, cut off sageness, cast away wisdom, and the world will be in perfect order.

The Yellow Emperor had ruled as Son of T'ien for nineteen years and his commands were heeded throughout the world, when he heard that Master Kuang Ch'êng was living on top of the Mountain of Emptiness and Identity. He therefore went to visit him. "I have heard that you, Sir, have mastered the Perfect Way. May I venture to ask about the essence of the Perfect Way?" he said. "I would like to get hold of the essence of *t'ien* and earth and use it to aid the five grains and to nourish the common people. I would also like to control the *yin* and *yang* in order to insure the growth of all living things. How may this be done?"

Master Kuang Ch'êng said, "What you say you want to learn about pertains to the true substance of things, but what you say you want to control pertains to things in their divided state. Ever since you began to govern the world, rain falls before the cloud vapors have even gathered, the plants and trees shed their leaves before they have even turned yellow, and the light of the sun and moon grows more and more sickly. Shallow and vapid, with the mind of a prattling knave—what good would it do to tell *you* about the Perfect Way!"

The Yellow Emperor withdrew, gave up his throne, built a solitary hut, spread a mat of white rushes, and lived for three months in retirement.

o   o   o   o

Autumn Floods (17)

o   o   o   o

Jo of the North Sea said, "You can't discuss the ocean with a well frog—he's limited by the space he lives in. You can't discuss ice with a summer insect—he's bound to a single season. You can't discuss the Way with a cramped scholar—he's shackled by his doctrines. Now you have come out beyond your banks and borders and have seen the great sea— so you realize your own pettiness. From now on it will be possible to talk to you about the Great Principle.

"Of all the waters of the world, none is as great as the sea. Ten thousand streams flow into it—I have never heard of a time when they stopped—and yet it is never full. The water leaks away at Wei-lü—I have never heard of a time when it didn't—and yet the sea is never empty. Spring or autumn, it never changes. Flood or drought, it takes no notice. It is so much greater than the streams of the Yangtze or the Yellow River that it is impossible to measure the difference. But I have never for this reason prided myself on it. I take my place with *t'ien* and earth and receive breath from the *yin* and *yang*. I sit here between *t'ien* and earth as a little stone or a little tree sits on a huge mountain. Since I can see my own smallness, what reason would I have to pride myself?

"Compare the area within the four seas with all that is between *t'ien* and earth—is it not like one little anthill in a vast marsh? Compare the Middle Kingdom with the area within the four seas—is it not like one tiny grain in a great storehouse? When we refer to the things of creation, we speak of them as numbering ten thousand—and man is only one of them. We talk of the Nine Provinces where men are most numerous, and yet of the whole area where grain and foods are grown and where boats and carts pass back and forth, man occupies only one fraction. Compared to the ten thousand things, is he not like one little hair on the body of a horse? What the Five Emperors passed along, what the Three Kings[30] fought over, what the benevolent man grieves about, what the responsible man labors over—all is no more than this!

o   o   o   o

"Calculate what man knows and it cannot compare to what he does not know. Calculate the time he is alive and it cannot compare to the time before he was born. Yet man takes something so small and tries to exhaust the dimensions of something so large! Hence he is muddled and confused and can never get anywhere. Looking at it this way, how do we know that the tip of a hair can be singled out as the measure of the smallest thing possible? Or how do we know that heaven and earth can fully encompass the dimensions of the largest thing possible?"

o   o   o   o

"Therefore the Great Man in his actions will not harm others, but he makes no show of benevolence or charity. He will not move for the sake of profit, but he does not despise the porter at the gate. He will not wrangle for goods or wealth, but he makes no show of refusing or relinquishing them. He will not enlist the help of others in his work, but he makes no show of being self-supporting, and he does not despise the greedy and base. His actions differ from those of the mob, but he makes no show of uniqueness or eccentricity. He is content to stay behind with the crowd, but he does not despise those who run forward to flatter and fawn. All the titles and stipends of the age are not enough to stir him to exertion; all its penalties and censures are not enough to make him feel shame. He knows that no line can be drawn between right and wrong, no border can be fixed between great and small. I have heard it said, 'The Man of the Way wins no fame, the highest virtue[31] wins no gain, the Great Man has no self.' To the most perfect degree, he goes along with what has been allotted to him."

o   o   o   o

Now do you say that you are going to make Right your master and do away with Wrong, or make Order your master and do away with Disorder? If you do, then you have not understood the principle of *t'ien* and earth or the nature of the ten thousand things. This is like saying that you are going to make *t'ien* your master and do away with Earth, or make *Yin* your master and do away with *Yang*. Obviously it is impossible. If men persist in talking this way without stop, they must be either fools or deceivers!

"Emperors and kings have different ways of ceding their thrones; the Three Dynasties had different rules of succession. Those who went against the times and flouted custom were called usurpers; those who went with the times and followed custom were called companions of righteousness."

o   o   o   o

Once, when Chuang Tzŭ was fishing in the P'u River, the king of Ch'u sent two officials to go and announce to him: "I would like to trouble you with the administration of my realm."

Chuang Tzŭ held on to the fishing pole and, without turning his head, said, "I have heard that there is a sacred tortoise[32] in Ch'u that has been dead for three thousand years. The king keeps it wrapped in cloth and boxed, and stores it in the ancestral temple. Now would this tortoise rather be dead and have its bones left behind and honored? Or would it rather be alive and dragging its tail in the mud?"

"It would rather be alive and dragging its tail in the mud," said the two officials.

Chuang Tzŭ said, "Go away! I'll drag my tail in the mud!"

When Hui Tzŭ[33] was prime minister of Liang, Chuang Tzŭ set off to visit him. Someone said to Hui Tzŭ, "Chuang Tzŭ is coming because he wants to replace you as prime minister!" With this Hui Tzŭ was filled with alarm and searched all over the state for three days and three nights trying to find Chuang Tzŭ. Chuang Tzŭ then came to see him and said, "In the south there is a bird called the Yüan-ch'u[34]—I wonder if you've ever heard of it? The Yüan-ch'u rises up from the South Sea and flies to the North Sea, and it will rest on nothing but the Wu-t'ung tree, eat nothing but the fruit of the Lien, and drink only from springs of sweet water. Once there was an owl who had gotten hold of a half-rotten old rat, and as the Yüan-ch'u passed by, it raised its head, looked up at the Yüan-ch'u, and said, 'Shoo!' Now that you have this Liang state of yours, are you trying to shoo me?"

o   o   o   o

Supreme Happiness (18)

Is there such a thing as supreme happiness in the world or isn't there? Is there some way to keep yourself alive or isn't there? What to do, what to rely on, what to avoid, what to stick by, what to follow, what to leave alone, what to find happiness in, what to hate?

This is what the world honors: wealth, eminence, long life, a good name. This is what the world finds happiness in: a life of ease, rich food, fine clothes, beautiful sights, sweet sounds. This is what it looks down on: poverty, meanness, early death, a bad name. This is what it finds bitter: a life that knows no rest, a mouth that gets no rich food, no fine clothes for the body, no beautiful sights for the eye, no sweet sounds for the ear.

People who can't get these things fret a great deal and are afraid—this is a stupid way to treat the body. People who are rich wear themselves out rushing around on business, piling up more wealth than they could ever use—this is a superficial way to treat the body. People who are eminent spend night and day scheming and wondering if they are doing right—this is a shoddy way to treat the body. Man lives his life in company with worry, and if he lives a long while, till he's dull and doddering, then he has spent that much time worrying instead of dying, a bitter lot indeed! This is a callous way to treat the body.

Men of ardor are regarded by the world as good, but their goodness doesn't succeed in keeping them alive. So I don't know whether their goodness is really good or not. Perhaps I think it's good—but not good enough to save their lives. Perhaps I think it's no good—but still good enough to save the lives of others. So I say, if your loyal advice isn't heeded, give way and do not wrangle. Tzǔ-hsü[35] wrangled and lost his body. But if he hadn't wrangled, he wouldn't have made a name. Is there really such a thing as goodness or isn't there?

What ordinary people do and what they find happiness in—I don't know whether such happiness is in the end really happiness or not. I look at what ordinary people find happiness in, what they all make a mad dash for, racing around as though they couldn't stop—they all say they're happy with it. I'm not happy with it and I'm not unhappy with it. In the end is there really happiness or isn't there?

I take inaction to be true happiness, but ordinary people think it is a bitter thing. I say: the highest happiness has no happiness, the highest praise has no praise. The world can't decide what is right and what is wrong. And yet inaction can decide this. The highest happiness, keeping alive—only inaction gets you close to this!

Let me try putting it this way. The inaction of *t'ien* is its purity, the inaction of earth is its peace. So the two inactions combine and all things are transformed and brought to birth. Wonderfully, mysteriously, there is no place they come out of. Mysteriously, wonderfully, they have no sign. Each thing minds its business and all grow up out of inaction. So I say, *t'ien* and earth do nothing and there is nothing that is not done. Among men, who can get hold of this inaction?

Chuang Tzǔ's wife died. When Hui Tzǔ went to convey his condolences, he found Chuang Tzǔ sitting with his legs sprawled out, pounding on a tub and singing. "You lived with her, she brought up your children and grew old," said Hui Tzǔ. "It should be enough simply not to weep at her death. But pounding on a tub and singing—this is going too far, isn't it?"

Chuang Tzǔ said, "You're wrong. When she first died, do you think I didn't grieve like anyone else? But I looked back to her beginning and the time before she was born. Not only the time before she was born, but the time before she had a body. Not only the time before she had a body, but the time before she had a spirit. In the midst of the jumble of wonder and mystery a change took place and she had a spirit. Another change and she had a body. Another change and she was born. Now there's been another change and she's dead. It's just like the progression of the four seasons, spring, summer, fall, winter.

"Now she's going to lie down peacefully in a vast room. If I were to follow after her bawling and sobbing, it would show that I don't understand anything about fate. So I stopped."

o   o   o   o

When Yen Yüan went east to Ch'i, Confucius had a very worried look on his face. Tzǔ-kung got off his mat and asked, "May I be so bold as to inquire why the Master has such a worried expression now that Hui has gone east to Ch'i?"

"Excellent—this question of yours," said Confucius. "Kuan Tzǔ[36] had a saying that I much approve of: 'Small bags won't hold big things; short well ropes won't dip up deep water.' In the same way I believe that fate has certain forms and the body certain appropriate uses. You can't add to or take away from these. I'm afraid that when Hui gets to Ch'i he will start telling the marquis of Ch'i about the ways of Yao, Shun, and the Yellow Emperor, and then will go on to speak about Sui-jên and

Shên-nung.[37] The marquis will then look for similar greatness within himself and fail to find it. Failing to find it, he will become distraught, and when a man becomes distraught, he kills."

o   o   o   o

Mastering Life (19)

o   o   o   o

Duke Huan was hunting in a marsh, with Kuan Chung as his carriage driver, when he saw a ghost. The duke grasped Kuan Chung's hand and said, "Father Chung,[38] what do you see?"

"I don't see anything," replied Kuan Chung.

When the duke returned home, he fell into a stupor, grew ill, and for several days did not go out.

A gentleman of Ch'i named Huang-tzŭ Kao-ao said, "Your Grace, you are doing this injury to yourself! How could a ghost have the power to injure you? If the vital breath that is stored up in a man becomes dispersed and does not return, then he suffers a deficiency. If it ascends and fails to descend again, it causes him to be chronically forgetful. And if it neither ascends nor descends, but gathers in the middle of the body in the region of the heart, then he becomes ill."

Duke Huan said, "But do ghosts really exist?"

"Indeed they do. There is the Li on the hearth and the Chi in the stove. The heap of clutter and trash just inside the gate is where the Lei-t'ing lives. In the northeast corner the Pei-a and Kuei-lung leap about, and the northwest corner is where the I-yang lives. In the water is the Kang-hsiang; on the hills, the Hsin; in the mountains, the K'uei; in the meadows, the P'ang-huang; and in the marshes, the Wei-t'o."

The duke said, "May I ask what a Wei-t'o looks like?"

Huang-tzŭ said, "The Wei-t'o is as big as a wheel hub, as tall as a carriage shaft, has a purple robe and a vermilion hat and, as creatures go, is very ugly. When it hears the sound of thunder or a carriage, it grabs its head and stands up. Anyone who sees it will soon become a dictator."

Duke Huan's face lit up and he said with a laugh. "*That* must have been what I saw!" Then he straightened his robe and hat and sat up on the mat with Huang-tzŭ, and before the day was over, though he didn't notice it, his illness went away.

o   o   o   o

You forget your feet when the shoes are comfortable. You forget your waist when the belt is comfortable. Understanding forgets right and wrong when the mind is comfortable. There is no change in what is inside, no following what is outside, when the adjustment to events is comfortable. You begin with what is comfortable and never experience what is uncomfortable when you know the comfort of forgetting what is comfortable.

o   o   o   o

External Things (26)

o   o   o   o

Chuang Chou's family was very poor and so he went to borrow some grain from the marquis of Chien-ho. The marquis said, "Why, of course. I'll soon be getting the tribute money from my fief, and when I do, I'll be glad to lend you three hundred pieces of gold. Will that be all right?"

Chuang Chou flushed with anger and said, "As I was coming here yesterday, I heard someone calling me on the road. I turned around and saw that there was a perch in the carriage rut. I said to him, 'Come, perch—what are you doing here?' He replied, 'I am a Wave Official of the Eastern Sea. Couldn't you give me a dipperful of water so I can stay alive?' I said to him, 'Why, of course. I'm just about to start south to visit the kings of Wu and Yüeh. I'll change the course of the West River and send it in your direction. Will that be all right?' The perch flushed with anger and said, 'I've lost my element! I have nowhere to go! If you can get me a dipper of water, I'll be able to stay alive. But if you give me an answer like that, then you'd best look for me in the dried fish store!'"

o   o   o   o

Chuang Tzŭ said, "If you have the capacity to wander, how can you keep from wandering? But if you do not have the capacity to wander, how can you wander? A will that takes refuge in conformity, behavior that is aloof and eccentric—neither of these, alas, is compatible with perfect wisdom and solid virtue. You stumble and fall but fail to turn back;

you race on like fire and do not look behind you. But though you may be one time a ruler, another time a subject, this is merely a matter of the times. Such distinctions change with the age and you cannot call either one or the other lowly. Therefore I say, the Perfect Man is never a stickler in his actions."

o   o   o   o

17

Sun Tzŭ: *The Art of War*

Know the enemy and know yourself.
—Sun Tzŭ, 3:31

The "Thirteen Chapters," as *The Art of War* is often called, was supposed to have been written about 500 B.C. Opinion today is that the book falls among the many early Chinese works of author or authors unknown. This much we know: Sun Tzŭ may have existed; whoever wrote the book was a military man; the consistent style and development of the thirteen chapters indicates that it was composed by one principal writer rather than several; the state of military technology and organization described therein puts the book in a time span between the earliest use in Chinese warfare of the crossbow (about 400 B.C.) and of cavalry (about 320 B.C.), the first of which he mentions, the second of which he does not. Therefore the book *Sun Tzŭ* tentatively takes its place somewhere in the fourth century B.C.

Whether or not the man ever existed, the writings that go under his name have interested many writers and military experts. In China and neighboring lands for more than 2000 years they have been held to be the most authoritative work on the art of war. To begin with, Han Fei Tzŭ (died 233 B.C.), the Legalist philosopher, notes that many a man, hoping to become a great tactician, studied *The Art of War*. Then there was a group of Chinese commentators, the most famous being Ts'ao Ts'ao (155–220 A.D.), the brilliant general, poet, and king of Wei (216–220 A.D.). Last among notable Chinese to profit from Sun Tzŭ's book has been Mao Tsê-tung, whose military doctrines draw inspiration from it. Outside China, Japan alone has issued over one hundred separate editions. It has found there its most dedicated disciples and was used as a text for the instruction of fighting men as early as 760 A.D. In France it was first published in 1772. The paraphrasing of Sun Tzŭ by military men even today occurs frequently and often too closely to be accidental. None of the paraphrasers or commentators has been able to improve on the pithy style of the master.

There is something of Sun Tzŭ's language and thought that recalls the *Tao-tê-ching*. The commander cultivates the *tao*. He is subtle and insubstantial, without trace, divinely mysterious, inaudible. Through him, the strong appear weak and the weak strong. His army has no definite shape; as water conforms to terrain, so the army flows around the enemy, spills over the ground, changes form with every rock and crevice.

But Sun Tzŭ pretends neither to Taoist nor to any other philosophical doctrine. What interests us about him are the ideas he advocates of the military's relation to ruler, state, and people. In great part these ideas reach the reader indirectly, for this experienced general does not mean to talk about them as the chief topics of his thirteen chapters. He means to talk principally about military subjects in themselves. Hence in the matter of military-political relations, *The Art of War* may be all the more trustworthy.

Sun Tzŭ's general attitude toward warfare differs from the attitudes of most of the classical philosophers. He does not deplore it as Mencius and specially Lao Tzŭ and Mo Tzŭ do; he does not raise it to a fundamental occupation as Lord Shang and Han Fei Tzŭ do. Neither does he distinguish between an aggressive or unjust war and a punitive expedition or a just war as do Mo Tzŭ, Mencius, and Hsün Tzŭ. The kind of war Sun Tzŭ openly detests is protracted war. It ruins states and peoples and armies. "No country has ever benefited from a long war," he declares. Nor does he try to give war some sort of cosmic significance. To most Chinese writers war appears as a disruption of the political harmony that T'ien intended men should live in. Since the author of *The Art of War* may be a general himself, it is not surprising that the book does not advance this argument; nor does it attempt to refute it. Sun Tzŭ accepts war as a crucial fact of life, too important to the state to be left unstudied.

SUN TZǓ: *THE ART OF WAR*

(Sun Tzǔ Ping Fa)

Selections

1. Estimates

Sun Tzǔ said:

1. War is a matter of vital importance to the State; the province of life or death; the road to survival or ruin. It is mandatory that it be thoroughly studied.

2. Therefore, appraise it in terms of the five fundamental factors and make comparisons of the seven elements later named. So you may assess its essentials.

3. The first of these factors is the *tao;* the second, weather; the third, terrain; the fourth, command; and the fifth, doctrine.

From Samuel B. Griffith, tr., *Sun Tzǔ: The Art of War* (Oxford: Clarendon Press, 1963), translation slightly modified.

4. By the *tao* I mean that which causes the people to be in harmony with their leaders, so that they will accompany them in life and unto death without fear of peril.[1]

5. By weather I mean the interaction of natural forces; the effects of winter's cold and summer's heat and the conduct of military operations in accordance with the seasons.

6. By terrain I mean distances, whether the ground is traversed with ease or difficulty, whether it is open or constricted, and the chances of life or death.

7. By command I mean the general's qualities of wisdom, sincerity, humanity, courage, and strictness.

8. By doctrine I mean organization, control, assignment of appropriate ranks to officers, regulation of supply routes, and the provision of principal items used by the army.

11. If you say which ruler possesses the *tao*, which commander is the more able, which army obtains the advantages of weather and terrain, in which regulations and instructions are better carried out, which troops are the stronger;

12. Which has the better trained officers and men;

13. And which administers rewards and punishments justly;

14. I will be able to forecast victory or defeat.

15. If a general who heeds my strategy is employed he is certain to win. Keep him! When one who refuses to listen to my strategy is employed, he is certain to be defeated. Dismiss him!

16. Having paid heed to the advantages of my plans, the general must create situations which will contribute to their accomplishment. By "situations" I mean that he should act expediently in accordance with what is advantageous and so control the balance.

17. All warfare is based on deception.

18. Therefore, when capable, feign incapacity; when active, inactivity.

19. When near, make it appear that you are far away; when far away, that you are near.

20. Offer the enemy a bait to lure him; feign disorder and strike him.

21. When he concentrates, prepare against him; where he is strong, avoid him.

22. Anger his general and confuse him.

23. Pretend inferiority and encourage his arrogance.

24. Keep him under a strain and wear him down.

25. When he is united, divide him.

26. Attack where he is unprepared; sally out when he does not expect you.

2. Waging War

Sun Tzǔ said:

1. Generally, in using troops: If one thousand fast four-horse chariots, one thousand four-horse wagons covered in leather, and one hundred thousand mailed troops are employed and if provisions must be transported for a thousand *li*, then with expenditures at home and in the field, on guest advisors, materials like glue and lacquer, and chariots and armor, it will cost one thousand pieces of gold before the one hundred thousand troops can move.

3. Victory is the main object in war. If this is long delayed, weapons are blunted and morale depressed. If troops attack cities, their strength will be exhausted.

4. If the army engages in protracted campaigns the resources of the state will not suffice.

5. When your weapons are dulled and ardour damped, your strength exhausted and treasure spent, neighbouring rulers will take advantage of your distress to act. And even though you have wise counsellors, none will be able to lay good plans for the future.

6. Thus, while we have heard of powerful speed in war, we have not yet seen a clever operation that was prolonged.

7. For no country has ever benefited from a protracted war.

9. Those adept in waging war do not require a second levy of conscripts nor more than one provisioning.

11. When a country is impoverished by military operations it is due to distant transportation; carriage of supplies for great distances renders the people destitute.

12. Where the army is, prices are high; when prices rise the wealth of the people is exhausted. When wealth is exhausted the peasantry will be afflicted with urgent exactions.

15. Hence the wise general sees to it that his troops feed on the enemy, for one bushel of the enemy's provisions is equivalent to twenty of his; one hundredweight of enemy fodder to twenty hundredweight of his.

19. Treat captives well, and care for them.

20. This is called "winning a battle and becoming stronger."

21. Hence what is essential in war is victory, not prolonged operations. And therefore the general who understands war is the minister of the people's fate and arbiter of the nation's destiny.

3. Offensive Strategy

Sun Tzŭ said:

1. Generally, in using troops: the best policy is to take a state intact; to ruin it is inferior to this.

2. To capture the enemy's army is better than to destroy it; to take intact a battalion, a company, or a five-man squad is better than to destroy them.

3. For to win one hundred victories in one hundred battles is not the highest skill. The highest skill is to beat the enemy without a fight.

4. Thus, what is of supreme importance in war is to attack the enemy's strategy;

5. Next best is to disrupt his alliances;

6. The next best is to attack his army.

7. The worst policy is to attack cities. Attack cities only when there is no alternative.

12. Consequently, in using troops: When ten to the enemy's one, surround him;

13. When five times his strength, attack him;

14. If double his strength, divide him.

15. If equally matched, engage him.

16. If weaker numerically, take the defensive;

17. And if in all respects unequal, elude him, for a small force is but booty for one more powerful.

18. Now the general is the protector of the state. If this protection is all-embracing, the state will surely be strong; if defective, the state will certainly be weak.

24. Now there are five circumstances in which victory may be predicted:

25. He who knows when to fight and when not to fight will be victorious.

26. He who understands how to use both large and small forces will be victorious.

27. He whose ranks are united in purpose will be victorious.

28. He who is prepared and lies in wait for an enemy who is not, will be victorious.

29. He whose generals are able and not interfered with by the sovereign will be victorious.

31. Therefore I say: "Know the enemy and know yourself; in a hundred battles you will never be in danger."

4. Dispositions

Sun Tzŭ said:

1. In ancient times the skillful warriors first made themselves invincible and awaited the enemy's moment of vulnerability.

2. Invincibility depends on one's self; the enemy's vulnerability on him.

3. It follows that those skilled in war can make themselves invincible but cannot cause an enemy to be certainly vulnerable.

11. And therefore the victories won by a master of war gain him neither reputation for wisdom nor merit for valour.

12. For he wins his victories without erring. "Without erring" means that whatever he does insures his victory; he conquers an enemy already defeated.

14. Thus a victorious army wins its victories before seeking battle; an army destined to defeat fights in the hope of winning.

15. Those skilled in war cultivate the *tao* and preserve the laws and are therefore able to formulate victorious policies.

16. Now the elements of the art of war are first, measurement of space; second, estimation of quantities; third, calculations; fourth, comparisons; and fifth, chances of victory.

17. Measurements of space are derived from the ground.

18. Quantities derive from measurement, figures from quantities, comparisons from figures, and victory from comparisons.

5. Power

Sun Tzŭ said:

1. Generally, management of many is the same as management of few. It is a matter of organization.

5. Generally, in battle, do the expected [thing] to engage; do the unexpected to win.

6. Now the resources of those skilled in the use of the unexpected are as infinite as the heavens and earth; as inexhaustible as the flow of the great rivers.

7. For they end and recommence; cyclical, as are the movements of the sun and moon. They die away and are reborn; recurrent, as are the passing seasons.

11. In battle there are only the expected and unexpected, but their combinations are inexhaustible.

12. The expected and the unexpected mutually reproduce, endlessly as in a circle.[2] Who can exhaust the possibilities?

20. Thus, those skilled at making the enemy move do so by creating a situation to which he must conform; they entice him with something he is certain to take, and with lures of ostensible profit they await him in strength.

21. Therefore a skilled commander seeks victory from the situation and does not demand it of his subordinates.

6. Weaknesses and Strengths

Sun Tzŭ said:

1. Generally, he who occupies the field of battle first and awaits his enemy is at ease; he who comes later to the scene and rushes into the fight is weary.

2. And therefore those skilled in war bring the enemy to the field of battle and are not brought there by him.

4. When the enemy is at ease, be able to harass him; when well fed, to starve him; when quietly encamped at rest, to make him move.

5. Go through territory that he does not make for; make for places he never thought you would make for.

6. That you may march a thousand *li*[3] without wearying yourself is because you travel where there is no enemy.

7. To be certain to take what you attack is to attack a place the enemy does not protect. To be certain to hold what you defend is to defend a place the enemy does not attack.

11. When I wish to give battle, my enemy, even though protected by high walls and deep moats, cannot help but engage me, for I attack a position he must succour.

12. When I wish to avoid battle I may defend myself simply by drawing a line on the ground; the enemy will be unable to attack me because I divert him from going where he wishes.

14. The enemy must not know where I intend to give battle. For if he does not know where I intend to give battle he must prepare in a great many places. And when he prepares in a great many places, those I have to fight in any one place will be few.

24. The ultimate in disposing one's troops is to become invisible. Then the most penetrating spies cannot pry in nor can the clever lay plans against you.

25. It is according to the shapes that I lay the plans for victory, but the multitude does not comprehend this, although everyone can see the outward aspects, none understands the way in which I have created victory.

26. Therefore, when I have won a victory I do not repeat my tactics but respond to circumstances in an infinite variety of ways.

27. Now an army may be likened to water, for just as flowing water avoids the heights and hastens to the lowlands, so an army avoids strength and strikes weakness.

28. And as water shapes its flow in accordance with the ground, so an army manages its victory in accordance with the situation of the enemy.

29. And as water has no constant form, there are in war no constant conditions.

31. Of the five elements,[4] none is always predominant; of the four seasons, none lasts forever; of the days, some are long and some short, and the moon waxes and wanes.

7. Manœuvre

Sun Tzŭ said:

1. Normally, when the army is employed, the general first receives his commands from the sovereign. He assembles the troops and mobilizes the people. He blends the army into a harmonious entity and encamps it.

18. Now gongs and drums, banners and flags are used to focus the attention of the troops. When the troops can be thus united, the brave cannot advance alone, nor can the cowardly withdraw. This is the art of employing a host.

21. Morale is high in early morning, flagging during the day, and spent by evening.

22. And therefore those skilled in war avoid the enemy when his spirit is keen and attack him when it is sluggish and his soldiers homesick. This is control of the moral factor.

23. In good order they await a disorderly enemy; in serenity, a clamorous one. This is control of the mental factor.

24. Close to the field of battle, they await an enemy coming from afar; at rest, an exhausted enemy; with well-fed troops, hungry ones. This is control of the physical factor.

26. Therefore, the art of employing troops is that when the enemy occupies high ground, do not confront him; with his back resting on hills, do no oppose him.

27. When he pretends to flee, do not pursue.

28. Do not attack his élite troops.

29. Do not gobble proffered baits.

30. Do not thwart an enemy returning homewards.

31. To a surrounded enemy you must leave a way of escape.

32. Do not press an enemy at bay.

8. The Nine Variables

Sun Tzŭ said:

1. In general, the system of employing troops is that the commander receives his mandate from the sovereign to mobilize the people and assemble the army.

2. Do not encamp in cut-off ground.

3. In communicating ground, unite with your allies.

4. You should not linger in desolate ground.

5. In enclosed ground, resourcefulness is required.

6. In death ground, fight.

7. There are roads not to follow; troops not to strike; cities not to assault; ground to be contested.

8. And there are commands of the sovereign not to be obeyed.

17. There are five qualities that are dangerous in the character of a general.

18. If bent on dying, he can be killed.

19. If determined to live, he can be captured.

20. If irascible, he can be made a fool of.

21. If finely honorable, he can be slandered.

22. If compassionate toward people, he can be harassed.

23. Now these five traits are serious faults in a general and calamitous in the conduct of war.

24. The ruin of the army and the death of the general are inevitable results of these shortcomings. They must be deeply pondered.

9. Marches

Sun Tzǔ said:

25. Humble words from envoys, but intensified preparations, are signs that the enemy is about to advance.

26. Fierce language and pretentious advances are signs that the enemy is about to retreat.

27. When the envoys speak in apologetic terms, he wants a respite.

28. When without a sworn agreement the enemy proposes a truce, he is deceptive.

32. When his troops lean on their weapons, they are famished.

33. When drawers of water drink before carrying it to camp, his troops are suffering from thirst.

34. When the enemy sees an advantage but does not advance to seize it, he is fatigued.

35. When birds gather above his camp sites, they are empty.

36. When at night the enemy's camp is clamorous, he is fearful.

37. When his troops are disorderly, the general's authority is weak.

38. When his flags and banners move about constantly he is in disarray.

39. If the officers are short-tempered they are exhausted.

40. When the horses are killed and their flesh eaten and when the troops neither hang up their cooking pots nor return to their shelters, the enemy is desperate.

41. When the troops continually gather in small groups and whisper together the general has lost the confidence of the army.

42. Too frequent rewards indicate that the general is at the end of his resources; too frequent punishments that he is in acute distress.

43. If the officers at first treat the men violently and later are fearful of them, the limit of indiscipline has been reached.

45. In war, numbers alone confer no advantage. Do not advance, relying on sheer military power.

47. If troops are punished before their loyalty is secured they will be disobedient. If not obedient, it is difficult to employ them. If troops are loyal, but punishments are not enforced, you cannot employ them.

48. Thus, command them with civility and imbue them uniformly with martial ardour and it may be said that victory is certain.

10. Terrain

Sun Tzŭ said:

1. Ground may be classified according to its nature as accessible, entrapping, indecisive, constricted, precipitous, and distant.

9. Now when troops flee, are insubordinate, distressed, collapse in disorder, or are routed, it is the fault of the general. None of these disasters can be attributed to natural causes.

18. If the situation is one of victory but the sovereign has issued orders not to engage, the general may decide to fight. If the situation is such that he cannot win, but the sovereign has issued orders to engage, he need not do so.

19. And therefore the general who in advancing does not seek personal fame, and in withdrawing is not concerned with avoiding punishment, but whose only purpose is to protect the people and promote the best interests of his sovereign, is the precious jewel of the state.

20. Because such a general regards his men as infants they will march with him into the deepest valleys. He treats them as his own beloved sons and they will die with him.

21. If a general indulges his troops but is unable to employ them; if he loves them but cannot enforce his commands; if the troops are disorderly and he is unable to control them, they may be compared to spoiled children, and are useless.

26. And therefore I say: "Know the enemy, know yourself; your victory will never be endangered. Know the ground, know the weather; your victory will then be total."

11. The Nine Varieties of Ground

Sun Tzŭ said:

1. In employing troops: Ground may be classified as dispersive, frontier, contested, communicating, focal, serious, difficult, encircled, and death.

12. Do not fight for the place of contention. . . .

28. Should one ask: "How do I cope with a well-ordered enemy host about to attack me?" I reply: "Seize something he cherishes and he will conform to your desires."

29. Speed is the essence of war. Take advantage of the enemy's unpreparedness; travel by unexpected routes and strike him where he has taken no precautions.

31. Plunder fertile country to supply the army with plentiful provisions.

33. Throw the troops into a position from which there is no escape and even when faced with death they will not flee. For if prepared to die, what can they not achieve? Then officers and men together put forth their utmost efforts. In a desperate situation they fear nothing; when there is no way out they stand firm. Deep in a hostile land they are bound together, and there, where there is no alternative, they will engage the enemy in hand-to-hand combat.

35. My officers have no surplus of wealth but not because they disdain worldly goods; they have no expectation of long life but not because they dislike longevity.

38. Now the troops of those adept in war are used like the "Simultaneously Responding" snake of Mount Ch'ang. When struck on the head its tail attacks; when struck on the tail, its head attacks, when struck in the centre both head and tail attack.

39. Should one ask: "Can troops be made capable of such instantaneous coordination?" I reply: "They can." For, although the men of Wu and Yüeh[5] mutually hate one another, if together in a boat tossed by the wind they would cooperate as the right hand does with the left.

42. The business of a general: to be serene and inscrutable, impartial and self-controlled.

43. He should be capable of keeping his officers and men in ignorance of his plans.

44. He prohibits superstitious practices and so rids the army of doubts. Then until the moment of death there can be no troubles.

45. He changes his methods and alters his plans so that people have no knowledge of what he is doing.

46. He alters his camp-sites and marches by devious routes, and thus makes it impossible for others to anticipate his purpose.

47. He fixes a date for rendezvous and after the troops have met, cuts

off their return route just as if he were removing a ladder from beneath them.

48. He leads the army deep into hostile territory and there releases the trigger.

49. He burns his boats and smashes his cooking pots; he urges the army on as if driving a flock of sheep, now in one direction, now in another, and none knows where he is going.

50. He assembles the army and throws it into a desperate position. So much for the business of the general.

55. Set the troops to their tasks without imparting your designs; use them to gain advantage without revealing the dangers involved. Throw them into a perilous situation and they survive; put them in death ground and they will live. For when the army is placed in such a situation it can snatch victory from defeat.

56. Now the crux of military operations lies in the pretence of accommodating one's self to the designs of the enemy.

61. Therefore at first be shy as a maiden. When the enemy gives you an opening be swift as a hare and he will be unable to withstand you.

12. Attack by Fire

Sun Tzŭ said:

1. There are five methods of attacking with fire. The first is to burn personnel; the second, to burn stores; the third, to burn equipment; the fourth, to burn arsenals; and the fifth, to use incendiary missiles.

15. Now to win battles and take your objectives, but to fail to exploit these achievements is ominous and may be described as "wasteful delay."

16. And therefore it is said that enlightened rulers deliberate upon the plans, and good generals execute them.

17. If not in the interests of the state, do not act. If you cannot succeed, do not use troops. If you are not in danger, do not fight.

18. A sovereign does not raise an army because he is enraged, nor does a general fight because he is resentful. For while an angered man may again be happy, and a resentful man again be pleased, a state that has perished cannot be restored, nor can the dead be brought back to life.

19. Therefore, the enlightened ruler is prudent and the good general is warned against rash action. Thus the state is kept secure and the army preserved.

13. Employment of Secret Agents

Sun Tzŭ said:

1. Now when an army of one hundred thousand is raised and dispatched on a distant campaign the expenses borne by the people together with the disbursements of the treasury will amount to a thousand pieces of gold daily. There will be continuous commotion both at home and abroad, people will be exhausted by the requirements of transport, and the affairs of seven hundred thousand households will be disrupted.

2. One who confronts his enemy for many years in order to struggle for victory in a decisive battle yet who, because he begrudges rank, honours, and a few hundred pieces of gold, remains ignorant of his enemy's situation, is completely devoid of humanity. Such a man is no general; no support to his sovereign; no master of victory.

3. Now the reason the enlightened prince and the wise general conquer the enemy whenever they move and their achievements surpass those of ordinary men is foreknowledge.

4. What is called "foreknowledge" cannot be elicited from spirits, nor from gods, nor by analogy with past events, nor from calculations. It must be obtained from men who know the enemy situation.

5. Now there are five sorts of secret agents to be employed. These are native, inside, double, expendable, and living.[6]

6. When these five types of agents are all working simultaneously and none knows their method of operation, they are called "The Divine Skein" and are the treasure of a sovereign.

13. He who is not sage and wise, humane and just, cannot use secret agents. And he who is not delicate and subtle cannot get the truth out of them.

14. Delicate indeed! Truly delicate! There is no place where espionage is not used.

21. The sovereign must have full knowledge of the activities of the five sorts of agents. This knowledge must come from the double agents, and therefore it is mandatory that they be treated with the utmost liberality.

22. Of old, the rise of Yin was due to I Chih, who formerly served the Hsia; the Chou came to power through Lü Ya,[7] a servant of the Yin.

23. And therefore only the enlightened sovereign and the worthy general who are able to use the most intelligent people as agents are certain to achieve great things. Secret operations are essential in war; upon them the army relies to make its every move.

18

The Legalists

Law is what shapes the people.
—*Book of Lord Shang*, 5:26

Chinese thinking from earliest times seems to have been apprehensive of legislation and even of written law, whether civil or criminal. Around the fourth century B.C. in China a new school rose to prominence called the Legalist. Its two best works are the *Book of Lord Shang* and the *Han Fei Tzŭ*. The state in which it wielded greatest influence was Ch'in, an uncouth, partly Tatar land far to the west, with a promising military future. The Legalists opposed the traditional Chinese particularistic attitude to law. They took a stand resembling the Graeco-Roman conception. Authority and law were to become coterminus and universal. Law was a force for unity. In lieu of the conflicting customs of disparate regions, there was to be one law everywhere.

As with many other philosophers of the time, the psychology of the Legalists was simple. To punish people, you must do what they hate; then they will act righteously. What do they hate? Penalties, physical pain, death. In this stimulus-response approach, the way to increase obedience is to increase punitive severity. Drawing further on the same psychology, the Legalists concluded that punishment for even the smallest offense should be cruel. The penalty for dumping ashes or refuse on the streets was the amputation of hands or feet. For if there are no small crimes, they reasoned, there can be no big crimes. A kind of reflex to criminality will be conditioned at the lowest level of crime which as a matter of course will operate also at the highest levels. The advantage is that the whole atmosphere of criminality which in itself creates the environment for crime will be thereby eliminated. Therefore, punish the smallest crime like the biggest one.

Given the degenerate state of affairs throughout the land, rites and tradition *(li)* obviously were not enough. There had to be law *(fa)*, swiftly enacted, clearly promulgated, strictly and uniformly enforced. The Legalists had to set up government as a legal machine that could be kept running by ordinary mortals.

In China the Legalists signalize the birth of political science in a modern sense. When discussing government and legislation, Lord Shang uses a number of terms with a current ring—political methods, figures or statistics, statistical methods, and a word *shih* that, whether translated as circumstances, conditions, trend, power, or influence, could easily make a keyword in the vocabulary of political science. As these various terms are used they clearly signify that ruling requires not law alone but also political methods consisting of both secret rules of power-handling and systematic rules of public administration.

Last but not least, ruling also requires research methods; in order to determine what laws should be enacted, a kind of policy research is required. Among the concepts of research there appears again the notion of statistical methods. "Statistics is the true method of ministers and rulers and the essential of a state," Lord Shang holds. And Han Fei Tzǔ adds, "Indeed, those who are most intelligent in governing by law rely on statistical methods and do not rely on men."

In the fourth century B.C., several states began to adopt Legalist ideas. The feudalistic system was to be supplanted by a centralized autocracy which would divide the country into administrative and military districts. The objective was to construct a strong bureaucratic state, girded for war, whose laws would be applied strictly and impartially to everyone and whose economic base would rest on farmers prepared at any time to march to battle.

The Legalists used to justify their system pragmatically—it worked, they thought. Doubtless, their policies won quick, visible successes. Increased military power brought them expansion at the cost of the less progressive bordering states. Ultimately, one state, Ch'in, the most Legalist of them all, conquered the others, and proclaimed itself the First Empire.

One of the First Emperor's steps to prevent disagreement over laws and orders was to try to destroy all philosophical writings and controversial literature including the great works of the Chou—the *Book of Docu-*

ments and the *Book of Songs*—in a holocaust of books. The attempt failed. Courageous scholars, risking the penalties of branding, forced labor, and death, hid books in walls and tombs to preserve them for posterity.

19

Lord Shang

Punish light crime severely.

—Lord Shang (*Han Fei Tzŭ*, 30)

It is quite possible that the *Book of Lord Shang*, though based on sayings and reports of Lord Shang (d. 338 B.C.), was put together later by administrative officials. Under the centralized autocracy the Legalists were creating, a new and enlarged bureaucracy had to be built up to supplant the old feudalistic government.

The work is attributed to the adviser of Duke Hsiao of the state of Ch'in, a man called Wei Yang or Kung-sun Yang (d. 338 B.C.). His name is associated with the phenomenal rise of Ch'in to supremacy over all of China, and he is given credit for most of the stern, radical Legalist measures of the Duke, who enfeoffed him as Lord Shang. He became respected, but also feared and hated. Once his protector died, Shang Yang was a marked man. Forced to rebel, he was slain, his head, arms, and legs pulled off by chariots driven in different directions, and his family exterminated.

The *Book of Lord Shang* itself is composed of twenty-five or more brief sections, some of which are lost. Mostly in essay form, simple and straightforward, it is often grim and gripping in its harshness.

THE *BOOK OF LORD SHANG*

(Shang Chün Shu)

Selections

The Elimination of Strength *(1:4)*

o   o   o   o

If in a country there are the following ten evils:[1] rites, music, odes, history, virtue, moral culture, filial piety, brotherly duty, integrity, and sophistry, the ruler cannot make the people fight and dismemberment is inevitable, and this brings extinction in its train. If the country has not these ten things and the ruler can make the people fight, he will be so prosperous that he will attain supremacy. A country where the virtuous

From J. J. L. Duyvendak, tr., *The Book of Lord Shang* (Chicago: University of Chicago Press, 1963).

govern the wicked will suffer from disorder, so that it will be dismembered; but a country where the wicked govern the virtuous will be orderly, so that it will become strong.

A country which is administered by the aid of odes, history, rites, music, filial piety, brotherly duty, virtue, and moral culture,[2] will, as soon as the enemy approaches, be dismembered; if he does not approach, the country will be poor. But if a country is administered without these eight, the enemy dares not approach, and even if he should, he would certainly be driven off; when it mobilizes its army and attacks, it will capture its objective, and having captured it, it will be able to hold it; when it holds its army in reserve, and makes no attack, it will be rich.

o   o   o   o

A country that has no strength and that practises knowledge and cleverness will certainly perish, but a fearful people, stimulated by penalties, will become brave, and a brave people, encouraged by rewards, will fight to the death. If fearful people become brave and brave people fight to the death the country will have no match; having no match, it will be strong, and being strong it will attain supremacy.

If the poor are encouraged by rewards, they will become rich and if penalties are applied to the rich, they will become poor. When in administrating a country one succeeds in making the poor rich and the rich poor, then the country will have much strength, and this being the case, it will attain supremacy.

o   o   o   o

Discussion about the People (2:5)

o   o   o   o

If, from a condition of rule and order, the people become lawless, and if one tries to rule this lawlessness, it will only increase; therefore, it should be ruled while it is still in a state of rule and order, then there will be true rule and order; if it is ruled, while it is in a state of lawlessness, lawlessness will remain.

It is the nature of the people to be orderly, but it is circumstances that cause disorder. Therefore, in the application of punishments, light offences should be regarded as serious; if light offences do not occur, serious ones have no chance of coming. This is said to be "ruling the people while in a state of law and order."

o   o   o   o

Opening and Debarring (2:7)

o   o   o   o

The guiding principles of the people are base and they are not consistent in what they value. As the conditions in the world change, different principles are practised. Therefore it is said that there is a fixed standard in a king's principles. Indeed, a king's principles represent one viewpoint and those of a minister another. The principles each follows are different but are one in both representing a fixed standard. Therefore, it is said: "When the people are stupid, by knowledge one may rise to supremacy; when the world is wise, by force one may rise to supremacy." That means that when people are stupid, there are plenty of strong men but not enough wise, and when the world is wise, there are plenty of clever men, but not enough strong. It is the nature of people, when they have no knowledge, to study, and when they have no strength, to submit.

o   o   o   o

Therefore, he who wishes to attain supreme sway by means of love, rejects punishments, and he who wishes to subjugate the feudal lords by means of force, relegates virtue to the background. A sage does not imitate antiquity nor does he follow the present time. If he were to imitate antiquity, he would be behind the times, and if he follows the present time, he is obstructed by circumstances.

o   o   o   o

Now you want to develop the people by imitating the ancient rulers, but the people of old were simple through honesty, while the people of today are clever through artificiality. Wherefore, if you wish to imitate the ancients, you will have orderly government by promoting virtue, and if you wish to imitate modern times, you will have laws by emphasizing punishments, and this is commonly distrusted. What the world now calls righteousness is the establishment of what people like and the abolishment of what they dislike, and what the world calls unrighteousness is the establishment of what people dislike and the abolishment of that in which they take delight.

o   o   o   o

Of old, people lived densely together and all dwelt in disorder, so they desired that there should be a ruler. However, why the empire was glad to have a ruler, was because he would create order. Now, having rulers but no law, the evil is the same as if there were no rulers, and having laws that are not equal to the disorders, is the same as if there were no law. The empire does not feel tranquil without a prince, but it takes pleasure in being stronger than the law, and thus the whole world is perturbed. Indeed, there is no greater benefit for the people in the empire than order and there is no firmer order to be obtained than by establishing a prince; for establishing a prince, there is no more embracing method than making law supreme; for making law supreme, there is no more urgent task than banishing villainy, and for banishing villainy, there is no deeper basis than severe punishments. Therefore those who attain supremacy, restrain by rewards and encourage by punishments, seek offences and not virtue, rely on punishments in order to abolish punishments.

Making Orders Strict (3:13)

o   o   o   o

A sage-prince understands what is essential in affairs, and therefore in his administration of the people, there is that which is most essential. For the fact that uniformity in the manipulating of rewards and punishments supports moral virtue is connected with human psychology. A sage-prince, by his ruling of men, is certain to win their hearts; consequently he is able to use force. Force produces strength, strength produces prestige, prestige produces virtue, and so virtue has its origin in force, which a sage-prince alone possesses, and therefore he is able to transmit benevolence and righteousness to the empire.

The Encouragement of Immigration (4:15)

o   o   o   o

Indeed, the trouble with Ch'in is, on the one hand, that if it raises soldiers and wages war, the country is poor, and on the other hand, if it remains quiet and farms, the enemy obtains respite. Your Majesty cannot combine success in these two fields. So, although for three generations it has waged successful wars, yet it has not subjected the empire. Now, if the old population of Ch'in are engaged in warfare, and if the newcomers are caused to occupy themselves with agriculture, then, even though the army may stay a hundred days outside the frontier, within the borders not a moment will be lost for agriculture. Thus, You may be successful both in enriching and in becoming strong.

When I speak of soldiers, I do not mean that all should be raised and mobilized to the last man, but according to the number of armies, soldiers, chariots, and cavalry that can be furnished within the territory, cause the old population of Ch'in to serve as soldiers and the new people to provide fodder and food. Should there be a state in the empire that does not submit, then Your Majesty should, herewith, in spring prevent their farming, in summer live on their produce, in autumn lay hold of their harvest, and in winter pickle their vegetables:[3] by the methods of the "Great Warfare" shake their fundamental means of existence and by those of the "Extensive Culture"[4] pacify their descendants. If Your Majesty follows this policy, then within ten years the various feudal lords will have no people from other countries[5] and wherefore, then, should Your Majesty be sparing in the conferment of titles or regard exemption from taxes[6] as a serious matter?

o   o   o   o

Should You now make exemptions from taxation for three generations, You would be able completely to subject the three Chin states.[7] This is not, like the virtuous kings, merely establishing the present times,[8] . . . but effecting that later generations shall be at the service of the king! This, however, does not mean that I do not welcome a sage, but it is difficult to await a sage.

Rewards and Punishments (4:17)

o   o   o   o

What I mean by the unification of punishments is that punishments should know no degree or grade, but that from ministers of state and generals down to great officers and ordinary folk, whosoever does not obey the king's commands, violates the interdicts of the state, or rebels against the statutes fixed by the ruler, should be guilty of death and should not be pardoned. Merit acquired in the past should not cause a decrease in the punishment for demerit later, nor should good behaviour in the past cause any derogation of the law for wrong done later. If loyal ministers and filial sons do wrong, they should be judged according to the full measure of their guilt, and if amongst the officials, who have to maintain the law and to uphold an office, there are those who do not carry out the king's law, they are guilty of death and should not be pardoned, but their punishment should be extended to their family for three generations.[9] Colleagues who, knowing their offence, inform their superiors will themselves escape punishment. In neither high nor low offices should there be an automatic hereditary succession to the office, rank, lands, or emoluments of officials. Therefore, do I say that if there are severe penalties that extend to the whole family, people will not dare to try how far they can go, and as they dare not try, no punishments will be necessary. The former kings, in making their interdicts, did not put to death, or cut off people's feet, or brand people's faces, because they sought to harm those people, but with the object of prohibiting wickedness and stopping crime, for there is no better means of prohibiting wickedness and stopping crime than by making punishments heavy.

o   o   o   o

Policies (4:18)

Of old, in the times of the Great and Illustrious Ruler,[10] people found their livelihood by cutting trees and slaying animals; the population was sparse and trees and animals numerous. In the times of Huang-ti,[11] neither young animals nor eggs were taken; the officials had no provisions and when the people died, they were not allowed to use outer coffins. These measures were not the same, but that they both attained supremacy was due to the fact that the times in which they lived were different. In the times of Shên Nung,[12] men ploughed to obtain food, and women wove to obtain clothing. Without the application of punishments or governmental measures, order prevailed; without the raising of mailed soldiers, he reigned supreme. After Shên Nung had died, the weak were conquered by force and the few oppressed by the many. Therefore Huang-ti created the ideas of prince and minister, of superior and inferior, the rites between father and son, between elder and younger brothers, the union between husband and wife, and between consort and mate. At home, he applied sword and saw, and abroad he used mailed soldiers; this was because the times had changed. Looking at it from this point of view, Shên Nung is not higher than Huang-ti, but the reason that his name was honoured was because he suited his time. Therefore, if by war one wishes to abolish war, even war is permissible; if by killing one wants to abolish killing, even killing is permissible; if by punishments one wishes to abolish punishments, even heavy punishments are permissible.

Of old, the one who could regulate the empire was he who regarded as his first task the regulating of his own people; the one who could conquer a strong enemy was he who regarded as his first task the conquering of his own people. For the way in which the conquering of the people is based upon the regulating of the people, is like the effect of smelting in regard to metal or the work of the potter in regard to clay; if the basis is not solid, then people are like flying birds or like animals. Who can regulate these? The basis of the people is the law. Therefore, a good ruler obstructed the people by means of the law, and so his reputation and his territory flourished.

o   o   o   o

If it is desired to do away with clever talkers, then all should control one another by means of the law, and should correct one another by means of mandates. Being unable to do wrong alone, one will not do wrong in the company of others. What is called wealth is to have receipts large and expenditure small. When there is moderation in dress, and frugality in food and drink, then expenditure is small. When women within and men outside[13] fulfill their duties completely, then receipts are large. What is called intelligence is for nothing to escape the sight, so that the multitude of officials dare not commit crimes nor the people to do wrong. Thus the ruler of men will repose on a rest-couch and listen to the sound of stringed and bamboo instruments, and yet the empire will enjoy order.

o   o   o   o

Weakening the People (5:20)

o   o   o   o

If the government takes such measures as the people hate, the people are made weak, and if it takes such measures as the people like, the people are made strong. But a weak people means a strong state and a strong people means a weak state. If the government takes such measures as the people like, they are made strong, and if strong people are made even stronger, the army becomes doubly weak; but if the government takes such measures as the people hate, they are made weak, and if weak people are made even weaker, the army becomes doubly strong. Therefore, by strengthening the people, one becomes doubly weak, and perishes; by weakening the people, one becomes doubly strong and attains supremacy.

o   o   o   o

External and Internal Affairs (5:22)

o   o   o   o

Of the internal affairs of the people, there is nothing harder than agriculture. Therefore an easy administration cannot bring them to it. What is called an easy administration? When farmers are poor and merchants are rich, when clever people gain profit and itinerant office-seekers are numerous. So the farmers, in spite of their extremely hard labour, gain little profit, and are worse off than merchants and shopkeepers and all manner of clever people. If one succeeds in restricting the number of these latter, then, even if one wished to, one could not prevent a state from becoming rich. Therefore is it said: "If one wishes to enrich the country through agriculture, then within the borders grain must be dear, taxes for those who are not farmers must be many, and dues on market-profit must be heavy, with the result that people are forced to have land. As those who have no land are obliged to buy their grain, grain will be dear, and those who have land will thus profit. When those who have land gain profit, there will be many who will occupy themselves with agriculture." When grain is dear, and the dealing in it is not profitable, while, moreover, heavy taxes are imposed, then people cannot fail to abolish merchants and shopkeepers and all manner of clever folk and to occupy themselves in the profit from the soil. So the strength of the people will be fully exerted in the profit from the soil. Therefore, he who organizes a state should let his soldiers have the full benefit of the profits on the frontiers and let the farmers have the full benefit from the profits of the market.

o   o   o   o

The Fixing of Rights and Duties (5:26)

The Duke questioned Kung-sun Yang,[14] saying: "Supposing that one established laws and mandates today, and wished that, tomorrow, all government servants and people, throughout the empire, should understand them clearly and apply them, so that all should be as one, and should have no selfish intentions—how can one bring this about?"

Kung-sun Yang replied: "There should be instituted, for the laws, government officers, who are able to understand the contents of the decrees and who should be the regulators of the empire. Then they should memorialize the Son of T'ien, whereupon the Son of T'ien would personally preside over the law and promulgate it. All should then issue to their inferiors the mandates they have received, and the law officers should preside personally over the law and promulgate it. When people venture to neglect practising the items, named in the promulgations of the officers presiding over the law, then each one is punished according to the item in the law which he has neglected. In the eventuality of these officers, who preside over the law, being transferred or dying, students should be made to read the contents of the law and a standard of knowledge should be fixed for them, so that, within a certain number of days, they should know the contents of the law, and, for those students who do not reach the standard, a law is made for punishing them.

Should anyone dare to tamper with the text of the law, to erase or add one single character, or more, he shall be condemned to death without pardon. Whenever government officials or people have questions about the meaning of the laws or mandates, to ask of the officers presiding over the law, the latter should, in each case, answer clearly according to the laws and mandates about which it was originally desired to ask questions, and they should, in each case, prepare a tablet of the length of one foot six inches, on which should be distinctly inscribed the year, month, day, and hour, as well as the items of law about which questions were asked, for the information of the government officials or of the people. Should the officers who preside over the law not give the desired information, they should be punished according to the contents of the law, that is, they should be punished according to the law about which the government officials or people have asked information. The officers, presiding over the law, should forthwith give to those government officials who ask information about the law, the left half of the document and they themselves should store carefully the wooden bindings with the right half of the document, keep them in a room and seal them with the seal of the chief of the office of laws and mandates. Later, on the death of the officer, affairs should be transacted according to these files.

"All the laws and mandates should be put together as a set, one set being kept in the palace of the Son of T'ien. Forbidden archives should be built for the laws, which are locked with lock and key to prevent admittance, and are sealed up; herein should be stored one set of the laws and mandates. Inside the forbidden archives they should be sealed with a seal forbidding their opening. Whoever ventures unauthorizedly to break the seals of the forbidden archives, or to enter the forbidden archives, to inspect the forbidden laws and mandates, or to tamper with one or more characters of the forbidden laws shall, in any of these cases, be guilty of death without pardon. Once a year laws and mandates shall be received for prohibitions and orders to be issued. The Son of T'ien shall set up three law officers, one in the palace, one in the office of the Chief Archivist together with a government official, and one in the chancery of the Grand Counsellor. In the various prefectures and subprefectures of the feudal lords, shall be instituted one law officer, together with government officials, all of whom shall be similar to the law officers in Ch'in. Thus the prefectures and subprefectures and the feudal lords shall all alike receive a knowledge of the laws and mandates in the archives, and moreover the afore-mentioned government officials and people, who are desirous of knowing the law, shall all address their inquiries to these law officers. Thus there shall be no one among the government officials and people of the empire, who does not know the law, and as the officials are clearly aware that the people know the laws and mandates, they dare not treat the people contrary to the law, nor dare the people transgress the law, as they would come into conflict with the law officers. If in their treatment of the people, the government officials do not act according to the law, the former should inquire of the law officer, who should at once inform them of the punishment for the illegal action in question fixed by the law. The people should then at once inform the government officials, formally, of the law officer's statement. Thus the government officials, knowing that such is the course of events, dare not treat the people contrary to the law, nor do the people dare infringe the law. In this way, government officials and the people of the empire, however virtuous or good, however sophistical or sagacious they may be, cannot add one word to twist the law, nor, though they may have a thousand pieces of gold, can they use one twenty-fourth of an ounce of it for such a purpose. Thus the knowing and crafty ones, as well as the virtuous and capable, will all force themselves to behave well and will do their best to restrain themselves and to serve the public weal. When people are stupid, they are easy to govern. All this originates from the fact that the law is clear, easy to know, and strictly applied.

"Law is the authoritative principle for the people and is the basis of government; it is what shapes the people. Trying to govern while eliminating the law is like a desire not to be hungry while eliminating food, or a desire not to be cold while eliminating clothes, or a desire to go east while one moves west. It is clear enough that there is no hope of realizing it.

"That a hundred men will chase after a single hare that runs away, is not for the sake of the hare, for when they are sold everywhere on the market, even a thief does not dare to take one away, because their legal title is definite. Thus if the legal title is not definite, then even men like Yao, Shun, Yü, or T'ang[15] would all rush to chase after it, but if the legal title is definite even a poor thief would not take it. Now if laws and mandates are not clear nor their titles definite, the men of the empire have opportunities for discussion; in their discussions they will differ and there will be no definiteness. If above the ruler of men makes laws, but below the inferior people discuss them, the laws will not be definite and inferiors will become superiors. This may be called a condition where rights and duties are indefinite. When rights and duties are indefinite, even men like Yao and Shun will become crooked and commit acts of wickedness, how much more then the mass of the people! This is the way in which wickedness and wrong-doing will be greatly stimulated, the ruler of men will be despoiled of his authority and power, will ruin his country and bring disaster upon the altar of the soil and grain.

"Now the former sages made writings and transmitted them to later generations, and it is necessary to accept these as authoritative, so that one may know what is conveyed by established terminology. Should they not be accepted as authoritative and should people discuss them according to ideas of their own mind, then until their death they will not succeed in understanding the terminology and its meaning. Therefore did the sages set up officers and officials for the laws and mandates, who should be authoritative in the empire, in order to define everyone's rights and duties, so that these being definite, the very crafty would become faithful and trustworthy, and the people would all become honest and guileless, each one restraining himself. For, indeed, the defining of everybody's rights and duties is the road that leads to orderly government, but the not defining of everybody's rights and duties is the road that leads to disorder. So where there is a tendency towards order, there cannot be disorder, and where there is a tendency towards disorder, there cannot be order. Indeed, where there is a tendency towards disorder and one governs it, the disorder will only increase, but where there is a tendency towards order and one governs it, there will be order. Therefore, the sage kings governed order and did not govern disorder.

"Indeed, subtle and mysterious words, which have to be pondered over, cause difficulty even to men of superior knowledge. There may be one case in ten millions, where the directing guidance of the law is not needed and yet it is correct in everything. Therefore, a sage governs the empire for the ten million cases. For, indeed, one should not make laws so that only the intelligent can understand them, for the people are not all intelligent, and one should not make laws so that only the men of talent can understand them, for the people are not all talented. Therefore, did the sages, in creating laws, make them clear and easy to understand and the terminology correct, so that stupid and wise, without exception, could understand them; and by setting up law officers and officers, presiding over the law, to be authoritative in the empire, prevented the people from falling into dangerous pitfalls. So the fact that when the sages established the empire, there were no victims of capital punishment, was not because capital punishment did not exist, but because the laws, which were applied, were clear and easy to understand. They set up law officers and government officials to be the authority, in order to guide them, and they knew that if the ten thousands of people all knew what to avoid and what to strive for, they would avoid misfortune and strive for happiness, and so restrain themselves. Therefore, an intelligent prince follows the existing conditions of order and so makes the order complete, with the result that the empire will enjoy great order."

20

Han Fei Tzŭ

If you do not regard conformity to law as right, you will
eventually observe no law.

—*Han Fei Tzŭ,* 20:54

Han Fei Tzŭ (d. 233 B.C.), a highly educated political thinker and
writer, was a noble of the state of Han in northwest China. The biogra-
phy contained in Ssŭ-ma Ch'ien's *Historical Records* (c. 100 B.C.) pictures
him as a moral man. He was incensed with the King of Han, who never
tried to improve the laws or to enrich the state and strengthen the army,
who chose and promoted "vermin," the frivolous and dissolute, putting
them over men of real ability; who permitted literati (Han Fei Tzŭ calls
them "itinerant witches and priests") to becloud the law; and who
treated the famous with favor. But when the country was in an emergency it was the poor, neglected warriors who were called to the colors.

Reform movements in the country, given life by the collapsing feudalistic system, influenced his thinking. He brought together the currents
that were pulling for a centralized state with positive law and gave them
shape in a comprehensive system. The ruler of the state of Ch'in evidently saw possibilities of statecraft in Han Fei Tzŭ's synthesis and put
some of them in practice. In time this king finished the conquest of the
warring states and became the first emperor of the newly unified China.

When Han Fei Tzŭ was invited to the court of Ch'in, the chief minister was Li Ssŭ. Apparently both men had earlier studied with the great
Confucian, Hsün Tzŭ. Jealousy, however, seems to have consumed the
prime minister. The story goes that Li Ssŭ, after slandering Han Fei
Tzŭ, saw to it that he was handed poison and ordered to commit suicide.
Han Fei Tzŭ complied. The historian Ssŭ-ma Ch'ien adds that the King
of Ch'in repented and ordered the scholar's release, but the pardon arrived too late.

Thus the second of the two great Legalist thinkers died at the hands of the Legalist state. Han Fei Tzŭ's ideas remained to influence later Chinese statecraft, but with him, self-proclaimed Legalist literature comes to an end.

Han Fei Tzŭ's works, numbering fifty-five treatises, are the fullest expression of Legalist thought. Though they contain the same political philosophy as the *Book of Lord Shang*, they are better organized, urbane, well-argued, and lightened with witty and telling stories and parables.

THE *HAN FEI TZŬ*

Selections

On the Difficulty in Speaking: A Memorial (1:3)

Thy servant, Fei,[1] is by no means diffident of speaking. As to why he has to hesitate in speaking: if his speeches are compliant and harmonious, magnificent and orderly, he is then regarded as ostentatious and insincere; if his speeches are sincere and courteous, straightforward and careful, he is then regarded as awkward and unsystematic; if his speeches are widely cited and subtly composed, frequently illustrated and continuously analogized, he is then regarded as empty and unpractical; if his speeches summarize minute points and present general ideas,

From W. K. Liao, tr., *The Complete Works of Han Fei Tzŭ*, 2 vols. (London: Probsthain, 1950).

being thus plain and concise, he is then regarded as simple and not discerning; if his speeches are very personally observing and well versed in the inner nature of mankind, he is then regarded as self-assuming and self-conceited; if his speeches are erudite and profound, he is then regarded as boastful but useless; if his speeches touch the details of housekeeping and estimate each item in terms of numerals, he is then regarded as vulgar; if his speeches are too much concerned with worldly affairs and not offensive in wording, he is then regarded as a coward and a flatterer; if his speeches are far from commonplace and contrary to human experience, he is then regarded as fantastic; if his speeches are witty and eloquent and full of rhetorical excellences, he is then regarded as flippant; if he discards all literary forms of expression and speaks solely of the naked facts, he is then regarded as rustic; and should he quote the *Book of Songs* or the *Book of Documents* from time to time and act on the teachings of the former sages, he is then regarded as a book chanter. These things explain the reason why thy servant, Fei, is diffident in speaking and worried about speaking.

Therefore, weights and measures, however accurate, are not always adopted; doctrines and principles, however perfect, are not always practised. Should His Majesty disbelieve the minister who speaks to the throne, the minister would be found guilty of a blunder or condemned to death.

For example, Tzŭ-hsü[2] schemed well but was killed by the King of Wu; Chung-ni[3] taught well but was detained by the Ruler of K'uang; and Kuan I-wu[4] was really worthy but was taken prisoner by the Ruler of Lu. Not that these three statesmen were not worthy, but that the three rulers were not intelligent.

In remote antiquity, when T'ang was the sanest and I Yin[5] the wisest of the age, though the wisest attempted to persuade the sanest, yet he was not welcomed even after seventy times of persuasion, till he had to handle pans and bowls and become a cook in order thereby to approach him and become familiar with him. In consequence T'ang came to know his worthiness and took him into service. Hence the saying: "Though the wisest man wants to persuade the sanest man, he is not necessarily welcomed upon his first arrival." Such was the case of I Yin's persuading T'ang. Again the saying: "Though the wise man wants to persuade the fool, he is not necessarily listened to." Such was the case of King Wên's persuading Chou.[6]

Thus, just as King Wên attempted to persuade Chou and was put in jail, Marquis I was broiled; Marquis Chiu's corpse was dried; Pi Kan had his heart cut open; and Earl Mei's[7] corpse was pickled.

Furthermore, I-wu was bound with chains. Ts'ao Ch'i absconded to Ch'ên. Pai-li Tzŭ begged on his way to the capital of Ch'in. Fu Yüeh was sold into slavery from place to place. Sun Tzŭ[8] had his feet cut off in Wei. Wu Ch'i wiped off his tears at Dike Gate, lamented over the impending cession of the Western River Districts to Ch'in, and was dismembered in Ch'u. Kung-shu Tso spoke of a man fit to be a pillar of the state but was regarded as unreasonable, so that Kung-sun Yang[9] absconded to Ch'in. Kuan Lung-p'êng was executed. Ch'ang Hung had his intestines chopped into pieces. Yin Tzŭ was thrown into a trap among brambles. The Minister of War, Tzŭ-ch'i, was killed and his corpse was floated on the Yangtze River. T'ien Ming was stoned to death. Mi Tzŭ-chien and Hsi-mên Pao quarrelled with nobody but were killed. Tung An-yü was killed and his corpse was exposed in the marketplace. Tsai Yü had to suffer the disaster caused by T'ien Ch'ang. Fan Chü had his ribs broken in Wei.

These tens of men were all benevolent, worthy, loyal, and upright persons in the world and followers of the right way and true path of life. Unfortunately they met such unreasonable, violent, stupid, and crooked masters, and lost their lives in the long run.

Then, why could these worthies and sages escape death penalties and evade disgrace? It was because of the difficulty in persuading fools. Hence every gentleman[10] has to remain diffident of speaking. Even the best speech displeases the ear and upsets the heart, and can be appreciated only by worthy and sage rulers. May Your Majesty therefore ponder over this memorial of thy servant!

Having Regulations: A Memorial (2:6)

o   o   o   o

Therefore, the intelligent sovereign makes the law select men and makes no arbitrary promotion himself. He makes the law measure merits and makes no arbitrary regulation himself. In consequence, able men cannot be obscured, bad characters cannot be disguised; falsely praised fellows cannot be advanced, wrongly defamed people cannot be degraded. Accordingly, between ruler and minister distinction becomes clear and order is attained. Thus it suffices only if the sovereign can scrutinize laws.

The wise man, on ministering to a ruler, faces the north[11] and swears an oath of his office, pledging "not to have two minds, never to reject any low commission in the court, and never to reject any hard job in the military camp, but to follow the instructions of his superior, to obey the law of the sovereign and empty his mind so as to wait for the royal decrees to come, and to have no dispute about them." Therefore, though he has a mouth of his own, he never speaks for his own advantage; though he has eyes of his own, he never sees for his private interest. Both his mouth and eyes are kept under his superior's control. In other words, who ministers to a ruler may be likened to the hand that is able to care for the head upward and for the feet downward, never fails to relieve them from extremes of cold and heat, and never fails to strike away even the Mo-yeh Sword [12] when it is near the body. Similarly, the intelligent ruler never employs worthy and clever ministers or wise and able men for any selfish purpose. Therefore, the people do not cross the village border to make friends and have no relatives living one hundred *li* away; high and low do not trespass against each other; the fool and the wise, each being content with his own lot, keep the scale and stand in perfect balance.[13] Such is the crowning phase of order, indeed!

o   o   o   o

The Two Handles (2:7)

o   o   o   o

Once in bygone days, Marquis Chao of Han[14] was drunk and fell into a nap. The crown-keeper, seeing the ruler exposed to cold, put a coat over him. When the Marquis awoke, he was glad and asked the attendants, "Who put more clothes on my body?" "The crown-keeper did," they replied. Then the Marquis found the coat-keeper guilty and put the crown-keeper to death. He punished the coat-keeper for the neglect of his duty, and the crown-keeper for the overriding of his post. Not that the Marquis was not afraid of catching cold but that he thought their trespassing the assigned duties was worse than his catching cold.

Thus, when an intelligent ruler keeps ministers in service, no minister is allowed either to override his post and get merits thereby nor to utter any word not equivalent to a fact. Whoever overrides his post is put to death; whoever makes a word not equivalent to a fact is punished. If everyone has to do his official duty, and if whatever he says has to be earnest, then the ministers cannot associate for treasonable purposes.

The lord of men has two difficulties to face: If he appoints only worthy men to office, ministers will on the pretence of worthiness attempt to deceive their ruler; if he makes arbitrary promotions of officials, the state affairs will always be menaced. Similarly, if the lord of men loves worthiness, ministers will gloss over their defects in order to meet the ruler's need. In consequence, no minister will show his true heart. If no minister shows his true heart, the lord of men will find no way to tell the worthy from the unworthy.

o   o   o   o

In these days, if the lord of men neither covers his feelings nor conceals his motives, and if he lets ministers have a chance to molest their master, the ministers will have no difficulty in following the examples of Tzŭ-chih and T'ien-ch'ang.[15] Hence the saying: "If the ruler's likes and hate be concealed, the ministers' true hearts will be revealed. If the ministers reveal their true hearts, the ruler never will be deluded."

Wielding the Sceptre (2:8)

o   o   o   o

The sceptre should never be shown. For its inner nature is non-assertion. The state affairs may be scattered in the four directions but the key to their administration is in the centre. The sage holding this key in hand, people from the four directions come to render him meritorious services. He remains empty and waits for their services, and they will exert their abilities by themselves. With the conditions of the four seas clearly in mind, he can see the *yang* by means of the *yin*. After appointing attendants on his right and left, he can open the gate and meet anybody. He can go onward with the two handles without making any change. To apply them without cessation is said to be acting on the right way of government.

Indeed, everything has its function; every material has its utility. When everybody works according to his special qualification, both superior and inferior will not have to do anything. Let roosters herald the dawn and let cats watch for rats. When everything exercises its special qualification, the ruler will not have to do anything. If the ruler has to exert any special skill of his own, it means that affairs are not going right.[16]

o   o   o   o

The Yellow Emperor[17] made the saying: "Superior and inferior wage one hundred battles a day." The inferior conceals his tricks which he uses in testing the superior; the superior manipulates rules and measures in splitting the influences of the inferior. Therefore the institution of rules and measures is the sovereign's treasure, the possession of partisans and adherents is the minister's treasure. Such being the situation, if the minister does not murder the ruler, it is because his partisans and adherents are not yet sufficient. Therefore, if the superior loses one or two inches, the inferior will gain eight or sixteen feet. The ruler in possession of a state never enlarges the capital. The minister following the true path never empowers his own family. The ruler following the right way never empowers any minister. Because, once empowered and enriched, the inferior will attempt to supplant the superior. So, guard against dangers and be afraid of eventualities. Install the crown prince quickly. Then many troubles find no way to appear.

To detect culprits inside the court and guard against crooks outside it, the ruler must personally hold his rules and measures. Make the powerful wane and the powerless wax. Both waning and waxing should have limitations. Never allow the people to form juntas and thereby deceive their superiors with one accord. Make the powerful wane like the moon, and the powerless wax like the heat of the bored fire. Simplify orders and dignify censures. Make the application of penal laws definite.

o   o   o   o

Eight Villainies (2:9)

In general there are eight ways whereby ministers are led to commit villainy:

The first is said to be "through the bribery of sharers of the same bed." What is meant by "through the bribery of sharers of the same bed"? In reply I say: By graceful ladies, beloved concubines, feminine courtiers, and pretty lads, the lord of men is bewildered. Counting on the sovereign's pleasant rest from governmental work and taking advantage of his being drunken and satiated, the sharers of the same bed would get from him what they want. This is the way to secure unfailing grants. Therefore, ministers bribe them in secret with gold and jewelry and thereby make them bewilder the sovereign. This is said to be "through the bribery of sharers of the same bed."

The second is said to be "through the bribery of bystanders." What is meant by "through the bribery of bystanders"? In reply I say: Actors, jokers, and clowns as well as attendants and courtiers would say, "At your service, at your service," before the sovereign has given any order, and say, "Yes, yes," before he has commanded them to do anything, thus taking orders ahead of his words and looking at his facial expressions and judging his needs by his colour in order thereby to render him service before he makes up his mind. Such people advance and withdraw *en bloc*, respond and reply with one accord, thus identifying their deeds and unifying their words so as to move the sovereign's mind. Therefore, ministers bribe them in secret with gold, jewelry, curios, and the like, and commit unlawful acts to their advantage and thereby make them beguile the sovereign. This is said to be "through the bribery of bystanders."

The third is said to be "through the entertainment of uncles and brothers." What is meant by "through the entertainment of uncles and brothers"? In reply I say: Sons by concubines are much loved by the sovereign; prime ministers and court officials are consulted by the sovereign. All such people exert their energies and exchange their ideas while the sovereign always listens to them. Ministers, accordingly, entertain concubines and their sons with music and beauties, and win the hearts of prime ministers and court officials with twisted words and sentences. Then through them they make promises and submit projects to the throne, so that when the tasks are accomplished, their ranks are raised, their bounties increased, and their minds thereby satisfied. In this way they make them violate the sovereign. This is said to be "through the entertainment of uncles and brothers."

The fourth is said to be "through fostering calamities." What is meant by "through fostering calamities"? In reply I say: The sovereign enjoys beautifying his palatial buildings, terraces, and pools, and decorating boys, girls, dogs, and horses, so as to amuse his mind. This will eventually bring him calamities. Therefore, ministers exhaust the energy of the people to beautify palatial buildings, terraces, and pools, and increase exactions and taxation for decorating boys, girls, dogs, and horses, and thereby amuse the sovereign and disturb his mind, thus following his wants and harvesting their own advantages thereby. This is said to be "through fostering calamities."

The fifth is said to be "through buying up vagabonds." What is meant by "through buying up vagabonds"? In reply I say: Ministers distribute money out of public revenues to please the masses of people and bestow small favours to win the hearts of the hundred surnames,[18] and thereby make everybody, whether in the court or in the market-place, praise them, and, by deluding the sovereign in this manner, get what they want. This is said to be "through buying up vagabonds."

The sixth is said to be "through the employment of fluent and convincing speakers." What is meant by "through the employment of fluent and convincing speakers"? In reply I say: The sovereign, with all avenues to news blockaded, rarely hears any disputes and discussions and is therefore apt to change his mind by eloquent persuaders. Accordingly, ministers find eloquent speakers from among the subjects of other feudal lords and feed able persuaders in the country, then make them speak about their self-seeking designs with skilfully polished words and fluent and convincing phrases, show the sovereign the direction of advantages and powers, overawe him with the location of calamities and disadvantages, manipulate all kinds of false sayings, and thereby deprave him. This is said to be "through the employment of fluent and convincing speakers."

The seventh is said to be "through the arrogation of authority and strength." What is meant by "through the arrogation of authority and strength"? In reply I say: The ruler of men maintains his authority and strength by keeping all officials and the hundred surnames on his side. Whatever he considers good is regarded as good by the officials and the people; whatever he never considers good is not regarded as good by the officials and the people. Ministers then gather bold swordsmen and desperate rascals to display their authority and make it known that whoever sides with them always gains and whoever does not side with them is bound to die, and thereby overawe the officials and the people and practise selfishness. This is said to be "through the arrogation of authority and strength."

The eighth is said to be "through the accumulation of support from the four directions." What is meant by "through the accumulation of support from the four directions"? In reply I say: The ruler of men, if his country is small, has to serve big powers, and, if his army is weak, has to fear strong armies. Any request by a big power the small country always has to accept; any demand by a strong army the weak army always has to obey. Accordingly, ministers raise exactions and taxations, exhaust public treasuries and armouries, empty the provisions of the country, and thereby serve big powers and utilize their influence to mislead the ruler. In serious cases, they would even send for foreign troops to assemble in the border-lands while they restrain their sovereign inside the country. Otherwise, they would invite special envoys from enemy states to molest their ruler and thereby overawe him. This is said to be "through the accumulation of support from the four directions."

These eight in general are the ways whereby ministers are led to commit villainy and the sovereigns of the present age are deluded, molested, and deprived of their possessions. Therefore, every sovereign should not fail to study them carefully.

o   o   o   o

Difficulties in the Way of Persuasion (4:12)

Difficulties in the way of persuasion, generally speaking, are not difficulties in my knowledge with which I persuade the ruler, nor are they difficulties in my skill of argumentation which enables me to make my ideas clear, nor are they difficulties in my courage to exert my abilities without reserve. As a whole, the difficulties in the way of persuasion lie in my knowing the heart of the persuaded in order thereby to fit my wording into it.

If the persuaded strives after high fame while you persuade him of big profit, you will be considered low-bred, accorded mean treatment, and shunned from afar. If the persuaded strives after big profit while you persuade him of high fame, you will be considered mindless and ignorant of worldly affairs and will never be accepted. If the persuaded strives after big profit in secret but openly seeks for high fame while you persuade him of high fame, you will be accepted in name but kept distant in fact; and, if you persuade him of big profit, your word will be adopted in secret but your person will be left out openly. These points should be carefully deliberated.

Indeed, affairs succeed if kept secret and fail if divulged. Though you never intend to expose the ruler's secrets, yet if you happen to speak of anything he wants to conceal, you are then in danger. When the ruler embarks openly on an enterprise but plans thereby to accomplish a different task, if the persuader knows not only its motive but also its purpose, he is then in danger. When the persuader has devised an extraordinary scheme which suits the ruler, if another wise man finds it out by inferring it from other sources and divulges the secret to the world, the ruler will think he has divulged the secret, wherefore he is in danger. If the persuader exhausts all his wisdom before his master's favour becomes thick, then though his persuasion prevails and has merits, his fruitful services will be forgotten with ease. If his persuasion takes no effect and has demerits, he will fall under suspicion. In such a case he is in danger. Supposing the ruler had an aptitude for certain faults and the persuader spoke plainly on propriety and righteousness and thereby challenged his vices, he would be in danger. If the ruler has taken a scheme from somebody else, which he assumes to be his own work, and the persuader happens to know the whole secret, he is in danger. Whoever forcibly persuades the ruler to do what he cannot do and not to do what he cannot stop doing, is in danger.

Therefore, if you talk about great men to him, he thinks you are intimating his defects. If you talk about small men to him, he thinks you are showing off your superiority. If you discuss an object of his love, he thinks you are expecting a special favour from it. If you discuss an object of his hate, he thinks you are testing his temper. If you simplify your discussion, he thinks you are unwise and will spurn you. If your discussion is lucidly wayward and extensively refined, he thinks you are superficial and flippant. If you omit details and present generalizations only, he thinks you are cowardly and incomplete. If you trace the principles of facts and use wide illustrations, he thinks you are rustic and arrogant. These are difficulties in the way of persuasion, which every persuader should know.

In general, the business of the persuader is to embellish the pride and obliterate the shame of the persuaded. If he has any private urgent need, you ought to encourage him with the cause of public justice. If the persuaded has a mean intention but cannot help it, you ought to praise its excellent points and minimize its harmfulness to the public. If he has a high ambition in mind but his real ability falls short of the mark, you ought to enumerate its mistakes, disclose its disadvantages, and esteem his suspension from realizing it. If he aspires to the pride of wisdom and talent, you ought to enumerate different species of the same genus with reference to every object of knowledge and thereby supply him with abundant information and let him derive ideas from you but pretend to ignorance of his derivation so as to elevate his wisdom.

If you want the persuaded to adopt your suggestion to cultivate interstate friendship, you ought to explain it in the light of a glorious cause and intimate its accord with his private interest. If you want to describe things dangerous and injurious to the state welfare, you ought to enumerate the reproaches and slanders against them first and then intimate their discord with his private interest.

Praise those men doing the same things as he does. Esteem the tasks under the same scheme as his tasks are. In regard to men having the same faults as he has, be sure to defend their harmlessness. In regard to men having met the same failures as he met, be sure to bring out their incurring no loss. If he makes much of his own strength, do not bring in any difficult task that impedes him. If he thinks his own decisions brave, do not point out their unlawfulness; that angers him. If he thinks his own scheme wise, do not recall his past failures which embarrass him. When your meaning is not offensive and your wording is not flippant, you are then under way to use all your wisdom and eloquence to persuade anybody. In this way you can become near and dear to him, avoid all suspicion, and exert your speech to the utmost.

I Yin[19] had to work as a cook and Pai-li Hsi had to go as a captive, both aiming thereby to approach their masters. These two men were sages. Still they could not help lowering themselves to such a humble level in order to introduce themselves to notice. Now take me as cook or captive. If you find it possible to take advice from me, carry out my suggestion, and thereby save the world, it is no shame to an able man.

Indeed, as days multiply in the long course of time and favour with the ruler grows well-grounded, when you are no longer suspected of devising schemes profoundly and not convicted in joining issue with the ruler on any point, then you may frankly weigh the relative advantages and disadvantages of the trend of the times and thereby forecast your meritorious services and straightly point out what is right and what is wrong in the course of government and thereby assert yourself. If ruler and minister stand together in such relationship, it is due to the success of persuasion.

o   o   o   o

The Difficulty of Pien Ho (4:13)

o   o   o   o

Lord Shang taught Duke Hsiao of Ch'in to organize groups of ten and five families, and establish the system of denunciation of crime and joint responsibility for offence, to burn the *Books of Poetry and History* and thereby make laws and orders clear, to bar the requests of private families and thereby encourage services to public offices, to prohibit idlers from purchasing official posts, and to celebrate farmers and warriors. The theory was carried into effect by Duke Hsiao with the immediate result that the sovereign thereby become glorious and secure and the state thereby became rich and strong. Eighteen years later the Duke passed away, whereupon Lord Shang was torn to pieces by chariots in Ch'in.

Ch'u, not employing Wu Ch'i, was dismembered and disturbed; Ch'in, practising the Law of Lord Shang, became rich and strong. Though the two philosophers' words turned out true, yet how came it that Ch'u dismembered Wu Ch'i and Ch'in tore Lord Shang to pieces by chariots? It was because the chief vassals had regarded law as annoyance and the masses had resented order.

o   o   o   o

Ministers Apt to Betray, Molest, or Murder the Ruler (4:14)

o   o   o   o

Scholars of the present age[20] in counselling the lord of men do not say, "Make use of the august and commanding position and thereby harass the wicked and villainous ministers," but all say, "Practise nothing but benevolence, righteousness, favour, and love!" Accordingly, rulers of the present age have praised the names of benevolent and righteous men but have never examined their realities, so that in serious cases they have ruined their states and lost their lives and in minor cases they have seen their territories dismembered and their ranks relegated.

o   o   o   o

There is a proverb saying, "Even the leper feels pity for the king." It is not a reverent saying. Nevertheless, since in antiquity there was no empty proverb, everybody should consider it carefully. It speaks for such sovereigns as are liable to molestation or murder.

If the lord of men does not have law and tact to control his ministers, then though he is still on the green margin of his life and has excellent talents, chief vassals will, as usual, gain influence, administer all state affairs at their will, and make all decisions on their own authority, everybody working to his own advantage. Fearing lest uncles and brothers of the sovereign or some heroic men should exercise the authority of the lord of men to suppress and censure them, they would depose worthy, full-grown rulers and set up young, weak ones on the throne, or set aside lawful heirs and place unlawful ones in their stead.

o   o   o   o

As witnessed in recent times, no sooner had Li Tai come into power in Chao, than he starved the Father Sovereign for one hundred days till he died; no sooner had Nao Ch'ih come into power in Ch'i, than he pulled out the sinews of King Min[21] and hanged him on the beam of the ancestral shrine where he died after one night.

Therefore, the leper, despite the boils and swellings all over his body, as compared with rulers of the Spring and Autumn Period,[22] never suffers such miseries as neck-strangling and thigh-shooting, and, as compared with rulers of recent times, never suffers such miseries as starvation to death and sinew-pulling. Thus, the mental agony and physical pain of the rulers molested and murdered certainly exceed those of the leper. From this viewpoint, though the leper feels pity for the king, there is good reason for it.

Portents of Ruin[23] *(5:15)*

1. As a rule, if the state of the lord of men is small but the fiefs of private families are big, or if the ruler's sceptre is insignificant but the ministers are powerful, then ruin is possible.

2. If the ruler neglects laws and prohibitions, indulges in plans and ideas, disregards the defence works within the boundaries and relies on foreign friendship and support, then ruin is possible.

3. If all officials indulge in studies, sons of the family are fond of debate, pedlars and shopkeepers hide money in foreign countries, and poor people suffer miseries at home, then ruin is possible.

4. If the ruler is fond of palatial decorations, raised kiosks, and embanked pools, is immersed in pleasures of having chariots, clothes, and curios, and thereby tires out the hundred surnames and exhausts public wealth, then ruin is possible.

5. If the ruler believes in date-selecting,[24] worships devils and deities, believes in divination and lot-casting, and likes fêtes and celebrations, then ruin is possible.

6. If the ruler takes advice only from ministers of high rank, refrains from comparing different opinions and testifying to the truth, and uses only one man as a channel of information, then ruin is possible.

7. If posts and offices can be sought through influential personages and rank and bounties can be obtained by means of bribes, then ruin is possible.

8. If the ruler, being easy-going, accomplishes nothing, being tender-hearted, lacking in decision, and, wavering between acceptance and rejection, has no settled opinion, then ruin is possible.

9. If the ruler is greedy, insatiable, attracted to profit, and fond of gain, then ruin is possible.

10. If the ruler enjoys inflicting unjust punishment and does not uphold the law, likes debate and persuasion but never sees to their practicability, and indulges in style and wordiness but never considers their effect, then ruin is possible.

11. If the ruler is shallow-brained and easily penetrated, reveals everything but conceals nothing, and cannot keep any secret but communicates the words of one minister to another, then ruin is possible.

12. If the ruler is stubborn-minded, uncompromising, and apt to dispute every remonstrance and fond of surpassing everybody else, and never thinks of the welfare of the Altar of the Spirits of Land and Grain[25] but sticks to self-confidence without due consideration, then ruin is possible.

13. The ruler who relies on friendship and support from distant

countries, makes light of his relations with close neighbours, counts on the aid from big powers, and provokes surrounding countries, is liable to ruin.

14. If foreign travellers and residents, whose property and families are abroad, take seats in the state council and interfere in civil affairs, then ruin is possible.

15. If the people have no confidence in the premier and the inferiors do not obey the superiors while the sovereign loves and trusts the premier and cannot depose him, then ruin is possible.

16. If the ruler does not take able men of the country into service but searches after foreign gentlemen, and if he does not make tests according to meritorious services but would appoint and dismiss officials according to their mere reputations till foreign residents are exalted and ennobled to surpass his old acquaintances, then ruin is possible.

17. If the ruler disregards the matter of legitimacy and lets bastards rival legitimate sons, or if the sovereign dies before he inaugurates the crown prince, then ruin is possible.

18. If the ruler is boastful but never regretful, makes much of himself despite the disorder prevailing in his country, and insults the neighbouring enemies without estimating the resources within the boundaries, then ruin is possible.

19. If the state is small but the ruler will not acquiesce in a humble status; if his forces are scanty but he never fears strong foes; if he has no manners and insults big neighbours; or if he is greedy and obstinate but unskilful in diplomacy; then ruin is possible.

20. If, after the inauguration of the crown prince, the ruler take in a woman from a strong enemy state,[26] the crown prince will be endangered and the ministers will be worried. Then ruin is possible.

21. If the ruler is timid and weak in self-defence and his mind is paralysed by the signs of future events; or if he knows what to decide on but dare not take any drastic measure; then ruin is possible.

22. If the exiled ruler is abroad but the country sets up a new ruler, or if before the heir apparent taken abroad as hostage returns,[27] the ruler changes his successor, then the state will divide. And the state divided against itself is liable to ruin.

23. If the ruler keeps near and dear to the chief vassals whom he has disheartened and disgraced or stands close by the petty men whom he has punished, then he will make them bear anger and feel shame. If he

goes on doing this, rebels are bound to appear. When rebels appear, ruin is possible.

24. If chief vassals rival each other in power and uncles and brothers are many and powerful, and if they form juntas inside and receive support from abroad and thereby dispute state affairs and struggle for supreme influence, then ruin is possible.

25. If words of maids and concubines are followed and the wisdom of favourites is used, and the ruler repeats committing unlawful acts regardless of the grievances and resentments inside and outside the court, then ruin is possible.

26. If the ruler is contemptuous to chief vassals and impolite to uncles and brothers, overworks the hundred surnames, and slaughters innocent people, then ruin is possible.

27. If the ruler is fond of twisting laws by virtue of his wisdom, mixes public with private affairs from time to time, alters laws and prohibitions at random, and issues commands and orders frequently, then ruin is possible.

28. If the terrain has no stronghold, the city-walls are in bad repair, the state has no savings and hoardings, resources and provisions are scarce, and no preparations are made for defence and attack, but the ruler dares to attack and invade other countries imprudently, then ruin is possible.

29. If the royal seed is short-lived, new sovereigns succeed to each other continuously, babies become rulers, and chief vassals have all the ruling authority to themselves and recruit partisans from among foreign residents and maintain interstate friendship by frequently ceding territories, then ruin is possible.

30. If the crown prince is esteemed and celebrated, has numerous dependents and protégés, develops friendships with big powers, and exercises his authority and influence from his early years, then ruin is possible.

31. If the ruler is narrow-minded, quick-tempered, imprudent, easily affected, and, when provoked, becomes blind with rage, then ruin is possible.

32. If the sovereign is easily provoked and fond of resorting to arms and neglects agricultural and military training but ventures warfare and invasion heedlessly, then ruin is possible.

33. If nobles are jealous of one another, chief vassals are prosperous,

seeking support from enemy states and harassing the hundred surnames at home so as to attack their wrongdoers, but the lord of men never censures them, then ruin is possible.

34. If the ruler is unworthy but his half-brothers are worthy; if the heir apparent is powerless and the bastard surpasses him; or if the magistrates are weak and the people are fierce; then the state will be seized with a panic. And a panic-stricken state is liable to ruin.

35. If the ruler conceals his anger, which he would never reveal, suspends a criminal case, which he never would censure, and thereby makes the officials hate him in secret and increases their worries and fears, and if he never comes to know the situation even after a long time, then ruin is possible.

36. If the commander in the front line has too much power, the governor on the frontier has too much nobility, and if they have the ruling authority to themselves, issue orders at their own will and do just as they wish without asking permission of the ruler, then ruin is possible.

37. If the queen is adulterous, the sovereign's mother is corrupt, attendants inside and outside the court intercommunicate, and male and female have no distinction, such a régime is called "bi-regal." Any country having two rulers is liable to ruin.

38. If the queen is humble but the concubine is noble, the heir apparent is low but the bastard is high, the prime minister is despised but the court usher is esteemed, then disobedience will appear in and out of the court. If disobedience appears in and out of the court, the state is liable to ruin.

39. If chief vassals are very powerful, have many strong partisans, obstruct the sovereign's decisions, and administer all state affairs on their own authority, then ruin is possible.

40. If vassals of private families are employed but descendants of military officers are rejected, men who do good to their village communities are promoted but those who render distinguished services to their official posts are discarded, self-seeking deeds are esteemed but public-spirited works are scorned, then ruin is possible.

41. If the state treasury is empty but the chief vassals have plenty of money, native subjects are poor but foreign residents are rich, farmers and warriors have hard times but people engaged in secondary professions[28] are benefited, then ruin is possible.

42. The ruler who sees a great advantage but does not advance to-

wards it, hears the outset of a calamity but does not provide against it, thus neglecting preparations for attack and defence and striving to embellish himself with the practice of benevolence and righteousness, is liable to ruin.

43. If the ruler does not practise the filial piety of the lord of men but yearns after the filial piety of the commoner, does not regard the welfare of the Altar of the Spirits of Land and Grain but obeys the orders of the dowager queen, and if he allows women to administer the state affairs and eunuchs to meddle with politics, then ruin is possible.

44. If words are eloquent but not legal, the mind is sagacious but not tactful, the sovereign is versatile but performs his duties not in accordance with laws and regulations, then ruin is possible.

45. If new ministers advance when old officials withdraw, the unworthy meddle with politics when the virtuous pass out of the limelight, and men of no merit are esteemed when hard-working people are disdained, then the people left behind will resent it. If the people left behind resent it, ruin is possible.

46. If the bounties and allowances of uncles and brothers exceed their merits, their badges and uniforms override their grades, and their residences and provisions are too extravagant, and if the lord of men never restrains them, then ministers will become insatiable. If ministers are insatiable, then ruin is possible.

47. If the ruler's sons-in-law and grandsons live behind the same hamlet gate with the commoners and behave unruly and arrogantly towards their neighbours, then ruin is possible.

Thus, portents of ruin do not imply certainty of ruin but liability to ruin.

o   o   o   o

Guarding against the Interior[29] (5:17)

o   o   o   o

Indeed, even the spouse who is so near and the son who is so dear to the sovereign are not trustworthy, much less can anybody else be trustworthy.

Besides, whether he be a ruler of ten thousand chariots or a ruler of one thousand chariots, the queen, the concubine, or the crown prince, even though he be the legitimate son, might hope for his early death. How do I know it is so? Indeed, man and wife, having no kinship between them, are intimate when mutually in love and distant when not in love. Hence the saying: "If the mother is loved, the son is held in the arms." If so, the contrary must run like this: "If the mother is unloved, the son is cast aside." Men fifty years old are as fond of women as usual, but women only thirty years old are falling off in beauty. If women falling off in beauty have to serve men still fond of the fair sex, then they will be neglected and their sons will doubt if they will remain heirs of their fathers. This is the reason why queens, princesses, and concubines crave the death of the rulers.

It is only when the mother is the queen dowager and the son is the sovereign that decrees never fail to prevail and prohibitions never fail to function. Then she finds as much pleasure between man and woman as at the time when the late ruler was still alive, and under no suspicion can she have all the powers of the ruler of ten thousand chariots to herself. For such a reason, poisoning with wine and hanging in secret are practised.

Hence it is said in T'ao-wu's *Spring and Autumn Annals*: "Of the lords of men, those who died of illness were not even half of those that died." If the ruler is ignorant of such a danger, seeds of disorder will multiply. Hence the saying: "If those who will profit by the ruler's death are numerous, then the lord of men is in danger."

o   o   o   o

For illustration, though the sun and the moon are surrounded by haloes, the causes of their eclipses are inside themselves. Similarly, though the ruler guards against what he hates, the causes of his calamity consist in what he loves.

For this reason, the intelligent sovereign would neither carry out any untenable task, nor eat any inordinate food, but would listen from all round and observe everybody closely in order thereby to scrutinize the faults of the interior and the exterior.

o   o   o   o

Facing the South[30] (5:18)

o   o   o   o

Those who do not know the right way to political order always say, "Never change ancient traditions, never remove existing institutions." Change or no change, the sage does not mind. For he aims only at the rectification of government. Whether or not ancient traditions should be changed, whether or not existing institutions should be removed, all depends upon the question whether or not such traditions and such institutions are still useful for present-day political purposes.

o   o   o   o

Generally speaking, men hesitate to change ancient traditions because they are diffident about affecting the peace of the people. Indeed, not to change ancient traditions is to inherit the traces of disorder; to accord with the mind of the people is to tolerate villainous deeds. If the people are stupid and ignorant of disorder and the superior is weak-spirited and unable to reform traditions and institutions, it is a failure in the process of government.

The lord of men must be intelligent enough to know the true path to order and severe enough to carry out his orders without reserve. Therefore, though he has to act contrary to the mind of the people, he should by all means establish an orderly government.

The basis of this argument is found in the "External and Internal Affairs" [31] by Lord Shang, who had iron spears and heavy shields around him whenever going out to provide against accidents. Likewise, when Kuo Yen began to assume the reins of government, Duke Wên had an official bodyguard. When Kuan Chung began to assume the reins of government, Duke Huan had an armoured carriage. Thus they all took precautions against mobs.

o   o   o   o

On Pretensions and Heresies: A Memorial (5:19)

o   o   o   o

Wherever private righteousness prevails, there is disorder; wherever public justice obtains, there is order. Hence the necessity of distinction between public and private interests.

Every minister cherishes both selfish motive and public justice. To refine his personality, improve his integrity, practise public creeds, and behave unselfishly in office, is the public justice of the minister. To corrupt his conduct, follow his desires, secure his personal interests, and benefit his own family, is the selfish motive of the minister. If the intelligent sovereign is on the Throne, every minister will discard his selfish motive and practise public justice. If the violent sovereign is on the Throne, every minister will cast public justice aside and act on his selfish motive. Thus, ruler and minister have different frames of mind.

The ruler keeps the minister in service with a calculating mind. So does the minister with a calculating mind serve the ruler. As both ruler and minister are equally calculating, each for himself, the minister never cares to injure his body and benefit the state, nor does the ruler want to injure the state and benefit the minister.

o   o   o   o

Collection of Sayings (11:32)

o   o   o   o

Mi Tzŭ-chien governed San-fu. Once Yu-jo saw him and asked him: "Why have you become so thin?" In reply Mi Tzŭ said: "His Highness, not knowing my inferiority and unworthiness, appointed me Governor of San-fu. The official duties are urgent. My mind is always worried over them. Therefore I have become thin." Thereupon Yu-jo remarked: "In bygone days Shun played the five-stringed guitar and sang the South Wind Poem but all-under-heaven [i.e., the world] was well governed. Now that San-fu is so tiny and you have worried about governing it, what can be done with all-under-heaven? Thus, if you have the right craft to rule the country, then even though you remain seated in the hall of the palace and retain the charming complexion of a girl, there will be no harm to political order. But if you have no tact to rule the country, then even though your body becomes exhausted and skinny, still there will not be help to political order."

o   o   o   o

To be sure, children, when they play together, take soft earth as cooked rice, muddy water as soup, and wood shavings as slices of meat. However, at dusk they would go home for supper because dust rice and mud soup can be played with but cannot be eaten. Indeed, tributes to the legacy of remote antiquity, are appreciative and eloquent but superficial; and admiration of the early kings for their benevolence and righteousness, cannot rectify the course of the state. Therefore, they can be played with but cannot be used as instruments of government, either.

o   o   o   o

Duke Hsiang of Sung fought with the Ch'us in the Cho River Gorge.[32] When the Sung forces had already formed in line, the Ch'u troops had not yet finished their lines. Thereupon the Right Minister of War, Kou Ch'iang, ran forward and advised the Duke, saying: "As the Ch'us are numerous and the Sungs are few, let us attack them when they are half crossing the River and not yet in line. They will certainly be defeated." "I have heard," said Duke Hsiang, "the gentleman would not wound the wounded, not capture men having two kinds of hair, not push people into danger, not drive people to bay, and not beat the drum towards enemies not yet in line. Now, the Ch'u troops have not completed their lines. If we attack them, we act against righteousness. Let them finish crossing the River and complete their lines. Then beat the drum and lead the army." "Your Highness does not love the people of Sung in leaving the confidential supporters in precariousness solely for the sake of righteousness." "If you do not return to your line," said the Duke, "I will enforce the martial law." The Right Minister returned to his line, when the Ch'u troops had already formed in line and established their positions. Then the Duke beat the drum. The Sung forces suffered a crushing defeat. The Duke was wounded in the thigh and died in three days. This is the calamity of yearning after benevolence and righteousness.

o   o   o   o

King Chao of Wei[33] wanted to have a hand in the official routine and said to the Lord of Mêng-ch'ang, "I, the King, want to have a hand in the official routine." "If Your Majesty wants to go through the official routine," said the Lord, "why does he not for trial learn and read the legal code?" King Chao, accordingly, started reading the code. After reading ten and some bamboo slips, he fell asleep. "I am unable to read this code," said the King. After all, if the ruler does not hold the august position and supreme handles firmly in hand but wants to perform the duties which the ministers ought to perform, is it not reasonable that he falls asleep in so doing?

o   o   o   o

Collection of Sayings (12:33)

o   o   o   o

Chieh Hu recommended his enemy to Lord Chien for premiership. The enemy thought he had by good luck forgiven him, and so went purposely to thank him. Thereupon Hu drew his bow, and, on receiving him, aimed at him, saying: "To be sure, I recommended you because I regarded your ability equal to the post. To have hatred for you is my private feud with you. I never on account of my feud with you kept you from my master." Hence the saying: "No private feud should go through public gates."

o   o   o   o

A Critique of the Doctrine of Position (17:40)

o   o   o   o

"Moreover, Yao and Shun as well as Chieh and Chou appear once in a thousand generations; whereas the opposite types of men are born shoulder to shoulder and on the heels of one another. As a matter of fact, most rulers in the world form a continuous line of average men. It is for the average rulers that I speak about authority. The average rulers neither come up to the worthiness of Yao and Shun nor reach down to the wickedness of Chieh and Chou. If they uphold the law and make use of their august position, order obtains; if they discard the law and desert their august position, chaos prevails. Now suppose you discard the position and act contrary to the law and wait for Yao and Shun to appear and suppose order obtains after the arrival of Yao and Shun, then order will obtain in one out of one thousand generations of continuous chaos. Suppose you uphold the law and make use of the august position and wait for Chieh and Chou to appear and suppose chaos prevails after the arrival of Chieh and Chou, then chaos will prevail in one out of one thousand generations of continuous order.

o   o   o   o

"Indeed, I do not consider it right to say that a swift horse and a solid carriage, when driven by bondmen and bondwomen, will be ridiculed by people, but, when driven by Wang Liang,[34] will make a thousand *li* a day. For illustration, if you wait for a good swimmer from Yüeh[35] to rescue a drowning man in a Central State, however well the Yüeh swimmer may do, the drowning person will not be rescued. In the same way, waiting for the Wang Liang of old to drive the horse of today is as fallacious as waiting for the man from Yüeh to rescue that drowning person. The impracticability is evident enough. But, if teams of swift horses and solid carriages are placed in readiness in relays fifty *li* apart and then you make an average coachman drive them, he will be able to drive them fast and far and cover one thousand *li* a day. Why should it then be necessary to wait for the Wang Liang of old?

o   o   o   o

Deciding between Two Legalistic Doctrines (17:43)

o   o   o   o

Tact is the means whereby to create posts according to responsibilities, hold actual services accountable according to official titles, exercise the power over life and death, and examine the officials' abilities. It is what the lord of men has in his grip. Law includes mandates and ordinances that are manifest in the official bureaux, penalities that are definite in the mind of the people, rewards that are due to the careful observers of laws, and punishments that are inflicted on the offenders against orders. It is what the subjects and ministers take as model. If the ruler is tactless, delusion will come to the superior; if the subjects and ministers are lawless, disorder will appear among the inferiors. Thus, neither can be dispensed with: both are implements of emperors and kings.

o   o   o   o

Six Contrarieties (18:46)

o   o   o   o

Therefore, the enlightened sovereign in governing the state would increase custodians and intensify penalties and make the people stop vices according to law but not owing to their own sense of integrity. For illustration, mothers love children twice as much as fathers do, but a father enforces orders among children ten times better than a mother does. Similarly, officials have no love for the people, but they enforce orders among the people ten thousand times better than their parents do. Parents heap up their love but their orders come to naught; whereas officials exercise force and the people obey them. Thus, you can easily make the choice between severity and affection.

Furthermore, what parents desire of children is safety and prosperity in livelihood and innocence in conduct. What the ruler requires of his subjects, however, is to demand their lives in case of emergency and exhaust their energy in time of peace. Now, parents, who love their children and wish them safety and prosperity, are not listened to; whereas the ruler, who neither loves nor benefits his subjects but demands their death and toil, can enforce his orders. As the enlightened sovereign knows this principle, he does not cultivate the feeling of favour and love, but extends his influence of authority and severity. Mothers love sons with deep love, but most of the sons are spoilt, for their love is over-extended; fathers show their sons less love and teach them with light bamboos, but most of the sons turn out well, for severity is applied.

o   o   o   o

Moreover, heavy penalties are not for the sole purpose of punishing criminals. The law of the intelligent sovereign, in suppressing rebels, is not disciplining only those who are being suppressed, for to discipline only the suppressed is the same as to discipline dead men only; in penalizing robbers, it is not disciplining only those who are being penalized, for to discipline only the penalized is the same as to discipline convicts only. Hence the saying: "Take seriously one culprit's crime and suppress all wickednesses within the boundaries." This is the way to attain order. For the heavily punished are robbers, but the terrified and trembling are good people. Therefore, why should those who want order doubt the efficacy of heavy penalties?

o   o   o   o

The learned men of today, one and all, cite the panegyrics in the classics, and, without observing closely the real facts, of the present age, say: "If the superior does not love the people and always levies exactions and taxations, then living expenses will become insufficient and the inferiors will hate the superior. Hence the chaos in the world." This means that if the superior lets the people have enough money to spend and loves them besides, then notwithstanding light punishment order can be attained. Such a saying is not true.

o   o   o   o

Take, for example, the beloved sons of wealthy families, who are given sufficient money to spend. Having sufficient money to spend, they spend it freely. Spending money freely, they indulge in extravagance. The parents, loving them so much, cannot bear to restrict them. Not restricted, they become self-willed. Being extravagant, they impoverish their families. Being self-willed, they practise violence. Such is the calamity of deep love and light penalty, even though there is enough money to spend.

o   o   o   o

Therefore, the intelligent sovereign, when governing the state, suits his policy to the time and the affairs so as to increase his financial resources, calculates taxes and tributes so as to equalize the poor and the rich, extends ranks and bounties for the people so as to exert their wisdom and ability, enlarges penal implements so as to forbid villainy and wickedness, and makes the people secure riches by virtue of their own efforts, receive punishments owing to their criminal offences, get rewards by performing meritorious services, and never think of any gift by beneficence and favour. Such is the course of imperial and kingly government.

o o o o

Eight Fallacies (18:47)

o o o o

The compassionate mother, in loving her little child, is surpassed by none. Yet, when the child has mischievous actions, she sends him to follow the teacher; when he is badly ill, she sends him to see the physician. For without following the teacher he is liable to penalty; without seeing the physician he is susceptible to death. Thus, though the compassionate mother loves the child, she is helpless in saving him from penalty and from death. If so, what preserves the child is not love.

The bond of mother and child is love, the relationship of ruler and minister is expediency. If the mother cannot preserve the family by virtue of love, how can the ruler maintain order in the state by means of love?

o o o o

Eight Canons (18:48)

o o o o

Those whose posts are high and responsibilities are great, should be held under surveillance by three means of control, namely, "taking hostages," "holding securities," and "finding sureties." [36] Relatives, wives, and sons can be taken as hostages; ranks and bounties can be held as securities; and the "three units and basic fives" [37] that are implicated in any of the members' illegal acts, can be found as sureties. Worthies refrain from evils for fear of "hostage-taking"; greedy people are transformed by the measure of "security-holding"; and culprits are harassed by the measure of "surety-using." If the superior does not exercise these means of control, the inferiors will dare to infringe upon his authority. If small culprits are not eliminated, he will have to censure great culprits.

When censuring culprits, if name and fact correspond to each other, he should immediately enforce the censure. If their life is detrimental to the state affairs and their death penalty is harmful to the ruler's name, then he should poison them through drinking or eating, otherwise send them into the hands of their enemies. This is said to "eliminate invisible culprits." [38] Harbouring culprits is due to the practice of misrepresentation. The practice of misrepresentation is due to the contempt for the law. If visible merits are always rewarded and disclosed crimes are punished, the practice of misrepresentation will stop. Him who gives no opinion of right or wrong, presents unreasonable persuasions and remonstrations, and shows contempt for the law, the ruler should not take into service.

Uncles, cousins, or worthy and excellent ministers, living in exile, are said to be "roaming calamities." Their menace comes from their provision of neighbouring enemies with numerous opportunities. Eunuchs and courtiers are said to be "profligate rebels." Their menace comes from their ill will caused by irritation and suspicion. To conceal anger, shelter criminals, and harbour them, is said to "increase commotions." The menace lies in the rise of men expecting godsends and making arbitrary promotions. To delegate equal authority to two chief vassals and maintain the balance of power between them without partiality, is said to "nourish calamities." The menace lies in the precipitation of family quarrels, intimidations, and regicides. To be careless and not to keep oneself godlike, is called to "lose prestige." Its menace lies in the rise of such treason as regicide by poisoning. These five are menaces, which, if the lord of men ignores them, will eventually precipitate such disasters as intimidation and regicide.

o   o   o   o

Keep detectives nearby the officials and thereby know their inner conditions. Send detectives afar and thereby know outer affairs. Hold to your clear knowledge and thereby inquire into obscure objects. Give ministers false encouragements and thereby extirpate their attempts to infringe on the ruler's rights. Invert your words and thereby try out the suspects. Use contradictory arguments and thereby find out the invisible culprits. Establish the system of espionage and thereby rectify the fraudulent people. Make appointments and dismissals and thereby observe the reactions of wicked officials. Speak explicitly and thereby persuade people to avoid faults. Humbly follow others' speeches and thereby discriminate between earnest men and flatterers. Get information from everybody and know things you have not yet seen. Create quarrels among adherents and partisans and thereby disperse them. Explore the depths of one culprit and thereby warn the mind of the many. Divulge false ideas and thereby make the inferiors think matters over.

In the case of similarities and resemblances, identify their common points. When stating anybody's faults, grasp the causes, know the due penalties, and thereby justify the exercise of your authority. Send out spies in secret to inspect the enemy states from time to time and thereby find their signs of decay. Gradually change envoys sent abroad and thereby break up their secret communications and private friendships with foreign states. Put every subordinate under surveillance by his immediate principal. Thus ministers discipline their vassals; vassals discipline their dependents; soldiers and officials discipline their troops; envoys discipline their deputies; prefects discipline their subordinates; courtiers discipline their attendants; and queens and concubines discipline their court maids. Such is said to be "the systematic thorough way."

If words are divulged and affairs leak out, then no statecraft will function at all.

o   o   o   o

The lord of men has the duty of devoting his attention to secrecy. For this reason, when his delight is revealed, his conduct will be slighted; when his anger is revealed, his prestige will fall to the ground. The words of the intelligent sovereign, therefore, are blockaded in such wise that they are not communicable outwards and are kept in such secrecy that they are unknowable.

o   o   o   o

Five Vermin: A Pathological Analysis of Politics (19:49)

In the age of remote antiquity, human beings were few while birds and beasts were many. Mankind being unable to overcome birds, beasts, insects, and serpents, there appeared a sage who made nests by putting pieces of wood together to shelter people from harm. Thereat the people were so delighted that they made him ruler of all-under-heaven and called him the Nest-Dweller. In those days the people lived on the fruits of trees and seeds of grass as well as mussels and clams, which smelt rank and fetid and hurt the digestive organs. As many of them were affected with diseases, there appeared a sage who twisted a drill to make fire which changed the fetid and musty smell. Thereat the people were so delighted that they made him ruler of all-under-heaven.

In the age of middle antiquity, there was a great deluge in all-under-heaven, wherefore Kung and Yü opened channels for the water. In the age of recent antiquity, Chieh and Chou were violent and turbulent, wherefore T'ang and Wu overthrew them.

Now, if somebody fastened the trees or turned a drill in the age of the Hsia-hou Clan, he would certainly be ridiculed by Kung and Yü. Again, if somebody opened channels for water in the age of the Yin and Chou Dynasties, he would certainly be ridiculed by T'ang and Wu. That being so, if somebody in the present age praises the ways of Yao, Shun, Kung, Yü, T'ang, and Wu, he would, no doubt, be ridiculed by contemporary sages.

That is the reason why the sage neither seeks to follow the ways of the ancients nor establishes any fixed standard for all times but examines the things of his age and then prepares to deal with them.

There was in Sung a man, who tilled a field in which there stood the trunk of a tree. Once a hare, while running fast, rushed against the trunk, broke its neck, and died. Thereupon the man cast his plough aside and watched that tree, hoping that he would get another hare. Yet he never caught another hare and was himself ridiculed by the people of Sung. Now supposing somebody wanted to govern the people of the present age with the policies of the early kings, he would be doing exactly the same thing as that man who watched the tree.

In olden times, men did not need to till, for the seeds of grass and the fruits of trees were sufficient to feed them; nor did women have to weave, for the skins of birds and beasts were sufficient to clothe them. Thus, without working hard, they had an abundance of supply. As the people were few, their possessions were more than sufficient. Therefore the people never quarrelled. As a result, neither large rewards were bestowed nor were heavy punishments employed, but the people governed themselves. Nowadays, however, people do not regard five children as many.

Each child may in his or her turn beget five offspring, so that before the death of the grandfather there may be twenty-five grandchildren. As a result, people have become numerous and supplies scanty; toil has become hard and provisions meager. Therefore people quarrel so much that, though rewards are doubled and punishments repeated, disorder is inevitable.

When Yao was ruling all-under-heaven, his thatched roof was untrimmed and his beam unplaned. He ate unpolished grain and made soup of coarse greens and wore deerskin garments in winter and rough fibre-cloth in summer. Even the clothes and provisions of a gate-keeper were not more scanty than his. When Yü was ruling all-under-heaven, he led the people with plough and spade in hands, till his thighs had no down and his shins grew no hair. Even the toil of a prisoner of war was not more distressful than his. Speaking from this viewpoint, indeed, he who abdicated the throne of the Son of T'ien in favour of others in olden times, was simply forsaking the living of a gate-keeper and the toil of a prisoner of war. Therefore the inheritance of all-under-heaven in olden days was not very great. Yet the prefect of today, upon the day of his death, hands down luxurious chariots to his descendants from generation to generation. Accordingly people think much of his position.

Thus, in the matter of leaving office, men make light of resigning from the ancient dignity of the Son of T'ien and consider it hard to quit the present post of a prefect. Really it is the difference between meagerness and abundance.

Indeed, those who dwell in the mountains and draw water from the valleys give water to each other on the occasion of festivals; those who live in swamps hire men to open channels for the water. Likewise, in the spring of famine years men do not even feed their infant brothers, while in the autumn of abundant years even strange visitors are always well fed. Not that men cut off their blood-relations and love passers-by, but that the feelings are different in abundance and in scarcity. For the same reason, men of yore made light of goods, not because they were benevolent, but because goods were abundant; while men of today quarrel and pillage, not because they are brutish, but because goods are scarce. Again, men of yore made light of resigning from the dignity of the Son of T'ien not because their personalities were noble, but because the power of the Son of T'ien was scanty; while men of today make much of fighting for office in government, not because their personalities are mean, but because the powers of the posts are great. Therefore the sage, considering quantity and deliberating upon scarcity and abundance, governs accordingly. So it is no charity to inflict light punishments nor is it any cruelty to enforce severe penalties: the practice is simply in accordance with the custom of the age. Thus, circumstances change with the age and measures change according to circumstances.

o   o   o   o

Evidently benevolence and righteousness once serviceable in olden times are not so at present. Hence the saying: "There are as many situations as there are generations." In the time of Shun the Miao tribes disobeyed. When Yü moved to send an expedition against them, Shun said: "By no means. As our virtue is not great, any resort to arms is not in accord with the *Tao*." Thenceforth for three years he cultivated the ways of civic training and then he made a parade of shields and battle-axes, whereupon the Miao tribes submitted. In a subsequent age, during the war with the Kung-kung tribes men using short iron weapons hardly reached their enemies while those whose armour was not strong suffered bodily injuries. It means that mere parade with shields and battle-axes once effective in olden times is not so at present. Hence the saying: "Situations differ, so measures change."

o   o   o   o

Now suppose there is a boy who has a bad character. His parents are angry at him, but he never makes any change. The villagers in the neighbourhood reprove him, but he is never thereby moved. His masters teach him, but he never reforms. Thus with all the three excellent disciplines, the love of his parents, the conduct of the villagers, and the wisdom of the masters, applied to him, he makes no change, not even a hair on his shins is altered. It is, however, only after the district-magistrate sends out soldiers in accordance with the law to search for wicked men that he becomes afraid and changes his ways and alters his deeds. So the love of parents is not sufficient to educate children. But if it is necessary to have the severe penalties of the district-magistrate come at all, it is because people are naturally spoiled by love and obedient to authority.

o   o   o   o

That being so, rewards should not be other than great and certain, thus making the people regard them as profitable; punishments should not be other than severe and definite, thus making the people fear them; and laws should not be other than uniform and steadfast, thus making the people comprehend them. Consequently, if the ruler in bestowing rewards makes no change and in carrying out punishments grants no pardon, but adds honour to rewards and disgrace to punishments, then both the worthy and the unworthy will exert their efforts.

That is not true at present. On the one hand, ranks are conferred for meritorious services; but on the other, official careers are scorned. Rewards are bestowed for diligent tillage, but hereditary occupations are slighted. Whoever declines appointment to office is shunned, but his contempt for worldly affairs is esteemed. Whoever transgresses prohibitions is convicted, but his boldness is admired. Thus there are nowadays opposed to each other the objectives of honour and disgrace as well as of reward and punishment. Small wonder laws and interdicts are ruined and the people are becoming more and more violent.

o o o o

Of old, there was in the Ch'u State a man named Chi-kung. Once his father stole a sheep, wherefore he reported to the authorities. Thereupon the prefect said, "Put him to death," as he thought the man was loyal to the ruler but undutiful to his father. So that man was tried and executed. From this it can be seen that the honest subject of the ruler was an outrageous son of his father.

o o o o

Therefore, incompatible things do not coexist. For instance, to reward those who kill their enemies in battle, and at the same time to esteem deeds of mercy and generosity; to reward with ranks and bounties those who capture enemy cities, and at the same time to believe in the theory of impartial love; to improve armour and encourage warriors as provisions against emergencies, and at the same time to admire the ornaments of the robes and girdles of the civil gentry; to depend upon the farmers for enriching the state and upon the warriors for resisting the enemies, and at the same time to honour the men of letters; and to neglect the men who respect the superior and revere the law, and at the same time to maintain gangs of wandering cavaliers and self-seeking swordsmen: out of such incompatible acts, how can a state attain order and strength? When the state is at peace, literati and cavaliers are supported; once an emergency arises, armed officers are taken into service. Thus, the privileged are not used; the used are not privileged. For this reason, men who ought to attend to public affairs neglect their duties, while wandering scholars daily increase in numbers. This is the reason why the age is full of chaos.

o   o   o   o

For such reasons, it is a common trait of the disorderly state that its learned men adore the ways of the early kings by pretending to benevolence and righteousness and adorn their manners and clothes and gild their eloquent speeches so as to cast doubts on the law of the present age and thereby beguile the mind of the lord of men; that its itinerant speakers[39] advocate deceptive theories and utilize foreign influence to accomplish their self-seeking purposes at the expense of their Altar of the Spirits of Land and Grain; that wearers of private swords gather pupils and dependents and set up standards of self-discipline and fidelity with a view to cultivating their fame but thereby violate the interdicts of the Five Ministries;[40] that the courtiers assemble inside the gates of private residences, use all kinds of bribes, and rely on influential men's access to the sovereign in order to escape the burden of military service; and that the tradesmen and craftsmen disguise worthless, broken articles as proper goods, collect useless luxuries, accumulate riches, wait for good opportunities, and exploit the farmers. These five types of men are the vermin of the state. Should the Lord of Mêng fail to get rid of such people as the five vermin and should he not patronize men of firm integrity and strong character, it would be no wonder at all if within the seas there should be states breaking up in ruin and dynasties waning and perishing.

Learned Celebrities:
A Critical Estimate of Confucians
and Mo-ists (19:50)

o   o   o   o

The learned gentlemen of the present age, when they speak on political order, mostly say: "Give the poor and the destitute land and thereby provide men of no property with enough." However, if there are men who were originally the same as others but have independently become able to be perfectly self-supporting, even without prosperous years or other income, it must be due to their diligence or to their frugality. Again, if there are men who were originally the same as others but have independently become poor and destitute without suffering from any misfortune of famine and drought or illness and malignancy or calamity and lawsuit, it must be due to their extravagance or to their laziness. Extravagant and lazy persons are poor; diligent and frugal persons are rich. Now, if the superior levies money from the rich in order to distribute alms among the poor, it means that he robs the diligent and frugal and rewards the extravagant and lazy. Naturally it is impossible to force people to speed up their work and also restrain their expenditure.

o   o   o   o

Suppose you keep a number of books, practise the art of speaking, gather a band of pupils, indulge in culture and learning, and discuss theories, then be sure sovereigns of this age will respect you therefore, saying, "To respect worthies is the way of the early kings." Indeed, those who are taxed by the magistrates are farmers while those who are fed by the superior are learned gentlemen. Being farmers, the former are more heavily taxed; being learned gentlemen, the latter are more liberally rewarded. Hence it is impossible to force the people to work hard and talk little.

o   o   o   o

Indeed, the sage, in ruling the state, does not count on people's doing him good, but utilizes their inability to do him wrong. If he counts on people's doing him good, within the boundary there will never be enough such persons to count by tens. But if he utilizes people's inability to do him wrong, an entire state can be uniformed. Therefore, the administrator of the state affairs ought to consider the many but disregard the few. Hence his devotion not to virtue but to law.

o   o   o   o

Loyalty and Filial Piety: A Memorial (20:51)

o   o   o   o

In antiquity the black-headed[41] were mindless and stupid. Therefore, it was possible to win their homage by means of empty fame. The people of today, however, are alert and astute and apt to preen themselves and disobey the superior. Therefore, the superior needs to encourage them with rewards, so that they will advance, and to terrify them with punishments, so that they will never dare to retreat.

o   o   o   o

Surmising the Mentality of the People: A Psychological Analysis of Politics (20:54)

o   o   o   o

Indeed, the administration of the state affairs requires the attention of the causes of human action so as to unify the people's mental trends; the exclusive elevation of public welfare so as to stop self-seeking elements; the reward for denunciation of crime so as to suppress culprits; and finally the clarification of laws so as to facilitate governmental procedures. Whoever is able to apply these four measures, will become strong; whoever is unable to apply these four measures, will become weak. Indeed, the strength of the state is due to the administration of its political affairs; the honour of the sovereign is due to his supreme power. Now, the enlightened ruler possesses the supreme power and the administrative organs; the ignoble ruler possesses both the supreme power and the administrative organs, too. Yet the results are not the same, because their standpoints are different. Thus, as the enlightened ruler has the supreme power in his grip, the superior is held in high esteem; as he unifies the administrative organs, the state is in order. Hence law is the origin of supremacy and penalty is the beginning of love.

o   o   o   o

Regulations and Distinctions (20:55)

o   o   o   o

Again, when governing the people, if you do not regard conformity to law as right, you will eventually observe no law. Therefore, the science and philosophy of politics should by all means emphasize the distinction between degrees of penalty and of reward.

o   o   o   o

For this reason, the state at the height of order is able to take the suppression of villainy for its duty. Why? Because its law comprehends human nature and accords with the principles of government.

If so, how to get rid of delicate villainy? By making the people watch one another in their hidden affairs. Then how to make them watch one another? By implicating the people of the same hamlet in one another's crime. When everyone knows that the penalty or reward will directly affect him, if the people of the same hamlet fail to watch one another, they will fear they may not be able to escape the implication, and those who are evil-minded, will not be allowed to forget so many people watching them. Were such the law, everybody would mind his own doings, watch everybody else, and disclose the secrets of any culprit. For, whosoever denounces a criminal offence, is not held guilty but is given a reward; whosoever misses any culprit, is definitely censured and given the same penalty as the culprit. Were such the law, all types of culprits would be detected. If the minutest villainy is not tolerated, it is due to the system of personal denunciation and mutual implication.[42]

o   o   o   o

AFTERWORD

The founding of the First Empire was a major event in world history. It was the first time the ideal of unity "within the Wall" had been realized. The First Emperor, Shih Huang Ti, had finished the Great Wall. It differentiated those outside the wall as barbarians beyond the pale. And the Ch'in, because of the awe with which people across Asia spoke of their achievements, probably lent their name to the country that has ever since been called China. People generally looked on Ch'in's rise to triumph and dominance of the new empire as proof of the efficacy of a strictly applied Legalism.

Yet when the First Emperor died while traveling in the eastern provinces in 212 B.C., his death had to be concealed for a number of reasons in which figured a future of palace intrigue and civil war. Despite the Legalist tradition he inherited, the Second Emperor, Er Shih, proved a poor successor. A few years after his father's death, he was forced by a eunuch official to commit suicide. Rebellion soon brought the First Empire down in a crash. Out of its wreckage arose the Han Dynasty.

NOTES

NOTES

2. Book of Documents

1. *Hsi* and *Ho*. Imperial ministers.
2. *Fang Ch'i*. Both he, and Ssŭ Yüeh below, were imperial ministers.
3. *The five rules* (or the "five instructions" or the "five classes"). Refers to the familial and social relations of ruler to minister, father and son, husband and wife, elder and younger brother, and friend and friend. See also Table 5 and note 4 below.
4. *The five punishments*. Usually decapitation, tattooing, castration, amputation of the hands or feet, and cutting off the nose.
5. *Kung Kung, Kun,* and *Huan Tou*. Imperial ministers. The first two were punished for failing to control the floods.
6. *Three years*. Actually only twenty-five months, this period became standard mourning.
7. *Within the four seas*. Like the phrase "all within the world," this expression has important political implications. The Chinese early conceived the idea that China was square-shaped, bounded on all sides by sea. All those within the pale were under the Chinese emperor. See note 8 below.
8. *The four gates*. Just as political territory was viewed in geometric harmony, so too was political or ceremonial architecture. Imperial buildings were constructed on square or rectilinear patterns, with four "gates" facing north, south, east, and west. The south was ritually most favored, and it was in this direction that the emperor faced when giving audience with ministers.
9. *Twelve Pastors*. Possibly imperial ministers, or officials charged with territorial rule.
10. *Chi Hsieh* and *Kao Yao*. Ministers of Emperor Shun.
11. *The hundred families*. Sometimes refers to the top families in the realm; sometimes to the people as a whole.
12. *Harmony*. The ancient idea of good government harmonizing with music, poetry, and dance appears especially in the *Hsün Tzŭ* and the Ritual Texts.
13. *Shun's guests*. The spirits of the royal ancestors.
14. *The five elements*. Fire, water, metal, wood, and soil.
15. *The three governing forces*. Heaven, Earth, and Man, a trinity that was greatly elaborated by later Confucian thought.
16. *Shang Ti*. When the Chou conquered the Shang they syncretized the Shang master-god, *Ti* or *Shang Ti* (usually translated as God or God on High by English-language translators), with their own *T'ien*. In the *Book of Documents, Ti* or *Shang Ti* is often referred to; yet *T'ien* is referred to three times as often. Later writings sometimes use both names but with varying nuances.

    The lord of Hsia. Last ruler of the Hsia Dynasty. His name was Chieh.

17. *Shao Kung* and *T'ai Kung.* These princes, Chou Kung, and other rulers mentioned in this political drama belong to the Chou Dynasty.
18. *T'ai Wang, Wang Chi,* and *Wên Wang.* I.e., their ancestors.
19. *Owe a great son to T'ien.* I.e., if their son, the king, must die . . .
20. *Reliance and resort.* The idea here is that if the ancestral sacrifices are not kept up or are destroyed by stronger forces, the family spirits, their name, and their past will die out.
21. *The jade disc and the tessera.* Only the reigning monarch could officiate with insignia at ceremonial functions.
22. *The prince.* Chou Kung or Duke of Chou, who is seeking to be prince regent to "the infant," King Ch'êng, King Wu's son and heir. The "two princes" are Shao Kung and T'ai Kung. The "criminal men" referred to later are the Kuan Shu group.
23. *The great Yin.* Another name for the Shang.
24. *The interior.* That is, the palace.
25. *The clan temple.* The spirits of royal ancestors.

3. Book of Songs

1. *Duke of Chou.* Successfully campaigned from northwestern China into the eastern lands of the Shang.
2. *Son of T'ien.* Usually translated as "the emperor." Here it refers to "the king."
3. *Nan-chung.* A Chinese general whose dates traditionally fall within the Western Chou Era, c. the reign of King Hsüan of Ch'i State, 827–782 B.C.
4. *Hsien-yün.* Tribe hostile to the Chou.
5. *The tablets.* The orders of the Son of T'ien.
6. *My heart is still.* Waley (the translator) suggests that this is a refrain from a bridal hymn sung by the wives.
7. *Hao.* One of the Chou capital cities in the early Western Chou Era. Waley notes that by the time this poem was written, Hao was no longer a capital but a cultural city.
8. *Shining Light.* Radiance surrounding the ancestral spirits.
9. *Impersonator of the Ancient.* In ancestral sacrifices a member of the family would play the role of the dead person, eating the ceremonial food, and bestowing blessings on the living family.
10. *King Wên.* Ch'ang, Wên Wang, the founder of the Chou Dynasty, who is often called "the accomplished king." (See Table 2.)
11. *God's charge.* T'ien's mandate to rule.
12. *Yin.* The Shang.
13. *Middle Kingdom.* China.
14. *Land of Kuei.* Modern Kuei Chou.
15. *Lord of Hsia.* In the *Book of Documents,* the title refer to Chieh, the last Hsia king.
16. *Two kingdoms.* Hsia and Shang.
17. *The west.* Land of the Chou.
18. *T'ai-po* and *Wang Chi.* Brothers. Wang Chi was King Wên's father.
19. *Mi, Yüan,* and *Kung.* Modern Kan Su, Shan Hsi, and Ho Nan. Chiefly in central northwestern China.
20. *Fit with strings.* To make musical instruments.
21. *Willow-tree.* Liu (willow) also means slaughter, according to the translator, Waley.
22. *Hou Chi.* God of Millet, ancestral God of the Chou. (See p. 6 and Table 2.)

23. *Hsia.* Another name for China.
24. *Blind men.* Like poets of ancient Greece, musicians of ancient China were often blind.
25. *Our guests.* Note the direct participation of both living and dead in ancestral ceremonies.
26. *Deep and wise was Shang.* According to the translator, this is a ballad of c. seventh-century origin B.C., composed by the people of Sung, traditionally descended from the Shang.
27. *Yü.* Traditionally Minister of Works under Emperor Shun.
28. *The dark king.* I.e., named Ch'i. He and Hsiang-t'u were early Shang leaders.
29. *T'ang.* Founded the Shang Dynasty by overthrowing Wei, Ku, K'un-wu, and Chieh of Hsia.

4. Book of Changes

1. *Ch'ien/The Creative.* This is the first hexagram. Hexagrams are composed of two trigrams. The lower one is called "inner." The one above is the "outer." The lines are numbered from one to six, commencing with the lowest.
2. *The Judgment.* Three Chinese sages were traditionally held to have given explanations for the sixty-four hexagrams. King Wên, at about 1143 B.C., is supposed to have given interpretations of the whole figures. Those remarks constituting "The Judgment" on the hexagrams are ascribed to him. The Duke of Chou, around 1120 B.C., interpreted the separate lines. In the selections the "a) line" is his. The Duke of Chou and King Wên's interpretations constitute the text of the *I Ching*. The third sage was Confucius. See note 3 below.
3. *The Image.* Confucius also was said to have done comprehensive work on the *I Ching*. "The Image," and the "Commentary on the Judgment" and the "b) lines," are supposed to be his work. These explanations of the *I Ching* are called *Appendixes* or the *Ten Wings*.
4. *Nine.* A line or stroke is called *yao*. The undivided —— is called *yang yao*. The divided — — is called *yin yao*. The Ch'ien trigram has three strokes ☰ and the K'un has six strokes ☷. But Yang contains Yin; hence Ch'ien is three plus six equals nine.
5. *Hidden dragon.* A symbol traditionally employed by the Duke of Chou to represent the superior man. From earliest times in China the dragon has been a sign of highest dignity and wisdom and has many other favorable connotations. See E. T. C. Werner, *A Dictionary of Chinese Mythology* (New York: Julian Press, 1961).
6. *Square.* The ancient Chinese tridimensional conception of the earth is as a great cube; hence, this represents earth.
7. *Order.* The Chinese character for order is *lü*, which also refers to a reedlike musical instrument. The literal meaning is, "The army marches forth to the sound of horns. If the horns are not in tune, the sign is bad."

5. The Spring and Autumn Annals *with the* Commentary of Tso

1. *Year IX.* 599 B.C., ninth year of the reign of Duke Hsüan of Ch'i (r. 607–590 B.C.).
2. *Year X.* 598 B.C.
3. *Year XI.* 597 B.C.

4. *Year XXV.* 547 B.C., twenty-fifth year of the reign of Duke Hsiang of Ch'i (r. 571–541 B.C.).
5. *The I.* Reference to the *Book of Changes.* For a discussion of divination in China, see pp. 63–68.

6. Book of Rites

Ritual Records

1. *Sage.* Here the emperor, or Son of T'ien, is given the honorary title of "sage."
2. *Personator of the departed.* Elsewhere, for example in the *Book of Songs,* he is called the Impersonator of the dead or of the ancient. See note 9, p. 394 above.
3. *The black-haired race.* The Chinese.
4. *Highly esteemed age.* The Hsia Dynasty, and the Shang and Yin Dynasties were two of the traditional Three Dynasties of Antiquity. (See Table 2.)
5. *The I.* Namely, the *I Ching, Book of Changes.* (See pp. 63–68.)

8. Confucius

The Analects

1. *The Master.* In the *Analects* Confucius is the Master. He did not write the *Analects;* they are supposed to preserve his words as handed down, selected, and compiled by students and others.
2. *Chi K'ang-tzŭ.* Head of the three most powerful families of Lu State, he controlled the actual ruler, the Duke of Lu. For this, and for his severe tax and war policies he was criticized by Confucius. He did, however, employ some of his disciples as officers. One of them, Jan Ch'iu, is thought to have been ostracized by Confucius for juggling the tax books. See note 18, p. 399 below.
3. *Master K'ung.* The Chinese name for Latinized Confucius is K'ung Fu Tzŭ. See note I, p. 401 below.
4. *The Book.* Possible reference to nonextant part of the *Book of Documents.*
5. *The East and North.* I.e., outside the pale of the central states.
6. *Archery.* One of the Six Arts of the gentlemen, the other five being: ceremonies, music, mathematics, charioteering, and writing.
7. *Tzŭ-kung.* Or *Ssŭ* (as Confucius calls him familiarly). One of Confucius's disciples, sometimes teased by the Master for his impetuous remarks.
8. *The Ospreys.* A reference to a love poem in the *Book of Songs* (see Waley, *Book of Songs,* 87).
9. *War Dance.* According to later Confucians, the Succession Dance mimed Shun's accession to the throne after Yao's abdication (both pre-Hsia legendary emperors); the War Dance mimed Wu's accession to the throne by military conquest (Chou's defeat of the Shang). See Table 2 and Chapter 1.
10. *Prosperity.* Quotation from one of the Chou poems.
11. *Ch'i-tiao K'ai.* Born 541 B.C. One of Confucius's disciples.
12. *Tzŭ-lu.* Or, familiarly, Yu; one of Confucius's favorite disciples.
13. *Mêng Wu Po.* Son of a Lu noble. Sent to study under Confucius.

14. *Tzŭ-lu (Yu)*, mentioned in 5:6 and note 12 above; *Jan Ch'iu*, see note 2 above; and Kung-hsi Ch'ih (Hua), whose expert knowledge of rites qualified him to arrange Confucius's funeral. These are the men Mêng Wu Po asks about.

15. *Tsai Yü.* A disciple.

16. *Tzŭ-ch'an.* Minister in Chêng State. Died when Confucius was twenty-nine.

17. *Chi Wên Tzŭ.* Reference to former Lu noble of the Chi family? Died seventeen years before Confucius was born.

18. *Hui* (also Yen Hui or Yen Yüan). Confucius's most brilliant student, though at times his complete acceptance of Confucius's teaching exasperated the Master. He impressed Confucius by his modesty and cheerful acceptance of the misfortunes of life, and by his enthusiasm for learning. He died at age twenty-nine.

19. *Chi K'ang-tzŭ.* See note 2 above. It seems the statesman is here screening men of office in his government.

20. *Po Niu* (also named *Jan Kêng*). A disciple. Later tradition has it that he was afflicted with leprosy; thus Confucius would not enter his house.

21. *Mêng Chih-fan.* The Master's most modest pupil.

22. *It.* The Way, the *tao.* See Chapter 13.

23. *Fan Ch'ih.* A disciple. He incurs the wrath of Confucius in an analect (2:12), not quoted here, in which he asks about farming. Confucius refers him to a gardener, and remarks behind his back that Fan is no gentleman.

24. *The Middle Use.* I.e., the golden mean.

25. *Even Yao and Shun could hardly criticize him.* A proverbial saying among later Confucians and other philosophers. Yao, Shun, Yü, and the early Chou rulers came to be known as the Ancients. See pp. 6–8.

26. *P'êng.* The Chinese Methuselah. Descended from a legendary emperor. Enfeoffed by Emperor Yao with the fief of P'êng. His real name was Ch'ien Kêng. He was born 1890 B.C. and disappeared into the west, aged seven hundred to eight hundred years.

27. *Sing.* For fuller description of various rites, see the *Book of Rites*, pp. 93–99, and the *Analects*, Book 10, and *Filial Piety*, pp. 182–200.

28. *Three Hosts.* The three divisions of the army.

29. *The Succession.* See note 9, above.

30. *Duke of Shê.* A principled nobleman of Ch'u who (according to the *Commentary of Tso*) had had an interview with Confucius.

31. *Huan T'ui.* A disreputable Minister of War in Sung, a state bordering on Lu. Huan T'ui is supposed to have tried to waylay and assassinate Confucius, perhaps because he feared the Master's influence on his brother, Ssŭ-Ma Niu, a disciple.

32. *T'ai Po.* Eldest son of the legendary ancestor of the Chou, Tan Fu. He renounced his succession to the throne in favor of his youngest brother, so the legend has it, and traveled into the deep south in search of medicinal herbs for his ailing father.

33. *Songs. Book of Songs.* See Table 3.

34. *It.* The Way.

35. *Rebel.* A theme later stressed by Mencius. (See p. 135 above).

36. *Ta-hsiang.* A village in Shan Tung province.

37. *K'uang.* A border town occupied at various times by the neighboring states of Wei, Chêng, Sung, and Lu. Confucius was held here in a case of mistaken identity with a troublemaker, Yang Huo, whom the townsmen were eager to catch.

38. *The Grand Minister.* Possibly P'i Tzŭ-yü of Wu State.

39. *Lao.* A disciple.

40. *The phoenix does not come; the river gives forth no chart.* The Master is saying that portents of the coming of a Sage are nowhere to be found.
41. *Nine Wild Tribes of the East.* A set phrase to refer to numerous uncivilized tribes to the remote east.
42. *Court.* Of the Duke of Lu.
43. *Three Armies.* Phrase signifying full military might of a kingdom.
44. *Who harmed none, was foe to none/ Did nothing that was not right.* As with many of his quotations, this comes from the *Book of Songs*, 67.

9. Mencius

1. *King Hui of Liang* (370–319 B.C.). Aging ruler of a declining state.
2. *Chariots.* The power of states was gauged by the number of chariots marshalled on the field of battle.
3. *Chin.* This state had held the hegemony of the central states in the seventh century. Only one hundred years later, its power was fragmented by the Hsiang family of Chin, who split the state into three—Han, Wei, and Chao. Mencius is here on a visit to the King of Wei. The three states waged jealous war between each other, wars they could ill afford at a time when Ch'in was moving from the west, and Ch'i and Ch'u threatened from the east and south.
4. *King Hsüan* (319–301 B.C.). He had friendly relations with many scholars to whom he gave audience at his court. Mencius here is invited to discuss political affairs, especially those concerning rulers of the not-too-distant past.
5. *Duke Huan of Ch'i* and *Duke Wên of Chin.* Two seventh-century-B.C. rulers who at different times won leadership of a loose confederacy of the central states when the royal house lost power. This political system (referred to variously as hegemony, paramountcy, or overlordship) had long been out of use by Mencius's time.
6. *Bell.* When a ruler wished to commemorate a special event such as a victory in war, diplomacy, and the like, a bronze bell was cast inscribed with the details of the circumstance, and then dedicated with the ceremony of sacrifice to family ancestors.
7. *But it is I who have surmised it.* See Waley, *Book of Songs*, 298, for this poem.
8. *And so ruled over the family and the state.* See Waley, *Book of Songs*, 245.
9. *Tsou.* Mencius's birthplace, a minor principality near Lu State where Confucius was born.
10. *Rites.* The Chinese term *li,* broadly signifying what is prescribed by ritual, propriety, sacrificial and other ceremonies, and manners, custom, and tradition as well. See Chapters 6 and 11.
11. *Mu.* One *mu* equals one-sixth of an acre.
12. *Meat.* Normally the fare of nobles and their families. The poorest classes ate vegetable dishes. Likewise, the upper classes wore silk, while the others wore hemp.
13. *Good and wise men.* I.e., nonmembers of the hereditary nobility, referring to ministers and political advisers of Ch'i and of other states.
14. *He was put to death by the whole country.* Mencius quotes liberally from the *Book of Documents* and the *Book of Songs*.
15. *T'êng.* A small principality whose ruler was not known as King but as Duke.
16. *Former Kings.* Mencius is referring to the model kings of antiquity. (See Table 2.)
17. *Benevolent.* Once the altars and ancestral shrine of a ruler were destroyed, his line was extinguished.

18. *Jan Ch'iu.* Reference to Confucius's disapproval of Jan Ch'iu's misappropriation of taxes while in the service of Chi K'ang-tzŭ of Lu State. See *Analects*, 11:16. Note: Ch'iu the steward is to be distinguished from the next Ch'iu, another name for Confucius.

19. *Composure.* For the ritual expressions of rulers giving audience, see *Analects*, Book 10.

20. *Kao Tzŭ.* A philosopher about whom little is known. His dates are c. 420–c. 350 B.C. Thought by some to have affinities with the Mo-ists, by others to share the views of Yang Chu, he is important here for the counterpoint with Mencius in the argument on human nature.

21. *Kung-tu Tzŭ.* A disciple, provocative when arguing with Mencius.

22. *King Yu* and *King Li.* Two kings of the Western Chou period (1111–771 B.C.). Yu favored his concubine, naming her son heir apparent. The legitimate son and heir overthrew Yu and moved the new government to Loyang in the east. Li was known as Li the Cruel for his acts of tyranny. He was deposed.

23. *Hsiang, the Lord of Wei,* and *Pi Kan.* Bad and good exemplars of early Confucian legend. The latter was killed by King Chou, last ruler of the Shang Dynasty.

24. *They would be drawn to superior virtue.* See Waley, *Book of Songs*, 142.

25. *Lung Tzŭ.* Nothing is known about this thinker.

26. Mencius supports his argument with famous names of the past:
I Ya. Cook to Duke Huan of Ch'i of the seventh century.
K'uang. Music master in Chin State.
Tzŭ-tu. The heart-throb of Chêng State.

27. *Chieh.* The last ruler of the Hsia Dynasty, his evil doings growing ever more elaborate with the passage of time. Chieh is said to have spent vast amounts of money to keep his concubine, Mo Hsi, amused. His ministers supported him with silent disapproval, only one of them having the nerve to speak out, for which he was executed.

28. Early heroes of political legend:
Shun. The son of a poor blind man.
Fu Yüeh. Too poor to pay for road repair, he paid in road repair labor; both he and Shun were summoned by Yao to office.
Chiao Chi. Became Minister to King Chou of the Shang Dynasty.
Kuan I-wu. Better known as Kuan Chung. Became Prime Minister to Duke Huan of Ch'i State (seventh century B.C.).
Sun-shu Ao. Prime Minister to Duke Chuang of Ch'u (late seventh century B.C.).
Po-li Hsi. Prime Minister to Duke Mu of Ch'in (second half of the seventh century B.C.).
These three states mentioned above had all acted as hegemons of the confederate states at different times.

29. *Families of Han and Wei.* I.e., great wealth and prestige.

30. *Po I* and *T'ai-kung.* Both were in the service of King Chou of Shang. Both switched loyalty to King Wên of Chou, who was mounting his eastern campaign.

31. *The rites.* The *Book of Rites*. See Chart 3 for a list of the Confucian Classics.

32. *T'ao Ying.* A disciple.

10. Hsün Tzŭ

1. *Book of Documents.* See Table 3 for a list of the Confucian Classics.

2. *Large clothes, wide girdles, and high hats.* Standard Confucian gear for several centuries.

3. *Mo Tzŭ* (c. 470–391 B.C.). One of the great philosophers. See Table 6 and Chapter 12.

4. *Defectives.* The five kinds of defectives were the deaf, the dumb, the crippled, the amputees, and the dwarfed or hunchbacked. See Table 5 for a list of some of the "fives" in Chinese literature; and notes 3 and 4, p. 393 above.

5. *Nobles.* In feudalistic society, it is of a noble to employ, of a commoner to serve.

6. *Service.* Corvée labor, service in the army, construction work, and the like.

7. *Travellers.* These would be interstate travellers, sometimes on friendly business, sometimes in the service of a hostile state and commissioned to spy.

8. *Circulation of valuables.* The currency of barter goods.

9. *Four seas.* See note 7, p. 393.

10. *Cornelian.* A reddish-colored quartz, a precious stone. "North sea," "south sea," and so forth is a stylistic way of referring to the remote points of the compass.

11. *Orphan, childless, a widower, or widow.* Another in the classifications of society; the four helpless ones.

12. *Lin-wu-chün.* Thought to be a general of Ch'u State.

13. *King Hsiao-ch'êng.* Reigned 265–245 B.C.

14. *Ts'ao-fu.* The preceding name, *I*, refers to Hou I, a master archer and chief of Tribe *I*, in the early Hsia Dynasty. A famous horse trainer of antiquity.

15. *T'ang and Wu.* T'ang, founder of the Shang Dynasty, ruled 1751–1738 B.C.; Wu Wang or Fa, the "Martial King," cofounder of the Chou Dynasty, ruled 1111–1104 B.C. See Table 2.

16. *Sun Wu* (fourth century B.C.) and *Wu Ch'i* (third century B.C.). Generals and authors of works on military science. (See Chapter 17.)

17. *The master.* Note the debate is recorded in third person, possibly by disciples.

18. *Li.* One *li* equals one-third of a mile. This *li* is written differently in Chinese characters from the *li* signifying rites, ceremonies, and good form, as in the *Book of Rites* or *I Li*.

19. *Mo-yeh.* A legendary sword endowed with magical qualities.

20. *Chieh* or *Chih.* Chieh was the last king of the Hsia Dynasty; his rule was damned as tyrannical by the Chou conquerors. See p. 19. Chih is "Bandit Chih," a famous robber and adventurer.

21. *Yin and Yang.* Originally these two terms may have meant dark and sunny. They later meant female and male. By the fourth century this was extended to mean the mutually dependent forces of nature. The terms were incorporated into philosophical writings of various schools. See Chapter 4.

22. *Yü.* Founder of the Hsia Dynasty. See Table 2.

23. *The sophists.* Hsün Tzŭ is referring to logicians and dialecticians of the School of Names or Logic. He criticizes the extremes of paradox and logic of such leading figures of the school as Hui Shih, King-sun Lung, and others.

24. *Chou.* I.e., King Chou of Shang. King Wu is the "Martial King." See note 15 above.

25. *The five flavours.* Bitter, sweet, sour, salty, and hot (peppery).

26. *Wu and Hsiang.* Musical forms of King Wu of Chou's time. The *Shao* and *Hu* of Emperor Shun and of Emperor T'ang's time.

27. *It.* Death.

28. *Joy.* In Chinese the character for music is the same as for joy, though both words have different pronunciations. The *Book of Music* (originally one of the *Six Classics*) has been lost. Some references to it are to be found in the *Book of Rites*, section 19. This essay by Hsün Tzŭ is a vigorous attack on Mo Tzŭ. (See pp. 243–44.)

29. *Ya* and *Sung.* The *Book of Songs* was set to music accompanied by dances. Songs were divided into three categories: *fêng, ya,* and *sung.* (See Chapter 3.)

30. *Arrangement of Officials.* A quotation from his own work, Book 9.

31. *Music is unchanging.* A quotation, like those that follow, from the *Book of Rites.*

32. *The five senses.* Sight, sound, smell, taste, and touch.

33. *Terms.* Here Hsün Tzŭ quotes from well-known works of the logicians. (See note 23 above.)

11. The Classic of Filial Piety

1. *Chung-ni.* Chinese names are many and complex. Confucius's surname or the name of the family into which he was born was K'ung. His personal name was Ch'iu. His social, outside-the-family name was Chung-ni.

2. *Tsêng Tzŭ* (505–437 B.C.). One of Confucius's most influential disciples. His family name was Tsêng, his personal name was Shên, and his social name was Tzŭ-yü. He is traditionally known as the author of both *The Great Learning* and the *Classic of Filial Piety.*

3. *Major Odes of the Kingdom.* One of the sections of the *Book of Songs.*

4. *Punishments.* See the *Book of Documents,* pp. 33–34.

The Doctrine of the Mean

1. *Tzŭ Ssŭ.* Confucius's grandson, who is credited with the elaboration of Confucian ideas in this text.

2. *Chung-ni.* See note 1, p. 401.

3. *Shun.* Emperor Shun, a legendary model king. (See Table 2.)

4. *Hui.* Yen Hui, one of Confucius's favorite disciples.

5. *Tzŭ-lu.* Another of Confucius's disciples.

6. *Manes.* The shades or spirits of particular dead persons.

7. *King Wên.* This section makes reference to the model kings of the Chou, founders of that ancient Chinese dynasty.

8. *Shang Ti.* For this religious term, see note 16, p. 393 above.

9. *Duke Ai.* Ruler of Lu State (494–468 B.C.). He appears as Confucius's student in the *Conduct of the Scholar,* pp. 210–15.

10. *Tortoise.* Tools of divination in ancient China. (See pp. 63–68.)

The Great Learning

1. *K'ang Kao, T'ai Chia,* and *Ti Tien.* All sections of the *Book of Documents* (see above, pp. 10–35).

2. *King T'ang.* Founder of the Shang Dynasty, ruling from 1751–1738 B.C. See Table 2.

3. *Ming-mang.* An approximation of the sound made by the oriole.

4. *Master Tsêng.* Tsêng Tzŭ, mention of whom will be found in the section on the *Classic of Filial Piety*, p. 184. He was one of Confucius's disciples.

5. *Yao and Shun.* Frequently associated pair of good legendary kings of antiquity. See Chapter 1. *Chieh and Chou.* In contradistinction, the pair of legendary bad kings, degenerate last members in their dynastic lines.

6. *Yin.* Another name for Shang. See Table 2.

7. *Book of Ch'u.* A chapter of the Chinese *Intrigues of the Warring States*, a work which has been assigned to the first century B.C.

8. *Ch'in Shih.* From the *Book of Documents.*

9. *Middle Kingdom.* Or *Chung Kuo*, the name given to the group of eleven states of the Spring and Autumn Period (722–481 B.C.) who felt themselves bound by ties of Chou culture and considered other neighboring states as rude, much as the Greek states thought of Macedonia. The term is often extended today, literarily, to mean China.

10. *Mêng Hsien Tzŭ.* A minister of Lu before Confucius's time.

The Conduct of the Scholar

1. *Ju.* One of the scholarly class of lesser aristocrats who were experts in the impressive, complex formalities of ceremonial life. Because of the importance in China of ceremonial observances and because of the weight Confucius had laid on the rites, his followers began to be called *ju* and have so been called ever since. There is no other name in Chinese for Confucians.

2. *Duke Ai of Lu.* Ruled as Duke of Lu State from 494–468 B.C.

3. *Scholar.* By Hsün Tzŭ's time, the long, flowing robe and tall, pointed cap were standard Confucian dress.

4. *A mat to be placed for him.* Customary style of seating in ancient China.

5. *Precious gem.* Reference to *Analects* 9:12.

6. *Windows.* For primitive and later styles of housing in ancient China, see Cheng Tê-k'un, *Archeology in China*, 3 vols. (Toronto: University of Toronto Press, 1963).

12. Mo Tzŭ

1. *Hsia.* As related in the *Book of Documents.* Yü founded the Hsia Dynasty, T'ang founded the Shang or Yin Dynasty. (See Table 2.)

2. *Ch'ing Chi.* Reference to a politician of Wu State who was murdered on the journey.

3. *Chieh.* In the references that follow, Chieh, the last ruler of the Hsia Dynasty, was defeated by T'ang, founder of the Shang Dynasty.

4. *Three Dynasties.* Properly speaking, Yao and Shun do not belong to the Three Dynasties of Antiquity since they predated them. The others do: Yü (Hsia), T'ang (Shang), and Wên and Wu (Chou). See Table 2.

5. *Yu and Li.* See note 22 to *Mencius*, p. 399.

6. *[T'ien].* Inserted by the translator. The Chinese text has no subject.

7. *The five grains.* Rice, millet, a variety of millet, wheat, and soy bean.

8. *The six animals.* Horse, ox, chicken, dog, pig, and sheep.

9. *Standard requirements.* See the *Book of Songs*, 202.

10. *Hsiang Nien.* A section of the *Book of Documents* no longer extant.

11. *Tao.* The *Way*, the right path in life. (See Chapter 13.)

12. *Pa, Yüeh, Ch'i,* and *Ching.* States of China in the fifth and fourth centuries B.C. Ching was another name for Ch'u State.

13. *Mount T'ai.* In the province of Shan Tung. It was anciently considered the highest mountain in the Middle Kingdom.

14. *Posterity.* See note 6, p. 398.

15. *Ta Ya.* That part of the *Book of Songs* composed of ceremonial songs. (See pp. 36, 41–60.)

16. *Kuo.* Open territory or land outside town walls.

17. *Li, chariots,* and *mu.* Chinese measurements in this passage. One *li* equals one-third of a mile (see note 18, p. 400); chariots were a standard of a ruler's wealth and power; one *mu* equals one-sixth of an acre.

18. *Prince of Miao.* (Declaration of Emperor Yao), pp. 12–14 above.

19. *Chiao Chih* and *Yu Tu.* The first is located in the south of Canton province; the second, in Hopei province.

20. *Tripod.* A sacrificial vessel with three legs.

21. *Lord.* Immolation was practiced in ancient China, especially during the rule of the Shang. By Mo Tzŭ's time it rarely occurred. Nonetheless it is said that at Emperor Huang-ti's funeral (210 B.C.), his entire harem was buried with him. On the practice of human sacrifice in China, see H. G. Creel, *The Birth of China* (New York: Ungar, 1964).

22. *Three years.* Twenty-five months.

23. *Five offices and six posts.* They represent the several departments of the government and differ with different dynasties.

24. *The cakes and wine will be unclean.* For sacrifice.

25. *Tu Po.* King Hsüan (827–783 B.C.) executed his minister Tu Po on false charges even though warned that Tu Po's spirit would avenge him. Three years later, according to the chronicles, Tu's apparition shot and killed Hsüan with bow and arrow before the eyes of the assembled feudal lords.

26. *Ch'in* and *shê.* Five- and twenty-five-stringed instruments.
    Yü. A flute.
    Shêng. A kind of Chinese bagpipe with seventeen reeds attached to a hollow gourd.

27. *Kung Mêng Tzŭ.* A Confucian.

28. *Lu's Question.* This chapter, a medley of interstate consultations between Mo Tzŭ and rulers, statesmen, and disciples, takes its name from Mo Tzŭ's meeting with the Lord of Lu.

29. *Wei Yüeh.* A disciple.

14. Tao-tê-ching

1. *Like a bowl.* Words in brackets are in amplification of the original text.

2. *Straw dogs.* Inexpensive common offerings burned in sacrifice to *T'ien* and *Ti* (Earth).

3. *Six family relationships.* Between father and son, elder and younger brother, husband and wife.

4. *Mother.* Commentators have said that *mother* means *tao,* but *mother* is used in different contexts with apparently different meanings. See sections 1, 25, 52, and 59 of the *Tao-tê-ching.*

5. *The right.* In peacetime, ritual performance is from left to right; in wartime, from right to left (*cf.* etymology of *sinister*).

6. *One.* Has various meanings in the *Tao-tê-ching.* It may signify the origin of every-

thing or the mystical unity or wholeness in diversity or a starting point for the idea of the complex growing out of the simple.

7. *Yin and yang.* See note 21, p. 400 above.
8. *Coarse cloth.* As opposed to the more refined and costly silk?
9. *Knot cords.* An ancient mnemonic practice, typically preliterate, in different parts of the world. Tying a knot in one's handkerchief to remember something is a vestigial modern example.

15. The Historical Yang Chu,
from the Book of Lieh Tzŭ

1. *Po-ch'êng Tzŭ-kao.* A feudal lord at the time of Emperor Yao.
2. *Paralyzed.* A tall story adapted from the account of Yü and the Great Flood related in the *Book of Documents.*
3. *Ch'in Ku-li.* A disciple of Mo Tzŭ.
4. *Mêng Sun-yang.* Yang's disciple.
5. *Kuan Yin.* Traditionally thought to have been Lao Tzŭ's contemporary. No work by him survives.
6. *Liang.* The princely name for Wei. (See note 3, p. 398.)
7. *Huang-chung* and *Ta-lü.* On ancient music, see L. Laloy, *La musique chinoise* (Paris: H. Laurens, 1910).
8. *Five Elements.* Earth, wood, metal, fire, and water. A third-century-B.C. thinker, Tsou Yen of Ch'i State, combined the Five Elements and *yin-yang* principles to form a new cosmology. Tung Chung-shu developed Tsou's ideas for the Han Dynasty. See Table 5 and note 4, p. 400, and notes 3 and 4, p. 393, above.

16. Chuang Tzŭ

1. *Hsü Yu.* One of the "Four Philosophers of the Mountain." The story goes that when Emperor Yao offered rulership to him, Hsü Yu fled Yao's presence and washed his ears of the defiling words he had heard. (See also Table 2.)
2. *Tzŭ-ch'i.* The dramatis personae of Chuang Tzŭ's stories are too numerous to identify. The more important ones will be singled out for explanation and returned (where possible) to their proper place in time. Tzŭ-ch'i here was a Taoist adept.
3. *The Great Clod.* One of Chuang Tzŭ's terms for the Way, the *tao;* the inexpressible absolute of the mystics.
4. *Tsung, Kuei,* and *Hsü-ao.* States that the legendary model-king Yao is supposed to have attacked.
5. *Recklessly.* One Chang Wu-tzŭ is talking to a certain Chü Ch'üeh-tzŭ.
6. *Yen Hui.* Confucius's favorite disciple. See note 18, p. 397.
7. *Hui Tzŭ* or *Hui Shih.* Philosopher of the School of Logic. Little is known about him except through the writings of other philosophers—for example, Mencius and Chuang Tzŭ. His dates are traditionally 420–350 B.C. He and Chuang Tzŭ seem to have been friends.
8. *Hard* and *white.* Reference to the paradoxes of the School of Logic.
9. *True Man.* Synonymous with such terms as the Sage, the Saint, the Perfect Man, and the Holy Man.
10. *Hu Pu-hsieh, Wu Kuang, Po I, Shu Ch'i, Chi Tzŭ, Hsü Yü, Chi To,* and *Shên-t'u Ti.* Famed men of the distant past who were revered by early Taoists.

11. *Yao and Chieh.* Saintly and sinful kings of the ancient past, according to Confucian canon.
12. *The Creator.* "He who creates things" *(Chao-wu).* Another special usage of Chuang Tzŭ's.
13. *Yin and yang.* For a discussion of those terms, see note 21, p. 400.
14. *Mo-yeh.* Famous magical sword of a king of Wu State, c. late sixth century B.C.
15. *Each other.* This is Confucius talking to Yen Hui, à la Chuang Tzŭ.
16. *Hsü Yu.* See note 1, above.
17. *Great Thoroughfare.* The Way, the *tao;* or the infinite, the absolute of mystical language.
18. *Yang-tzŭ Chü.* Perhaps a reference to the early philosopher Yang Chu (fourth century B.C.). (See Chapter 15 above.)
19. *Lao Tan.* Generally taken to be one and the same as Lao Tzŭ, though he may possibly have been another early philosopher.
20. *Huang-chung* and *ta-lü.* Standard pitch-pipes.
21. *Tsêng* and *Shih.* Disciples of Confucius; the former is credited with the *Classic of Filial Piety.* (See Chapter 11 above.)
22. *Yang* and *Mo.* Yang Chu and Mo Tzŭ respectively. (See Chapters 12 and 15 above.)
23. *Yü.* Emperor Shun of antiquity becomes in later times a model of kingly virtue, of which a frequently quoted example is his choice of successor to the throne—not on a hereditary basis but on merit.
24. *Ho Hsü.* One of the kings of antiquity.
25. *Lao Tan.* See note 19 above.
26. *Yellow Emperor.* This allusion to a legendary Chinese ruler goes contrary to usual Taoist practice, since he is typically cited as founder of Taoism.
27. *Dark City.* See the *Book of Documents,* "Declaration of Emperor Yao," pp. 12–14.
28. *Mo-ists.* Followers of Mo Tzŭ, and later adherents to the Mo-ist School of Philosophy. See Chapter 12 above.
29. *Cangues.* Portable pillories fastened onto the neck of criminals.
30. *Five Emperors* and *Three Kings.* See Table 2; also for reference to the Three Dynasties below.
31. *Highest virtue.* A play on the homophones *tê* (virtue) and *tê* (gain, or acquisition). See note 8, p. 179, in B. Watson, *Complete Works of Chuang Tzŭ.*
32. *Sacred tortoise.* The shell of a tortoise was often used in divination; see Chapter 4.
33. *Hui Tzŭ.* See note 7 above.
34. *Yüan-ch'u.* The Chinese names refer to rare and exotic things.
35. *Tzŭ-hsü.* A minister of Wu State who lost his life by constantly warning his king of imminent danger, thus incurring his suspicion.
36. *Kuan Tzŭ.* Prime Minister to Duke Huan of Ch'i State (seventh century B.C.). See note 4, p. 407, below.
37. *Sui-jên and Shên-nung.* Model kings of antiquity, and mythological culture heroes, respectively.
38. *Father Chung.* Kuang Chung (d. 645 B.C.) the chief minister of Duke Huan of Ch'i (r. 685–643 B.C.), who used to call him "Father Chung."

17. Sun Tzŭ: The Art of War

1. *Tao.* For Sun Tzŭ the *tao* has less the philosophical or religious meaning of the way

of true standards or of the nature or virtue (although these elements remain part of the connotation), than a political meaning. The *tao* is that way of right acting that unites people to their leaders, the path that a true ruler or commander walks. See p. 247.

2. *In a circle.* The *yin-yang.* See discussions on pp. 65 and 400, note 21.
3. *Li.* About one-third of a mile. See note 18, p. 400.
4. *The five elements.* See Table 5.
5. *Wu and Yüeh.* Southern states of the Warring States era.
6. *Native, inside, double, expendable,* and *living.* These are, respectively: ordinary enemy natives spying against their own country; enemy officials bought over; enemy agents bought over; one's own agents misinformed in order to divulge false information to the enemy; one's own agents returning from a mission alive.
7. *I Chih* and *Lü Ya.* Exemplary figures in Confucian tradition. The former was an official connected with the takeover of the Hsia Dynasty by the virtuous Shang King, T'ang the Successful; the latter, with the takeover of the Shang Dynasty by the two Chou kings, Wên and Wu.

19. Lord Shang

1. *Ten evils.* Most of these evils pertain to the Confucian school.
2. *Moral culture.* Philosophers' writings were composed on bamboo slips and collated to form books. It is possible that the copyist-editor here carelessly omitted "integrity and sophistry."
3. *Vegetables.* In the sense of making them inedible.
4. *Extensive Culture.* Reference to the nonextant chapters of the *Book of Lord Shang*? I.e., conquer the rebellious states in war or acculturate them by economic measures.
5. *Other countries.* Since, in the classical formula of good government, there will be a massive emigration to Ch'in State.
6. *Taxes.* A means of encouraging emigration.
7. *Three Chin states.* Han, Wei, and Chao.
8. *Present times.* Shang Yang interprets the governmental policies of the kings of antiquity to be suitable for their own time. He promises a more enduring plan.
9. *Three generations.* This could mean death to either parents, brothers, wife and children; or to father, son, and grandson; or to father's brothers, brothers, sons' brothers.
10. *The Great and Illustrious Ruler.* Reference to Fu Hsi, inventor of fishing and hunting. (See Table 2.)
11. *Huang-ti.* The Yellow Emperor.
12. *Shên Nung.* Patron of agriculture and commerce; follows Fu Hsi in time and precedes Huang-ti. See Table 2.
13. *Women within and men outside.* Women in the home, men in the fields.
14. *Kung-sun Yang.* Shang Yang.
15. *Yao, Shun, Yü, and T'ang.* The honorable sages of antiquity.

20. Han Fei Tzŭ

1. *Fei.* Han Fei Tzŭ.
2. *Tzŭ-hsü.* Escaped to Wu State from Ch'u when his father and brother were exe-

cuted. Managed to persuade Wu's ruler to attack Ch'u in revenge. Later served Ch'u, but incurred suspicion and was forced to commit suicide.
3. *Chung-ni.* Confucius.
4. *Kuan I-wu.* Kuan Tzŭ. He was captured by Lu and sent to Ch'i State in a prisoner's cart. Later became Prime Minister of Ch'i's ruler, Duke Huan (seventh century B.C.), whom he helped to a powerful position among the states of the time. A work bearing his name consists now of a conglomeration of seventy-six (once, eighty-six) texts of different dates, content, and styles.
5. *I Yin.* Counsellor to Emperor T'ang of the Shang Dynasty. One version of his rise to power says that he ingratiated himself with T'ang by his excellent cooking.
6. *Chou.* King Wên (the Enlightened) launched a campaign against King Chou, last of the Shang. His successor, King Wu, finally overthrew the Shang and established the Chou Dynasty. See above, p. 6.
7. *Marquis I, Marquis Chiu, Pi-kan, Earl Mei.* King Chou's ministers.
8. *Sun Tzŭ.* I.e., Sun Pin, presumed descendant of Sun Tzŭ, author of *The Art of War.* See pp. 318–319. Sun Pin was also a military strategist.
9. *Kung-sun Yang.* Shang Yang, author of the *Book of Lord Shang.* See pp. 333–349.
10. *Gentleman.* Extended from the sense of Confucian gentleman to mean the educated man, the scholar-official.
11. *Faces the north.* The Chinese ruler always faced south in court audiences, his minister facing him. "To face south" means to rule from the throne. "To face north" means "to have an audience with His Majesty."
12. *Mo-yeh.* A legendary sword. See note 14, p. 405.
13. *Perfect balance.* Legalist utopian passage with strains of the *Book of Documents* ("Counsels of Minister Kao Yao"), and *Tao-tê-ching,* 80. See pp. 16–18 and 274 above.
14. *Marquis Chao of Han.* Reigned 358–333 B.C.
15. *Tzŭ-chih* and *T'ien-ch'ang.* Deceitful ministers.
16. *Right.* Han Fei Tzŭ was strongly influenced by Taoist teachings and wrote the first commentary on the *Tao-tê-ching.*
17. *The Yellow Emperor.* Legendary founder of Taoism, the semidivine Huang-ti. See pp. 6, 8 and Table 2.
18. *Hundred surnames.* The ordinary people.
19. *I Yin.* See note 5 above.
20. *Scholars of the present age.* Reference to the Confucians and Mo-ists.
21. *Li Tai.* Became Grand Assistant to King Hui-wên of Chao in 298 B.C.
Father Sovereign. Title given himself by King Wu-ling of Chao after abdicating in favor of his younger son, Ho, in 298 B.C. Ho later became King Hui-wên. In 295 B.C., Li Tai took to the field for his king to put down a revolt led by Ho's brother, and killed the rebellious prince and locked the father up inside the palace until he starved to death.
Nao Ch'ih. Military commander from Ch'u, appointed prime minister by King Min of Ch'i in 284 B.C.
King Min. Ruler of Ch'i killed in 283 B.C. by Nao Ch'ih in a traitorous agreement with the enemy forces of Yen.
22. *Spring and Autumn Period.* 722–481 B.C. For accounts of these and other feuds between the states, see above, Chapter 7.
23. *Portents of ruin.* The enumeration of portents from 1–47 is an addition of the translation.

24. *Date-selecting.* Favorable days for ceremonial.
25. *Altar of the Spirits of Land and Grain.* Sacrifice to earth deities for good crops.
26. *Enemy state.* I.e., such action would cause anxiety lest the offspring of the foreign consort be favored over the legitimate son and heir.
27. *Hostage returns.* It was not uncommon practice for the heir apparent to be sent as hostage to reinforce a pact or to guarantee interstate policy.
28. *Secondary professions.* The primary occupation was farming/military service. The secondary, commerce, finance, scholarly activity, etc.
29. *Interior.* The *interior* refers to the queen, concubines, heir apparent, children of the ruler, and court retinue. The *exterior* (outside the palace's inner sanctum) refers to the ministers and office-holders.
30. *Facing the south.* See note 11 above.
31. *External and Internal Affairs.* For a selection from this chapter of the *Book of Lord Shang*, see pp. 344–345.
32. *Cho River Gorge.* 638 B.C. An example of ancient chivalry practiced by one of the original feudal states toward a parvenu state of the southern region, Ch'u. The chivalrous action had to do with the Duke waiting until the Ch'u troops were ready to fight. An action similar to that at the famous battle of Fontenoy (May 11, 1745) where the British commander allegedly invited the French to fire first (and the French just as courteously refused). The Anglo-allied forces, like those of the Duke of Sung, lost the battle. The Duke of Sung has become a byword for a kind of ineffectual Old World courtesy. "We are not like the Duke of Sung," said Mao Tsê-tung.
33. *Wei.* Not to be confused with the state of Wei formed after Chin State split up.
34. *Wang Liang.* Legendary charioteer of antiquity.
35. *Yüeh.* Deep Southeast.
36. *Finding sureties. Cf.* note 27 above.
37. *Three units and basic fives.* Reference to the division of the state into three units for military administration and into five families for local administration.
38. *Eliminate invisible culprits.* Political opposition and the like, which is not classified as crime but is an irritant to the state.
39. *Itinerant speakers.* The traveling teachers of the different schools of thought who sought to influence the ruler to adopt their policies and methods of government. See Chapter 7.
40. *Five Ministries,* War, Education, Revenue, Public Works, and Justice.
41. *The black headed.* Chinese people. The origin of the phrase is undecided; it may refer either to the bare-headed commoners as distinct from the hat-wearers of the ruling classes, or to the first immigrants to China subservient to their new rulers.
42. *The system of personal denunciation and mutual implication.* This system, known as the *pao-chia*, did take shape in China in the Sung Dynasty around 1070 A.D.

A GUIDE TO
FURTHER READING

General and Reference Works

Balazs, Etienne. *Chinese Civilization and Bureaucracy.* Translated by H. M. Wright. Edited by Arthur F. Wright. New Haven: Yale University Press, 1964.
———. *Political Theory and Administrative Reality in Traditional China.* London: School of Oriental and African Studies, University of London, 1965.
Beasley, W. G., and Pulleyblank, E. G., eds. *Historians of China and Japan.* Historical Writing on the Peoples of Asia. London: Oxford University Press, 1961.
Birch, Cyril, and Keene, Donald, eds. *Anthology of Chinese Literature.* New York: Grove, 1965.
Bodde, Derk. *China's Cultural Tradition, What and Whither?* Source Problems in World Civilizations. New York: Holt, 1957.
Chan, Wing-tsit. *An Outline and an Annotated Bibliography of Chinese Philosophy.* New Haven: Yale University Press, 1959.
———. *Religious Trends in Modern China.* New York: Columbia University Press, 1953.
———, tr. *A Source Book in Chinese Philosophy.* Princeton: Princeton University Press, 1963.
Chang, Chung-li. *The Chinese Gentry.* Seattle: University of Washington Press, 1955.
Ch'en, Kenneth K. S. *Buddhism in China: A Historical Survey.* Princeton: Princeton University Press, 1964.
Chi, Ch'ao-ting. *Key Economic Areas in Chinese History.* London: Allen and Unwin, 1936.
Couling, Samuel. *The Encyclopedia Sinica.* London: Oxford University Press, 1917.
Creel, Herrlee Glessner. *Chinese Thought from Confucius to Mao Tse-tung.* Chicago: University of Chicago Press, 1953.
———. *Sinism: A Study of the Evolution of the Chinese World-View.* Chicago: Open Court, 1929.
Cressey, George Babcock. *China's Geographic Foundations: A Survey of the Land and Its People.* New York: McGraw-Hill, 1934.
Dawson, Raymond, ed. *The Legacy of China.* Oxford: Clarendon Press, 1964.
Day, Clarence B. *Chinese Peasant Cults.* Shanghai: Kelly & Walsh, 1940.
———. *The Philosophers of China, Classical and Contemporary.* New York: Philosophical Library, 1962.
DeBary, W. Theodore, Chan, Wing-tsit, and Watson, Burton, eds. *Sources of Chinese Tradition.* New York: Columbia University Press, 1960.
deGroot, Jan Jakob Maria. *Religion in China; Universism: A Key to the Study of Taoism and Confucianism.* New York: Putnam, 1912.

deGroot, Jan Jakob Maria. *The Religion of the Chinese*. New York: Macmillan, 1910.

Dubs, Homer H. *A Roman City in Ancient China*. London: The China Society, 1957.

Eberhard, Wolfram. *A History of China from the Earliest Times to the Present Day*. Translated by E. W. Dickes. London: Routledge & Kegan Paul, 1950.

————. *Guilt and Sin in Traditional China*. Berkeley: University of California Press, 1969.

Fairbank, John King, ed. *Chinese Thought and Institutions*. Chicago: University of Chicago Press, 1957.

————. *The Chinese World Order*. Cambridge: Harvard University Press, 1968.

Fei, Hsiao-t'ung. *Peasant Life in China*. New York: Dutton, 1939.

Fitzgerald, Charles Patrick. *China, A Short Cultural History*. 4th ed., rev. New York: Praeger, 1958.

Fung, Yu-lan. *A History of Chinese Philosophy*. Translated by Derk Bodde. 2 vols. Princeton: Princeton University Press, 1952.

Gernet, Jacques. *Daily Life in China: On the Eve of the Mongol Invasion 1250–1276*. Translated by H. M. Wright. New York: Macmillan, 1962.

Giles, Herbert A. *A Chinese Biographical Dictionary*. London: Bernard Quaritch, 1898.

————. *A Chinese-English Dictionary*. 2d ed. 2 vols. New York: Paragon, 1964.

Goodrich, L. Carrington. *A Short History of the Chinese People*. New York: Harper, 1943.

————. *A Syllabus of the History of Chinese Civilization and Culture*. 5th ed., rev. New York: China Society of America, 1950.

Granet, Marcel. *Chinese Civilization*. Translated by Kathleen E. Innes and Mabel R. Brailsford. New York: Alfred A. Knopf, 1930.

————. *Festivals and Songs of Ancient China*. Translated by E. D. Edwards. New York: Dutton, 1932.

Ho, Ping-ti. *The Ladder of Success in Imperial China: Aspects of Social Morality 1368–1911*. New York: Columbia University Press, 1962.

Hou, Fu-wu. *Chinese Political Traditions*. Washington: Public Affairs Press, 1965.

Hsiao, Kung-Chuan. *Rural China*. Seattle: University of Washington Press, 1960.

Hsu, Francis L. K. *Under the Ancestors' Shadow*. New York: Columbia University Press, 1948.

Hucker, Charles O., ed. *Chinese Government in Ming Times*. New York: Columbia University Press, 1969.

————. *The Traditional Chinese State in Ming Times (1368–1644)*. Tucson: University of Arizona Press, 1961.

Hughes, E. R., tr. *Chinese Philosophy in Classical Times*. 2d ed., rev. New York: Dutton, 1942.

Hughes, E. R., and Hughes, K. *Religion in China*. London: Hutchinson's University Library, 1950.

Hu, Shih. *The Development of Logical Method in Ancient China*. Shanghai: Oriental Book Co., 1922.

James, H. F., ed. *China*. The Annals of the American Academy of Political and Social Science, vol. 152. Philadelphia: American Academy of Political and Social Science, 1930.

Kao, George. *Chinese Wit and Humor*. New York: Coward McCann, 1946.

Karlgren, Bernard. *The Chinese Language: An Essay on Its Nature and History*. New York: Ronald Press, 1949.

Kirby, E. Stuart. *Introduction to the Economic History of China*. New York: Macmillan, 1953.

Kracke, Edward A., Jr. *Civil Service in Early Sung China, 960–1067 A.D.* Cambridge: Harvard University Press, 1953.

Lach, Donald F. *Asia in the Making of Europe.* 2 vols. Chicago: University of Chicago Press, 1965.

Lang, Olga. *Chinese Family and Society.* New Haven: Yale University Press, 1946.

Lattimore, Owen. *Inner Asian Frontiers of China.* New York: American Geographical Society, 1940.

Levenson, Joseph R. *Confucian China and Its Modern Fate: A Trilogy.* 1 vol. Berkeley: University of California Press, 1968.

Lin, Mousheng. *Men and Ideas: An Informal History of Chinese Political Thought.* New York: John Day Company, 1942.

Lin, Yutang, ed. *The Wisdom of China.* London: The New English Library Ltd., 1963.

Loewe, Michael. *Imperial China.* London: Allen and Unwin, 1966.

Mathews, R. H. *Chinese-English Dictionary.* American ed., rev. Cambridge: Harvard University Press, 1963.

MacNair, Harley Farnsworth, ed. *China.* Berkeley: University of California Press, 1946.

Meskill, John, ed. *The Pattern of Chinese History.* Boston: Heath, 1965.

Mote, Frederick W. *Intellectual Foundations of China.* New York: Alfred H. Knopf, 1971.

Needham, Joseph. *Grand Titration.* Toronto: University of Toronto Press, 1971.

————. *Science and Civilization in China.* 6 vols. to date. Cambridge: Cambridge University Press, 1954–1971.

Olschki, Leonard. *Marco Polo's Asia.* Translated by J. A. Scott. Berkeley: University of California Press, 1960.

Payne, Robert, ed. *The White Pony: An Anthology of Chinese Poetry from the Earliest Times to the Present Day.* New York: New American Library, 1960.

Reischauer, Edwin O. *Ennin's Travels in T'ang China.* New York: Ronald Press, 1955.

————, and Fairbank, John King. *A History of East Asian Civilization.* 2 vols. Vol. 1: *East Asia: The Great Tradition.* Vol. 2: *East Asia: The Modern Transformation.* Boston: Houghton Mifflin, 1960.

Rickett, W. Allyn. *Kuan-tzu: A Repository of Early Chinese Thought.* Hong Kong: Hong Kong University Press, 1965.

Schwartz, Harry. *China.* New York: Atheneum, 1966.

Sun, E-tu Zen, and de Francis, John. *Chinese Social History: A Translation of Selected Studies.* Washington, D.C.: American Council of Learned Societies, 1956.

Suzuki, Daisetz Teitaro. *A Brief History of Early Chinese Philosophy.* London: Probsthain, 1914.

Tawney, R. H. *Land and Labor in China.* New York: Harcourt, Brace & World, 1932.

Tseu, Agustinus A. *The Moral Philosophy of Mo-tze.* Taipei: China Printing, 1965.

Tung, Tso-pin. *Chronological Tables of Chinese History.* 2 vols. Hong Kong: Hong Kong University Press, 1960.

Watson, Burton, tr. *Records of the Grand Historian of China.* 2 vols. New York: Columbia University Press, 1962.

Weber, Max. *The Religion of China: Confucianism and Taoism.* Translated by Hans H. Gerth. Glencoe: The Free Press, 1951.

Werner, E. T. C. *A Dictionary of Chinese Mythology.* New York: Julian Press, 1961.

Wiens, H. J. *China's March toward the Tropics.* Hamden, Conn.: Shoe String Press, 1954.

Wilhelm, Richard. *Short History of Chinese Civilization.* Translated by J. Joshua. London: Harrap, 1929.

Williams, C. A. S. *Outlines of Chinese Symbolism and Art Motives.* Shanghai: Kelly & Walsh, 1932.

Williamson, Henry R. *Mo Ti, A Chinese Heretic.* Tsinan (China): University Press, 1927.

Wittfogel, Karl A. *Oriental Despotism: A Comparative Study of Total Power.* New Haven: Yale University Press, 1957.

Wright, Arthur F., ed. *Studies in Chinese Thought.* Chicago: University of Chicago Press, 1937.

Yang, C. K. *Chinese Communist Society: The Family and the Village.* 1-vol. ed. Cambridge, Mass.: MIT Press, 1965.

——. *Religion in Chinese Society: A Study of Contemporary Social Functions of Religion and Some of Their Historical Factors.* Berkeley: University of California Press, 1961.

Yang, Lien-Shang. *Studies in Chinese Institutional History.* Cambridge: Harvard University Press, 1963.

1. Literature of Kings: The Six Classics

Chêng, Tê-k'un. *Archeology in China.* 3 vols. Toronto: University of Toronto Press, 1963.

Creel, Herrlee Glessner. *The Birth of China: A Study of the Formative Period of Chinese Civilization.* New York: Ungar, 1964.

——. *The Origins of Statecraft in China, VI, The Western Chou Empire.* Chicago: University of Chicago Press, 1970.

Granet, Marcel. *Festivals and Songs of Ancient China.* Translated by E. D. Edwards. New York: Dutton, 1932.

Karlgren, Bernard, tr. *The Book of Documents.* Stockholm: Museum of Far Eastern Antiquities, 1950.

——. *The Book of Odes.* Stockholm: Museum of Far Eastern Antiquities, 1950.

Legge, James, tr. *The Shoo King or the Book of Historical Documents.* The Chinese Classics, vol. 3. Oxford: Clarendon, 1865.

——. *She King or the Book of Poetry.* The Chinese Classics, vol. 4. Oxford: Clarendon, 1871.

——. *The Ch'un Ts'ew with the Tso Chuen.* The Chinese Classics, vol. 5. Hong Kong: Hong Kong University Press, 1960.

Pound, Ezra, tr. *The Confucian Odes: The Classic Anthology Defined by Confucius.* New York: James Laughlin, 1959.

Rickett, W. Allyn, tr. *Kuan-tzu: A Repository of Early Chinese Thought,* vol. 1. Hong Kong: Hong Kong University Press, 1965.

Ross, John. *The Original Religion of China.* Edinburgh: Oliphant, Anderson and Ferrier, 1909.

Steele, John, tr. *The I-li or Book of Etiquette and Ceremonial.* Taipei: Ch'eng-Wen Co., 1966.

Waley, Arthur, tr. *The Book of Songs.* Boston: Houghton Mifflin, 1937.

Watson, Burton. *Early Chinese Literature.* New York: Columbia University Press, 1962.

Watson, William. *China before the Han Dynasty.* New York: Praeger, 1961.

Wilhelm, Hellmut. *Change: Eight Introductory Lectures on the I Ching.* New York: Pantheon Books, 1960.

Wilhelm, Richard. *The I Ching or Book of Changes.* Translated by Cary F. Baynes. Bollingen Series, XIX. 3rd ed. Princeton: Princeton University Press, 1967.

Willetts, William, *Chinese Art.* 2 vols. Baltimore: Penguin Books, 1958.

2. The Age of Contending Philosophies

Crump, J. I. *Intrigues of the Warring States: Studies of the Chan-kuo Ts'e.* Ann Arbor: The University of Michigan Press, 1964.

Hsu, Cho-yun. *Ancient China in Transition.* California: Stanford University Press, 1965.

Hughes, E. R. *Chinese Philosophy in Classical Times.* Everyman Library, no. 973. London: Dent, 1942.

Walden, Arthur. *Three Ways of Thought in Ancient China.* New York: Macmillan, 1939.

Walker, Richard Louis. *The Multi-State System of Ancient China.* Hamden, Conn.: Shoe String Press, 1953.

3. Confucius

Collis, Maurice. *The First Holy One.* New York: Knopf, 1948.

Creel, Herrlee Glessner. *Confucius, the Man and the Myth.* New York: John Day, 1949.

Hsu, Leonard Shih-lien. *The Political Philosophy of Confucius.* London: Routledge, 1932.

Legge, James, tr. *Confucian Analects, etc.* The Chinese Classics, vol. 1. Oxford: Oxford University Press, 1893.

Lin, Yutang, tr. *The Wisdom of Confucius.* New York: Modern Library, 1938.

Liu, Wu-chi. *Confucius, His Life and His Time.* New York: Philosophical Library, 1955.

————. *A Short History of Confucian Philosophy.* Baltimore: Penguin, 1955.

Pound, Ezra, tr. *Confucian Analects.* London: Owen, 1956.

Soothill, William Edward. *The Analects of Confucius.* Yokohama: Published by the author, 1910.

Shryock, John Knight. *The Origin and Development of the State Cult of Confucius.* New York: Paragon, 1966.

Waley, Arthur, tr. *The Analects of Confucius.* London: George Allen and Unwin Ltd., 1938.

Wilhelm, Richard. *Confucius and Confucianism.* Translated by George H. and A. P. Danton. London: Paul, 1931.

Wright, Arthur F., ed. *Confucianism and Chinese Civilization.* New York: Atheneum, 1964.

————. *The Confucian Persuasion.* Stanford: Stanford University Press, 1960.

Wright, Arthur F., and Twitchett, Denis, eds. *Confucian Personalities.* Stanford: Stanford University Press, 1962.

4. Mencius

Dobson, W. A. C. H., tr. *Mencius.* Toronto: University of Toronto Press, 1963.

Faber, E. *The Mind of Mencius, or Political Economy Founded on Moral Philosophy.* London: Trubner, 1882.

Legge, James, tr. *The Life and Works of Mencius.* London: Trubner, 1875.

Richards, Ivor Armstrong. *Mencius on the Mind: Experiments in Multiple Definition.* London: Kegan, Paul, Trench, Trubner, 1932.

Ware, James R., tr. *The Sayings of Mencius.* New York: New American Library, 1960.

5. Hsün Tzŭ

Dubs, Homer H., tr. *History of the Former Han Dynasty.* By Pan Ku. 3 vols. Baltimore: Waverly, 1938–53.

Dubs, Homer H., tr. *Hsüntze, the Moulder of Ancient Confucianism*. London: Probsthain, 1927.
————. *The Works of Hsüntze*. London: Probsthain, 1928.
Forke, Alfred, tr. *Lun Heng: The Critical Essays of Wang Ch'ung*. New York: Paragon Book Gallery, 1962.
Forke, Alfred. *The World Conception of the Chinese: Their Astronomical, Cosmological and Physico-Philosophical Speculations*. London: Probsthain, 1925.
Watson, Burton, tr. *Hsün Tzu: Basic Writings*. New York: Columbia University Press, 1963.

6. Filial Piety *and* Ritual Texts

Chai, Ch'u, and Chai, Winberg, eds. *Li Chi (Book of Rites)*. Translated by James Legge. New York: University Books, 1967.
Hughes, E. R., tr. *The Great Learning and the Mean-in-Action*. New York: Dutton, 1943.
Legge, James, tr. *The Shu King, the Religious Portions of the Shih King, the Hsiao King. Sacred Books of the East*, F. Max Muller, ed., vol. 3. London: Oxford University Press, 1885.
————, tr. *The Li Ki*. Sacred Books of the East, F. Max Muller, ed., vols. 27 and 28. London: Oxford University Press, 1885.
Makra, Mary Lelia, tr. *The Hsiao Ching (or Classic of Filial Piety)*. New York: St. John's University Press, 1961.

7. *Mo Tzŭ*

Mei, Yi-pao. *Motse: The Neglected Rival of Confucius*. London: Probsthain, 1934.
————, tr. *The Ethical and Political Works of Motse*. London: Probsthain, 1929.
Tomkinson, L., tr. *The Social Teachings of Meh Tse*. Tokyo: Asiatic Society of Japan, 1927.
Watson, Burton, tr. *Mo Tzu: Basic Writings*. New York: Columbia University Press, 1963.

8. Tao-tê-ching *and the Taoists*

Blakney, R. B., tr. *The Way of Life*. New York: New American Library, 1955.
Carus, Paul, tr. *The Canon of Reason and Virtue: Being Lao-Tze's Tao Teh King*. Chicago: Open Court, 1945.
Chan, Wing-tsit, tr. *The Way of Lao Tzu, A Translation and Study of the Tao tê-ching*. New York: Bobbs-Merrill, 1963.
Creel, Herrlee Glessner. *What Is Taoism? and Other Studies in Chinese Cultural History*. Chicago: University of Chicago Press, 1970.
Duyvendak, J. J. L., tr. *Tao Tê Ching: The Book of the Way and Its Virtue*. London: Murray, 1954.
Forke, Alfred, tr. *Yang Chu's Garden of Pleasure*. London: Murray, 1912.
Fung, Yu-Lan, tr. *Chuang Tzu*. Shanghai: Commercial Press, 1933.
Giles, Lionel, tr. *Musings of a Chinese Mystic*. London: Murray, 1947.
————, tr. *Taoist Teachings from the Book of Lieh Tzu*. London: Murray, 1925.
Graham, Charles, tr. *The Book of Lieh Tzu*. London: Murray, 1961.
Lau, D. C., tr. *Lao-Tzu: Tao tê ching*. Baltimore: Penguin, 1963.
Legge, James. *The Texts of Taoism*. 2 vols. Oxford: Clarendon Press, 1891.
Lin, Yutang, tr. *The Wisdom of Laotse*. New York: The Modern Library, 1948.
Merton, Thomas, tr. *The Way of Chuang Tzu*. New York: New Directions, 1965.

Waley, Arthur. *The Way and Its Power*. London: Allen & Unwin, 1934.

Watson, Burton, tr. *The Complete Works of Chuang Tzu*. New York: Columbia U. Press, 1968.

Welch, Holmes. *The Parting of the Way: Lao Tzu and the Taoist Movement*. Boston: B Press, 1956.

9. Sun Tzŭ: The Art of War

Giles, Lionel, tr. *Sun Tzu on the Art of War: The Oldest Military Treatise in the World*. London: Luzac, 1910.

Griffith, Samuel B., tr. *Sun Tzu: The Art of War*. Oxford: Clarendon, 1963.

Phillips, Thomas R., ed. *Roots of Strategy: A Collection of Military Classics*. Harrisburg, Pa.: Military Service Publications, 1941.

10. The Legalists and the First Empire

Bodde, Derk. *China's First Unifier: A Study of the Ch'in Dynasty as Seen in the Life of Li Ssu*. Leiden: Brill, 1938.

————. *Statesman, Patriot, and General in Ancient China*. New Haven: American Oriental Society, 1940.

Ch'u, T'ung-tsu. *Law and Society in Traditional China*. The Hague: Mouton & Co., 1965.

Duyvendak, J. J. L., tr. *The Book of Lord Shang*. Chicago: University of Chicago Press, 1963. (First pub., London: Probsthain, 1928.)

Liao, W. K., tr. *The Complete Works of Han Fei Tzu*. London: Probsthain, 1959.

Watson, Burton, tr. *Han Fei Tzu: Basic Writings*. New York: Columbia University Press, 1964.

INDEX
of Subjects

Philosophers, philosophy, ix, 8, 63–64, 109–11, 149, 171, 183, 248, 276, 282, 319, 404
Pleasures, 277. *See also* Desires.
Poetry, 16, 36–62, 247, 250, 393, 395
Political advisers, 110, 114, 124, 129–130, 135–36, 138, 140, 144, 147, 211–12, 217, 288–91, 314–15, 352–54, 360–63, 398, 408
Political Philosophy, ix, x, 63–84, 94, 113, 128–29, 147, 351, 388; of the Chou, 8, 10–11
Political science, 334, 388
Population, 341, 382
Portents. *See* Divination
Poverty, 23, 117, 123–24, 129, 135–36, 158, 215, 231, 261, 267, 300, 312, 316, 386. *See also* Asceticism
Praxis. *See* Activism-Quietism
Promise. *See* Duty, Obedience
Property, 58, 234, 386. *See also* Riches
Profit, 118, 152, 360–61, 365. *See also* Riches
Propaganda. *See* Rhetoric
Prudence, 119, 122, 186, 189, 207, 255–256, 331, 367. *See also* Danger, Mean, Sage, Wisdom
Psychology. *See* Emotions, Mind, Senses
Public welfare, 387
Punishment/reward, 6, 14–15, 17–19, 21, 26–29, 33–35, 52, 75–76, 101, 131, 135, 137, 139, 153, 155, 164–65, 223–24, 226–27, 234, 240, 242–43, 296, 308–309, 328–29, 333–35, 338, 340, 342–43, 345–47, 353–56, 365–66, 375–77, 381–83, 388, 393, 399, 405–406. *See also* War, punitive

Quiet, Quietism. *See* Activism-Quietism

Rank(s), 79, 103, 106–108, 117, 119, 121–24, 126, 146–47, 152, 154, 157–59, 164, 169, 172–74, 190–91, 193–94, 197, 219–21, 238, 264–65, 343, 380; by age, 107, 153, 173, 195; by birth, 140, 150, 153; of emperor, 165–66; feudal, 153; heredity, 6; by merit, 6, 136, 140, 144, 148, 150, 220–27, 249, 366, 374, 384, 398; political, 185–87; by purchase, 365; of scholar, 213
Reality, Realism, ix, 172–74, 197–200, 247, 264, 284–85, 287, 302, 373; philosophical, 173–75, 197, 199. *See also* Knowledge, Mind, Sleeping/awake
Reason. *See* Mind

Rectification of terms. *See* Language
Regicide, 131, 150, 364, 379. *See also* Tyrannicide.
Religion, 6, 10, 18–19, 46–52, 56, 59–61, 80, 102, 113, 124, 145, 147, 150–151, 168, 182, 185–86, 192–94, 216–17, 222–26, 233–35, 239–42, 283, 393; religion and the state, *see* Mandate of T'ien, Succession; *see also* Ancestors, God, Rites, Sacrifice, Spirits, Tao, T'ien
Research methods, 334
Resistance, passive, 249
Revolt, revolution, 19, 28, 51, 57–58, 83–86, 100, 124, 158, 179, 193, 245, 367, 376–77, 379, 389, 406–407
Rhetoric, 8, 16, 306, 352, 359, 360–63, 365, 369, 385. *See also* Language
Riches, 23, 79, 106, 113, 117, 122, 124, 129–30, 139, 148, 158–59, 176, 190–91, 196, 208–209, 211–12, 254, 265, 267, 311, 330, 360–61, 365, 377
Right/wrong, 57, 286–87, 298, 311, 313. *See also* Good/evil
Rigid/flexible, 256, 270, 274, 316–17
Rites, 15, 18, 24, 31–33, 36, 53, 61, 93–108, 113, 117, 121, 123–26, 136, 138, 141, 146–47, 150, 166–69, 172–73, 182–83, 186, 192–93, 215, 236–38, 246–47, 264, 296, 299–300, 303, 305, 312–13, 334, 337–40, 393–94, 397–99, 402–403, 414; theory of, 100
Ritual Records, 93–94, 100–108, 182–83; as part of Classics, 93; date of, 94
Ruler, 25, 43–45, 76, 81–84, 116, 147, 182, 184–87, 244, 259, 264–65, 271, 289–91, 314–16, 353, 407; duties of, 196–97; and family, 94, 107, 113, 137; importance of, 155, 163, 165–66
Ruler, the average, 374–75
Ruler, the bad, 29, 40–41, 59, 85–92, 114, 131–36, 144, 163, 219, 221, 225, 230–31, 261, 271, 273, 316, 353–55, 363–64, 371–72, 399, 402, 405
Ruler, the good, ix, 16–17, 20, 25–27, 40, 46–52, 54–57, 61–62, 78, 85, 114, 124, 129–30, 132–36, 138, 146, 149–150, 153–56, 160–61, 163, 191–95, 200, 202–208, 220, 230–31, 247, 252, 255–57, 260–61, 266, 269, 271, 273, 278–80, 301, 316–17, 331–32, 340, 355–57, 371–72, 377–78, 387, 399, 405; as teacher, *see* Teacher, Education. *See also* Kings, ancient model; Sage, Scholar
Ruling class, ix, 114, 408

INDEX
of Persons and Places